Intern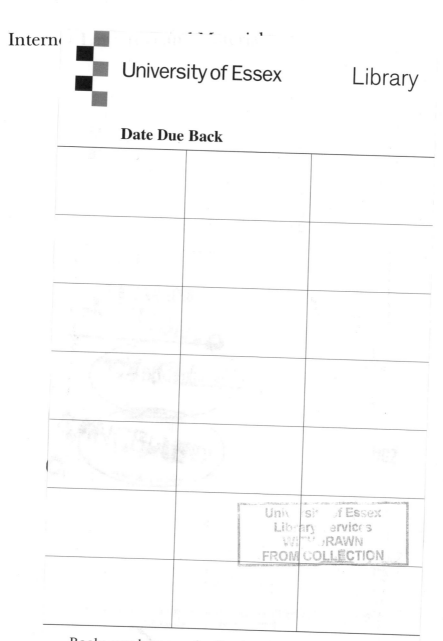

University of Essex   Library

Date Due Back

Books may be renewed online (or telephone 01206 873187)
Unless they have been recalled.

Form No. L.43 April 2004

Law in Context

Editors: William Twining (University College, London) and
Christopher McCrudden (Lincoln College, Oxford)

Internet Law
Text and Materials

Chris Reed
Professor of Electronic Commerce Law and Head of the Information Technology Law Unit at the Centre for Commercial Law Studies, Queen Mary and Westfield College, University of London

Butterworths
London, Edinburgh, Dublin
2000

United Kingdom	Butterworths, a Division of Reed Elsevier (UK) Ltd, Halsbury House, 35 Chancery Lane, LONDON WC2A 1EL and 4 Hill Street, EDINBURGH EH2 3JZ
Australia	Butterworths, a Division of Reed International Books Australia Pty Ltd, CHATSWOOD, New South Wales
Canada	Butterworths Canada Ltd, MARKHAM, Ontario
Hong Kong	Butterworths Hong Kong, a division of Reed Elsevier (Greater China) Ltd, HONG KONG
India	Butterworths India, NEW DELHI
Ireland	Butterworth (Ireland) Ltd, DUBLIN
Malaysia	Malayan Law Journal Sdn Bhd, KUALA LUMPUR
New Zealand	Butterworths of New Zealand Ltd, WELLINGTON
Singapore	Butterworths Asia, SINGAPORE
South Africa	Butterworths Publishers (Pty) Ltd, DURBAN
USA	Lexis Law Publishing, CHARLOTTESVILLE, Virginia

A member of the Reed Elsevier plc group

© Chris Reed 2000
reprinted 2001

A CIP Catalogue record for this book is available from the British Library.

ISBN 0 406 98141 8

Typeset by Doyle & Co, Colchester.
Printed and bound in Great Britain by Hobbs the Printers Ltd, Totton, Hampshire.

Visit Butterworths LEXIS *direct* **at: http://www.butterworths.com**

Preface

The genesis of this book lies in the author's experience in teaching computer law to students. Many of the ideas expressed here have been developed in discussion and team teaching with my colleagues of the Information Technology Law Unit, Dr Ian Walden, Lars Davies, Christopher Millard, John Angel, Laura Edgar and Gavin Sutter. Their contributions have been made over a period of years, and cannot now be separately identified. However, I am conscious that much of what is of value in this book is attributable to their own work, and gratefully acknowledge their otherwise uncredited efforts. Of course, all errors and misunderstandings remain my own responsibility. Thanks are also due to Julia Hörnle of the Information Technology Law Unit, who secured the permissions for the extracts quoted in the book. I also take this opportunity to acknowledge the assistance of Mark Lewis of Tite & Lewis, whose advice on my practice work in the Internet law field has been invaluable and who has been kind enough to read and comment on some of the chapters.

Finally, mention must be made of the collective contribution of the hundreds of students who have painstakingly listened to my lectures on the topics considered in the book and have challenged and refined my thinking. In particular I must thank those of the 1999/2000 University of London LLM cohort who have provided research assistance on specific topics: Roux de Villiers (Alternative dispute resolution – Chapter 9.3.3); Sajan Poovayya (Localisation and applicable law and forum – Chapter 7.1.3); and Anne Flanagan (Trade marks and domain names – Chapter 3.2); and also Mr Juan Avellan, PhD researcher at the Information Technology Law Unit, for information on electronic signatures and identity certification (Chapters 5, 6.1).

Chris Reed
August 2000

Acknowledgments

I am grateful to the following persons and bodies for permission to reproduce extracts from the materials in which they hold copyright:

American Bar Association	Digital Signature Guidelines
Australian Parliament and Government	Australian legislation. All legislative material herein is reproduced by permission but does not purport to be the official or authorised version. It is subject to Commonwealth of Australia copyright. The Copyright Act 1968 permits certain reproduction and publication of Commonwealth legislation. In particular, s.182A of the Act enables a complete copy to be made by or on behalf of a particular person. For reproduction or publication beyond that permitted by the Act, permission should be sought in writing from the AusInfo. Requests in the first instance should be addressed to the Manager, Legislative Services, AusInfo, GPO Box 1920, Canberra ACT 2601 or by e-mail: Cwealthcopyright@dofa.gov.au.
GlobalSign (formerly BelSign)	BelSign 1999 website information
Internet Society	Requests for Comment (RFCs)
Teree E. Foster	Viktor Mayer-Schönberger and Teree E. Foster, *Free Speech and the Global Information Infrastructure,* 56 Michigan Telecommunications and Technology Law Review [Vol. 3:45 1996–1997] 45
A. Michael Froomkin	'The Essential Role of Trusted Third Parties in Electronic Commerce', 75 Oregon L. Rev. 49 (1996) © A. Michael Froomkin, 1996. All rights reserved.
Christopher Kuner	Translation of German Multimedia Law
ICANN	Uniform Domain Name Dispute Resolution Policy © ICANN 1999

Viktor Mayer-Schönberger	Viktor Mayer-Schönberger and Teree E. Foster, *Free Speech and the Global Information Infrastructure*, 56 Michigan Telecommunications and Technology Law Review [Vol. 3:45 1996–1997] 45
New Yorker	Cartoon by G. Steiner, Chapter 5
OECD	The Application of the Permanent Establishment Definition in the Context of Electronic Commerce: Proposed Clarification of the Commentary on Article 5 of the OECD Model Tax Convention (Revised Draft For Comments), Working Party No. 1 on Tax Conventions and Related Questions, OECD Committee on Fiscal Affairs (March 2000). OECD Model Tax Convention The Taxation Of Global Trading Of Financial Instruments: A Discussion Draft, OCDE/GD(97)29
Chip Salzenberg, Gene Spafford, Mark Moraes	'What is Usenet?' ftp://rtfm.mit.edu/pub/usenet-by-group/news,answers/what-is/part1
Singapore Parliament	Electronic Transactions Act
UK Department of Trade and Industry	'Building Confidence in Electronic Commerce' (URN 99/642, 5 March 1999) http://www.dti.gov.uk/cii/elec/elec_com.html Crown Copyright is reproduced with the permission of the Controller of Her Majesty's Stationery Office
UK Internet Watch Foundation	IWF Constitution
World Intellectual Property Organisation	*The Management of Internet Names and Addresses: Intellectual Property Issues*, Interim Report of the WIPO Internet Domain Name Process (WIPO, December 23, 1998) Copyright Treaty
Yee, K	'location.location.location: a Snapshot of Internet Addresses as Evolving Property', 1997(1) *Journal of Information, Law and Technology*

Contents

Table of UK Statutes

References in this Table to *Statutes* are to Halsbury's Statutes of England (Fourth Edition) showing the volume and page at which the annotated text of the Act may be found. Page references printed in **bold** type indicate where the section of the Act is set out in part or in full.

Table of Statutes — Foreign Jurisdictions

Page references printed in **bold** type indicate where the section of the Act is set out in part or in full.

Table of European Communities Legislation

Page references printed in **bold** type indicate where the section of the Legislation is set out in part or in full.

Table of Conventions and Agreements

Page references printed in **bold** type indicate where the section of the Legislation is set out in part or in full.

List of Cases

Y

Z

Introduction

1   AIMS AND METHODOLOGY

The most difficult task when writing a legal text is deciding what to leave out. This difficulty is compounded at least a hundred-fold when the subject of the book is Internet law. The reason for this becomes apparent when the so-called 'Cyberspace fallacy' is examined more closely.

The Cyberspace fallacy states that the Internet is a new jurisdiction, in which none of the existing rules and regulations apply. This jurisdiction has no physical existence; it is a virtual space which expands and contracts as the different networks and computers, which collectively make up the Internet, connect to and disconnect from each other. The geographical locations where activities occur are often purely fortuitous, dictated by the then current configuration of the Internet. The world-wide accessibility of the Internet means that no one legal jurisdiction has de jure or de facto control of these activities. From all this, it is concluded that no jurisdiction has *any* control.

A moment's thought reveals the fallacy. All the actors involved in an Internet transaction[1] have a real-world existence, and are located in one or more legal jurisdictions. The computing and communications equipment through which the transaction takes place is also located in legal jurisdictions, even though it may be difficult to identify precisely which equipment was in fact used. It is inconceivable that a real-world jurisdiction would deny that its laws potentially

---

1   Terminology will be a constant difficulty in this book. It is likely to be many years until there has been sufficient legislative and judicial activity to develop an internationally agreed terminology for Internet activities. It is therefore necessary to define terms as the book progresses – to assist the reader, these terms will be defined in footnotes where appropriate. A further problem is that many words carry with them a set of legal associations which may be inappropriate in the context of the Internet. I have therefore attempted to select terms which carry as few of these associations as possible. Thus far, there are three terms which require definition: 'Internet' means the then subsisting virtual network created by the internetworking of other networks, connected using the TCP/IP protocol or other means of open access to information. Readers must remember that the Internet has little or no fixed existence or infrastructure, and its configuration changes from second to second. 'Actor' means any person (legal or natural) who sends or receives information via the Internet. This includes intermediaries who receive and pass on information. Actors may not be acting consciously – in many instances the actor will be acting via one or more computers which are programmed to exchange information without any human intervention. 'Transaction' means an exchange of information between two actors. The legal effects of that exchange of information are a separate matter, and it should not be assumed that a transaction has any legal effects at all.

applied to the transaction. In fact, because the Internet is accessible from almost everywhere in the world,[2] transactions whose real-world analogues would have been restricted to only one or two jurisdictions may potentially be subject to *every* jurisdiction – this is particularly clear in the case of advertising via a Web site.[3] It may be that the Internet, rather than being unregulated, is in fact the most heavily regulated 'place' in the world.

It follows that a definitive work on Internet law would need to expound all the laws of all the countries which might potentially have an impact on Internet transactions. Such a book would be almost impossible to produce, and would in any case be grossly repetitive of legal analysis already accessible in standard works. For example, a sale via the Internet of a music CD from a Ruritanian seller to a Ruritanian buyer, with all the electronic messages passing through a Ruritanian Internet service provider, is clearly a sale of goods subject to Ruritanian law. No useful purpose would be served by rehashing the standard work on the Ruritanian Commercial Code.

It also follows that a book which expounds the law of one jurisdiction, as it relates to the Internet, is likely to be of limited utility.[4] An Internet transaction, even though it appears to take place between actors in the same jurisdiction, may in fact involve other jurisdictions.[5] Furthermore, because the Internet provides the cheapest mechanism for dealing with customers outside one's own jurisdiction, most Internet commerce enterprises will have a substantial number of foreign customers.

What then will this book leave out? The answer is, those elements of the law which are equally applicable to a real-world transaction. However, the difficulties of identifying which laws apply to the transaction and which states have jurisdiction over it must not be underestimated – these will be examined in Chapter 7. What the book will attempt to deal with is the law which is applicable only or mainly to the Internet, together with those aspects of the law which apply to Internet transactions in very different ways from their applicability to real-world activities. The aims of the book are thus:

- to analyse the fundamental issues which are raised by the advent of the Internet as a global communications mechanism;
- to identify the challenges to existing laws and regulations which this new communications mechanism poses, illustrating them by examples drawn from as wide a range of jurisdictions as possible;
- to identify trends in the development of the law in respect of each of these issues; and
- to analyse potential mechanisms for addressing the challenges.

How far these aims have been achieved, only the reader can judge.

So far as methodology is concerned, I have not adopted any jurisprudential, political or social theory as an aid to discussion. It seems to me far too early to

---

2   Or even from outer space.
3   See in particular Chapter 7.1.3.4 and 7.2.1.3.
4   Inevitably, given the author's physical location in the UK, the book refers to more UK legal materials than those from any other jurisdiction. The intention, however, is to give a fair picture of the state of the law on a global basis, even if there is some geographical bias in that picture.
5   For example, information exchanged between two subscribers to CompuServe (at least before its acquisition by AOL) always passed through computers located in the US, even if both subscribers were accessing the network from the UK.

attempt an analysis of Internet law based on a theory which predicates particular results as desirable. As the book will, I hope, demonstrate, some Internet activities are effected through mechanisms which are so different from those to which the law is designed to apply that achieving *any* result is difficult, let alone a particular, desired result.[6] Instead, the book adopts a bottom-up method of analysis; first identifying the new types of activity which appear to fall outside existing categories of law, then assessing how far the existing law is extendable to cover those activities and what results it produces, and finally assessing the global consensus (if any) which appears to be emerging as to how those new activities should be addressed by the law. This is not to say that the book is entirely value free, or that it does not make suggestions as to the desirability of particular solutions; but to the extent that explicit values are used to assess the developing law, these are mainly those of consistency, effectiveness in achieving the law's aims, and enforceability.[7] More perceptive readers will no doubt identify the implicit and unconscious value assumptions which inform the author's opinions.

So far as possible, the law is stated as at 1 January 2000. However, the law in this area is now moving at such a pace that some of the materials discussed here may have been overtaken by later developments which escaped the author's notice. Where possible, developments between 1 January and 31 March 2000 have been incorporated. Readers should be warned that the legal materials examined in each chapter are not the only applicable materials on the topic, but have been selected as representative of the current state of global development in the area. The most that this book can claim to offer, therefore, is an overview of the current state of Internet law as seen from one commentator's perspective together with some predictions as to its future development.

2   THE TECHNICAL AND ECONOMIC CONTEXT

Internet law needs to be understood in both its technical and economic context. Those new to the topic might be forgiven for thinking that the former is the most important – after all, the Internet is one of the most 'technical' phenomena around. In fact, the technical detail is often comparatively unimportant. The fundamental technical characteristic which affects the law, and which it is vitally important to understand, is that the Internet is nothing more than a method of transporting digital information. The consequences of that transport usually have legal effects, but the precise mechanism used to transport the information will in many cases be legally irrelevant.

There are two consequences of this technical characteristic which have a far-reaching effect on the law, however. The first might be described as global equivalence – all computers which are connected to the Internet are equally close to, and accessible to, any Internet user. National boundaries may have

---

6   This is particularly apparent in the field of taxation of electronic commerce – see Chapters 7.2 and 8.1.

7   These assessments are made on the collective effects of the global set of laws under discussion, not on any one country's laws. Because of the global and undifferentiated reach of any Internet activity, a self-consistent system of national law may still be 'undesirable' if it is radically different from the other laws of the world, irrespective of its merits when examined in isolation.

some meaning at the level of the physical infrastructure of the Internet, but so far as users and service providers are concerned they hardly exist. Indeed, a service provider who wishes for some reason[8] to customise that service for different jurisdictions may find it nearly impossible to do so. The second consequence arises from the fact that information is transported only in digital form. This makes it possible for actions to be taken as a result of a digital transmission of information, based on automated decision-making without any human intervention or thought (other than that necessary to set the parameters of the automated decision-making in advance). Much of our existing law is based on attributing consequences to human behaviour and decisions, and its application may prove difficult when the human element is absent.

This is not to say that the detailed technical operation of the Internet is always unimportant; in some instances, its effect on the law is dramatic. This occurs when the law's impact is based not on the mere fact of information interchange, but on the way in which the interchange took place. Contract formation[9] is merely the most obvious example. In those circumstances a detailed understanding of the technical context of the transaction at issue can be vital, as the apparent flow of information (so far as the human user is concerned) may be very different from what is occurring at the hardware and software level. The technical issues are examined further in Chapter 1.

Finally, so far as the technical context is concerned, an important new characteristic of the Internet is that it makes far greater use of intermediaries for the communications process than previously. These intermediaries work in unexpected ways, and their relationships with the communicating parties are also new and often undefined in law. Chapter 2 examines this issue further.

However, the economic context is far more important to the current and future shape of Internet law. This economic context arises from the technical characteristics of global equivalence, digital transmission and automated decision-making, identified above. It is now generally recognised that the advent of the Internet is creating a fundamental change in the way that many commercial activities are, or will soon be, undertaken. The precise nature of that change is as yet unknowable – we are only just now at the stage which the telephone reached about a century ago[10] and the computer half a century back.[11] Some of the economic effects of these three technical characteristics can already be seen, however:

- Global equivalence means that any Internet business has access to a global marketplace. Previously, globalisation of a business was a slow and expensive

---

8 Eg to remove the risk of non-compliance with, or subjection to, a particular country's laws – see Chapters 7 and 8.

9 See Chapter 6.2.

10 At the time, no-one seems to have envisaged that the telephone would become a mass communication device, and economic models for its use were predicated on particular types of service. For example, a Budapest telephone service was set up in 1893 whose main purpose was to provide on-line news and entertainment to subscribers; in the 1920s and 1930s it had over 10,000 subscribers – *Economist*, 31 December 1999, p 85.

11 Around that time the chairman of IBM is reputed to have predicted that the world market for computers in the year 2000 could exceed 100. My university department, the Centre for Commercial Law Studies at Queen Mary & Westfield College London, owns about that many.

process, which required the establishment of branches or agencies in each country where customers were to be solicited. Now, the costs of setting up a theoretically global business are almost identical to those of setting up a purely national one,[12] although the practical difficulties of establishing a global brand so as actually to reach customers are still substantial. From the customer's perspective, all Internet businesses are equally 'local', as the transaction costs of ordering from each are the same. As a result all Internet businesses have, or should have, global ambitions.

- The digital transmission of information has three main economic consequences. The first is that the costs of communication have been lowered very substantially. The cost of an international business letter, excluding staff costs, is likely to be in the region of US $1, and international faxes longer than a single page will probably be even more costly. An individual email or Web page access is so cheap that its cost is almost impossible to quantify. The second consequence is that a digital communication from a customer can automatically be integrated into a business's other information systems, cutting out a large element of staff costs. For example, the customer becomes the business's data entry clerk, and the roles of bookkeeper, invoice issuer and stock controller also disappear. The third consequence is perhaps the most fundamental – because information can be transmitted in its 'pure' state, rather than recorded on some data carrier such as a book, a disk or a CD-ROM, it becomes economic to sell it in small packages, rather than as the larger bundle of information necessary to achieve the price which makes production and carriage of the data carrier economic. This opens up the possibility of a new type of economic good, the 'information product', and thus a brand new area of economic activity.
- Automated decision making also has substantial economic effects. The most obvious of these is the reduction of staff costs – the minimum size for the sales and marketing staff of a business selling digitised music on-line via a website requires is precisely zero! Less obvious, though perhaps of more economic significance, is the saving to be made from integrating sales and marketing with all other facets of the business, such as stock control, purchasing, payment receipt and accounting. This is particularly relevant in business-to-business electronic commerce.

These economic drivers produce a very different business model from the traditional one, in which a business entering a new national market needed to establish local branches or agencies, engage staff, develop a local distribution system and engage in local advertising. All these were clearly subject to local law, and differences from the laws of the other places in which the business operated could be accommodated comparatively easily. The new business model for the Internet is of an enterprise which operates each of its functions from one locality only, servicing its global operations from that one place. In doing so, it bypasses the traditional mechanisms of dedicated staff and premises on which much of national law impacts. Furthermore, it may operate in new ways,

---

12 Leaving aside legal and regulatory compliance costs, which are highly significant on a global scale.

in particular by making use of new types of intermediary service which do not fit easily into existing legal categories and by disintermediating the agencies traditionally used to reach customers.

Chapter 1

The Internet as a distributed environment

One of the great dangers when examining a technical subject is misuse of the collective noun. For example, for many years some biologists argued that evolution worked, in part at least, through natural selection at the level of the species. 'Species', however, is a collective noun for the whole set of individual members of that species, and it is now clear that the evolutionary mechanism works only at the level of individual species members, or even at the lower level of the individual genes which have determined that individual's characteristics.[1] For the purposes of evolutionary study, treating a species as a discrete entity is simply incorrect.

The word 'Internet' is, perhaps surprisingly, also a collective noun. This fact is obscured because we tend to speak of 'the' Internet; as a result it is very difficult not to think of it as a single entity.[2] For the purposes of legal analysis, however, this single entity perspective is almost always misleading. It leads to a number of assumptions, all of which are false:

- that there is a recognisable controller of the Internet, who might ultimately be responsible for it;
- that the Internet has a fixed, definable infrastructure;
- that the information and services obtainable via the Internet are provided by that entity called 'the Internet'.

This perspective leads to the following picture of the Internet, in which users interact via a mysterious mechanism which is none the less self-contained:

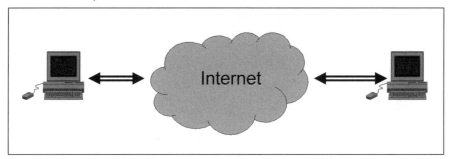

---

1   Dawkins *The Extended Phenotype* (Oxford: Oxford University Press, 1982) p 99 ff.
2   In about 1997, rumours circulated that the senior partner in a City of London law firm (unnamed) had inquired in all seriousness 'I've been reading a lot about something called the Internet; should *we* get one?'.

To understand the legal implications of the Internet we must step back from this perception of it as a single entity and ask ourselves three questions:

- What functions does the Internet perform?
- How does it perform them?
- Which legal or natural persons are involved, and what is their role?

THE FUNCTIONS OF THE INTERNET[3]

The basic function performed by the Internet is extremely simple – it transports digital information from one computer to another, and nothing more. In other words, at the functional level the Internet is no more than a communications technology. The meaning of the information communicated via the Internet is completely irrelevant to its transport; that meaning is determined by the software which receives the information. Any type of information which can be translated to digital form can be transported – the most common types of information are text, numerical data, images, sounds and video.

Any additional functions which are effected via the Internet are not performed by the Internet itself. They are *services* which are provided by one or more of the players involved. All these services are performed by the exchange of digital information.

PERFORMANCE OF THOSE FUNCTIONS

The transport function is performed by copying the digital information from one computer to another until a copy reaches the receiving computer. The information, however, is not sent in a continuous stream. Instead, the sending computer splits the information into discrete packets or datagrams, each addressed to the receiving computer, which reassembles the information once the packets have arrived. The intermediate computers work simply on the addresses of each packet, forwarding it to another computer until it reaches its destination. There is no need for these packets to follow the same route, or to arrive at the same time or in any particular order.

THE PLAYERS

From all this, it follows that there will be more persons involved in any transmission of information than simply the sender and receiver. The packets containing the information transmitted will have been copied by one or more intermediary computers, which may not be the same computers for each packet. At this stage, for the purposes of legal analysis it is simplest to divide the players in an Internet information exchange into two groups:

- The parties to the exchange, ie the computers of sender and recipient which are at either end of the transmission.
- Intermediaries, ie all the other computers which receive and pass on packets.

A more detailed analysis of the players is attempted in Chapter 2.

---

3   The definitive set of specifications for the Internet and its operations is the 'Requests for Comment' (RFC) series of documents maintained by the Internet Architecture Board. A useful index with links to the text of RFCs can be found at http://www.it.kth.se/docs/rfc/.

TYPES OF CONNECTION

All the intermediaries mentioned above will be *hosts,* ie they are (for the time being) permanently connected to other hosts and are passing addressed packets back and forth. The parties to the exchange, however, may have different types of access:

Crocker *To Be 'On' the Internet* (March 1995) Network Working Group, RFC 1775, p 2[4]

2.   LABELS FOR INTERNET ACCESS

The following definitions move from 'most' to 'least' Internet access, from the perspective of the user (consumer). The first term is primarily applicable to Internet service providers. The remaining terms are primarily applicable to consumers of Internet service.

Full access

This is a permanent (full-time) Internet attachment running TCP/IP, primarily appropriate for allowing the Internet community to access application servers, operated by Internet service providers. Machines with Full access are directly visible to others attached to the Internet, such as through the Internet Protocol's ICMP Echo (ping) facility. The core of the Internet comprises those machines with Full access.

Client access

The user runs applications that employ Internet application protocols directly on their own computer platform, but might not be running underlying Internet protocols (TCP/IP), might not have full-time access, such as through dial-up, or might have constrained access, such as through a firewall. When active, Client users might be visible to the general Internet, but such visibility cannot be predicted. For example, this means that most Client access users will not be detected during an empirical probing of systems 'on' the Internet at any given moment, such as through the ICMP Echo facility.

Mediated access

The user runs no Internet applications on their own platform. An Internet service provider runs applications that use Internet protocols on the provider's platform, for the user. User has simplified access to the provider, such as dial-up terminal connectivity. For Mediated access, the user is on the Internet, but their computer platform is not. Instead, it is the computer of the mediating service (provider) which is on the Internet.

Messaging access

The user has no Internet access, except through electronic mail and through netnews, such as Usenet or a bulletin board service. Since messaging services can be used as a high-latency – i.e., slow – transport service, the use of this level of access for mail-enabled services can be quite powerful, though not interactive.

A REVISED PERSPECTIVE OF THE INTERNET

From all this we can see that the Internet is not an entity, but a communications infrastructure. To the extent that it *is* a thing, it is a network of networks, all internetworking with each other by passing data packets.[5] The internetwork expands and contracts as connections are made and broken.

Users communicate with each other across this infrastructure using client/ server technology. This means that one communicating party runs client software, which requests information, and the other runs server software which meets that request. A clear example of this is viewing a Web page. The user enters the address (URL)[6] of the page into his browser software (eg Netscape Navigator or Internet Explorer). This is the client software. It generates a request for the page, which is sent via the Internet to the computer on which the page is stored. Web server software running on that computer responds to the request by sending the packets which make up the page to the browser software. The browser then reassembles them and displays the page.

Thus a more accurate model of the Internet, and the one which lawyers must adopt is as follows:

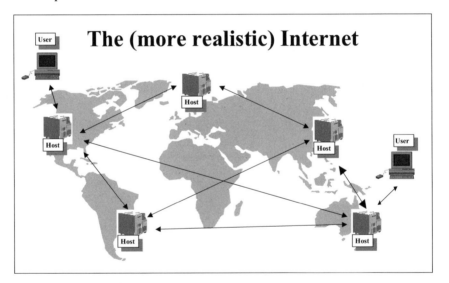

The (more realistic) Internet

1.1 PACKET SWITCHING, COPYING AND THE INCHOATE NATURE OF INTERNET 'DOCUMENTS'

A user's client software and the other party's server software are able to exchange packets of information across the Internet because all the computers involved use common *protocols* to define how a packet should be dealt with. A protocol is, in essence, an algorithm for recognising and dealing with a piece of information. Different manufacturers will implement those algorithms in the appropriate ways for their particular hardware or software, but the 'public' face which the hardware or software shows to other Internet computers will always be the same.

5   See Lars Davies 'The Internet and the Elephant' (1996, April) International Business Lawyer 151.
6   Uniform Resource Locator, made up of the domain name + directory structure + filename – eg www.ccls.edu/itlaw/index.html.

R Braden (ed) *Requirements for Internet Hosts – Communication Layers* **(October 1989) Network Working Group, RFC 1122, p 8**[7]

1.1.3 INTERNET PROTOCOL SUITE

To communicate using the Internet system, a host must implement the layered set of protocols comprising the Internet protocol suite. A host typically must implement at least one protocol from each layer.

The protocol layers used in the Internet architecture are as follows:

- *Application Layer*
  The application layer is the top layer of the Internet protocol suite. The Internet suite does not further subdivide the application layer, although some of the Internet application layer protocols do contain some internal sub-layering. The application layer of the Internet suite essentially combines the functions of the top two layers – Presentation and Application – of the OSI reference model.
  We distinguish two categories of application layer protocols: user protocols that provide service directly to users, and support protocols that provide common system functions . . .

- *Transport Layer*
  The transport layer provides end-to-end communication services for applications . . . TCP is a reliable connection-oriented transport service that provides end-to-end reliability, resequencing, and flow control. UDP is a connectionless ('datagram') transport service . . .

- *Internet Layer*
  All Internet transport protocols use the Internet Protocol (IP) to carry data from source host to destination host. IP is a connectionless or datagram internetwork service, providing no end-to-end delivery guarantees. Thus, IP datagrams may arrive at the destination host damaged, duplicated, out of order, or not at all. The layers above IP are responsible for reliable delivery service when it is required. The IP protocol includes provision for addressing, type-of-service specification, fragmentation and reassembly, and security information.
  The datagram or connectionless nature of the IP protocol is a fundamental and characteristic feature of the Internet architecture. Internet IP was the model for the OSI Connectionless Network Protocol . . .

- *Link Layer*
  To communicate on its directly-connected network, a host must implement the communication protocol used to interface to that network. We call this a link layer or media-access layer protocol . . .

Of these layers of protocols, the most important for communications across the Internet infrastructure are the Transport and Internet layers. The most commonly used transport protocol is Transport Control Protocol (TCP). TCP controls the exchange of packets between hosts; it sets out mechanisms for checking whether a packet has arrived, for checking to ensure it has not been corrupted in transit, and for re-sending it if transmission fails. The Internet Protocol (IP) sets out the rules for determining what the receiving host should do with the packet. It defines the addressing system, the numbering of packets (to ensure reassembly of the complete transmission), etc. Communications infrastructures which use this technology, such as the Internet, are known as TCP/IP networks. Hosts dealing with packets do so purely on the TCP/IP elements of those packets, and do not concern themselves with the contents of the packets.

The Applications layer protocols define the type of information contained in the collection of packets and what is to be done with it. Probably the best known such protocol is HTTP, the HyperText Transfer Protocol[8] which is the basis of the World Wide Web. Other important applications layer protocols include SMTP and POP,[9] used for email, and FTP.[10]

An analogy which might be helpful is to consider a physical letter being sent from London to New York:

- The address on the letter corresponds, roughly to the IP information contained in a data packet.
- Each step in the postal delivery examines that address, and then uses the appropriate mechanism to transfer the letter to the next stage of the delivery process. That mechanism corresponds to the TCP information in a packet. Thus the local sorting office might place the letter in a sack marked 'International' and send that sack to a central sorting office. The central office would empty out the sack, and sort the letters into other sacks – 'New York', 'Paris', etc. Eventually a sack containing the letter will arrive in New York, and the letter will be sorted into another sack for the appropriate delivery round.
- Finally the letter arrives, and the addressee's name is used by some person within the building to determine which person in that building is to receive the letter. This name is roughly equivalent to the Applications layer protocol, which determines the client software application to which the packet should be sent.[11]

Of course, all but the smallest Internet communications consist of a number of packets, and there is no requirement that they should all follow the same route to their destination. Indeed, the original purpose of the TCP/IP technology was to produce a 'bomb-proof' defence network, so that if any one host were destroyed or ceased to function the packets would simply be re-routed round the gap in the network.

---

8   HTTP is developed and controlled by the World Wide Web Consortium, http://www.w3.org.
9   Simple Mail Transfer Protocol and Post Office Protocol respectively.
10 File Transfer Protocol.
11 For example, it is perfectly possible on a PC for the user to run several client applications simultaneously – eg checking email using POP, downloading a file using FTP and viewing a Web page using HTTP. As each packet arrives, the PC's Internet access software examines the Application layer information, and then directs the packet to the appropriate piece of client software. It does not matter that the stream of packets arriving at the PC is a mixture of POP, FTP and HTTP packets, as the Application layer protocol information enables them to be sorted out.

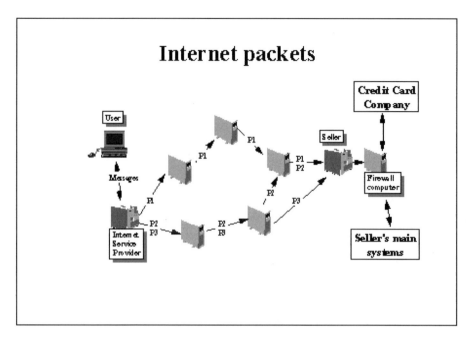

However, unlike the postal service the 'original' packet never arrives. Each computer which handles a packet does so by making and passing on copies, and discarding the packets it received. This copying is fundamental to all communications between computers and immediately raises two obvious legal issues:

- How can we apply traditional legal distinctions between originals and copies of documents to a communications technology in which these distinctions are meaningless?
- How far should intermediaries be held liable for the contents of packets (eg for copyright infringement, breach of obscenity laws, etc) when their role is merely to copy and retransmit those packets in accordance with their TCP/IP information?

A final point which should be examined under this heading is the conceptual mismatch between a physical document, something which the law has understood for millennia, and its digital equivalent. The physical document is, normally,[12] a piece of paper which exists in one space-time location only. It can be copied, in which case there are two documents, the original and a copy. The equivalent digital document, however, is simply a set of binary data, conveniently conceptualised as 1s and 0s. It is more accurate to say that it is stored, rather than 'exists', and may well be stored in multiple locations. Worse, that storage is almost certainly always of a copy.

A simple example may be illustrative. Suppose that a reader of this book sends me an email with a word processing file attached. The word processing 'document' was created as a representation of words on a screen, but underlying

---

12 English law has been sufficiently flexible to recognise a photograph of a tombstone as a document for evidential purposes: *Lyell v Kennedy (No 3)* (1884) 27 Ch D 1.

that screen display was a set of digital numbers, representing the visible symbols, stored in the working memory (RAM) of the author's computer. At some point that set of numbers was saved to disk as a file, and the information in RAM and on the screen was discarded. When the email was sent, the author's e-mail software made a copy of the file in memory, split it into packets, and sent those packets out via the Internet. Different host computers copied and re-transmitted those packets on their journey. Finally my email software retrieved the message (reassembled from packets by the mailbox software running on my College's mail server) and I detached the file and saved it to my hard disk.

The result of all this activity is that the digital document now exists in multiple locations; but, for all practical purposes, it is the *same* document. It has identical information content to the 'original' (whichever version that was), and cannot be distinguished from any other copy by, as would be the case for a hard copy document, noting the difference in the physical medium (the paper for a hard copy document). That physical medium is purely fortuitous – if I change my computer, and copy all the files from the old to the new computer, it seems artificial to say that I have deleted one copy and created a new one. Indeed, we talk of 'moving' files from one storage location to another, recognising that for our purposes it continues to be the same document even though it has actually been copied.

The law, however, is closely rooted in the physical world. Fundamental concepts such as 'ownership' depend on the physical uniqueness of the thing owned. We have no difficulty in deciding that I own a particular diskette, but it is much harder to determine what, if anything, my ownership rights are in respect of a digital document stored on that disk.[13]

1.2   THE CO-OPERATIVE NATURE OF INTERNETWORKING AND THE DISTRIBUTED NATURE OF INFRASTRUCTURE OWNERSHIP

This packet switching method of transporting information, using a common set of protocols, means that there is no necessity for complicated rules governing the relationship between Internet hosts. That relationship is nothing more formal than an agreement for mutual co-operation. Each host operator has impliedly agreed with each other host operator that it will accept and re-transmit packets addressed to the other, and at most that it will use reasonable efforts to do so.[14] The primary technical and operational requirements for host operators are set out in the RFCs.[15]

13 Some idea of the conceptual difficulties involved can be seen from the attempts of the English courts to come to grips with property issues in this context. In *Cox v Riley* (1986) 83 Cr App Rep 54 the courts held that deletion of programs stored on a magnetic storage medium amounted to criminal damage to property, the property being the storage medium. The position was later altered by statute, Computer Misuse Act 1990, s 3, substituting a new offence of unauthorised access to a computer with intent to modify its contents. In *R v Lloyd* [1985] QB 829 the question arose whether multiple copying of a cinema film master could amount to theft of that film; the court held that theft could only be committed if the copying was so extensive as to render the master valueless. See further Chapter 6.1.1.

14 This might have the effect of creating a contract between each host operator and every other – see eg the English case of *Clarke v Earl of Dunraven* [1897] AC 59, where the House of Lords held that by entering a sailing race, each competitor made a contract with every other competitor to abide by the rules of the race.

15 See in particular J Van Bokkelen *Responsibilities of Host and Network Managers – A Summary of the 'Oral Tradition' of the Internet* (August 1990) Network Working Group, RFC 1173.

When a transmission host receives a packet, it asks itself (if we allow ourselves to anthropomorphise the machine) one simple question – 'Is this packet for me?':

- If the answer is 'Yes', it passes the packet to the appropriate software application running on the host. Thus, an HTTP packet would be passed to the Web server to which it was addressed.
- If the answer is 'No', it passes the packet to another host to which it is connected. Routing tables indicate which of the connected hosts lies on the most efficient route to the packet's destination, but if the connection to that host is temporarily inoperative the packet will be passed to a different host.

This process means that the packet is likely to arrive, but gives no guarantee as to its arrival time.[16] For this reason, the Internet is sometimes described as a 'best efforts' network.

R Braden (ed) *Requirements for Internet Hosts – Communication Layers* **(October 1989) Internet Engineering Task Force, Network Working Group, RFC 1122, p 6**[17]

1.1 THE INTERNET ARCHITECTURE

. . .

1.1.1 INTERNET HOSTS

A host computer, or simply 'host', is the ultimate consumer of communication services. A host generally executes application programs on behalf of user(s), employing network and/or Internet communication services in support of this function . . .

An Internet communication system consists of interconnected packet networks supporting communication among host computers using the Internet protocols. The networks are interconnected using packet-switching computers called 'gateways' or 'IP routers' by the Internet community, and 'Intermediate Systems' by the OSI world. The RFC 'Requirements for Internet Gateways'[18] contains the official specifications for Internet gateways. That RFC together with the present document and its companion[19] define the rules for the current realization of the Internet architecture.

Internet hosts span a wide range of size, speed, and function. They range in size from small microprocessors through workstations to mainframes and supercomputers. In function, they range from single-purpose hosts (such as terminal servers) to full-

16 New protocols such as the Point To Point protocol have been developed to permit real-time communications via a consistent series of hosts – see RFC 1661.
17 Copyright © The Internet Society 1995. All Rights Reserved. This document and translations of it may be copied and furnished to others, and derivative works that comment on or otherwise explain it or assist in its implementation may be prepared, copied, published and distributed, in whole or in part, without restriction of any kind, provided that the above copyright notice and this paragraph are included on all such copies and derivative works. However, this document itself may not be modified in any way, such as by removing the copyright notice or references to the Internet Society or other Internet organizations, except as needed for the purpose of developing Internet standards in which case the procedures for copyrights defined in the Internet Standards process must be followed, or as required to translate it into languages other than English. The limited permissions granted above are perpetual and will not be revoked by the Internet Society or its successors or assigns. This document and the information contained herein is provided on an "AS IS" basis and THE INTERNET SOCIETY AND THE INTERNET ENGINEERING TASK FORCE DISCLAIMS ALL WARRANTIES, EXPRESS OR IMPLIED, INCLUDING BUT NOT LIMITED TO ANY WARRANTY THAT THE USE OF THE INFORMATION HEREIN WILL NOT INFRINGE ANY RIGHTS OR ANY IMPLIED WARRANTIES OF MERCHANTABILITY OR FITNESS FOR A PARTICULAR PURPOSE.
18 RFC 1009, now obsoleted by RFC 1812.
19 R Braden (ed) *Requirements for Internet Hosts – Application and Support* (October 1989) Internet Engineering Task Force, Network Working Group, RFC 1123.

service hosts that support a variety of online network services, typically including remote login, file transfer, and electronic mail . . .

1.1.2   ARCHITECTURAL ASSUMPTIONS

The current Internet architecture is based on a set of assumptions about the communication system. The assumptions most relevant to hosts are as follows:

(A)   The Internet is a network of networks.
Each host is directly connected to some particular network(s); its connection to the Internet is only conceptual. Two hosts on the same network communicate with each other using the same set of protocols that they would use to communicate with hosts on distant networks.

(B)   Gateways don't keep connection state information.
To improve robustness of the communication system, gateways are designed to be stateless, forwarding each IP datagram independently of other datagrams. As a result, redundant paths can be exploited to provide robust service in spite of failures of intervening gateways and networks.

All state information required for end-to-end flow control and reliability is implemented in the hosts, in the transport layer or in application programs. All connection control information is thus co-located with the end points of the communication, so it will be lost only if an end point fails.

(C)   Routing complexity should be in the gateways.
Routing is a complex and difficult problem, and ought to be performed by the gateways, not the hosts. An important objective is to insulate host software from changes caused by the inevitable evolution of the Internet routing architecture.

(D)   The system must tolerate wide network variation.
A basic objective of the Internet design is to tolerate a wide range of network characteristics – e.g., bandwidth, delay, packet loss, packet reordering, and maximum packet size. Another objective is robustness against failure of individual networks, gateways, and hosts, using whatever bandwidth is still available. Finally, the goal is full 'open system interconnection': an Internet host must be able to interoperate robustly and effectively with any other Internet host, across diverse Internet paths.

The 'design'[20] of the Internet means that its different physical elements can be, and are, owned by different entities. Some of these are belong to Governments, some to academic institutions, and others to corporations or even private individuals. No single entity can, or could hope to, control the actions of such a heterogeneous and distributed community.[21] The primary rule is that packets should be passed on; and the only sanction for failure to comply with the basic open standards for communications is that one's own communications will not have the technical characteristics which enable them to be carried via other hosts.

The legal relationship between hosts is as diverse as the ownership of the Internet infrastructure. There are two primary requirements to become a host:

- to operate using Internet standards, such as TCP/IP; and
- to be connected to at least one other host.

---

20 'Many members of the Internet community would argue that there is no architecture, but only a tradition, which was not written down for the first 25 years . . .': B Carpenter (ed) *Architectural Principles of the Internet* (June 1996) Network Working Group, RFC 1958, p 2.

21 'Fortunately, nobody owns the Internet, there is no centralized control, and nobody can turn it off. Its evolution depends on rough consensus about technical proposals, and on running code. Engineering feed-back from real implementations is more important than any architectural principles.' B Carpenter (ed) *Architectural Principles of the Internet* (June 1996) Network Working Group, RFC 1958, p 4.

The interconnection agreement between any pair of hosts is a private one,[22] and the obligations of the parties, including any charging mechanism, will differ widely. Some interconnections are provided on a commercial basis, others are co-operative. There can thus be no charging mechanism for an Internet transmission as a whole. The essence of the co-operative packet switching process is that each part of the infrastructure bears its own costs.

1.3 HOSTING, MIRRORING AND OTHER HIDDEN ELEMENTS OF THE INTERNET

The distributed nature of the Internet infrastructure and its co-operative methods of working means that much of what goes on is hidden from the non-technical user. For end-to-end communications, the description in parts 1.1 and 1.2 of this chapter is probably sufficient for most legal purposes. However, when Internet *resources* raise legal questions, these hidden elements of the Internet become very relevant.

The term 'resource' is used to mean any information or facility (such as computing facilities, use of software, etc) which is accessible via the Internet. The most visible resources are information resources, such as Web pages or files accessible via FTP, but it is also possible to use the Internet to run programs on remote computers or to search remote databases.

In relation to physical world resources, the law makes substantial use of the concepts of ownership, possession and control. Although these may be partitioned between different actors (eg a motor car may be owned by X but driven, and thus possessed and controlled, by Y), the number of actors involved is always finite and determinable. Internet resources are very different – they allow multiple actors to have possession and control, often in effect simultaneously, whilst in many cases this fact is invisible to users of the resource. This distribution of legally significant powers raises difficult issues, which are examined in more depth in Chapters 3, 5 and 8 in particular.

1.3.1 Resource hosting

Resource hosting provides a particularly clear example of this phenomenon. Most individuals who wish to make a resource available via the Internet will not themselves be operators of a host. They therefore need to come to some arrangement with a host to enable the resource to be stored on the host's computers and made accessible via its servers.

The kinds of issues which resource hosting raises can be demonstrated by examining a simple example, the website[20] of the gliding club of which I am a member:

- The Web pages making up the site are stored on the computers of LineOne.net, which hosts the site. They are accessed from LineOne's Web server. Demon thus has 'possession' of those resources, and also exercises some control over them in that it could delete them from its computers or disable access via its Web server.

---

22 With a few exceptions such as JANET, the UK's Joint Academic NETwork, where the interconnect terms for all academic institutions connected to JANET are identical.

- However, effective control over those resources is exercised by myself. Under my contract with LineOne I can add to or substitute any of those resources, and LineOne agrees to host any website I care to place on its server up to a certain size. This is the only formal relationship between any of the parties to this example. The resources also exist on my PC, from which I upload them to the site, although that PC is not a host and thus users cannot access the resources from me directly.
- The Web pages were authored by another club member, who thus 'owns' them (at least in the copyright sense). He too 'possesses' copies, but again his computer is not a host. However, he has no access to the relevant part of the LineOne host computer, and thus cannot control changes to the website.
- Any user who visits the site will make copies of the Web pages he views in the RAM of his computer, and probably in the cache of his browser software. He too will 'possess' the resources.

From the user's perspective, this division and multiplication of rights and powers is invisible. The website appears to 'belong' in all respects to the gliding club, although a technically sophisticated user might notice that the URL of the site indicates that it is hosted by LineOne . However, if the website were viewed from within a frame[1] on another Web page via a link, the hosting could only be discovered by examining the source code of the page containing the link. None of this matters to the user so far as accessing the resources is concerned.

If, though, a dispute arises over the contents of the website, it becomes essential to discover all the actors involved and their different rights and powers. Suppose that there is an allegation that the website contains defamatory material. The author of the page might have a defence based on privilege, but that defence would probably not be available to the others involved. LineOne might have a defence that it was an innocent distributor, based on its purely ministerial acts in making the resource accessible.[2] The liabilities and defences of the various actors can only be analysed once their precise roles have been ascertained.

1.3.2   Mirroring

The Internet has many bottlenecks, communications links where the traffic is sometimes so heavy that access to resources becomes slow and unreliable. The transatlantic links are typical. European users generally notice that access to US resources is more difficult after lunch, when the US begins to wake up. US users find European resources easier to access in the evenings, when Europeans are asleep.

One technical solution is the mirroring of sites, making and maintaining identical copies on either side of the bottleneck. Hosts then translate a user request for a resource into a request addressed to the most local mirror site, and the resource is fetched from that site.

From a technical and informational perspective mirroring is entirely sensible; the resources are the same at each site. From a legal perspective, identical resources in different geographic locations may have different legal consequences. To give two simple examples:

23 http://website.lineone.net/~rattlesden.
 1 See Chapter 3.3.3 for a discussion of framing.
 2 Note that defamation law varies widely, and the laws of different jurisdictions would produce different results in this example. See Chapter 4 for further discussion.

- A resource on a US site may, so far as that site's host is concerned, comply with trade mark law, but the identical resource on a UK site may infringe a UK trade mark.
- A data resource on a German site may not infringe any copyrights because it attracts no protection under German copyright law, but the same resource on an Australian mirror site may be an infringement because the resource attracts an Australian copyright.

1.3.3   Other hidden elements

1.3.3.1   *Caching*

Some resources are so much in demand that a particular host may find that it is constantly requesting copies on behalf of its client users. An obvious method of reducing network traffic, computing time, and thus costs, is for the host to store a copy of that resource on its own server, and to meet user requests by providing a copy of *that* copy. This is known as caching, and provides a good technical solution provided it incorporates some mechanism for ensuring that the cached resource is updated if the master version changes. The decision to cache a resource is made automatically by software, on the basis of the number of user requests, and is not the result of a conscious decision by the host operator.

Caching also takes place at the user level in many cases. Most browser programs set themselves up to retain temporary copies of all the resources a user has examined, so as to save the effort of fetching the resource again if a site is revisited. Users may be surprised to discover quite how much third party information is stored on the hard disk of their PC.[3]

However, caching can complicate the legal analysis substantially. An action which appears to copy a resource from location A may in fact copy it from location B, or there may be no copying at all (other than from local hard disk into RAM). Additional copies of resources may be stored in caches world-wide – this may be a problem for copyright owners, or may equally present an opportunity.[4]

1.3.3.2   *Java and Active-X*

Recent technological developments have enabled website authors to attach small programs to their Web pages. When the user downloads the page, the program which accompanies it runs on the user's computer. One use of such a program is to request resources from third party servers, which can then be incorporated in the Web page or downloaded to the user's disk. The best known of these technologies are Java[5] and Active-X.[6]

---

3   For Windows 95/98 users, this is usually in the c:\Windows\Temporary Internet Files directory.
4   In the *Netcom* case (*Religious Technology Centre v Netcom On-Line Communications Services Inc* 907 F Supp 1361 (ND Cal 1995) – see Chapter 4.2.1 for further discussion) the plaintiff brought a copyright infringement action against an Internet Service Provider (ISP) in respect of cached copies. The action failed under US law on the grounds of lack of knowledge on the part of the ISP, but had it succeeded it would have enabled the plaintiffs to pressurise other ISPs to block access to that resource. The question of whether a host should be immune from such an action is discussed in Chapter 4.3.2.1.
5   See http://www.sun.com/java/.
6   See http://www.microsoft.com.

From the user's perspective, these resources are being delivered from the website which he accessed. In reality, however, the user is unknowingly performing the acts which access the third party resource. Questions of who is legally responsible for these acts have still to be determined by law.

1.4   THE DISTRIBUTION OF COMPUTING PROCESSES AND THE VIRTUAL SITE

In this chapter the term 'server' has been used extensively. The reader might think that a server is a single, physical computer. This is not necessarily the case. Because the Internet is a network of networks, a particular domain name or its underlying IP address[7] only locates a gateway to that network, which *will* be a single computer. The resources managed by the server, however, may be spread over multiple computers in that network, or even on computers on other networks. The server software itself may not run on the gateway computer. It is not necessary for these computers to be in the same jurisdiction.

Thus, for example, the domain name ibm.com points to a gateway in the US. However, IBM's own network spreads across many countries, and resources may be situated on computers in those countries. This is entirely opaque to the user, who sees the resources as being delivered from ibm.com.

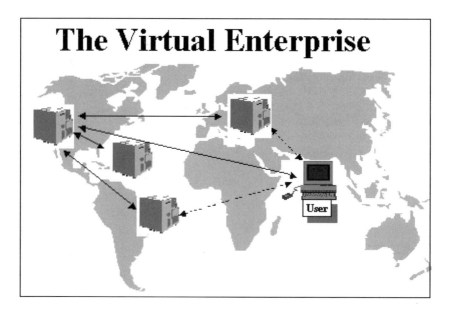

The Virtual Enterprise

The same effect is possible using the Internet itself. There is no reason why an enterprise should not conduct its activities from a virtual site, with the various parts of its digital activities scattered around the world and communicating with each other via the Internet. For example, a business selling downloadable software and accepting credit card payments might structure itself so that orders

7   See Chapter 3.1 for further detail.

are accepted and processed in the US, card payments processed in Luxembourg, delivery made from a Brazilian server, and accounts stored in Madagascar. All communications with customers could be routed through the US server, or if preferred could be controlled by a Java applet running on the customer's computer which communicates directly with the other servers. This structure can be made almost infinitely flexible, with the physical locations changing as required.There are many reasons why a virtual, distributed business structure might be adopted. One highly relevant factor will be that such a structure enables the business to avoid the adverse impact of particular national-level laws and regulations. Tax law is an obvious example, but export controls, copyright laws, record keeping regulations and data protection laws might equally make such a structure advantageous. Some of these issues are addressed in Chapter 10.

1.5 PENETRATING THE CLOUDS

We have moved some distance in this chapter from the amorphous picture of the Internet with which we began. But when presented with a real problem, all the lawyer knows initially is that the Internet was involved. How is the problem to be analysed?

The answer comes from the Internet's fundamental function, as a communications technology. The lawyer's first task must be to build a clear picture of the communications which have taken place, and which led to the problem. By mapping out these communications, the various actors involved, and the roles they played, can be identified. Only then should any attempt be made to classify the problem in legal terms. Because so much of the communications activity of the Internet is otherwise invisible, what initially looked like a simple problem under US copyright law may turn into a complex problem involving unfair competition, contract and criminal laws of several jurisdictions. Alternatively, the apparently complex problem may reveal itself to be extremely simple. Until this mapping of communications has taken place, however, the lawyer cannot even attempt to guess the true nature of the problem.

Chapter 2

From each according to his ability: actors and activities in the Internet world

The process of mapping the flow of Internet communications and determining the roles played by the actors in a transaction is complex, even in the simplest of cases. This is because it is almost never true that only two parties are involved. Every Internet transaction requires the participation of multiple intermediaries, and may well involve more than two actors. Each of these plays its own part in carrying out the transaction.

From the perspective of the naïve observer, it may not be at all obvious that multiple parties are involved, or what their roles are. A legal analysis of the Internet transaction, however, requires an understanding of all those whose activities[1] play a part in the transaction. It is perfectly possible that some action which appears to have been performed by X was in fact carried out by Y, and this will clearly be relevant to the rights and obligations of those involved.

To clarify the investigation of these players and their roles, this chapter will make frequent reference to a simple, hypothetical transaction in which software is sold on-line. In the physical world this transaction is comparatively simple. The buyer enters a shop, agrees to buy the software from the seller, hands over cash, and leaves in possession of a copy of the software. The Internet equivalent is at first sight nearly as simple. The buyer visits the seller's website, selects the software he wishes to purchase, makes payment through some mechanism such as a credit card, and receives the software as a file download. However, for this transaction to be effected, dozens of third parties have also needed to play a part.

2.1 PRINCIPAL ACTORS

The principal actors in an Internet transaction are the easiest to recognise. All Internet transactions work by the transmission of information from one place to another, so the primary actors involved are the sender of that information and its recipient. There may be legal consequences to the exchange of information, so that, for example, they become buyer and seller, licensor and licensee, etc. From the perspective of a legal analysis, however, the most important step is to identify the communications which have taken place and to determine who, in each case, was the sender and the recipient.

---

1 Remembering that in most cases these activities are not the direct result of conscious human decisions, but are carried out automatically by software.

A surprisingly small proportion of Internet communications take place as a result of the unsolicited sending of information. The most obvious example is electronic mail, or email, where the sender transmits a message to a known email address. Other examples might appear to be the new 'push' or Web broadcasting ('webcasting') technologies, which are largely used for news-type distribution of information, but in fact these only provide information on receipt of a request from the user.[2] In almost all cases, information is only sent in response to a request from the ultimate recipient, or, more accurately, that recipient's software.

Thus, a user who wishes to view a Web page needs to instruct his software to fetch that page from the host on which it is stored. The Web page address is entered into the user's browser software, and that software sends a packet to the host named in the address, requesting the page. Software running on the host then transmits the page to the user's computer, using the return address contained in the requesting packet.

In most cases, this immediately complicates the legal analysis. Sometimes the website proprietor and the host will be one and the same, so that we do not need to concern ourselves whether the proprietor or the host should be considered in law as the sender of the Web page. However, in many cases the website proprietor stores his website on a resource host, from which the Web pages are made available to users. Who, then, is the sender? On a technical analysis this must be the host, whose software has responded to the user's request by transmitting the Web page to him. However, that host will rarely, if ever, exercise any control over the contents of the website. The proprietor determines which Web pages are stored on the resource host, and uses the host's services to make those pages available. From this perspective it is the proprietor who sends the page to the user, using the facilities of the host to do so.

In such a scenario, it is unhelpful to ask who the sender of the information is. Instead, we need to recognised that there are three actors involved in the transaction:

- the controller of the resource (in this case a Web page), who determines its information content and who is permitted to have access to it (eg by requiring a password for access to the site);
- the resource host, who stores the Internet-accessible copies of that resource and, on request, transmits copies to the requesting address; and
- the user (in this case the viewer of the website), who requests access from the resource host and receives the resource from that host.

It must also be recognised that the controller's website could be split across multiple resource hosts. In our example, the Web page through which the user places his order for the software could be stored on host A, but the downloadable copy of the software stored on host B. A diagram of the transaction would then look as follows:

---

2   The reason the information appears to be unsolicited is because the user's software is set up to make periodic requests without further authorisation from the user – see http://www.whatis.com/webcasti.htm.

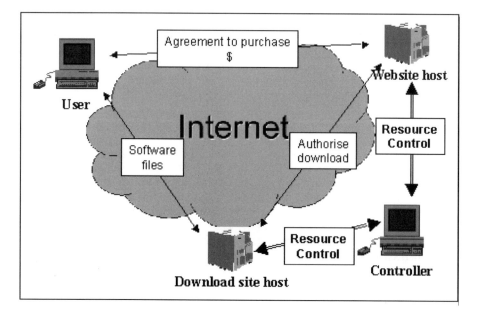

Furthermore, it must not be forgotten that there are hidden elements of the Internet, such as the mirroring and caching of websites (see Chapter 1.3). It is perfectly possible that the user's initial request for the seller's Web page was fulfilled from a cached copy, held by a different host. Once the user filled in his order details, that information would be sent to the controller's resource host for processing, and probably a further Web page confirming the order would be received from that source.

In our hypothetical example it is easy to see that the relationship of buyer and seller is formed between the user and the controller. However, if the software or the content of the Web pages infringes some third party's rights, the functions performed by the resource host and the other hosts involved immediately become relevant to the legal analysis. These questions are examined in detail in Chapter 4.

2.2 INFRASTRUCTURE PROVIDERS

The communications infrastructure of the Internet falls into two categories:

- The underlying physical structure of wires, switches and other communications paths which carry information between hosts. These are controlled and managed by organisations such as telecommunications companies, or in some cases infrastructure leased from telecommunications companies is assembled by backbone organisations such as JANET (the UK's Joint Academic Network). From a legal perspective these organisations are merely owners and operators of the physical equipment which transports information, and play little part in any legal analysis. They will not be considered further in this book.
- The facilitating infrastructure of the Internet, which consists of the transmission, routing and directory services which allow the transmission of TCP/IP packets to their destination. These services are provided across

the physical infrastructure by intermediary service providers, whose roles are considered below.

2.3 INTERMEDIARIES

Intermediaries, in the Internet context, are organisations whose services are used to facilitate a transaction between communicating parties. In our on-line software sale example, the website host and the download site host are both intermediaries without whom the transaction could not be effected. As the remainder of this section demonstrates, there are many other intermediaries who might become involved in the transaction.

2.3.1 Transmission hosts

We have already seen in Chapter 1.2 that an Internet communication will only be successful if its constituent packets are passed from host to host until they reach their destination. In this book, a host which is receiving and passing on a packet is termed a 'transmission host'.

In most cases there will be no direct relationship between the end user and the transmission hosts involved in the communication[3] – indeed, the end user will probably be unaware of which hosts have been involved – and so it might be thought that the role of transmission host would have few legal consequences. However, because transmission hosts transmit packets by copying them and re-sending copies, the question of their liability for the information content of the packets has received substantial legal attention – see Chapter 4.2.

An indeterminate number of transmission hosts will have been involved in our hypothetical software sale, but for the sake of clarity they are omitted from the diagram reproduced above. The grey cloud labelled 'Internet' represents these hosts.

2.3.2 Resource hosts

A user who wishes to make information resources, such as Web pages and other files, available on demand will need to use the services of a resource host. All that a resource host does is to provide space on its disk storage for the user's resources, and then runs software (such as a Web server) which handles requests from other users for access to those resources.

The differences between the types of resource host lie mainly in the matter of who controls the resources residing on the host's disk storage.

2.3.2.1 Website host

The website host is the most visible type of host to non-technical Internet users, as its domain name appears in the URL of the sites visited by that user. Most ISPs provide website space to their subscribers and run Web server software which allows other users to gain access to the site's resources via the HTTP

---

3   With the exception of each end user's access provider – see 2.3.3.1 below.

protocol. Normally, the host creates a directory in which the subscriber's website is stored, and which makes up part of the site's URL. In that directory the subscriber places his Home Page (often index.html or home.html) which contains links to the other pages which comprise the site. The subscriber is usually free to create sub-directories to ease management of the site, and to add to or delete from the site at will.

The primary controller of the website is clearly its proprietor, who normally adds to and deletes from the site via password-controlled FTP. The resource host retains ultimate control, and can delete files or prevent access to the site subject to any contractual terms in the subscriber agreement.[4] However, in practice the host will not examine the content of the files which make up that site unless a complaint is received from a third party.

The resource host is a very visible target if any of the resources on its servers infringe third party rights, as it possesses copies of those resources, has some control over their use, and could in theory (though not in practice) examine the information content of the user's resources before they are made available to other Internet users. These issues are considered in depth in Chapter 4.2.

2.3.2.2   *Newsgroup host*

A newsgroup is a discussion forum, in which Internet users can read and post messages and reply to postings from other users. Newsgroups can be private, or of limited distribution, but the most visible and widely disseminated newsgroups form part of Usenet. A newsgroup is simply a database containing user postings.[5] What makes Usenet so global in scope is that multiple hosts each carry selected newsgroups, add postings they have received to their own copies of the newsgroup database, and periodically swap updates with other Usenet hosts. Thus, a posting to, say, news.demon.co.uk will quickly propagate to all the other news servers which carry the newsgroup in which the posting was made.

Some newsgroups are moderated, so that their control is in the hands of a particular individual or organisation. However, in most cases there is no such moderation, and the contents of the newsgroup reflect the collective input of its readers.

Chip Salzenberg, Gene Spafford, Mark Moraes 'What is Usenet?' ftp:// rtfm.mit.edu/pub/usenet-by-group/news,answers/what-is/part1

AN APPROXIMATE DESCRIPTION

Usenet is a world-wide distributed discussion system. It consists of a set of 'newsgroups' with names that are classified hierarchically by subject. 'Articles' or 'messages' are 'posted' to these newsgroups by people on computers with the appropriate software – these articles are then broadcast to other interconnected computer systems via a wide variety of networks. Some newsgroups are 'moderated'; in these newsgroups, the articles are first sent to a moderator for approval before appearing in the newsgroup. Usenet is available on a wide variety of computer systems and networks,

---

4   See Chapter 1.3 for a practical example of the control and ownership issues inherent in a website.
5   In most cases, postings more than a few weeks old are deleted from the newsgroup itself and may be moved to an archive.

but the bulk of modern Usenet traffic is transported over either the Internet or
UUCP.

. . .

WHAT USENET IS

Usenet is the set of people who exchange articles tagged with one or more universally-
recognized labels, called 'newsgroups' (or 'groups' for short). There is often confusion
about the precise set of newsgroups that constitute Usenet; one commonly accepted
definition is that it consists of newsgroups listed in the periodic 'List of Active
Newsgroups' postings which appear regularly in news.lists.misc and other newsgroups.
A broader definition of Usenet would include the newsgroups listed in the article
'Alternative Newsgroup Hierarchies' (frequently posted to news.lists.misc). An even
broader definition includes even newsgroups that are restricted to specific geographic
regions or organizations. Each Usenet site makes its own decisions about the set of
groups available to its users; this set differs from site to site.

(Note that the correct term is 'newsgroups'; they are not called areas, bases, boards,
conferences, round tables, SIGs, echoes, rooms or usergroups! Nor, as noted above,
are they part of the Internet, though they may reach your site over it. Furthermore,
the people who run the news systems are called news administrators, not sysops. If
you want to be understood, be accurate.)

DIVERSITY

If the above definition of Usenet sounds vague, that's because it is.

It is almost impossible to generalize over all Usenet sites in any non-trivial way.
Usenet encompasses Government agencies, large universities, high schools, businesses
of all sizes, home computers of all descriptions, etc, etc.

(In response to the above paragraphs, it has been written that there is nothing
vague about a network that carries megabytes of traffic per day. I agree. But at the
fringes of Usenet, traffic is not so heavy. In the shadowy world of news-mail gateways
and mailing lists, the line between Usenet and not-Usenet becomes very hard to
draw.)

CONTROL

Every administrator controls his own site. No one has any real control over any site
but his own.

The administrator gets her power from the owner of the system she administers.
As long as her job performance pleases the owner, she can do whatever she pleases,
up to and including cutting off Usenet entirely. Them's the breaks.

Sites are not entirely without influence on their neighbors, however. There is a
vague notion of 'upstream' and 'downstream' related to the direction of high-volume
news flow. To the extent that 'upstream' sites decide what traffic they will carry for
their 'downstream' neighbors, those 'upstream' sites have some influence on their
neighbors' participation in Usenet. But such influence is usually easy to circumvent;
and heavy-handed manipulation typically results in a backlash of resentment.

. . .

IF YOU ARE UNHAPPY . . .

Property rights being what they are, there is no higher authority on Usenet than the
people who own the machines on which Usenet traffic is carried. If the owner of the
machine you use says, 'We will not carry alt.sex on this machine', and you are not
happy with that order, you have no Usenet recourse. What can we outsiders do, after
all?

That doesn't mean you are without options. Depending on the nature of your
site, you may have some internal political recourse. Or you might find external pressure
helpful. Or, with a minimal investment, you can get a feed of your own from
somewhere else. Computers capable of taking Usenet feeds are down in the $500

range now, UNIX-capable boxes are going for under $1000 (that price is dropping fast, so by the time you read this, it may already be out-of-date!) and there are several freely-redistributable UNIX-like operating systems (NetBSD, FreeBSD, 386BSD and Linux from ftp sites all around the world, complete with source code and all the software needed to run a Usenet site) and at least two commercial UNIX or UNIX-like systems in the $100 price range.

No matter what, though, appealing to 'Usenet' won't help. Even if those who read such an appeal are sympathetic to your cause, they will almost certainly have even less influence at your site than you do.

By the same token, if you don't like what some user at another site is doing, only the administrator and owner of that site have any authority to do anything about it. Persuade them that the user in question is a problem for them, and they might do something – if they feel like it, that is.

If the user in question is the administrator or owner of the site from which she posts, forget it; you can't win. If you can, arrange for your newsreading software to ignore articles from her; and chalk one up to experience.

2.3.2.3   FTP site host

An FTP[6] site is a collection of information resources which are accessed by downloading them to the user's disk storage.[7] The host's system administrator controls those who are permitted to upload resources to the site through passwords, but it is generally up to the site's controller to determine whether general access is permitted (through anonymous login) or whether access is restricted to those with passwords. In terms of the legal issues involved, FTP sites can be considered as pretty much equivalent to websites.

2.3.2.4   DNS host

DNS (Domain Name System) hosts provide an important part of the logical communications infrastructure of the Internet. In order to access a server, such as a website or FTP site, the user's software needs to know that site's IP address. IP addresses are sets of four binary numbers, usually written as eg 138.1.22.11. However, users cannot easily remember numerical addresses of this kind, and so providers of Internet resources are permitted to register domain names such as ccls.edu, alphanumeric identifiers for their servers. DNS hosts maintain databases which match domain names to IP addresses, and when a user enters a domain name into his software, that software sends a request to a DNS host which looks up the domain name and returns the corresponding IP address.[8] The software then uses the IP address to access the resource. Domain names are considered further in Chapter 3.1 and 3.2.

Although the DNS lookup service provided by DNS hosts is fundamental to the operation of the Internet, it raises few if any legal issues. All the DNS host does is to provide an address; what the user then does in respect of the resources

---

6   For an explanation of FTP see Kessler and Shepard *A Primer On Internet and TCP/IP Tools and Utilities* Request for Comments 2151, p 15 ff, available from www.ietf.org.

7   Though modern browser software can sometimes be used to display the requested file rather than saving it to disk for later viewing.

8   If the DNS host's database does not have an entry for that domain name, the DNS host interrogates other DNS hosts until it finds (or fails to find) a match for the name, and then adds the name and the corresponding IP address to its database. Thus domain name entries gradually propagate around the system of DNS databases.

available from that address has no connection with the DNS host. However, the allocation of domain names has raised substantial legal questions – see Chapter 3.2.

2.3.3   Communication services

Internet intermediaries can provide a wide range of services to users, the most important of which are those services which allow Internet communications to take place. Unless the user is also a host, it will need to use these intermediary services in order to send information and access resources.

2.3.3.1   Internet Service Providers

End users can only send and receive Internet communications if they are connected to the Internet. An Internet Service Provider (ISP) is normally[9] a host which is connected full-time to other hosts, and which provides access and other services to its subscribers. Subscribers will connect to the ISP through various means, including dial-up connections across the public telecommunications network, and once connected will have access to such Internet resources and facilities as the ISP provides. Some ISPs provide mainly access and ancillary services, such a mailbox and website space. Others may offer a range of additional resources to subscribers only, in addition to providing access to the wider Internet – America On Line (AOL)[10] is a well-known example of the latter category.

ACCESS

Access to the Internet is the most fundamental service provided by an ISP. Once the user is connected to the ISP, the ISP acts as a transmission host by passing packets to and from the user. Some ISPs provide unrestricted access to all Internet resources, whereas others may restrict the resources which can be accessed, eg to provide a 'family-friendly' service.[11]

---

9   In the past, systems known as 'bulletin boards' provided a limited range of Internet services. A bulletin board is simply a computer which is connected to the public telecommunications network and to which subscribers obtain dial-up access to use the resources held on the bulletin board. Some bulletin boards would, through an arrangement with an Internet host, offer such services as email to their subscribers. Periodically, the bulletin board would connect to the host and transfer and receive email. Effectively, the bulletin board had its own email account with the host (eg board@host.co.uk) from which it could send and receive email. Once the board had received its email, software would make the relevant messages available to its users, whose email addresses might read user1.board@host.co.uk, user2.board@host.co.uk, etc.

   Generally speaking, bulletin boards could not provide real-time services such as access to the World Wide Web, but only store and forward services such as email and Usenet news. Most bulletin boards have now become Internet hosts.
10   http://www.aol.com.
11   Probably the best-known example of such an ISP was Prodigy, http://www.prodigy.com. Its family-friendly policy led it into problems of defamation liability in *Stratton Oakmont Inc v Prodigy Services Co* 23 Media L Rep 1794 (NY Sup Ct, May 25 1995) – see Chapter 4.2.3.1.

MAILBOX

The second fundamental service provided by an ISP is the user's mailbox. This is simply a structured storage space on the ISP's computers in which received email is stored and from which sent email is transmitted. Received email waits in that storage space until the user connects to the ISP and decides to download his email, at which time it is marked as 'read' and may be deleted.

The mailbox is necessary because the user is not a full-time connected host – thus if an email message were delivered direct to his computer, communication would often fail because his computer would not be connected and ready to receive it. This inherent delay in email communication raises some interesting contract formation issues which are discussed in Chapter 6.2.

USER RESOURCE HOSTING

ISPs often provide their users with disk space in which to create a resource site, normally a website, which the ISP then make available via its Web server – see 2.3.2.1 above. ISPs may also permit their users to create FTP sites, use the ISP's server for hosting a newsgroup, etc.

ACCESS TO ISP RESOURCES

Finally, the ISP is likely to provide some resources which are accessible only to its users. These may be minimal, eg automated email help or some internal Web pages containing useful information for users. In some cases, however, ISPs provide access to more substantial resources, often provided by third parties, and may charge for access to them. Examples might include commercial newsfeeds or commercial database access.

2.3.3.2   *Directory services*[12]

If a user knows the URL of a resource he can obtain access to it. Without the URL, however, that resource is effectively hidden from the user. This problem is overcome through hosts who offer directory services to Internet users. These fall into two types: structured directories and Web crawler databases.

STRUCTURED DIRECTORY

Structured directories list Web resources under a tree hierarchy. The directory structure is established by the proprietor of the directory, and resource controllers then register their resources, choosing an appropriate category within the directory structure. These directories usually include search facilities as well.

The first and best-known structured directory was Yahoo! (http://www.yahoo.com). A screenshot from the directory is shown below. The Address line in the browser window shows that we have travelled three steps down the directory tree, into Government, then to Law, and then to Technology. The display indicates that below Technology are six sub-classifications: Information, Intellectual

---

12 See also Kessler and Shepard *A Primer On Internet and TCP/IP Tools and Utilities* Request for Comments 2151, p 35, available from www.ietf.org.

Property, Internet, Journals, Technology Transfer and Telecommunications. Within each of these are found links to relevant resources.

Users normally use structured directories by browsing through potentially relevant categories until an interesting resource is discovered, and then accessing that resource via the hyperlink on the directory's Web page.

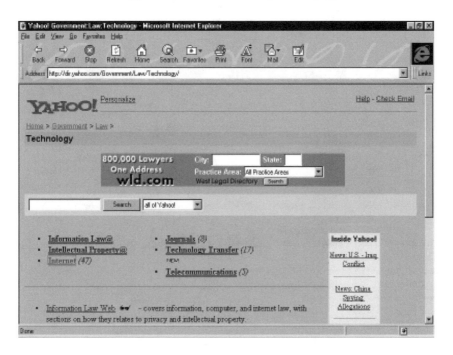

WEB CRAWLER

Structured directories generally list only those resources which have been registered by their controllers. Many important resources are not registered, or the category of registration is not guessable by the user. An alternative way of finding resources is to use a Web crawler such as AltaVista, http://www.altavista.com.

Web crawlers use their 'spare' time, when some of their computing capacity is not being used by searchers, to access websites. At each website they perform two functions:

- First, the Web crawler accesses a page and creates a concordance of it, by producing a list of all the words on the page with the exception of common words, such as 'a' and 'the'. This concordance is then used to update the master concordance database held by the Web crawler's server, adding the page's URL to the master database entry for each word which occurs on the page.
- Second, the Web crawler follows every link on that page to another Web page, and then performs steps one and two on the new page.

When a user searches for a resource, he enters some words into the opening Web page from the Web crawler site. These words are then looked up in the concordance, and every URL for pages on which those words occur is returned. The result is a list of resources which contain the search words, and may thus be relevant.

A screen capture of the search results from AltaVista for 'internet law' is shown below. There were 30,134 matches, so the search probably needs to be refined to produce a manageable number of matches. Most Web crawlers allow quite complicated searches, eg 'internet and (copyright near infringement) and (17 USC)', which should retrieve references to copyright infringement under US law which have some involvement with the Internet.

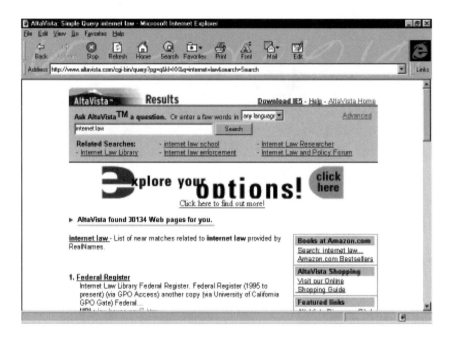

OTHER DIRECTORY SERVICES

Before the arrival of the World Wide Web, search tools for Internet resources were developed which are still available, although they are less easy to use than Web-based directories. The three most important are probably Archie, which searches for filenames, Gopher, which allows the user to browse menus of resources, and WAIS[13] which allows free-text searching of databases. These tools are increasingly less used by ordinary users, and so are not described here.[14]

2.3.3.3   Anonymising

Some Internet users wish to remain anonymous, either because of privacy concerns or in an attempt to avoid unsolicited advertising email ('spam'). Or,

---

13 Wide Area Information Service.
14 For detailed descriptions see Krol *The Whole Internet User's Guide and Catalog* (2nd, Sebastopol CA: O'Reilly & Associates, 1994) Chapters 9, 11 and 12; Kessler and Shepard *A Primer On Internet and TCP/IP Tools and Utilities* Request for Comments 2151, p 30, available from www.ietf.org.

of course, the user may be up to no good, or merely shy. Whatever the reason for the desire for anonymity, services are available to achieve this end. Anonymising services are of two types:

- Anonymous remailers,[15] who receive email from the user requiring anonymity, strip out all message headers which would indicate the origin of the email, and re-send it to its addressee. The anonymous remailer retains records of the sender's identity so that any reply can be routed to the sender of the original message, but promises not to disclose that information.
- Anonymous Web surfing services.[16] When a user requests a Web page, that request identifies the user's access provider and possibly the user's computer. Anonymous Web surfing services send the request as from their own computers but pass on the received Web page to the user. Again, the service provider needs to retain some records of the user's identity, but because there is no substantial delay between requesting a Web page and receiving it, these records need only to be maintained from the time of the user's request until the time the Web page is transmitted to him.

2.3.4   Transaction facilitation services

In order to facilitate an Internet communications transaction, particularly if it is a commercial transaction, additional services may be required. This section does not attempt an exhaustive list of such services, but briefly describes the most common.

2.3.4.1   *Domain name allocation*

In our hypothetical example, the seller of software will probably require its own domain name to assist it in doing business. The domain name is the primary method by which users identify and access websites, and is matched to the IP address (which is the actual method by which resources are accessed) through the DNS system – see 2.3.2.4 above.

Domain names are allocated by domain name registries, either at the country level (eg .uk) or at the global level (.com, .org, etc). In the early days of the Internet these domain names were seen as mere identifiers, and so were allocated on a first come first served basis with no checking to see if some other person had a better 'right' to the name. Once commercial activity began on the Internet, however, disputes began to arise over domain name registrations, with commercial organisations demanding the 'return' of names which were associated with their commercial activities, and in particular names which matched their trade marks. See Chapter 3.2 for further discussion.

2.3.4.2   *Identity services*

Internet actors are whoever they say they are; in other words, there is no necessary connection between a user's chosen on-line identity and his physical

---

15 See eg http://www.replay.com.
16 See eg http://www.anonymizer.com.

world identity. In the early days of the Internet this did not matter too much – the community was small, and if the 'real' identity of a user needed to be discovered this could probably be done through personal contacts.

In the commercial world, however, identification of the parties who are doing business is often vital. For this reason, service providers known as Certification Authorities have evolved, who take evidence of a user's physical world identity and, by electronic means, certify that identity to others. Additional bodies known as Registries, who make copies of ID Certificates available (particularly those identifying Certification Authorities), are also arriving on the scene. These identification services have received substantial legislative attention – see Chapter 5 – and the ID Certificates issued to users play an important role in enabling legally effective electronic signatures to be produced, as discussed further in Chapter 6.1.2.

2.3.4.3 *Payment*

Commercial activity requires some mechanism for making payments, and immediate commercial transactions such as on-line supplies of software require immediate payment systems. All payment systems, with the exception of physical cash, require the transformation of a debt held by the payer to a debt held by the payee. The traditional debtors for payment transactions are the banks[17] and credit card companies.

Internet commerce began by using the existing credit card system, which had developed methods of remote, immediate payment for telephone sales (the 'not present' credit card transaction). Initiatives are now under way in an attempt to develop cheaper and more secure payment mechanisms, which in particular will be suitable for low value payments and thus allow micro information transactions (such as the supply of an image or a share price) to be carried out economically. These require the invention of new types of intermediary, and the resulting legal issues are discussed in Chapter 4.

2.4   THE DISTRIBUTED ENTERPRISE

We saw in Chapter 1.4 that the communications technology of the Internet makes it possible for a commercial enterprise to distribute itself both logically and physically around the globe. What should now also be apparent is that the enterprise cannot perform all the functions necessary to carry out a commercial transaction between itself and its customers without making use of a large number of intermediaries. Not only are the enterprise's constituent elements distributed among its component parts, but the functions necessary to perform the transaction are distributed among those component parts together with the various intermediaries involved.

In our simple software sale, both buyer and seller will have involved several intermediaries:

---

17 The banking system is, generally speaking, both too slow and too expensive for Internet transactions and, save for high value transactions, only available for transfers which do not cross national boundaries.

- The buyer will probably have used:
  - an ISP to gain access to the Internet and to send and receive packets;
  - a directory service to discover the URL of the seller's website;
  - a DNS service to discover the IP address for that URL;
  - numerous transmission hosts to transport his messages to the seller;
  - a Certification Authority to issue an ID Certificate; and
  - a payment service provider to pay the seller.
- The seller will probably have used:
  - an ISP to gain access to the Internet. That ISP will probably have acted as resource host for the seller's website.
  - a domain name registry to obtain his domain name;
  - an additional resource host, which stores the software for downloading;
  - numerous transmission hosts to transport his messages and the software to the buyer;
  - a Registry to check the buyer's identity; and
  - a payment service provider to receive payment.

Thus, if we redraw the diagram of our hypothetical transaction from 2.1 above, omitting the actual communication paths but identifying the types of relationship involved, we see a much more complex picture:

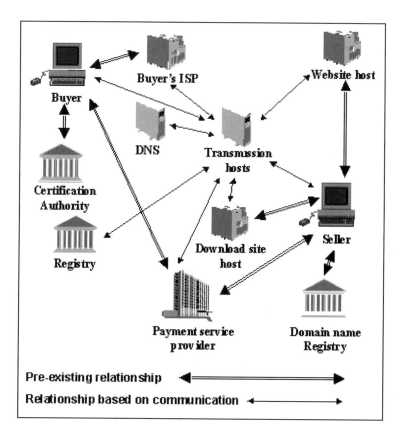

There are two things which are particularly interesting about this diagram. The first is that there is a very small number of pre-existing relationships. Some, but not all, of these will be contractual. In general, as the remainder of this book hopes to demonstrate, those pre-existing relationships are quite similar to their physical world equivalents, and do not present major difficulties in analysing and applying the law.

The second thing is more important; the vast majority of relationships which come into existence during the course of the transaction arise because of some electronic communication between those involved, and the communications almost always pass through transmission hosts. These relationships are thus indirect, and in most cases arise without prior contact, or indeed any formal contact, between the communicating parties. These relationships are new; they are not found in physical world transactions. It would perhaps not be an exaggeration to say that a large part of the new Internet law, whose development is tracked and predicted in this book, is concerned with analysing the legal nature of those relationships and determining and developing the legal rules which apply to them.

Chapter 3

An infinity of scarce resources: ownership and use of Internet resources

3.1   EXPLORING THE PARADOX

The Internet may well be the largest information resource which has ever existed. In theory, there is no limit to its growth. Of course, it will always in fact be finite, but on the scale of human usage it may in practice be treated as potentially infinite. This is true both of the network itself, and of the information resources available via that network.

To take a simple example, accessing a server via the Internet requires one to know its IP address. This is expressed as four binary numbers, each of eight bits (four octets).[1] In theory, therefore, the maximum number of servers which can be connected to the Internet is 2^{32} or in decimal notation 4,294,967,296. To put this in context, the current population of the world is estimated at just under six billion,[2] so that there are probably enough potential IP addresses to allow every adult to run his or her own server. But if this number of potential servers becomes insufficient, each person (including children) in the estimated world population of around 11 billion in 2150 could be allocated nearly 100 IP addresses by modifying the address format to five octets.

Internet users will know that server addresses are identified to humans by domain names. These are expressed in alphanumeric form (eg ccls.edu), and a computer known as a Domain Name Server matches these names to the numerical IP addresses. If a domain name were limited to only eight characters (treating upper and lower case letters as equivalent and including the numerals 0–9), there would be nearly three trillion potential domain names. And domain names can be much longer.

The paradox arises because, although the available quantity of this particular resource is so large (and can be made larger) that in practice we can treat it as infinite, each particular instance of the resource *must* be unique. It is not possible for two servers to be allocated the same IP address, or two IP addresses the same domain name,[3] otherwise the addressing technology would not be able to identify which server was being referred to. Thus, although the total quantity of the resource is great, each particular instance is as scarce as it is possible to be.

---

1   Normally written as decimal numbers, eg 138.1.22.11.
2   'World Population Projections to 2150', Population Division of the Department of Economic and Social Affairs at the United Nations Secretariat, 1 February 1998, http://www.undp.org/popin/wdtrends/execsum.htm.
3   Although a single IP address can be mapped to multiple domain names.

As a result, problems which do not exist in the physical world, or which are comparatively easily coped with, become almost insoluble in the Internet world. Domain names are an excellent example. 'Smith' is a common Anglo-Saxon surname possessed by hundreds of thousands of people. Thousands of businesses trade under the name Smith. The physical world can cope with this duplication. In the Internet world, however, the permissible number of Smith domain names is very small. In the .uk division, the domain name which is likely to be most attractive to a business is smith.co.uk. Once that domain name has been allocated, all other Smiths need to devise alternatives. There are trillions of them, but to a person trading under the name of Smith, q3ewz99m.co.uk is clearly far less attractive or memorable than smith.co.uk.[4]

Competition for scarce resources means that a legal mechanism for allocating those resources is necessary. This is clearly understood in respect of scarce physical world resources such as land, and the necessary mechanisms for allocating ownership and use rights over land have been developed over the centuries. The Internet has created new scarce resources, and new ways of using scarce resources, leaving the law to follow behind in developing methods of resource allocation. The issues to be examined in this chapter are therefore (a) how far the existing legal resource allocation mechanisms can cope with the Internet; and (b) the new resource allocation mechanisms which are under development.

Scarcity of Internet resources derives from a combination of factors:

- Technical uniqueness, as in the case of IP addresses and domain names.
- Semantic uniqueness. The domain name smith.co.uk has meaning to the human mind, whilst the name q3ewz99m.co.uk does not. A white on blue logo is easily readable; a pale blue on paler blue logo is not.
- Economic uniqueness. Trading names and trade marks are the clearest example here. The ability to sell one's goods and services under the name 'Coca Cola' is of much higher value than being forced to sell them under the name 'NewBrand Cola'.
- Origin uniqueness. A legal opinion from Professor Smith of Loamshire University is (probably) of greater value than one from Mr Smith the shopkeeper, and is certainly perceived as more valuable.

The remainder of this chapter will concentrate on two categories of Internet resources, both of which are fundamental to the World Wide Web: domain names, which are characterised by technical, semantic and origin uniqueness; and Web-accessible information resources, which are characterised by origin and economic uniqueness.

3.2   DOMAIN NAMES

The technological function of a domain name is very simple. It is no more than a label for an IP address. When an Internet user enters a domain name into a software application, such as a browser program or an FTP client, the

---

4   The Smiths have ingeniously extended their domain name space by adding prefixes or suffixes to their names – see eg A&B Smith Company, www.absmith.com; Smith International Inc., www.smith-intl.com; Smith Micro Software, www.smithmicro.com; Smith Sign Company, smithsign.com. Another alternative is to incorporate a brand or product name into the URL in place of the company name, eg thus Smith Turf Farms have a site at www.zoysiagrass.com.

software sends that name to one of a number of Domain Name Server (DNS) computers. The DNS searches in its database for the IP address which matches the domain name, and then returns the IP address to the requesting software application. Once the software has received the IP address, it can be used to communicate with the server to which the domain name refers. This is the reason why domain names must be unique; if they labelled more than one IP address, it would be uncertain which server was to be contacted.

For the user, however, the domain name has additional functions. To begin with, it is usually memorable in a way in which IP addresses are not. The domain name for Harvard University's Web server, www.harvard.edu, is far easier to remember than its IP address 128.103.60.55. Domain names can be selected by the operator of the server, and are normally chosen in part to be memorable.

Second, domain names are usually chosen to have a semantic association with operator of the server. The most common choice is the name of the organisation, as in harvard.edu, demon.net and wipo.int. Alternatively, the name may be chosen to describe the activities of the organisation; for example, the domain name lawyers.com is registered to Martindale-Hubbell, producer of the Martindale-Hubbell Law Directory.

Third, domain names may be similar to the registered trade marks or unregistered trading names of a commercial enterprise. 'IBM' and 'Microsoft' are registered as trade marks in a number of jurisdictions, and are closely matched by their domain names ibm.com and microsoft.com.

It is these additional purposes that domain names serve which give rise to legal disputes.[5] The uniqueness of each domain name means that a number of different server operators may well desire the same name. Additionally, an enterprise which has some exclusivity in a name for trading purposes may well object to a different organisation using that name as its domain name.

3.2.1 Initial allocation of domain names

Domain names are allocated by a process of simple registration with the appropriate registrar and payment of the required fee. The server owner devises an appropriate domain name and then checks with an on-line database, operated by one of the registrars, to see if that name has already been taken. If the name is not already registered, it can normally be assigned to the server owner immediately. This 'first come, first served' process of allocating domain names has been held valid by the courts of several jurisdictions.[6]

---

5   'Precisely because they are easy to remember and to identify, however, domain names have come to acquire a supplementary existence as business or personal identifiers. As commercial activities have increased on the Internet, domain names have become part of the standard communication apparatus used by businesses to identify themselves, their products and their activities. Advertisements appearing in the media now routinely include a domain name address, along with other means of identification and communication, such as the corporate name, trademark and telephone and facsimile numbers. But, whereas the telephone and facsimile numbers consist of an anonymous string of numbers, without any other significance, the domain name, because of its purpose of being easy to remember and to identify, often carries an additional significance which is connected with the name or mark of a business or its product or services.' *The Management of Internet Names and Addresses: Intellectual Property Issues*, Interim Report of the WIPO Internet Domain Name Process (WIPO, 23 December 1998), p 3.

6   See eg *Pitman Training Ltd v Nominet UK* [1997] FSR 797; *Interstellar Starship Services Ltd v Epix Inc* Civ No 97-107-FR (D Or 1997); *Alice c Alice* (Cour d'Appel de Paris, 4 December 1998, overturning the *TGI* decision summarised in note 2, p 52).

No other searches are undertaken to check whether the domain name is in use for some other purpose, such as a trade name. So far as the Internet infrastructure is concerned, a domain name is simply an alias for an IP address, and the only type of confusion which needs to be avoided is the issuance of duplicate domain names.

The Management of Internet Names and Addresses: Intellectual Property Issues, **Interim Report of the WIPO Internet Domain Name Process (WIPO, December 23, 1998), pp 2–3**

THE DOMAIN NAME SYSTEM

4.   The domain name system (DNS) serves the central function of facilitating users' ability to navigate the Internet. It does so with the aid of two components: the domain name and its corresponding Internet Protocol (IP) number. A domain name is the human-friendly address of a computer that is usually in a form that is easy to remember or to identify, such as *www.wipo.int.* An IP number is the unique underlying numeric address, such as 192.91.247.53. Distributed databases contain the lists of domain names and their corresponding IP numeric addresses and perform the function of mapping the domain names to their IP numeric addresses for the purpose of directing requests to connect computers on the Internet. The DNS is structured in a hierarchical manner which allows for the decentralized administration of name-to-address mapping. This last new characteristic has provided the basis for the remarkable speed at which new computers can be added to the Internet, while ensuring their accurate name resolution.

5.   The DNS has been administered by IANA, pursuant to principles that were described in Request for Comments (RFC) 1591 of March 1994.[7] The DNS operates on the basis of a hierarchy of names. At the top, are the top-level domains, which are usually divided into two categories: the generic top-level domains (gTLDs) and the country code top-level domains (ccTLDs).

6.   There are, at present, seven gTLDs. Three of these are open, in the sense that there are no restrictions on the persons or entities that may register names in them. These three gTLDs are *.com, .net* and *.org.* The other four gTLDs are restricted, in the sense that only certain entities meeting certain criteria may register names in them. They are *.int,* which is restricted to use by international organizations; *.edu,* which is restricted to use by four-year, degree-granting colleges and universities; *.gov,* which is restricted to use by agencies of the federal government of the United States of America; and *.mil,* which is restricted to use by the military of the United States of America.

7.   There are at present 249 ccTLDs. Each of these domains bears a two letter country code derived from Standard 3166 of the International Standardization Organization (IS0 3166),[8] for example, *.au* (Australia), *.br* (Brazil), *.ca* (Canada), *.eg* (Egypt), *.fr* (France), *.jp* (Japan) and *.za* (South Africa). Some of these domains are open, in the sense that there are no restrictions on the persons or entities who may register in them. Others are restricted, in that only persons or entities satisfying certain criteria (for example, domicile within the territory) may register names in them.

---

7   See http://wipo.isi.edu/in-notes/rfc1591.text. A number of other RFCs have also provided guidance for the administration of the DNS.
8   The attribution of a country code to a domain by IANA entailed no recognition of the status of the territory designated by the country code. As stated in RFC 1591, 'The IANA is not in the business of deciding what is and what is not a country'.

8. Functionally, there is no distinction between the gTLDs and the ccTLDs. A domain name registered in a ccTLD provides exactly the same connectivity as a domain name registered in a gTLD. Nor can it be said that the gTLDs are open, whereas the ccTLDs are restricted. As mentioned, there are open gTLDs and ccTLDs, which contain no restrictions on use, and restricted gTLDs and ccTLDs, which restrict use to persons or entities responding to certain criteria.

9. At the date of publication of this Interim Report [December 1998], nearly 4.8 million domain names have been registered worldwide.[9] Of these, approximately 1.4 million have been registered in the ccTLDs. The approximate weekly volume of new registrations is 70,000.

Domain names must not be confused with property rights in names, such as trade marks. A domain name is acquired through simple contract with a registry,[10] and any rights which the holder has in respect of the name derive from that contract.[11]

3.2.2 Legal rights in names – an inevitable conflict

The fundamental nature of domain names gives rise to an inevitable conflict between holders of legal rights to particular names. The reason for the conflict is that domain names must be *absolutely* unique, while names in which legal rights subsist are only *relatively* unique. In other words, although there can only be one holder of the domain name smith.com, there may be (and are) multiple persons and organisations with legal rights in the name 'Smith'. Over the years the law has evolved mechanisms for partitioning the 'Smith' name space between the users of the name; but it is technically impossible for the smith.com name space to be partitioned, for the reasons given above.

Legal rights in names derive from two sources:

- registration of the name as a trade mark, which gives exclusive rights to use the name for particular purposes within a defined geographical area; and
- actual use of the name for trading, which in most jurisdictions confers some limited rights to prevent others from using the name in such a way as to misappropriate the claimant's trade reputation.

3.2.2.1 Trade marks

A trade mark is a sign, or combination of signs, which is used to distinguish the goods or services of one undertaking from those of another undertaking.[12] The sign may take a number of forms, though in relation to domain names the only signs of relevance are those which consist of the alphanumeric characters capable of constituting a domain name, in effect words. For a sign to constitute a trade mark, it must normally be registered as such by a national trade mark registry. Throughout the industrialised world the basic principles under which

---

9 Statistics from Netnames Ltd http://www.domainstats.com.
10 The definitive list of registrars is held at http://www.internic.net.
11 See eg the Network Solutions Service Agreement, http://www.networksolutions.com/legal/service-agreement.html.
12 See eg Art 2 of Directive 89/104/EEC of 21 December 1988 to approximate the laws of the Member States relating to trade marks.

registration is granted have been agreed in international treaties,[13] but the rights granted by registration are purely national rights.[14]

The trade mark system, however, recognises that it would be inappropriate to grant the exclusive right to use a name or other sign to just one undertaking, even within a single jurisdiction. The basis of trade marks is that they *distinguish* goods and services from those of other undertakings,[15] and there is clearly no danger of confusion if the same mark is used by different undertakings for quite different goods and services. This problem is normally dealt with by adopting the Nice Classification,[16] which sets out 42 categories of goods and services. A trade mark is registered within one or more of these categories, and confers exclusive rights to use the mark within the jurisdiction in relation to goods and services falling within the registered categories. The trade mark is only infringed by another's use of the same mark if that use is (a) in the course of trade, and (b) the mark is used in relation to the same or similar goods or services.[17] A number of cases have already held that the mere registration of a domain name which is identical to a mark, and use of that domain name for eg a website, does not without more amount to commercial use of the trade mark.[18]

This system for allocating rights in names works reasonably well in the physical world, which can be partitioned both geographically and by categorising the goods or services on offer. There is far less partitioning in the Internet. The conflicts with the domain name system may be classified into two types.

The first type of conflict arises in relation to the allocation of domain names, because there are insufficient names to satisfy each trade mark holder:

- Within each country-code top level domain (ccTLD) such as .uk there are potentially 42 different trade mark holders who might all want the domain name trademark.co.uk. The general approach which seems likely to be adopted is that the 'first come, first served' principle should apply, leaving the remaining 41 trade mark holders dissatisfied but with no remedy.[19]
- The same is true of the global top level domain (gTLD).[20] The problem here is very much worse, as every undertaking which does business internationally, or has ambitions to do so, will want a .com registration.

13 Most importantly the Paris Convention and the Trade Mark Law Treaty, both administered by WIPO – www.wipo.org.

14 The main exception to this is the European Union's Community Trade Mark, established by Council Regulation 40/94/EC on the Community trade mark, which grants exclusive rights to use the mark throughout the EU.

15 An application to register a trade mark will be denied if the mark is not sufficiently distinctive of the applicant's products, eg because it is a word commonly used as a generic description for that type of product. Thus no law firm could register the trade mark 'Lawyer'. Similarly, geographic names are usually refused registration – see eg *Yorkshire Copper Works Ltd v Trade Mark Registrar* (1953) 71 RPC 150 (UK House of Lords).

  Additionally, most trade mark registries operate search and opposition procedures to ensure that there is no overlap with existing trade mark holders, and that current users of the proposed mark can make objection to its registration.

16 Set out in the Nice Agreement Concerning the International Classification of Goods and Services for the Purposes of the Registration of Marks, an international treaty administered by WIPO – www.wipo.org.

17 See eg UK Trade Marks Act 1984, s 10.

18 *Panavision International LP v Toeppen*, 945 F Supp 1296, 1303 (CD Cal. 1996); *Academy of Motion Picture Arts & Sciences v Network Solutions Inc*, 989 F Supp 1276, 1997 WL 810472 (CD Cal, 22 December 1997); *Lockheed Martin Corp v Network Solutions Inc*, 985 F Supp 949 (CD Cal 1997).

19 See eg the UK case of *Pitman Training Ltd v Nominet UK* [1997] FSR 797.

20 See eg the US litigation in *Roadrunner v Network Solutions* Docket No 96-413-A (ED Va, 26 March 1996) and the UK litigation in *Prince plc v Prince Sports Group Inc* [1998] FSR 21.

- To complicate matters still further, non-trade mark holders may register a domain name which is identical to the trade mark. Use of that domain name will normally only infringe the trade mark if it is used in the course of trade in respect of the relevant goods or services.[1]

The second type of conflict occurs because the Internet is a global, not a geographical, network. In the physical world, holders of similar trade marks issued in different jurisdictions are rarely exposed to conflict because their systems for marketing are normally country-based, and thus match the geographical boundaries of the trade mark.[2] However, the domain name system allows every server connected to the Internet to be accessed from anywhere else, which means that any trade marks registered in the domain owner's jurisdiction are displayed in other jurisdictions where different persons may hold the mark.[3] A good example of the potential conflict is the domain name Avnet, used by a number of organisations in the information technology field. Avnet.com is used by an Arizona semiconductor and computing services company; avnet.co.nz by a similar company in New Zealand; avnet.org belongs to a New Jersey ISP; and avnet.it gives access to the server of an Italian network services organisation. All these servers are accessible from the other jurisdictions.

Even if there is no actual trade mark infringement, eg because the lines of business are sufficiently dissimilar that the goods and services fall into different trade mark classes, there is nonetheless a danger of trade mark dilution. This occurs when the mark becomes so commonly used that it is less effective, or even completely ineffective, as a mechanism for distinguishing the goods and services of the holder from those of competitors.[4] In recent years, specific provisions making dilution an infringement of the mark have become widespread.[5]

Yee K 'location.location.location: a Snapshot of Internet Addresses as Evolving Property' 1997(1) *Journal of Information, Law and Technology*[6] § 7.1

Dilution focuses protection on a famous mark itself rather than on likelihood of consumer injury. In traditional trademark protection, the focus is in protecting consumers against a 'likelihood of confusion.' In contrast, the focus of dilution is not injury to the potential consumer, but injury to the value of the mark itself and its associated good will. While traditional trademark law protects consumers from a likelihood of confusion, the FTDA affords owners of marks an injunctive remedy

1 *Avnet Inc v Isoact Ltd* [1998] FSR 16, at 19–20.
2 Conflicts tend only to occur when both holders seek to expand to a new country – see eg *Anheuser-Busch Inc v Budejovicky Budvar* [1984] FSR 413, concerning the rival claims of the Czech and US beer manufacturers to the exclusive right to use the name Budweiser in the UK.
3 Thus the www.budweiser.com server, operated by the US brewer, is accessible from the Czech Republic. Assuming the Czech brewer has registered the name Budweiser as a trade mark in that jurisdiction, the US brewer is potentially infringing Czech trade mark law.
4 If the dilution is sufficiently extensive, the holder may lose the mark – see eg UK Trade Marks Act 1994, s 46(1):
     '(1) The registration of a trade mark may be revoked on any of the following grounds . . .
     (c) that, in consequence of acts or inactivity of the proprietor, it has become the common name in the trade for a product or service for which it is registered;
     (d) that in consequence of the use made of it by the proprietor or with his consent in relation to the goods or services for which it is registered, it is liable to mislead the public, particularly as to the nature, quality or geographical origin of those goods or services.'
5 See eg UK Trade Marks Act 1994, s 10(3), US Federal Trademark Dilution Act 1995, 15 *USC* s 1125(c) (1996).
6 http://elj.warwick.ac.uk/jilt/intprop/97_1yee/.

against newcomers whose marks merely cause 'a dilution of the distinctive quality of the mark'.[7]

Under the FTDA, trademark owners must establish four elements for a prima facie case of federal dilution: (1) 'commercial use in commerce' by a (2) newcomer using the mark after it has become (3) 'famous' in way that (4) has the effect of 'diluting' the identifying power of the famous mark.

The requirement that the defendant's use be 'commercial use in commerce' involves a two step analysis. First, the defendant must meet the Lanham Act's definition of 'use in commerce', that is, use in the regular course of interstate trade. For goods, this means the mark must appear on the goods or their containers or labels; for services, the mark must appear in relevant promotional materials. Second, the defendant's use must be 'commercial,' that is, in speech that proposes 'a commercial transaction'.[8] Thus noncommercial speech like in reviews, parodies, and artistic expressions are not actionable under the Dilution Act.

The FTDA lists eight factors for determining whether a mark is famous: distinctiveness, the duration, extent, and geographic extent of its use and publicization, the channels of trade of its use; its recognition in the channels of trade; the nature and extent of similar marks used by third parties; whether and how the mark was federally registered.[9] While statute does not specify the relative weights accorded to these factors, these factors are similar to the traditional likelihood-confusion analysis, which may provide guidance on the application of these factors.

The FTDA defines dilution as the 'lessening of the capacity of a famous mark to identify and distinguish goods and services, regardless of the presence or absence of: (1) competition between the owner of the famous mark and the other parties, or (2) likelihood of confusion, mistake, or deception'.[10] Thus, the FTDA extends for 'famous' marks the traditional Lanham Act protection to providing for claims against non-competing and non-confusing uses if they diminish the effectiveness of the mark.

Historically, courts have recognised three types of dilution: blurring, tarnishment, and disparagement. Dilution by blurring anticipates the 'whittling away' of a senior mark owner's mark by use of a similar mark even if on a dissimilar product. In *Jaguar Cars Ltd v Skandrani*[11] the court found a likelihood of dilution between Jaguar cologne and the automobile. Dilution by tarnishment occurs when use of a junior mark degrades the senior mark by associating to it an undesirable image. In *Chemical Corporation of America v Anheuser-Busch Inc*[12] the slogan 'Where there is life . . . there's bugs' tarnished the beer manufacturer's mark 'Where there is life . . . there's Bud'. Disparagement occurs when a junior user alters the plaintiff's mark in an undesirable way. In *Deere & Co v MTD Products Inc*[13] the junior user diluted the Deere logo by an unflattering depiction of it in comparative advertising.
. . .

The FTDA has already been tested in several cases.[14] In *Hasbro v Internet Entertainment Group Ltd*, Hasbro alleged that defendant's domain name 'candyland.com' infringed on Hasbro's trademark in the children's board game Candy Land. Hasbro argued that operation of defendant's site, which featured adult entertainment, diluted its famous mark and successfully persuaded a federal court on 9 February 1996 to enjoin the use of 'candyland.com'.[15]

In another dispute,[16] Avon Products Inc gained control over 'avon.com' after bring an action under the FTDA and successfully persuading Internic to terminate the defendant's use of 'avon.com'.

7   15 USC § 1125(c)(1).
8   *Virginia State Board of Pharmacy v Virginia Citizens Consumer Council Inc*, 425 US 748 (1976).
9   15 USC § 1125(c)(1)(A)–(H) (1996).
10 15 USC § 1127 (1996).
11 18 USPQ 2d 1626 (SD Fla 1991).
12 306 F 2d 433 (5th Cir 1962).
13 41 E 3d 39 (2d Cir 1994).
14 See list at http://www.law.gwu.edu/lc/internic/recent/rec2.html.
15 40 USPQ 2d (BNA) 1479 (1996).
16 *Avon Products Inc v David K Les et al* Case No 96 Civ 1213 (SDNY, 20 February 1996).

3.2.2.2 Unregistered trade names

Even if a trade name is not registered as a trade mark, the user of the name may have a remedy if a competitor uses the name in such a way as to suggest a commercial connection with him or his products. This remedy is not based on proprietary rights in the name, but on the effect of the competitor's conduct. In essence, the use of the name by the competitor must potentially mislead purchasers of the goods or services in question into believing that the plaintiff has endorsed, or is in some way connected commercially with, the defendant's goods or services. The claim would therefore be based upon the defendant's misappropriation of the plaintiff's trade reputation, and thus fall under the general heading of unfair competition law.[17] Unfair competition law will only provide a remedy where both parties are engaged in business. English law has no general rules against unfair competition, so complaints on this ground would be limited to those falling within the tort of passing off.[18]

However, several civil law jurisdictions have a more strongly developed law of parasitic or unfair competition which provides a remedy for unfair, misleading or disparaging conduct in the course of business. Thus, for example, the Belgian Law of 14 July 1991 on Unfair Practices and the Protection of Consumers arts 22–29 provides a remedy for commercial communications which create confusion with other traders.[19] Article 1 of the German Act Against Unfair Competition prohibits in general terms misleading conduct in the course of business as an act of unfair competition. Similar provisions are found in art 260 (formerly art 212) of the Portuguese Código da Propriedade Industrial 1940 as amended.

Unfair competition law is not purely a civil law phenomenon, at least as regards misappropriation of trade reputation. In Australia, s 52 of the Commonwealth Trade Practices Act 1974 provides:

'A corporation shall not, in trade or commerce, engage in conduct that is misleading or deceptive or is likely to mislead or deceive.'

and this has been developed through case law to deal with a wide range of unfair competition issues. In the US, s 43(a) of the Lanham Act[20] appears to be developing along similar lines to the Australian law. Section 43(a) provides a remedy for the use in commerce of:

---

17 An internationally agreed definition of the basic principle of unfair competition law is set out in art 10*bis*(2) of the Paris Convention for the Protection of Industrial Property (Stockholm Act 1967):
    'Any act of competition contrary to honest practices in industrial or commercial matters constitutes an act of unfair competition.'
For a comprehensive digest of world unfair competition laws see John R Olsen and Spyros M Maniatis, *Trade Marks: World Law & Practice* (London: FT Law and Tax, 1996) at § 22 of each national summary.
18 This action is more limited than general unfair competition laws, and is based on misrepresentations as to the goods or services of the proprietor which are likely to cause damage to that person's goodwill – *Erven Warnink BV v J Townsend & Sons (Hull) Ltd* [1980] RPC 31.
19 It also provides a remedy against communications which contain disparaging statements (even if true) which relate to another trader or his products or services, and against unfair comparative advertising. These might be relevant to a claim that linking to the plaintiff's website is an act of unfair competition – see part 3.3 below.
20 15 USC § 1125(a). See further US Restatement (Third) of Unfair Competition (1993) §§ 2–8.

'. . . any word, term, name, symbol, or device . . . or any false designation of origin, false or misleading description of fact, or false or misleading representation of fact . . .'

which is likely to cause confusion, mistake or deception as to the connection or relationship between the parties. The authorities indicate that the Lanham Act goes beyond trade mark infringement and creates a federal statutory tort which gives broad protection against various forms of unfair competition and false or misleading advertising.[1] In particular, the courts have given remedies for parasitic competitive practices which attempt to take advantage of another's commercial reputation, particularly in the field of media-related marketing.[2]

It seems probable, however, that simply adopting a domain name which is used by the plaintiff as a trade name will not be sufficient to found an action unless the plaintiff has registered that name as a trade mark. In the Australian case of *McIlhenny Co v Blue Yonder Holdings Pty Ltd (formerly) Tabasco Design*[3] the plaintiff manufacturer of Tabasco sauce alleged that the use of the word 'Tabasco' in the name of the defendant design company indicated a commercial connection between them and was thus an infringement of s 52 of the Commonwealth Trade Practices Act 1974. There were no visual similarities between the Tabasco sauce label and the defendant's logo, and the court held that the parties' fields of activity were so different that no misleading or deceptive conduct resulted.

3.2.2.3   *Trade name protection and free speech*

Protection of a trade name against its use by another as a domain name requires proof of false or misleading conduct on the part of the domain name holder, and thus provides no remedy against innocent, non-confusing use. A claim for trade mark infringement must demonstrate that the domain name has been used in the course of trade in relation to goods or services falling within the trade mark's registered classifications.[4] A claim based on unfair competition must normally show that the business use of the domain name misappropriated the plaintiff's trade reputation. These limitations allow a wide range of non-actionable uses of the word or words which constitute the domain name.[5]

More extensive protection of domain names, and trade names generally, would immediately create a conflict with the fundamental principle of freedom of speech, the best known example of which is possibly the First Amendment to the US Constitution. Indeed, this conflict has already come before the US courts. The Georgia Computer Systems Protection Act 1991[6] purported to create a new criminal offence of transmitting data which uses a name, trade name, logo, etc falsely to identify the transmitter, or which falsely states or implies that the transmitter has permission or is authorised to use the name, etc. It

---

1   *Colligan v Activities Club of New York Ltd* 442 F 2d 686 (1971); *Alfred Dunhill Ltd v Interstate Cigar Co Inc* 499 F 2d 232 (1974); *Estate of Elvis Presley v Russen* 513 F Supp 1339 (1981).
2   *Dallas Cowboys Cheerleaders Inc v Pussycat Cinema Ltd* 604 F 2d 200 (1979); *Woody Allen v National Video Inc* 610 F Supp 612 (1985).
3   (1997) 149 ALR 496.
4   Eg UK Trade Marks Act 1994, s 10.
5   For a discussion of the conflict between free speech principles and trade marks, in the context of domain names, see *Planned Parenthood Federation of America Inc v Richard Bucci d/b/a Catholic Radio*, 1997 42 USPQ 2d (BNA) 1430 (1997).
6   Ga Code 1981, 16 September 1990 to 16 September 1994.

would thus have criminalised many previously permissible domain names. In June 1997 the Georgia Computer Systems Protection Act was held void as unconstitutional in *ACLU of Georgia v Miller*.[7]

It seems likely that the conflict between the domain name system and the legal protection of trade marks and trade names will be unable to be resolved by legislation. Instead, the legal focus in the coming years will be on methods of resolving that conflict.

3.2.3 Resolution of domain name disputes

Lars Davies *A Model for Internet Regulation? – Constructing a Framework for Regulating Electronic Commerce* (London: Society for Computers and Law, 1999), p 35[8]

One possible solution to the problem caused by the scarce capacity of the gTLDs or generic top level domains would be to dissolve the '.com' and '.org' domains, instead requiring the right holders to register under the ccTLDs or country top level domains in which they hold registered trade marks. This would solve a large section of conflicts where conflicting right holders hold marks in different jurisdictions. It would do little to alleviate the problems caused by similar or the same marks registered by different right holders within the same jurisdiction for different classes[9] or between users who might legitimately use the same or similar mark.[10] As a realistic proposal it would fail, however, as domain name holders in these gTLDs would strongly resist losing their registrations.

One radical solution that was proposed by an independent group of users was to set up a completely new name system, based on the domain name system technology, where name holders could themselves decide on the domains that they wished to register, including the top level domains. The system was designed to be completely self sufficient and independent from the existing domain name system[11] and would have its own rudimentary dispute resolution mechanism.

Another proposal, and one which has found many advocates is one which calls for the expansion of the numbers of gTLDs that are currently available. The different proposals have called for varying numbers of new gTLDs, from three to over one hundred. Some have even called for specific proposals to have a special gTLD for registered trademarks and gTLDs for specific classes of business.[12] Though these are

---

7 Case 1:96-cv-2475-MHS (ND Ga, 20 June 1997). Judgment available at http://www.aclu.org/court/aclugavmiller.html.

8 Available in electronic form from http://www.scl.org.

9 *Avnet Incorporated v Isoact Ltd* [1998] FSR 16.

10 *Pitman Training Ltd v Nominet UK* [1997] FSR 797. Though it came before the Trade Marks Act 1994 the case of *Anheuser-Busch Inc v Budejovicky Budvar* [1984] FSR 413 is an interesting case which highlights these problems quite well.

11 Such a system is very easy to establish and would use the same technology and software that the current domain name system uses. The current domain name system uses a defined set of root servers, servers that know the Internet locations of all the servers that service the top level domains. All clients and name servers can have access to the root servers. All that a new system would need be a different set of root servers. In January 1999 an attack on the current domain system comprised of re-mapping the pointers in the domain name system to a new set of root servers that only accesses a small proportion of existing domains. For a short time the Internet did not operate correctly as clients and name servers could not map the majority of DNS names to IP addresses.

12 This is, to some degree, akin to partitioning of marks under the 42 classes of the Nice Classification. However, it does not achieve the same purpose as the Nice Classification partitions marks within each independent jurisdiction. To achieve a similar effect with the domain name system the 42 classes under the Nice Classification would each need their own separate domains under each ccTLD. This would not only prove somewhat cumbersome, requiring the registrars to become involved more closely with trade mark law and practice, something which most would refuse to do, but could also prove unacceptable to the marketing departments within businesses.

seductive arguments the result would be to essentially multiply the domains in which conflict would arise. One particular proposal from the WIPO suggested the creation of a gTLD specifically for registered trade marks with a second level domain of randomly assigned number strings to help differentiate between identical trade marks belonging to separate rights holders. The more memorable the number string the higher the registration fee. This again would most probably result in conflict over who could register the second level domains with squabbles over certain memorable number strings a certainty.

The World Intellectual Property Organisation has recognised the problems raised by the clash between the domain name system and trade marks. As a consequence the WIPO Arbitration and Mediation Centre is developing an on-line Internet based system for administering commercial disputes involving intellectual property. Though this may well be expanded to cover the areas under the remit of the WIPO, the Centre will initially concentrate on domain name disputes. The dispute resolution mechanism is unique in that it is designed to be used on-line, both for document exchange and for filing, though original documentary evidence will still need to be filed in a physical form, and for real-time communications between the various parties involved. The dispute resolution mechanism is simply aimed at providing an inexpensive and efficient service and does not, in any way, seek to take the place of national jurisdictions. It is simply a service which users can agree to use instead of taking the dispute before a national court.

Two domain name registration systems have agreed to use the Centre's services, the INternet One system, which allocated domains under the '.io' domain, and the new international system proposed by the Generic Top Level Domain Memorandum of Understanding or gTLD-MoU.[13] These two systems are attempting to introduce an operations framework to resolve domain name and trade mark disputes.

The United States government recently published its plans to overhaul the administration of the IP number allocation and domain name systems in a statement of policy.[14] The United States government has proposed to withdraw from its role in administering the IP number allocation and domain name administration and hand the role over to a private not-for-profit corporation to be established in the United States.[15] The proposal does not resolve the conflicts between trade marks and domain names. Rather it notes the issues in a salient manner[16] and calls for the World Intellectual Property Organisation to initiate a balanced and transparent process to deal with the issues. This will most likely involve the WIPO Arbitration and Mediation Centre and the procedures that are currently being developed.

13 The Generic Top Level Domain Memorandum of Understanding is an international governance framework that domain name registrars can sign up to in which policies for administering and developing the domain name system are developed and deployed by its members. The World Wide Web address for the gTLD-MoU is http://www.gtld-mou.org.
14 *Management of Internet Names and Addresses*, Docket Number 980212036-8146-02, published by the National Telecommunications and Information Administration. A copy is available on-line at http://www.ntia.doc.gov.
15 This is totally in line with the first principle enunciated in the *Framework for Global Electronic Commerce*, published by the US Department of Commerce, namely that 'the private sector should lead'. The United States government is very keen to promote self-regulation wherever this proves possible. The lack of governmental representation on the board of the proposed corporation, there will not be any, has predictably drawn fire from the European Commission.
16 'In trademark/domain name conflicts, there are issues of jurisdiction over the domain name in controversy and jurisdiction over legal persons (the trademark holder and the domain name holder). This document does not attempt to resolve questions of personal jurisdiction in trademark/domain name conflicts. The legal issues are numerous, involving contract, conflict of laws, trademark, and other questions. In addition, determining how these various legal principles will be applied to the borderless Internet with an unlimited possibility of factual scenarios will require a great deal of thought and deliberation. Obtaining agreement by the parties that jurisdiction over the domain name will be exercised by an alternative dispute resolution body is likely to be at least somewhat less controversial than an agreement that the parties will subject themselves to the personal jurisdiction of a particular national court. With this in mind, the references to jurisdiction in this policy statement are limited to jurisdiction over the domain name in dispute, and not to the domain name holder.'

This review of a selection of the proposals for reforming the domain name system demonstrates that technical change is unlikely to overcome the basic conflict with legal rights in trade names. This leaves two possible mechanisms for resolving disputes: mediation and/or arbitration, and litigation.

3.2.3.1 RESOLUTION OUTSIDE THE COURT SYSTEM

Because of the contractual nature of the relationship between the holder of a domain name and the registry, it is possible to provide in that contract for some initial dispute resolution by the registry itself. The Internet Corporation for Assigned Names and Numbers[17] (ICANN) has produced a Dispute Resolution Policy to which all domain name registries now adhere.

Uniform Domain Name Dispute Resolution Policy (As Approved by ICANN 24 October 1999, © ICANN 1999)[18]

1. PURPOSE

This Uniform Domain Name Dispute Resolution Policy (the 'Policy') has been adopted by the Internet Corporation for Assigned Names and Numbers ('ICANN'), is incorporated by reference into your Registration Agreement, and sets forth the terms and conditions in connection with a dispute between you and any party other than us (the registrar) over the registration and use of an Internet domain name registered by you. Proceedings under Paragraph 4 of this Policy will be conducted according to the Rules for Uniform Domain Name Dispute Resolution Policy (the 'Rules of Procedure'), which are available at www.icann.org/udrp/udrp-rules-24oct99.htm, and the selected administrative-dispute-resolution service provider's supplemental rules.

. . .

3. CANCELLATIONS, TRANSFERS, AND CHANGES

We will cancel, transfer or otherwise make changes to domain name registrations under the following circumstances:

a. subject to the provisions of Paragraph 8, our receipt of written or appropriate electronic instructions from you or your authorized agent to take such action;
b. our receipt of an order from a court or arbitral tribunal, in each case of competent jurisdiction, requiring such action; and/or
c. our receipt of a decision of an Administrative Panel requiring such action in any administrative proceeding to which you were a party and which was conducted under this Policy or a later version of this Policy adopted by ICANN. (See Paragraph 4(i) and (k) below.)

We may also cancel, transfer or otherwise make changes to a domain name registration in accordance with the terms of your Registration Agreement or other legal requirements.

4. MANDATORY ADMINISTRATIVE PROCEEDING

This Paragraph sets forth the type of disputes for which you are required to submit to a mandatory administrative proceeding. These proceedings will be conducted before one of the administrative-dispute-resolution service providers listed at www.icann.org/udrp/approved-providers.htm (each, a 'Provider').

---

17 'The Internet Corporation for Assigned Names and Numbers (ICANN) is the non-profit corporation that was formed to assume responsibility for the IP address space allocation, protocol parameter assignment, domain name system management, and root server system management functions performed under US Government contract by IANA and other entities.' http://www.icann.org.

18 http://www.icann.org/udrp/udrp-policy-24oct99.htm.

a. Applicable disputes. You are required to submit to a mandatory administrative proceeding in the event that a third party (a 'complainant') asserts to the applicable Provider, in compliance with the Rules of Procedure, that
    (i)   your domain name is identical or confusingly similar to a trademark or service mark in which the complainant has rights; and
    (ii) you have no rights or legitimate interests in respect of the domain name; and
    (iii) your domain name has been registered and is being used in bad faith.
   In the administrative proceeding, the complainant must prove that each of these three elements are present.
b. Evidence of registration and use in bad faith. For the purposes of Paragraph 4(a)(iii), the following circumstances, in particular but without limitation, if found by the Panel to be present, shall be evidence of the registration and use of a domain name in bad faith:
    (i)   circumstances indicating that you have registered or you have acquired the domain name primarily for the purpose of selling, renting, or otherwise transferring the domain name registration to the complainant who is the owner of the trademark or service mark or to a competitor of that complainant, for valuable consideration in excess of your documented out-of-pocket costs directly related to the domain name; or
    (ii) you have registered the domain name in order to prevent the owner of the trademark or service mark from reflecting the mark in a corresponding domain name, provided that you have engaged in a pattern of such conduct; or
    (iii) you have registered the domain name primarily for the purpose of disrupting the business of a competitor; or
    (iv) by using the domain name, you have intentionally attempted to attract, for commercial gain, Internet users to your web site or other on-line location, by creating a likelihood of confusion with the complainant's mark as to the source, sponsorship, affiliation, or endorsement of your web site or location or of a product or service on your web site or location.
c. How to demonstrate your rights to and legitimate interests in the domain name in responding to a complaint. When you receive a complaint, you should refer to Paragraph 5 of the Rules of Procedure in determining how your response should be prepared. Any of the following circumstances, in particular but without limitation, if found by the Panel to be proved based on its evaluation of all evidence presented, shall demonstrate your rights or legitimate interests to the domain name for purposes of Paragraph 4(a)(ii):
    (i)   before any notice to you of the dispute, your use of, or demonstrable preparations to use, the domain name or a name corresponding to the domain name in connection with a bona fide offering of goods or services; or
    (ii) you (as an individual, business, or other organization) have been commonly known by the domain name, even if you have acquired no trademark or service mark rights; or
    (iii) you are making a legitimate noncommercial or fair use of the domain name, without intent for commercial gain to misleadingly divert consumers or to tarnish the trademark or service mark at issue.

. . .

k. Availability of court proceedings. The mandatory administrative proceeding requirements set forth in Paragraph 4 shall not prevent either you or the complainant from submitting the dispute to a court of competent jurisdiction for independent resolution before such mandatory administrative proceeding is commenced or after such proceeding is concluded. If an Administrative Panel decides that your domain name registration should be canceled or transferred, we will wait ten (10) business days (as observed in the location of our principal office) after we are informed by the applicable Provider of the Administrative Panel's decision before implementing that decision. We will then implement the decision unless we have received from you during that ten (10) business day period official documentation (such as a copy of a complaint, file-stamped by the clerk of the court) that you have commenced a lawsuit against the complainant in a jurisdiction to which the complainant has submitted under Paragraph 3(b)(xiii) of the Rules of Procedure. (In general, that jurisdiction is either the location of our principal office or of your address as shown in our Whois database. See Paragraphs 1 and 3(b)(xiii) of the Rules of Procedure for details.) If we receive such documentation within the ten (10) business day period, we will not implement the Administrative Panel's decision, and we will take no further action, until we receive (i) evidence satisfactory to us of a resolution between the parties; (ii) evidence satisfactory to us that your lawsuit has been dismissed or withdrawn; or (iii) a copy of an order from such court dismissing your lawsuit or ordering that you do not have the right to continue to use your domain name.

5.   ALL OTHER DISPUTES AND LITIGATION

All other disputes between you and any party other than us regarding your domain name registration that are not brought pursuant to the mandatory administrative proceeding provisions of *Paragraph 4* shall be resolved between you and such other party through any court, arbitration or other proceeding that may be available.

6.   OUR INVOLVEMENT IN DISPUTES

We will not participate in any way in any dispute between you and any party other than us regarding the registration and use of your domain name. You shall not name us as a party or otherwise include us in any such proceeding. In the event that we are named as a party in any such proceeding, we reserve the right to raise any and all defenses deemed appropriate, and to take any other action necessary to defend ourselves.

7.   MAINTAINING THE STATUS QUO

We will not cancel, transfer, activate, deactivate, or otherwise change the status of any domain name registration under this Policy except as provided in Paragraph 3 above.

The basic principles of this dispute policy can be summarised as follows:

- the 'first come, first served' method of allocating domain names remains fundamental;
- however, a trade mark proprietor in any jurisdiction who makes a genuine complaint of bad faith registration[19] is entitled to relief under the policy if the mandatory administrative proceeding finds in his favour;
- the administrative proceeding does not act as arbiter on the question whether the use of the domain name does in fact infringe the trade mark, but merely whether it is identical or confusingly similar to the trade mark and whether the other requirements are met,[20] and
- if the defendant also has a registered trade mark, the complaint should fail as the defendant will have a right or legitimate interest in the domain name under clause 4(a)(ii) of the policy.

---

19 Thus a mere allegation that a domain name is identical to a trade mark is insufficient – the proprietor of the mark must allege that the registrant has no legitimate interest in the domain name and that it acted in bad faith.

20 Though see ICANN Rules for Uniform Domain Name Dispute Resolution Policy http:// www.icann.org/udrp/udrp-rules-24oct99.htm Rule 15(a), which allows the panel to take into account any principles of law that it deems applicable.

The World Intellectual Property Organisation has proposed that an administrative dispute resolution procedure should be developed, operating largely on-line, which would mediate between the parties in dispute over the domain name.[1] This procedure would be an alternative to litigation or arbitration. The principles to be applied when resolving disputes should be:

> *The Management of Internet Names and Addresses: Intellectual Property Issues* Interim Report of the WIPO Internet Domain Name Process (WIPO, 23 December 1998), p 56

199. GUIDING PRINCIPLES

Review of the cases which have been decided in national courts concerning domain names and intellectual property rights indicates that seven principles can be identified which could serve as a basis of reference for decision-makers in reaching decisions. These principles are:

(i) The rights and interests of the parties. These would include not only intellectual property rights that the parties may have in, or in relation to, the name, but also any other rights and interests.[2]

(ii) The use of the domain name. Relevant questions here are whether the holder is actually using the domain name, and, if so, any goods, services or purposes in connection with which the domain name is being used; whether such use is commercial or non-commercial, or relates to public service; the extent of public recognition of the domain name; and the contents of the web pages or email messages associated with the domain name. The intended use of the domain name by the third party complainant would also be taken into consideration and balanced against the interests of the domain name holder.[3]

---

1   *The Management of Internet Names and Addresses: Intellectual Property Issues,* Interim Report of the WIPO Internet Domain Name Process (WIPO, 23 December 1998), p 46 ff.

2   See eg *Pitman Training Ltd v Nominet UK* [1997] FSR 797 (*http://www.open.gov.uk/lcd/scott.htm*) (court weighed the competing interests of two companies legitimately trading under the name 'Pitman' in a dispute over the rights to the domain name *pitman.co.uk.* The domain name was reassigned to the original owner in view of the 'first-come, first-served' principle); *Alice c Alice,* (TGI de Paris, Ord Référé, 12 March 1998 (see http://www.legalis.net/legalnet/judiciaire/ decisions/ord_120398.htm) (in a conflict between the holder of a domain name who also had an independent right in the name and the owner of a trademark registered at an earlier time, the tribunal decided in favour of the trademark owner, thus not following the first-come, first-served principle) [*author's note: this decision has since been overturned – see note 6, p 39*]); *Planned Parenthood Federation of America Inc v Richard Bucci d/b/a Catholic Radio,* 1997 US Dist LEXIS 3338 (1997) (where defendant registered a domain name very similar to the trademark of Planned Parenthood and used the site primarily to criticise or make political statements, the court balanced the interests in protection of free speech against the likelihood of confusion arising from the use of the domain name, before granting an injunction to enjoin use of the domain name).

3   *Panavision International LP v Toeppen,* No 97-55467 (9th Cir, April 1998) (Court of Appeals determined that registering trademarks as domain names and attempting to sell them constitutes 'commercial use' under United States law); *Pitman Training Ltd v Nominet UK* [1997] FSR 797 (see http://www.open.gov.uk/lcd/scott.htm) court found that, in light of the facts in that case, use of the domain name was insufficient to establish a passing off action); *Interstellar Starship Services Ltd v Epix Inc,* Civ No 97-107-FR (Dor 1997) (see *http://www.bna.com/e-law/cases/epix.html*) (court found that in the absence of a risk of confusion, use of the domain name 'epix.com' did not infringe the registered trademark 'EPIX'); *Toy R'Us Inc v Eli Abir and Web Site Management,* 1997 US Dist LEXIS 22431 (1997) (court granted an injunction to prevent the defendant's use of the domain name toysareus.com, including to solicit international business or seeking to sell the domain name to foreign purchasers for use in foreign markets, on the grounds of infringement of a famous trademark); *Epson,* District Court of Dusseldorf (34 191/96, April 4 1997) (court held that even though the person had not used the domain name 'epson.de' for email or web page, there was a concrete threat that he would do so later, and stated that to establish a likelihood of confusion it was irrelevant what kind of products or services were offered on the web site; the products to be compared were the web sites as such, regardless of the content of the website).

(iii) The length of time of registration. If the domain name has been registered and used by the domain name holder for a considerable period, and the third party complainant has waited for a long time before disputing the domain name, this could affect the outcome of the case.
(iv) The nature of the top-level domain in which the domain name is registered. This factor could have a bearing on the resolution of the dispute, although the gTLDs as they currently exist are not sufficiently differentiated (nor in practice are registrations differentially made by users) for this to become an important factor in the immediate future.
(v) Abusive registration of the domain name. The definition of what might constitute an abusive registration of a domain name is discussed in the next chapter. The issues identified in that discussion would be taken into account here and any indications that the domain name was registered abusively would be a ground for decision.
(vi) Identical or confusingly similar. It should be considered whether the domain name is identical or confusingly similar to the intellectual property right asserted in the claim, or whether any use of the domain name either avoids or compounds any such confusion.[4]
(vii) First-come, first-served principle. This principle reflects the accepted current practice for registering domain names and would remain an important factor to be weighed, of particular relevance in cases where no clear outcome is likely to follow from an application of the previous factors.[5]

3.2.3.2   Resolution through the courts

The primary role of the courts is to decide whether the use of a domain name infringes the plaintiff's trade mark registered in that jurisdiction or, where a registry has reallocated or removed a domain name, whether the registry's action was correct. These matters can be determined under well-established principles of trade mark or contract law.

More difficult is the resolution of a new phenomenon which has arisen from the Internet's domain name system – the prospective registration of domain

---

4   *Sté Coopérative Agricole Champagne Céréales c/ JG*, (TGI de Versailles, Ord Référé, 14 April 1998) (see http://www.legalis.net/legalnet/judiciaire/tgi_versailles_0498.htm) (Tribunal Found that the use of the *dénomination sociale* of a company by another individual working in the same area created a risk of confusion); *Commune d'Elancourt c/ Loic L*, TGI de Versailles, Ord Référé, 22 October 1998 (see http://www.legalis.net/legalnet/judiciaire/decisions/ord_221098.htm) (Tribunal found that a site named 'Elancourt Bienvenue à Elancourt' created confusion with the site of the city of Elancourt 'Ville d'Elancourt', and ordered the individual to stop using the former denomination); *Heidelberg*, Munich District Court, 1996 CR 353 (court, in a conflict concerning the domain name 'heidelberg.de' between the City of Heidelberg and a computer company providing a website containing information on the City of Heidelberg, stated that the computer company 'use of the name would harm the interest of the city of Heidelberg because most Internet users would associate the site with the city; the fact that the city of Heidelberg could use a different domain name was considered irrelevant since the computer company has no right to the name 'Heidelberg' in a first place); *Tractebel*, T Co de Bruxelles, 6 June 1997, (where the domain name coincided with the name of the company 'Tractebel', the Tribunal ruled that it would not deprive the domain name holder of his rights in the domain name) (decision on appeal).
5   *Pitman Training Ltd v Nominet UK* [1997] FSR 797 (see http://www.open.gov.uk/lcd/scott.htm) (two companies trading under the name 'Pitman' disputed rights to the domain name *pitman.co.uk*, which had been originally assigned to Pitman Publishing, but erroneously reassigned to Pitman Training/PTC. The domain name was reassigned to the original owners in view of the 'first-come, first-served' principle).

names which might be wanted by commercial enterprises, with a view to selling the registration to those enterprises at a substantial profit. This activity has been described as 'domain name piracy', 'cyberpiracy' and 'cybersquatting'.[6]

The problem with cybersquatting is that the domain name holder has not actually used the domain name in respect of the trade mark holder's goods or services; in other words, he has committed no direct act which infringes the trade mark. This has not prevented the courts from providing a remedy to the trade mark holder on various grounds, including trade mark dilution,[7] passing off[8] and unfair competition.[9]

Two important appellate decisions illustrate the different grounds on which cybersquatting can be restrained. In the US, the 9th Circuit Court of Appeals decided *Panavision International LP v Toeppen*[10] on the basis of dilution of a famous trade mark. Here the defendant had registered over 100 trade marks as domain names, and had several times offered to sell them to the trade mark owners, including offering to sell the domain panavision.com to the plaintiff. He did not use these marks in relation to the goods or services in respect of which the marks were registered – for example, the website www.panavision.com contained photographs of the town of Pana, Illinois. In spite of this care on the defendant's part, the court held him guilty of infringing the Federal Trademark Dilution Act, 15 USC. § 1125(c), which provides:

> The owner of a famous mark shall be entitled . . . to an injunction against another person's commercial use in commerce of a mark or trade name, if such use begins after the mark has become famous and causes dilution of the distinctive quality of the mark . . .

The important distinction between this provision and ordinary trade mark infringement is that in the case of famous marks, *any* commercial use may amount to dilution, not merely use in respect of the registered class of goods or services. The court determined that the defendant's conduct in registering marks and attempting to sell them constituted a commercial use of the marks,[11] and thus fell within the statute.

In the UK, the cybersquatting issue came before the Court of Appeal in *Marks & Spencer plc and others v One In A Million Ltd.*[12] The facts were very similar to the *Panavision* case, as the defendants had registered numerous trade marks

---

6 See eg the US National Telecommunications and Information Administration White Paper, *Statement of Policy on the Management of Internet Names and Addresses* (5 June 1998) section 8, http://www.ntia.doc.gov/ntiahome/domainname/6_5_98dns.htm.

7 *Avery Dennison Corpn v Sumpton*, 999 F Supp 1337 (CD Cal 1998).

8 *Oggi Advertising Ltd v McKenzie*, CP147/98 (unreported, High Court of Auckland, 5 June 1998); *Cardservice International Inc v McGee*, 950 F Supp 737 (ED Va 1997).

9 *Epson*, District Court of Dusseldorf (Case 34 O 191/96, 4 April 1997) (case also decided on grounds of threatened infringing use of a trade mark); *Commune d'Elancourt c Loïc L*, TGI de Versailles, 22 October 1998.

10 Case No 97-55467 (9th Cir, April 1998).

11 See also *Intermatic Inc v Toeppen*, 947 F Supp 1227, 1230 (ND Ill, 1996). In the German case of *Epson*, District Court of Dusseldorf (Case 34 O 191/96, 4 April 1997) the defendant had engaged in similar conduct, registering the domain name epson.de and offering to sell it to the plaintiff, with a threat that it would otherwise be sold to others. The court held that this was a threatened use of the mark 'Epson' in the course of trade, and thus sufficient to allow the grant of an injunction to prevent the threatened trade mark infringement.

12 [1998] FSR 265. Also reported elsewhere sub nom *British Telecommunications plc v One in a Million Ltd.*

of British companies as domain names, including marksandspencer (both .com and .co.uk), bt.org, britishtelecom.co.uk and virgin.org, and had offered to sell them to the plaintiffs. Again, there was no directly infringing use of the marks in relation to the plaintiffs' goods or services. Here, the court decided in favour of the plaintiff on the basis of the defendant's passing off:

- because any future use of a domain name which was similar or identical to household names such as those of the plaintiffs would inevitably amount to passing off, the plaintiffs were entitled to injunctions against such activity if there was evidence that it might take place; and
- the defendants had made explicit threats to sell the domain names to 'any other interested party', and this was held to constitute an implicit threat to use the domain names to pass off another's goods and services.

The court granted a permanent injunction to prevent use or sale of the domain names, and ordered that the domain name registrations be transferred to the plaintiffs.

Cybersquatting has increasingly been recognised as a problem which needs to be solved, as entrepreneurs take advantage of the reputations of others to register domain names which may attract members of the public. Of particular concern is the growing practice of registering the names of celebrities, particularly where the domain name is used for a pornography site.[13] The US legislature has already addressed this issue in the Anticybersquatting Consumer Protection Act 1999[14] (ACPA) which amends the US Trademark Act of 1946. It creates civil liability for bad-faith registration with intent to profit of domain names that are identical or confusingly similar to distinctive trademarks[15] or which dilute famous trademarks.[16] Personal names are also protected.[17] Remedies under the Act include injunctive relief, the forfeiture or cancellation of the domain name,[18] actual damages or profits, or elective statutory damages of between $1,000 and $100,000 per domain name.[19] A non-exhaustive list of factors to be considered in determining whether bad faith exists includes:

- the prior bona fide use of the name in the offering of goods or services;
- the provision of material and false contact information when applying for the domain registration;
- the person's offer to sell or otherwise assign the domain name to the mark for financial gain without having used it in connection with the bona fide offering of goods and services; and
- the registration of multiple domain names which the person knows are identical or confusingly similar to distinctive marks or dilute famous marks.[20]

These factors are similar to those set out in cl 4(b) of the ICANN Uniform Domain Name Dispute Resolution Policy.[1]

13 'How the Net pirates almost stole my good name', *Mail on Sunday* 19 March 2000.
14 See Pub L 106–113 (1999).
15 15 US C 1125(a)(d)(1)(A)(I).
16 15 US C 1125(a)(d)(1)(A)(II).
17 15 US C 1129(b).
18 15 US C 1116.
19 15 US C 1117
20 15 US C 1125(a)(D)(1)(B)(i).
 1 http://www.icann.org/udrp/udrp-policy-24oct99.htm – see •• above.

The ACPA was used in *Sporty's Farm LLC v Sportsman's Market Inc*[2] to uphold an appeal decided under the Federal Trademark Dilution Act.[3] In that case the plaintiff was a mail order company which sells products to pilots and aviation enthusiasts, and which had used and registered as a trademark the logo 'sporty's'. A competitor, Omega, entered the aviation-product business under the name of Pilot's Depot and registered the domain name 'sportys.com' with NSI. Following complaints by the plaintiff, Omega sold the domain name to its newly-formed wholly owned subsidiary Sporty's Farm, which sold Christmas trees, and which began advertising on a 'sportys.com' web page.

The Court of Appeals for the Second Circuit affirmed the lower court's injunction requiring Sporty's Farm to relinquish the domain name to plaintiff, applying the new anticybersquatting law. It concluded that it did not need to decide whether 'sporty's' was a famous mark, as was necessary under the Federal Trademark Dilution Act, because it was an inherently distinctive mark, satisfying a qualitative test that can be applied before a mark has been used. The domain name 'sportys.com' was indistinguishable from 'sporty's' because domain names cannot contain apostrophes, and thus met the ACPA test of 'confusingly similar,' if not 'identical'.

In deciding that Omega's registration evinced a 'bad faith intent to profit', the court found that intention from the facts that:

- neither Omega nor Sport's Farm had any intellectual property rights in 'sportys.com' at the time it was registered;
- the domain name was not the legal name of Omega, the party that registered it;
- Sporty's Farm was not formed and did not begin using the domain name until months later and after suit had been filed; and, most importantly
- there was clear evidence that the purpose of the domain name registration was to compete with the plaintiff in its aviation products market.

It seems probable that most jurisdictions will face similar issues, and will resolve them in similar ways at least so far as bad faith registrations by commercial competitors are concerned. However, there are as yet no clues as to how the law will, or should, deal with registrations by non-commercial organisations or persons, who by definition cannot be guilty of trademark infringement.

3.2.4 Can the conflict be resolved?

There seems to be a consensus among commentators that the conflict between the domain name and trade mark systems is irreconcilable where both parties act in good faith. Even if trade mark holders were always to be given priority, it is impossible to match a unique domain name to the theoretically possible 42 x (number of trade mark jurisdictions) holders of the same mark.

However, although the conflict cannot be resolved it seems that the current approaches being adopted by domain name registries, the courts and international organisations such as WIPO will ameliorate its effects. Infringing uses of domain names registered subsequent to trade marks will be resolved primarily at the domain name registry level, the courts are rapidly developing

---

2   53 USPQ 1570, WL 124389 (2d Cir, 2000).
3   See above and 3.2.1 .

techniques for dealing with cybersquatting, and arbitration and mediation are likely to assist conflicting legitimate users of trade names to reach an accommodation with each other.[4] What is increasingly clear is that domain names, with their global reach, are in some respects more fundamental to Internet commerce than trade marks – indeed, commercial organisations which are entering the field of Internet commerce are now choosing their domain name first,[5] before embarking on a programme of trade mark registration.

3.3   MAKING USE OF THIRD PARTY INFORMATION RESOURCES

The domain name system is not the only aspect of the Internet which produces problems of this kind. The very nature of the client/server technology which underpins the Internet exhibits a different aspect of the paradox that resources can be simultaneously plentiful and scarce.

The fundamental philosophy of the Internet is that a resource whose URL is known should be accessible from any connected computer unless its controller[6] has taken technical steps to make it inaccessible. The different services available via the Internet allow a user to access these resources in different ways. Thus Telnet permits him to issue commands to a remote computer, while FTP permits the transfer of files to and from that remote computer. The only information the user needs is the location of the resource and the type of service available in respect of the resource.

Until quite recently, a user would need to receive this information directly (eg from an email or a printed text) and enter it manually into the relevant application in order to access the resource. This meant that there was often a direct relationship between the user and the controller of the resource, and the nature of that relationship would normally answer most of the legal questions which might arise in respect of the way in which the resource was used.[7] However, the advent of the World Wide Web has enabled Web page authors to make the necessary information available indirectly, through the HTML source code of their page. As a result, the user does not access the resource consciously and directly from the server of the resource's controller; instead, that access is controlled, indirectly, by the Web page author. This raises the new question of the legal relationship between the resource controller and the Web page author who wishes to provide access to it (the 're-user').

---

4   The ICANN mediation and arbitration procedures are attracting a large number of disputes ('Hundreds of Net Disputes in International Mediation', *NY Times*, 24 February 2000, http://www.nytimes.com/library/tech/00/02/cyber/articles/24domain.html) but the high costs of the service may act as a deterrent – see further Chapter 9.3.4.

5   Though accompanied by a precautionary prior trade mark registration to ensure that they do not lose use of the domain name under the various domain name registry dispute policies – see part 3.2.3.1 above. Tunisia is a favoured jurisdiction for such precautionary registrations because it offers particularly speedy registration without onerous searches for conflicting marks.

6   The 'controller' of a resource means the person who is responsible for making that resource available via the Internet and who determines the technical and legal conditions for access to the resource. This person may or may not be the owner of any copyright or other right which subsists in the resource.

7   In essence, by allowing the user to have access to the resource, the controller granted an implied licence to the user in respect of the resource. In some cases there would also be an express agreement about what use could be made of the resource, eg if the user needed an account name and/or password to access the resource.

From the controller's perspective, the resources on his server are unique. Initially at least, they exist only on the server, and are accessible only through the controller's own Web pages. However, the Internet technologies allow (in theory) an infinite number of copies of those resources to be made, and an infinite number of new access paths to be created. This may diminish the value of the resource to the controller.[8] To a Web page author, however, re-use of the resource saves time and effort in creating his own resources, and he may additionally benefit from the resource's economic or origin uniqueness by using it to attract viewers[9] to his own Web pages.

In the physical world the only effective way of using a third party's information resources is by copying them. A re-user, however, may do this with Internet resources in three distinct ways:

- by copying the resource and using that copy in the Web page;
- by including the resource in his Web page through an automated link, which is invisible to the viewer of the page unless the HTML source code is examined; or
- by including a visible link to the resource in the Web page, which allows the viewer of the page to access the resource by selecting that link.

If a controller objects to the re-use of his resource, he may be faced with the assertion that his action in making the resource available via the Internet has granted the re-user a licence to re-use it. It is therefore necessary to begin by examining whether such a licence could exist, and if so what its terms might be.

3.3.1 Licences to re-use Web resources

3.3.1.1 *Express licences*

In some cases the controller of a Web resource expressly grants his viewers an express licence to re-use the resource. For example, the software house Adobe, which produces the Acrobat Reader software, expressly permits free distribution of that software. Adobe also licenses the use of the 'Includes Adobe Acrobat' logo in respect of that distribution.[10] Express licensing of texts is also quite common – the European Commission's website contains the following licence, accessible via a link labelled 'Copyright'[11] on most (but not all) of the site's pages:

Copyright Notice

© EUROPEAN COMMUNITIES, 1995–1999

The European Commission maintains this server to enhance public access to information about its initiatives and EU policies in general.

---

8 For example:
- the resource may be a means of attracting viewers to an advertising website;
- the resource may be a work from which the controller receives royalties, or which if re-used out of context diminishes the author's reputation;
- the resource may be a trade mark logo, re-use of which creates the danger of trade mark dilution.

9 A 'viewer' is a user of the World Wide Web – he views Web pages using his Web browser software, eg Netscape Navigator or Internet Explorer.

10 See http://www.adobe.com/prodindex/acrobat/distribute.html.

11 http://europa.eu.int/geninfo/copyright_en.htm.

> Reproduction is authorized, except for commercial purposes, provided the source is acknowledged.
>
> Information on EUROPA does not necessarily engage the responsibility of the European Institutions. While our goal is to keep this information timely and accurate, we cannot guarantee either. If errors are brought to our attention, we will try to correct them.
>
> Some of the documents and multimedia sequences on this server might contain references, or pointers, to information maintained by other organisations. Please note that we do not control and cannot guarantee the relevance, timeliness or accuracy of these outside materials.

To the extent that a licence grants permission to make and re-use copies of the resource, it requires no further analysis. More complicated, however, is the effect of any negative provisions of the licence which forbid particular activities in relation to the resource. In particular:

- If the user would, in the absence of any express licence, have acquired an implied licence to use the resource, the express licence can only restrict that right if it is brought to the attention of the user.[12] Where the restriction is set out on the Web page from which the resource is obtained, or embedded in the resource itself, there will be no question that it was brought to the user's attention. However, a controller who set out the express licence on his site's home page only would be unable to demonstrate that the licence was brought to the attention of users who arrived at other pages on the site via hyperlinks from a different website.

- The express licence cannot prevent the user from performing those acts which would not require a licence, eg copying public domain material or making fair use of copyright-protected material.

3.3.1.2 Implied licences

A licence to copy or otherwise use a work can often be implied from the circumstances in which the owner made the work available to the alleged licensee. For example, in the UK case of *Saphena Computing Ltd v Allied Collection Agencies Ltd*[13] the court held that by supplying the source code of software to a purchaser, the software owner had impliedly licensed the purchaser to copy and make adaptations of that code for the purposes of the purchaser's business. These purposes would include repair, maintenance and enhancement of the software.

A licence can only be implied from evidence that the resource's controller has granted an implied licence to other Web users.[14] Such evidence might consist of the controller's acts of:

- placing the page on a Web server which makes the resource accessible; and

---

12 The basic principle is that an implied licence may only be terminated by reasonable notice: *Trumpet Software Pty Ltd v OzEmail Pty Ltd* [1996] 34 IPR 481; *Redwood Music Ltd v Chappell & Co Ltd* [1982] RPC 109; *Martin-Baker Aircraft Co Ltd v Canadian Flight Equipment Ltd* [1955] 2 QB 556.

13 [1995] FSR 616.

14 The mere fact that a copyright work is accessible does not of itself evidence the grant of a licence. 'Silence as to the imposition of a restriction is not, in our view, necessarily indicative of a grant of freedom from restriction.' *Computermate Products (Australia) Pty Ltd v Ozi-Soft Pty Ltd* (1988) 83 ALR 492, 498.

- linking to that page from some other Web page which is linked to the World Wide Web.[15]

The effect of doing this is to make the resource accessible to all Web users, and the necessary implication is that the controller has granted those users at least the right to obtain initial access to the resource. The difficult question which then has to be addressed is whether the controller has granted more extensive permission to use the resource.

Where a licence is implied from a contract between the parties, it has been held that the licence extends no further than is necessary to give business efficacy to the contract, which means it permits the performance of otherwise infringing acts only to the extent necessary to allow the work to be used for the purposes which were in the contemplation of the parties when the contract was made.[16] The test is clearly an objective one; what is relevant is the licence which appears to observers to have been granted, not what the licensor subjectively intended (if anything).

There appears to be no UK case law on gratuitous implied licences, but *Copinger*, the standard UK work on copyright, suggests that the same principles should apply as for contractual licences.[17] The Australian courts have held that where a copyright work is made available for a particular purpose, that can carry with it an implied licence to copy to the extent necessary for that purpose. In *FAI Insurances Ltd v Advance Bank Australia Ltd*[18] the parties were engaged in a battle for control of the board of the bank. Proxy forms for voting at the annual general meeting were distributed to shareholders by the bank, and FAI distributed a rival version, based on the bank's form but with different voting instructions. The court held that the bank had granted all shareholders an implied licence to copy the form for the purpose of voting at the meeting, and thus FAI's copying did not infringe.

A detailed analysis of the approach to be taken when construing an implied licence in respect of information technology products was undertaken in the Australian case of *Trumpet Software Pty Ltd v OzEmail Pty Ltd*[19] In that case the defendant included the plaintiff's software, Trumpet Winsock, on a diskette which the defendant had arranged to be distributed free with a computer magazine. Amendments were made to the configuration files of the software which resulted in it connecting by default to the defendant as Internet Service Provider, and which also suppressed notices that Trumpet Winsock was distributed as shareware. The diskette additionally contained other software relating to the use of the defendant's service.

One element of the defence to the plaintiff's action for copyright infringement was an assertion that, by marketing Trumpet Winsock as shareware,

---

15 The act of placing a Web page on a Web server only makes it *theoretically* available to users – in practice, nobody will know it exists so nobody will access it. The normal method of constructing a website is to create a 'home' page, which has links (direct or indirect) to all the other pages on the site, and then to register that page with a public directory such as Yahoo!. Users who visit the site then create additional links to the parts of it they find interesting; as a general rule, the more links there are to a site, the more users will visit it. For example, there appeared to be about 10,500 links to the Queen Mary & Westfield College website 'www.qmw.ac.uk' as at April 1999.

16 *Blair v Osborne and Tomkins* [1971] 2 QB 78 (Court of Appeal).

17 *Copinger & Skone James on Copyright* (14th London: Sweet & Maxwell, 1999), pp 5–208.

18 (1968) 68 ALR 133.

19 [1996] 34 IPR 481 (Federal Court of Australia).

the plaintiff had impliedly granted to any potential distributor an unrestricted licence to distribute the software.[20] Heerey J held that any such licence would be subject to terms, which should be identified by adopting the same approach as for implied contractual terms. A condition would be implied if (i) it was necessary to give business efficacy in the light of the fundamental purpose of the work, and (ii) it was so obvious as to go without saying.[1] In determining these matters, evidence of trade usage was admissible, though in this case it was not sufficiently unambiguous to establish custom in the legal sense. Applying these principles the judge found that the distribution licence contained an implied term that the software should be distributed in its entirety and unamended, but did not contain a term that no other software should accompany Trumpet Winsock. The defendant's distribution fell outside the terms of the licence, as files had been amended, and was thus an infringement of copyright.

We can conclude, therefore, that making a resource available via the Internet grants an implied licence to users to make limited use of the resource. At a minimum, the licence permits the initial copying of the resource into RAM (and probably into the user's browser software cache), and also personal use of the resource as appropriate.[2] What is less clear is whether that implied licence will extend to:

- retaining a copy of the resource for future personal use;
- distributing copies of the resource to others;
- re-using the resource in one's own Web page; or
- writing HTML source code which permits others to gain access to the resource.

These issues are examined further below. The relevant test will be what a reasonable Web user would have been led, by the controller's actions, to believe he was permitted to do in respect of the resource.

3.3.2 Direct copying of the resource

The first step in analysing the relationship between the controller of the resource and the re-user is to determine what, if any, rights the controller has to prevent copying and re-use. These rights will fall into one of two classes:

- Property rights in the resource, normally intellectual property rights. The most likely such rights are copyrights and trade marks. The proprietor of those rights (who may or may not be the controller of the resource) will be able to bring an action for any infringement of the rights against any person who infringes.
- Contractual rights. These will arise when the controller of the resource makes it available subject to conditions, in circumstances such that the courts will construe a contractual obligation on the part of the person accessing the resource to comply with those conditions. Agreement to the conditions may be express, eg by clicking on an 'I Agree' button on the

---

20 On the facts, the court held that any such licence had been revoked during the negotiations between the parties prior to distribution of the diskette.
1 [1996] 34 IPR 481, 500.
2 Eg viewing an image, playing a sound file, etc.

Web page through which the resource is accessed, or may be implied from the act of accessing the resource in the knowledge that conditions are imposed. It is important to note here that these contractual rights will only be enforceable against a party to the contract, and not against any other person who uses the resource.

3.3.2.1   *Initial copying*

In most cases the author's initial copying of the resource will be lawful. If the controller expressly permits a user to have access to the resource, eg by making available a Web page which contains a link to the resource, he will have granted a licence to copy[3] it and to display or otherwise gain access to the information (in the case of a sound file, for example, the licence would be to make the sounds audible). The licence may also extend to storing a copy of the resource on the user's computer for later access. Where the terms of the licence are not express, it will be a question for the courts to determine the permissions granted to the user.[4]

If the user copies the resource and makes private use of it in breach of his contractual obligations or the controller's property rights, this is unlikely to be detectable by the controller and thus no legal action will ensue. The initial copying only becomes visible if the Web page author re-uses that resource.

3.3.2.2   *Re-use*

Re-use of another's resources is a common phenomenon of the World Wide Web. Web page authors are, as a general rule, not lawyers, and are only dimly aware of the existence of intellectual property and contractual rights. Additionally, there is a commonly held view that Internet resources are free for re-use, that the controller's act in making them accessible somehow places them in the public domain.

This, of course, is very far from the truth. If the resource is subject to intellectual property rights, the proprietor of those rights will potentially have an action against the re-user. The nature of that action can best be analysed from a concrete example, and because the most extensive rights in Internet resources are conferred by copyright law, the analysis will concentrate on the copyright aspects of the action. Actions based on breach of contract will be rare because of the difficulty of proving the existence of a contract between the controller and the re-user.

Let us assume that the re-user decides to produce a Web page which incorporates text copied from controller A and an image copied from controller B. To achieve this the author will place two files on his Web server: the HTML source code of the page ('My_Page.html'), including A's text, and in a separate file B's image ('Image_B.gif'). The source code might read as follows:

---

3   Because access to all information resources via the Internet takes place by copying them to the RAM of the user's computer.

4   See the Australian cases of *FAI Insurances Ltd v Advance Bank Australia Ltd* [1968] 68 ALR 133, *Trumpet Software Pty Ltd v OzEmail Pty Ltd* [1996] 34 IPR 481.

```
<html>
<head>
<title>My_Page</title>
</head>
<body>
<b><p>MY PAGE</p></b>
<p>This document describes the products and services of A Inc. A Inc. is
the world leader in widget production. A's widgets are far superior to our
competition in the following respects (comparison with Widgets produced
by B Inc.):</p>
<br>
– price<br>
– quality<br>
– availability<br>
<p><img src='Image_B.gif' width=140 height=120></p>
</body>
</html>
```

If the viewer accesses this page, the HTML file is sent to his computer and his
browser software builds the following display:

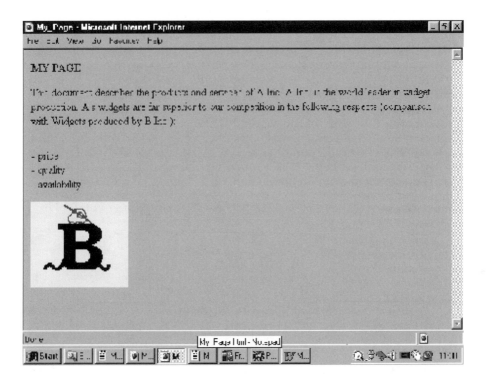

There are three types of copyright infringement by the re-user which might
have occurred during this process:

- The storage of copies of controller A's text (in the file 'My_Page.html') and controller B's image on the author's server may have amounted to the making of unauthorised copies. This act is an infringement of copyright in most jurisdictions.[5]
- The transmission of these copies to the viewer. This act also infringes copyright.[6]
- Authorising or inciting the viewer to infringe copyright.[7] When the viewer's computer receives the files it makes copies of them in RAM, and the fact that the viewer is not aware that he is receiving unauthorised copies is irrelevant to the question of infringement.

It must be borne in mind that these acts will not always infringe copyright in the works in question. There may be a general licence to copy, transmit and authorise further copying of the work.[8] The re-user may also have the right to make the copies in question because his copying amounts to fair use of the works, eg the copies are made for the purpose of criticism or review and are fair in relation to that purpose.[9] It is worth noting that commercial re-use, which is far more likely to give rise to a dispute than private re-use, is not necessarily unfair.[10]

3.3.3 Incorporation of the resource through an automated link

Thus far, we have not gone beyond the bounds of established legal principles. The method of obtaining access to the resource in question is new, but its use falls within reasonably well-established legal concepts of copyright and contract. However, the technology of the Internet does not *require* direct copying in order to make use of a third party resource. It is equally possible to incorporate a resource into a Web page in such a way that the copying is effected not by the re-user, but by the viewer of the page.

The way in which this is achieved is to author a Web page which automatically loads the Web resource from other servers. All that is necessary is to include the hypertext reference to that resource in the appropriate way. A simple example, using frames technology, might be as follows:

---

5 Art. 9(1) of the Berne Convention provides:
   'Authors of literary and artistic works protected by this Convention shall have the exclusive right of authorising the reproduction of these works, in any manner or form.'
   See eg UK Copyright, Designs and Patents Act 1988, ss 16 and 17 (exclusive right to make copies); US Copyright Act 1976 (17 USC § 101 et seq), § 106(1) (exclusive right to reproduce the work).
6 UK Copyright, Designs and Patents Act 1988, s 18 (issuing copies to the public); 17 USC § 106(3) (distribution of copies to the public).
7 See eg UK Copyright, Designs and Patents Act 1988, s 16(2).
8 See part 3.3.1.1 above.
9 See eg 17 USC § 107, UK Copyright, Designs and Patents Act 1988, ss 29–30.
10 See eg *BBC v British Satellite Broadcasting Ltd* [1992] Ch 141, *Campbell v Acuff-Rose Music Inc* 510 US 569, 591 (1994).

```
<html>
<head>
<title>My Page</title>
</head>
<frameset rows='210,*'>
    <frame src="http://www.A_server.com/Publicity/Text_A.html"
    frameborder=0 scrolling=auto>
    <frame src="http://www.B_server.com/Images/Image_B.gif"
    frameborder=0 scrolling=no>
</frameset>
</html>
```

The result of this source code is that when the viewer's browser receives the page's HTML code, it divides the screen into two parts, or frames. In the upper frame it requests controller A's own Web page, which contains the re-used text, *directly from controller A's server,* and displays it in that frame. It does the same from controller B's server with the image 'Image_B.gif' and displays that in the lower frame. The result is as follows:

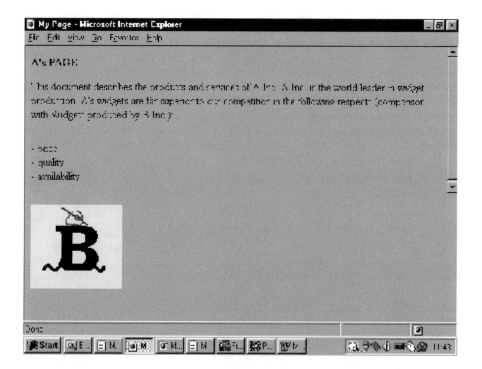

A comparison of the two pages reveals that they are very similar, and careful coding of the framing page could make them more nearly identical.

What has happened here is very interesting from a legal perspective. The re-user has not made any direct copy of the two Web resources. Instead, he has sent HTML code to the viewer, and the effect of that code on the viewer's browser software is to instruct that browser software to request the resources direct from the respective controller's servers. In other words, the person who makes the direct copies is the viewer, not the author. And yet the result is pretty much the same.

It is by no means clear that the re-user's Web page infringes the resource controller's rights. He has not copied the resources himself. However, if the viewer, who has copied the resources, is in breach of the controller's' rights, the author may be secondarily liable for inciting or authorising that breach.[11]

Unfortunately, from the resource controller's perspective, it follows from the analysis in part 3.3.1.2 above that the viewer has an implied licence to access the resources. Even if the resources were made available coupled with an express licence term which limited access, for example licensing access only via the respective controller's Web page, the viewer is ignorant of this restriction because he has never visited that Web page, or even if he has, does not realise that the resource is being requested by his browser software from the controller's server.[12]

However, this analysis of the implied licence may only be true for what might be described as 'published' resources. As we have seen, the test for determining the terms of implied licences is what the reasonable Web user has been led by the controller to believe he can do with the resource. Where the resource is a complete Web page, the reasonable user will believe he is entitled to view that page; he has been led to that belief by the controller's actions in making the page accessible via the Web. A closer examination of most Web pages, however, reveals that they are made up of discrete elements, which are loaded by the HTML source code and assembled to produce the complete page. Would a reasonable Web user have been led to believe that he was being granted a licence to access each of those elements separately, or only to access them as a collection? The answer would seem to be the latter. In the *Trumpet Winsock*[13] case the court held that a reasonable shareware distributor would understand that the software had to be distributed as an entirety, and not as separate component parts, and the same reasoning should apply to a Web page. The fact that the controller of the resource has made the location of the resource known by including the relevant HTML code in his own pages does not imply the grant of a licence to third parties to make their own use of the 'unpublished' resource.[14]

It follows that, in our second example, there may be a distinction between controller A's Web page and controller B's image. If controller B only made the image available as a sub-element of a Web page, as is most likely, he did not grant the viewer an implied licence to access it separately from the rest of that page. The image is, in effect, an unpublished resource, and there is no implied licence to access it on its own. The viewer has copied and displayed that image, without a licence to do so, and is thus in breach of B's copyright. This breach was authorised or incited by the defendant re-user, through his page's source code, and thus he too is in breach of copyright.

11 See eg *CBS Songs Ltd v Amstrad Consumer Electronics Ltd* [1988] AC 1013. This case, which concerned the sale of twin-deck audio cassette recorders, decided that providing the means to infringe copyright would only amount to authorisation or incitement if the means provided had no non-infringing use. In the case of a Web page which loads infringing resources, the viewer cannot choose to use it for a different purpose.

12 The only way the viewer can discover the origin of the resources which make up the Web page is by examining the source code of the page. By the time this can be done, the resources will probably have been accessed.

13 *Trumpet Software Pty Ltd v OzEmail Pty Ltd* [1996] 34 IPR 481 – see part 3.3.1.2 above for discussion.

14 *Computermate Products (Australia) Pty Ltd v Ozi-Soft Pty Ltd* (1988) 83 ALR 492, 498.

3.3.4 User-selected linking

The remaining method by which a Web author may use an Internet resource is by incorporating a user-selected hyperlink to the resource on his Web page. This is achieved by a simple line in the HTML source code:

<a href="http://www.server.com/resource.html">Resource Title</a>

The effect of this is to display the words 'Resource Title' on the page in highlighted form (usually underlined). If the viewer clicks on that part of the screen, his browser software sends a request to the server named in the code for that particular resource, and when it is received, displays it on the screen. Instead of a title, the page could use an image to indicate the hyperlink:

<a href="http://www.server.com/resource.html"><img src='Click_Button.gif'></a>

These lines of source code would produce the following screen display:

The normal result of clicking on these links would be a display of the resource as a new page, although if the link were within a frame on the original Web author's page, the resource would be displayed within that frame,[15] with the remainder of the referring page remaining visible.

These links are very like the references in the footnotes to this book. They give the viewer the address where the resource can be found, but leave it to the

---

15 Unless the source code of the referring page or of the resource (if it were an HTML page) contained code preventing its display in a frame.

viewer to decide whether to examine it. At first sight it would seem that no objection to this type of linking could possibly be raised. However, in 1996 the possibility that linking to another's website might be unlawful was raised for the first time in the Scottish case of *Shetland Times v Shetland News*.[16] A few months later similar actions were filed in the US in *Washington Post Co v Total News Inc*,[17] and *Ticketmaster Corp v Microsoft Corp*.[18] Each plaintiff objected to the links to its site from the defendant's Web pages.[19]

The *Shetland Times* case arose because the defendant's website contained links to news stories carried by the plaintiff's website. By following a link, the viewer was taken direct to the plaintiff's news stories, rather than first accessing the *Shetland Times* home page which carried advertising. Because the links on the *Shetland News* site reproduced the headlines of the *Shetland Times* news stories, the action was for breach of copyright in those headlines.

The facts of *Total News* were similar, but with the added factor that the links were selected from within frames. The *Total News* website[20] was designed to act as a gateway to other news services available via the World Wide Web. A viewer visiting the site would see displayed on the screen of his browser three frames:

- a frame containing buttons labelled with the names of the news services which could be accessed via the site;
- a frame in which news stories were displayed; and
- a frame containing advertising.

When the viewer selected a particular news service, Web pages from the server operating that service were displayed in the news stories frame, but the other two frames remained visible. The effect was that a viewer could read a news story from, eg the *Washington Post*, but would continue to see the *Total News* advertising (and, as a side effect, would either not see the advertising on the news service's website, or would see it with reduced prominence). This action was based on misappropriation, trademark dilution and infringement, copyright violation and other related tortious acts.

In *Ticketmaster* there was no allegation of copyright infringement, the action being based on misrepresentation of the business connection between the parties, unfair competition and trade mark dilution. Microsoft had linked to the Ticketmaster site, which gave details of entertainment in Seattle, and again the links by-passed the advertising pages.

The common factor in these cases was that in each the plaintiff was attempting to generate revenue via advertising on its website. This advertising often resides on a site's home page, through which viewers who visit the site can access other items, each of which has its own page. The links were perceived by the respective plaintiffs as a threat to their advertising revenue, and thus led to the litigation.

---

16 [1997] FSR 604. The websites involved are at http://www.shetland-times.co.uk and http://www.shetland-news.co.uk.

17 No 97 Civ 1190 (PKL) (SDNY, complaint filed 20 February 1997).

18 Case no 97-3055 DDP (CD Cal, 12 April 1997).

19 See Raysman and Brown 'Dangerous Liaisons: The Legal Risks of Linking Web Sites' New York Law Journal, 8 April 1997; Sampson 'Hyperlink at Your Own Risk' New York Law Journal, 24 June 1997.

20 http://www.totalnews.com.

Legal action was not the only option open to the plaintiffs in these cases, because they could have re-fashioned their websites to prevent the offending links.[1] However, the fact that a plaintiff can take practical steps to prevent infringement of his rights by a defendant is not a justification for the infringement of those rights. Additionally, many proprietors of websites will not have the technical expertise to control linking. Because advertising revenue is at present one of the main ways of financing a Web presence, the issue of controlling Web links is of major practical importance. Furthermore, a website proprietor may also wish to protect his image or reputation, and thus will object to certain links on that ground even if he has no advertising revenue to protect.

Each of these cases was settled,[2] so they offer no firm precedents. However, the arguments raised indicate that there are three grounds on which a website proprietor might be able to resist linking:

- trespass;
- breach of copyright; and
- unfair competition.

3.3.4.1 Trespass

Trespass, on closer examination, turns out to offer little help to the resource controller. Trespass to land is the unjustified interference with another's right to possession of that land[3] and trespass to goods is the unjustified interference with or denial of the owner's right to possession of the goods.[4] A website per se is intangible, and thus accessing or using it cannot itself be a trespass; that act might, however, amount to a trespass to the goods (the server or servers) on which the website is stored, or to the land where those servers are situated.[5]

Trespass only provides a remedy against interferences with goods or land which adversely affect the plaintiff's right of possession.[6] In the case of land the

---

1 For example, it is possible to include a CGI (Common Gateway Interface) or Perl script as part of a Web page, effectively a computer program, which assembles the page dynamically. This script will hide the URL of the resource, and can automatically direct the viewer to the page containing advertising, or incorporate advertisements into the requested page as it is sent to the viewer. Additionally, there are technological measures which can be used to prevent a linked-to page being displayed within a frame.

2 In essence, in each case the defendant was permitted to continue linking to the site, but agreed to acknowledge the plaintiff's site in the link and not to link in such a way as to by-pass or dilute the effect of the plaintiff's advertising.

3 *Ward v Macauley* (1791) 4 Term Rep 489, England and Wales; US Restatement (Second) of Torts § 158 (1965), US.

4 The technical distinctions between trespass, detinue and conversion are not examined here; the distinction between these torts is in essence based on whether the defendant's acts interfere with the plaintiff's current, continued or future possession, and the courts have gradually eroded the differences in pleading and procedure applicable in such cases. The US Restatement (Second) of Torts treats all these as trespasses to chattels.

5 Trotter Hardy has suggested that the theories of property which underlie the law of trespass would justify the courts in extending the doctrine of trespass to include unauthorised access to a website – I Trotter Hardy 'The Ancient Doctrine of Trespass to Web Sites' (1996) J Online L art 7, http://www.wm.edu/law/publications/jol/hardy.html. See, however, the contrary argument in Reed 'Controlling World Wide Web Links: property rights, access rights and unfair competition' (1998) 6 Indiana Journal of Global Legal Studies 167, 174 ff.

6 See eg US Restatement (Second) of Torts §§ 159–161 (1965); *Clerk & Lindsell on Torts* (17th edn, London: Sweet & Maxwell, 1995) 17-07.

interference must be direct, and thus the indirect use of the land on which the computer hosting the website is situated, by a viewer who requests a file, is not actionable.

However, trespass to goods may be indirect, and includes 'using or intermeddling with a chattel in the possession of another'[7] and acts by which 'the possessor is deprived of the use of the chattel for a substantial time'[8] When a viewer accesses a URL, eg by clicking on a link, he indirectly issues commands to the Web server and uses a fraction of processing time in running those commands. However, if the use still allows the plaintiff to retain possession and use of the chattel it will not amount to a trespass.[9] The amount of computer time required to fulfil the viewer's request for a file is so small that the proprietor's other computing activities will be almost totally unaffected.

Even if trespass theory were to be developed to encompass the transient interferences with land or goods involved in accessing a website, the person who creates the link to that website does not himself perform any interfering act. He could of course be liable for inciting the viewer to trespass. However, in most cases the website proprietor encourages the presence of the viewer, and only objects to the existence of the link. If the viewer is not a trespasser, the link cannot be an actionable incitement to trespass.

3.3.4.2   Breach of copyright

Copyright is the second legal means through which a controller might restrict links to his site. Copyright is the exclusive right to make or distribute copies of a work; and the entire technical basis of the Internet, and thus the World Wide Web, is that information is passed between computers in the form of copies. Under the Berne Convention, the owner of copyright in a work created in one country is entitled to national treatment in all other Berne Convention countries,[10] which means that a copyright infringement action can be brought in the alleged infringer's own jurisdiction where injunctive remedies will more easily be enforceable.

Copyright will only provide the controller with a remedy if a copyright-protected work has been copied and the re-user is responsible for that copying. The question which therefore needs to be answered is what, if any, works are copied when one website links to another.

The text of a Web page is protected as a literary work,[11] any graphic images as artistic works[12], any linked sound or video files as sound recordings or films,[13] and the whole as a compilation.[14] It follows that copying of the whole or a

---

7   US Restatement (Second) of Torts § 217(a) (1965).

8   US Restatement (Second) of Torts § 218(b) (1965).

9   *Moore v Regents of the University of California* 793 P 2d 479 (Cal, 1990), cert denied 499 US 936 (1991), use of plaintiff's rare cells in developing patented invention. Similarly, under English law an indirect use will only be actionable as a conversion if the use is so extensive as to deny the owner's right to continued possession – *Hiort v Bott* (1874) LR 9 Exch 86; *Clerk & Lindsell on Torts* (17th edn, London: Sweet & Maxwell, 1995) paras 13-38, 13-39.

10 Article 5(1) of the Berne Copyright Convention (Paris Revision 1971 as amended).

11 UK Copyright, Designs and Patents Act 1988, s 3(1); 17 USC § 102(a)(1).

12 UK Copyright, Designs and Patents Act 1988, s 4(1); 17 USC § 102(a)(5) (pictorial, graphic and sculptural works).

13 UK Copyright, Designs and Patents Act 1988, s 5(1); 17 USC § 102(a)(6).

14 17 USC § 103(a). A compilation is a literary work under UK Copyright, Designs and Patents Act 1988, s 3(1).

substantial part of any Web page is an infringement of copyright in the work or works copied. However, a re-user who provides a link to the Web page does not copy any of these things.

To investigate what might be copied, we need to examine links more closely. The HTML source code required to link to another Web page would read something like:

<a href="http://www.controller.com/Web_Site/Pages/About.html">About the Controller</a>

This link consists of five elements, composed at different times and assembled according to the various technical conventions of the Internet:

- the HTML elements of the URL (<a href="...."></a>), which are common to all URLs;
- the domain name of the Web server on which the page resides, devised by the operator of that server when the domain name was registered ('www.controller.com');
- the directory structure of the Web server ('/Web_Site/Pages/'), chosen by the controller for convenience of maintaining the website;
- the filename of the HTML file containing the Web page, which might be generated automatically by the software used to create the page (eg '~w198037.html') or chosen to reflect the content of the page (eg 'About.html'); and
- the title of the page ('About the Controller'), devised by its author and included between the <title> and </title> elements of the page's source code. This is the text which will appear, highlighted, on the screen of the viewer of a referring page, and it could be substituted by any other text (eg 'A link to a page giving information on the Controller') or an image. This text is the only optional element of the link – all four other elements *must* be present for the link to work.

The easiest way to create a link is for the re-user to view the page in question and then instruct his browser software to bookmark that page. The browser software assembles the elements listed above and includes them in the source code of a Web page held on the viewer's computer (often called 'bookmark.html'). The re-user can then copy the link's source code from his bookmarks page to the referring page, ie the page containing the link, which he is constructing. Creating a link in this way will always copy the original title of the linked-to page into the link. The controller's copyright could be infringed by this process if:

- the page title is protected as a literary work; or
- the URL is protected as a literary work; or
- the combination of the two is a compilation, and thus protected as a literary work.

As a general rule, titles of works are not protected. They attract no copyright protection under US law,[15] nor do short phrases and slogans unless they exhibit a minimal level of creativity sufficient to take them outside s 102(b) of the Copyright Act.[16] Additionally, because the title text element of a link is largely

15 *Warner Bros Pictures Inc v Majestic Pictures Corp* 70 F 2d 310 (2d Cir, 1934).
16 *Arica Institute Inc v Palmer* 770 F Supp 188 (SDNY 1991), affd 970 F 2d (2d Cir, 1992); *Kanover v Marks* 91 USPQ 370 (SDNY, 1951).

functional, acting as a label which identifies to the viewer the work which can be accessed via that link, it will only be protected by copyright if it exhibits a higher level of originality than is normally required for literary works.[17] UK law adopts a very similar approach, requiring for protection as a literary work that the text must exhibit a de minimis element of skill, judgment and labour, though not necessarily any literary merit,[18] and afford some information, instruction or literary enjoyment to the reader.[19] In other cases the following were held not to be works for the same reason: a trivial advertisement slogan,[20] an advertisement consisting of four, commonplace sentences,[1] a short extract,[2] the title of a song, used as the title of a film by the defendant,[3] and most titles of books, newspapers and plays.[4] As a general rule, a Web page title would need to be lengthy and creative before it was likely to attract copyright.

Authoring the URL requires no labour, skill or judgment, and is generally undertaken by the viewer's browser software. Additionally, as explained above, the re-user has no choice about including the HTML elements, the server name, the directory path and the file name. This should be sufficient to prevent copyright arising in almost any URL.[5] The same arguments apply to protecting the complete link as a compilation, as combining the title and URL of a linked-to page requires insufficient skill, labour, judgment or creativity to attract protection.

In civil law jurisdictions, Web links are even less likely to be actionable. Civil law systems protect *authors'* rights, as opposed to copyrights, and the subject matter of protection is 'intellectual creations' rather than the more utilitarian protection given in common law jurisdictions. The clearest example is probably German law, where under art 2(2) of the Copyright Law (*Urheberrechtsgesetz*) the standard of originality required for protection is 'personal intellectual creations'.[6] Furthermore, in the case of utilitarian works (into which category a link would surely fall) German law requires an even higher standard for

---

17 *Abli Inc v Standard Brands Paint Co* 323 F Supp 1400 (CD Cal, 1970).
18 *Ladbroke (Football) Ltd v William Hill (Football) Ltd* [1964] 1 WLR 273.
19 *Exxon Corporation v Exxon Insurance Consultants International Ltd* [1982] Ch 119. See also *Hitachi Ltd v Zafar Auto and Filter House* [1997] FSR 50, 58 (Copyright Board, Karachi, Pakistan; no copyright in the word 'Hitachi').
20 'Youthful appearances are social necessities, not luxuries' *Sinanide v La Maison Kosmeo* (1928) 139 LT 365.
 1 *Kirk v Fleming (J&R) Ltd* [1928-35] Mac CC 44.
 2 *Noah v Shuba* [1991] FSR 14.
 3 *Francis, Day and Hunter Ltd v Twentieth Century Fox Corpn Ltd* [1940] AC 112.
 4 *Dicks v Yates* (1881) 18 Ch D 76; *Licensed Victualler's Newspaper Co v Bingham* (1888) 38 Ch D 139; *Miss World (Jersey) Ltd v James Street Productions Ltd* [1981] FSR 309.
 5 This is particularly clear under US copyright law, where the compulsory combination of elements required to produce a URL will prevent it exhibiting the minimum level of creativity required for copyrightability by *Feist Publications Inc v Rural Telephone Service Co Inc* 499 US 340 (1990). In addition, and irrespective of any creativity, the functional elements of the URL are likely to be excluded from copyrightability by 17 USC § 102(b) via the idea/expression merger doctrine. Those functional elements are the only way in which the URL can be expressed if it is to perform its function of enabling access to the Web resource. Therefore, on the assumption that the 'abstraction, filtration and comparison' test of *Computer Associates International Inc v Altai Inc* 982 F 2d 693 (2d Cir, 1992) applies to URLs as well as to software, all these functional elements would be filtered out before the comparison for infringement purposes began. The result is that the only possible protected element of the URL under US law is its title.
 6 Similarly, the French Intellectual Property Code requires originality in the form of an 'intellectual creative process'.

protection, that the work exhibits a degree of creativity which is higher than the average level in the field in question.[7] Whether assessed under the normal civil law standard, or the higher level for utilitarian works, Web links will almost never exhibit the necessary degree of intellectual creation required to attract protection.[8]

A national curiosity, which arose in the *Shetland Times* case, was the argument that websites fall within the special UK rules on copyright in cable broadcasts. The definition of 'cable programme service' in s 7(1) of the UK Copyright, Designs and Patents Act 1988 is clearly wide enough to encompass websites, and the plaintiff argued that its Web page headlines received copyright protection as cable programmes which was infringed by their inclusion in the defendant's cable programme service (the *Shetland News* website).[9] There is insufficient space here to review the argument in detail, but in the author's opinion Web page headlines are unlikely to be protected as cable programmes for the same reasons that they are not protected as literary works.[10] However, a copyright infringement action on this basis against a UK-based re-user might be successful if the re-user used a link to incorporate the whole resource automatically (see part 3.3.3 above).

3.3.4.3   Unfair competition

The three cases on Web linking which were described earlier in this chapter demonstrate very clearly that the plaintiffs in each did not really object to links to their websites. The real cause for complaint was that (a) the links by-passed their revenue-generating pages, and more importantly (b) that the defendants were enhancing their own websites by virtually incorporating elements of the plaintiffs' sites. The basis of the complaints was that the defendants' conduct was calculated to benefit from the plaintiff's resources – in other words, that the links constituted unfair competition. This action will only be available, assuming the relevant jurisdiction has the appropriate type of unfair competition law, if both websites relate to a business.

Unfair competition has already been examined in this chapter in the context of disputes over domain names.[11] Most unfair competition laws, including the tort of passing off,[12] concern themselves mainly with misappropriation of trade

---

7 Thus at one time, software was only protected if it exhibited this high level of originality – *Inkasso-Programm*, BGH decision of 9 May 1985, 1986 IIC 681; *Betriebssystem*, BGH decision of 4 October 1990, 1991 IIC 723. The originality requirements for software have since been harmonised in the European Union by Directive 91/250/EEC on the legal protection of computer programs, OJ L 122/42, 17 May 1991, which requires the program to be the author's 'own intellectual creation' (art 1(3)).

8 Though a Web link might receive some minimal protection from direct copying under the provisions protecting non-original writings in the Netherlands Copyright Act, art 10:1(1), and a collection of links would be protected under the catalogue rule in the Nordic countries (see eg art 5 of the Danish Copyright Act).

9 UK Copyright, Designs and Patents Act 1988, s 20(c).

10 See further Reed 'Controlling World Wide Web Links: property rights, access rights and unfair competition' (1998) 6 Indiana Journal of Global Legal Studies 167, 184 ff.

11 See part 3.2.2.2 above.

12 A passing off action under English law is likely only to assist a controller where the offending link results in a diminution of the plaintiff's trading reputation or goodwill. The normal effect of a link is, if anything, to enhance the plaintiff's reputation because the fact of being linked to demonstrates his importance. A successful action for passing off is likely to be rare.

reputation.[13] However, some laws go further and also provide a remedy for acts committed in the course of business which (a) fall outside the norms of honest or good faith competitive conduct, and (b) cause damage to the plaintiff's business.[14] Unfair competition laws in this second category will potentially provide a remedy for the misappropriation of work product, and thus may give a remedy for Web links which are intended by the re-user to take unfair advantage of the controller's information resources.[15]

The basis of an unfair competition action would be an assertion that the link made unfair use of the controller's trade reputation, by leading viewers of the page containing the link to believe:

- that the linked-to resources are the work product of the proprietor of the referring page; or
- that the controller of the linked-to resource has some business connection with the proprietor of the referring page.

No court has yet determined the circumstances in which Web links contravene unfair competition law, but a series of cases under s 52 of the Australian Commonwealth Trade Practices Act 1974 about character merchandising and media spin-off marketing gives some indication of their likely approach. The most recent decision in this line is *Twentieth Century Fox Film Corp v South Australian Brewing Co Ltd*,[16] where the defendants marketed a product called 'Duff' beer, intending to create a link in the mind of consumers between the beer and the cartoon programme 'The Simpsons'. It was clear on the evidence, however, that the product would not lead consumers to believe that it was authorised or licensed by the owners of 'The Simpsons'. In his judgment, Tamberlin J said:

> On a literal reading of s. 52 of the Act, the deliberate creation by the breweries of an association by use of the name 'Duff' between the breweries' beer can and 'The Simpsons' program, in circumstances where there is no association and indeed, where such an association is contrary to the express policy of the producers, amounts to misleading and deceptive conduct. There is no necessity to demonstrate that the viewer or consumer must think in specific terms of permission or allowance in order to constitute deceptive conduct. The intentional use of the name 'Duff Beer' which produces the false association is sufficient, in my view.

There must, however, be actual or likely misleading or deception of viewers or consumers[17], and the court is more likely to find a breach of s 52 of the Trade Practices Act where there is evidence of an intention to mislead.[18] Indeed,

---

13 See art of the 1382 French Civil Code, prohibiting acts which cause confusion with another's products or business, on which many unfair competition laws are based.
14 See eg art 1365 of the Indonesian Civil Code which prohibits, inter alia, acts or omissions which are contrary to honest usage, good faith and good conduct; art 2598 of the Italian Civil Code which prohibits directly or indirectly making use of means not in conformity with the principles of professional ethics and which are likely to damage the business of others.
15 'Unfair competition provides a means of countering the undesirable effects of misuse of another's exploits...' Anselm Kamperman Sanders *Unfair Competition Law* (Oxford: Clarendon Press, 1997) p 22.
16 (1996) 66 FCR 451. See also *Pacific Dunlop Ltd v Hogan* (1989) 23 FCR 553 where the court found a TV advert containing a character which clearly referred to the eponymous hero of the film 'Crocodile Dundee' to be misleading and deceptive because viewers would believe the actor Paul Hogan had a commercial connection with the product.
17 *Parkdale Custom Built Furniture Pty Ltd v Puxu Pty Ltd* (1982) 149 CLR 191.
18 *Bridge Stockbrokers Ltd v Bridges* (1984) 4 FCR 460.

intention to mislead is inherent in the basic concept of unfair competition; honest and unintentionally misleading commercial conduct is far less likely to amount to an actionable act of unfair competition.

It is easy to see how links to the controller's website might lead a viewer to believe that there is some commercial connection between the controller and the re-user. This is particularly likely if the viewer is technically unsophisticated, and does not notice that the domain name of the linked to site is different from the domain name of the referring site, or does not realise that this difference may mean that the sites are operated by different entities.

This does not mean that deceptive linking will always be actionable. There is no globally uniform consensus on a minimum level of protection against unfair competition, and national laws differ widely, both in their underlying philosophy of what interests are protected and what types of act are considered unfair. Because the true nature of most objections to links is likely to be that they mislead viewers, however, an action based on unfair competition is always worth investigating.

3.3.4.4 *An implied licence to create links?*

As we have seen in part 3.3.1.2 above, the controller's act of making a resource available via the Internet may grant an implied licence to re-use that resource. If a link falls within the terms of the implied licence, the controller will be unable to take any action in respect of the link until he has given reasonable notice to terminate that licence.[19] We must therefore investigate what the terms of that licence might be, adopting the test of what a reasonable user of the Internet has been led to believe he is permitted to do in respect of the resource.

The first assumption that the Internet user would make is that the controller wanted his resource to be accessible. If the resource is a Web page, the primary means of making it accessible is to ensure that there are links to it.[20] Indeed, the first act of an author of a new website is normally to register the home page, and perhaps other pages with a Web directory such as Yahoo!,[1] which will make accessible a link to the website in a structured directory. Yahoo! only catalogues URLs which have been registered with it,[2] and thus does not always provide complete information about the contents of a site. This function is performed by Web crawlers such as Alta Vista,[3] which follow links from pages they have already examined, retrieve the source code of the linked-to page, and then store that page's URL with automatic indexing of its contents. All regular users of the Web are aware of these tools, and know that their own pages will be indexed unless they use technological means to prevent indexing.

Indeed, the World Wide Web takes its name from the philosophy underlying the HTML language, which was designed as a means of interconnecting Web pages and other resources like a spider's web. The Web only exists because of interconnections between pages. This, and the fact that a page's accessibility increases as more links are made to it, would further lead the reasonable Internet

---

19 *Trumpet Software Pty Ltd v OzEmail Pty Ltd* [1996] 34 IPR 481.
20 In theory the controller could simply publicise the URL by posting it to an electronic or physical bulletin board, but in practice almost all Web pages are found by following links.
1 http://www.yahoo.com.
2 Although it has recently added a Web crawler function to its site.
3 http://www.altavista.com.

use to believe that a Web page author expects his page to be linked to if it contains something of interest.

All this suggests that making a Web page available via the Internet confers an implied licence on other Web page authors to make links to that page, unless the nature of the page[4] is such that merely making it theoretically accessible does not, of itself, indicate the grant of a licence.

A controller who wishes to prevent all links, or links in certain circumstances, has two possible courses of action:

- He could use a scripting language, such as CGI or Perl, to force all viewers to enter through a 'front' or home page or to assemble a page dynamically (eg to ensure that advertisements were displayed).
- He could attempt to negate any potential implication of a licence by including a notice on the Web page notice that no licence is in fact granted, or is only granted subject to restrictions. However, that notice might not be sufficient to negate the implication of a licence in respect of Web crawlers. Because no human reads the text content of the page, a notice on the page could only operate as constructive, rather than actual, notice that no licence was given. It is arguable that as it is possible for a website operator to exercise some control over the activities of Web crawlers through a file titled 'robots.txt' in the root directory of the Web server,[5] a notice on the Web page itself would be insufficient to deny a licence to Web crawler operators.

3.4   FROM PROPERTY TO PROPRIETY

What this chapter has attempted to demonstrate is that the Internet's infinity of scarce resources makes property rights less useful. It may be that the law will eventually develop concepts of global property rights which can be used to exclude others from Internet resources. At present, though, the territorial nature of those rights and the ways in which the technology allows infinite use of resources without infringing property rights means that resource controllers (including trade name proprietors) need to look for new ways of protecting their interests.

Because the essence of the Internet is that it makes it possible to access resources globally, these new methods of protection cannot be based on absolute rights to exclude others from a resource. Making the resource available via the Internet is incompatible with exclusivity. The attention of lawyers needs to shift from rights in a resource to the behaviour of that resource's users.

It seems that the law is beginning (or at least, shows signs of beginning) to develop concepts of what constitutes unacceptable behaviour in respect of another's resources. Merely adopting that person's trade name as your Internet identity is permissible; but using it to cause confusion with his goods or services, or attempting to secure payment for transferring it to him, is not. Linking to a resource that has been made available by its controller is acceptable; but linking to unpublished resources, framing published resources with one's own

---

4   Eg an unpublicised page, not pointed to by any other page on the website.
5   This file can be used to limit or deny access to all or part of the website. However, some Web crawlers are 'badly behaved', and will ignore the file and index all the Web pages on the site anyway.

advertising or including them in one's own resources for gain is likely to be unacceptable.

In the earliest days of the Internet there were many suggestions that the user community would police itself,[6] so that the law's intervention would be unnecessary. That belief has turned out to be unfounded. However, the basis on which the law intervenes in disputes over resources seems likely to be that of community standards; but probably the standards of the Internet user community, and not the physical world community with which the courts were previously familiar.

6   See eg John Perry Barlow 'Coming Into the Country' (1991 March) Communications of the ACM p 19.

Chapter 4

New actors on a new stage: intermediary liability in the Internet world

As we have seen in Chapters 1 and 2, the Internet technologies require the participation of intermediaries to make transactions possible. Although intermediaries such as banks or commercial agents play an important part in physical world commerce, there are fundamental differences between physical world and Internet intermediaries:

- Physical world intermediaries are conscious actors in the transaction, whereas Internet intermediaries are often unconscious actors.
- Physical world intermediaries have a prior, legal relationship with one of the primary actors; Internet intermediaries more commonly have no preexisting relationship.

In essence, Internet intermediaries play one of two roles in an information transaction. They may provide services to one or more of the parties, including fundamental communications services such as access, information storage, etc. Alternatively, they may provide some additional service which facilitates a transaction between end users, eg identifying one of the parties,[1] providing search facilities, etc. Liability for providing defective services of this kind will be based on established legal principles, although the application of those principles to previously unknown types of service may not be obvious.

More important, though, is the role of intermediaries in relaying information through TCP/IP packet switching. This raises the question of their potential liability for the third party information content of those packets. Although these intermediaries operate via software which processes information automatically and in ignorance of its content or the nature of the transaction, in some cases they are the most easily identified targets for legal action if information content which they carry infringes a third party's rights.[2] This

---

1 Thus, for example, a bank which is providing information about its customer's account will wish to be certain that it is in fact the customer who has requested that information.
2 There are essentially three reasons why an intermediary might be the preferred target of an aggrieved plaintiff:
   - the originator of the offending information content has insufficient assets to pay substantial damages (the 'deep pockets' concept);
   - the originator of the offending information is in a foreign jurisdiction, while the intermediary is in the plaintiff's home jurisdiction; or
   - an action against the originator is unlikely to prevent further dissemination of the offending information, eg because he or she will simply move the information to another server, whereas

chapter will also examine the circumstances in which an intermediary might be held liable, and the developing consensus on the limitations which can or should be placed on that liability.

4.1 SERVICE PROVIDER LIABILITY

An intermediary who provides services in respect of an Internet transaction runs two separate liability risks. The first is the risk that his actions or inaction in the course of providing the service may cause loss to a communicating user or third party. The second risk is that he might be held responsible for the content of the information he has transmitted, either being forced to pay compensation to the person aggrieved by the content, or even committing a criminal offence. This part of the chapter concentrates on the first risk.

4.1.1 Liability for communication failure

Any claim that an intermediary should compensate the communicating parties for a transmission failure will need to identify a duty on the part of the intermediary to avoid that failure. In the absence of legislation imposing liability on intermediaries, such a duty could only arise in contract or via the law of tort.

The discussion of the relationships between the players in an Internet transaction in Chapter 1.2 demonstrates that in most cases there will be no contractual relationship between an intermediary and a communicating party. The obvious exception is the relationship between each communicating party and its ISP. Many of those relationships will be governed by express contracts[3] whose terms will define the ISP's liability for communications failures.

---

action against the intermediary may result in complete or partial blocking of access to the information. This is the reason why the Bavarian Lander government took action against CompuServe in 1995 to require CompuServe to stop providing access from within Germany to neo-Nazi newsgroups. From the Bavarian government's perspective this was a success, as CompuServe was initially forced to suspend world-wide access to those newsgroups – CompuServe press release of 28 December 1995 'CompuServe Suspends Access to Specific Internet Newsgroups', http://www.eff.org/pub/Alerts/Foreign_and_local/cserv.press_rel. See further U Sieber 'Criminal Liability for the Transfer of Data in International Networks – New Challenges for the Internet (part I)' (1997) 13 Computer Law and Security Report, p 151.

3   But by no means all. Probable non-contractual relationships include:
*   the relationship between academics or students and the University computing services department which provides them with Internet access;
*   the relationship between employees and their employer's ISP. In this case it will be necessary to distinguish between communications made in furtherance of the employer's business, in which case they will be the employer's communications and thus within the terms of the contract, and private communications (if these are permitted) where the relationship with the ISP, if any, will normally be tortious.

If the contract contains no express terms as to liability, or the express terms are void as exclusion clauses (see 4.3.1 below), the laws of most jurisdictions will imply a term that the ISP must take reasonable care in the provision of services to its user.[4] Thus, the ISP would be liable for failing to process an outgoing or incoming communication, but only if the failure should have been avoided. Merely proving failure will be insufficient by itself, as all normal[5] computing technology fails at times, often for no apparent reason. In most cases, an ISP would probably not be liable to its customers unless the transmission defect was caused by the ISP's failure to be sufficiently careful in selecting the hardware and software which comprises its system, or a failure to take sufficient care in operating the system. Provided the hardware and software are from reputable sources, then unless the ISP is also the designer of the hardware or software a defect in either will not normally render it in breach of its obligations of care.

Other intermediaries who are involved in the transaction will certainly have no express contract with a communicating party. The only ways in which those intermediaries might owe a contractual duty is:

- If the courts are prepared to imply a contract between the intermediary and the communicating party. The implication of such contracts is not unknown, at least in the common law jurisdictions, even where the parties have had no previous dealings. For example, in the English case of *Clarke v Earl of Dunraven*[6] the House of Lords held that a yacht owner's act of entering for a sailing race created an implied contract between himself and all the other entrants in which they agreed to abide by the rules of the race. It seems unlikely, though, that a court would be prepared to adopt the same reasoning to imply a contract between an Internet transmission host and a user whose packets were received by the host for onward transmission. In a yacht race with at most a few hundred entrants, all engaged in the same enterprise, the creation of a contractual nexus between them on the basis of a set of express terms of which all are aware does not produce an unmanageable set of legal relationships. The implication of contracts between a transmission host and all users whose packets arrive at the host's servers would produce millions of individual contracts, none of whose terms could easily be identified as they would all need to be implied by the courts.
- If the applicable law[7] recognises the concept of enforceable contractual obligations for the benefit of a third party, this might create a contractual duty owed by a transmission host to the customers of those ISPs with which it has an express interconnection agreement (eg if it provides the ISP with a connection to the Internet on a chargeable basis). However, most laws which recognise this concept require the term to confer a right on the third party expressly,[8] rather than by implication, and it seems unlikely that transmission hosts would agree to express terms conferring such rights.

---

4   Eg UK Supply of Goods and Services Act 1982, s 13.
5   The position might be different for safety-critical systems, where failure could threaten life or health.
6   [1897] AC 59.
7   See Chapter 7.1.

Even if such a contractual duty were found to exist, again it would be at most a duty to take reasonable care in the forwarding of packets. Proof of breach would always be extremely difficult.

A tortious duty of care is even less likely to be imposed on the intermediary. The losses resulting from an information transaction are normally likely to be purely financial losses, and most jurisdictions will only impose a duty of care to avoid such losses where there is a pre-existing (though non-contractual) relationship between the parties.[9] As we have seen in Chapter 1, the basic workings of the Internet mean that a user cannot predict which intermediaries will be involved in the transaction, with the exception of the access providers for each of the communicating parties, so there seems to be no basis for imposing such a duty on the other transmission hosts involved. In the unlikely event that an Internet transaction has the capacity to give rise to physical injury or property damage, because the intermediaries involved have no knowledge of the nature of the transaction it will not be foreseeable that a failure on their part might cause such loss. Foreseeability of this kind is normally a prerequisite for a duty to arise.

Finally, even if a particular intermediary did owe a duty to one or other of the communicating parties, it is normally not foreseeable that breach of that duty will cause loss. This is because the packet-switching technology of the TCP/IP protocols is designed to ensure that packets find their way around a malfunctioning transmission host and still arrive, and that lost packets are re-sent. In the common law jurisdictions at least, this will mean that there is insufficient causal link between the breach and the loss, which will be unrecoverable as being too remote.[10]

4.1.2 Other services

It is far too early to list all the additional services which will be offered by intermediaries, although a discussion of the services which are already available is contained in Chapter 2 and some further predictions have been made:

> **UK Department of Trade and Industry, 'Building Confidence in Electronic Commerce' (URN 99/642, 5 March 1999) p. 17, http://www.dti.gov.uk/cii/elec/elec_com.html**
>
> **POSSIBLE ROLES FOR INTERMEDIARIES IN THE ELECTRONIC MARKETPLACE**
>
> **Benefits for the consumer**
> - Guarantees of: order fulfilment, fitness for purpose etc.
> - Collection and management of purchasing preference information (through data capture on transactions routed through the intermediary and without effort by the consumer) and its release under direct consumer control.
> - Management of commodity purchases, at 'best buy' prices from multiple sources. (eg stationery for a Small or Medium Enterprise, or non-perishable goods for a domestic consumer).

---

8 See eg UK Contracts (Rights of Third Parties) Act 1999, s 1(1).
9 See eg *Caparo Industries plc v Dickman* [1990] 2 AC 605.
10 *Wagon Mound* [1961] AC 388.

- Management of inventory and updating (for example on software purchased or for insurance purposes).

Benefits for vendors
- Guarantees of payment.
- Local customer service and support.
- Authorised access to detailed consumer preference information, to be used in highly targeted one to one marketing and follow up.
- Access to authoritative, anonymised, data on general market development and trends.

Many of these services are merely electronic versions of services already provided in the physical world, and in those cases the law will require little development to provide an adequate framework for determining the rights and responsibilities of the parties. Services are intangible, like information, and the Internet merely provides a new mechanism for delivering those services which can be provided solely by transferring information around the world. The legal difficulties which do arise will almost certainly arise not from the law regulating the service itself, but from the fact that services delivered via the Internet can be supplied from foreign jurisdictions and via a distributed enterprise. These issues are considered in Chapters 7 and 8.

Some services, however, are completely new, and have no physical world analogues. Chapter 2 has attempted to identify some of the most important of these. Three are worthy of mention here because they are fundamental to the proper operation of the Internet as a communications mechanism, and for this reason have attracted legislative or judicial attention:

- Domain name allocation enables users to navigate the Internet.[11] Because of the overlap and conflict between domain names as addresses and business names as identifiers of commercial actors, many disputes have arisen. It is interesting to note that the litigation on this point, discussed in depth in Chapter 3.1, has upheld the self-imposed immunities of domain name registries, which refuse to become involved in determining disputes over name allocation other than by providing interim solutions pending final determination by the courts.
- Directory services enable users to discover the existence of Internet resources. Because they are analogous to physical world directories, it is at first sight hard to see how liability might arise, other than through false entries which amount to defamation or some similar wrong. However, there is one important difference between Internet directory services and physical world directories – in addition to providing the address of a resource, an Internet directory also provides the means of access to that resource via a hyperlink. There is therefore some danger that these intermediaries will be seen as involved in some way in the distribution of infringing resources, and thus liable to the person whose rights have been infringed. The US has taken specific action to give the providers of directory services immunity

---

11 In technical terms it is irrelevant, as all communications are addressed by reference to IP addresses. However, because humans cannot easily remember numerical addresses, the domain name system provides the essential interface between the computers which communicate and the humans who wish to send and receive those communications.

from copyright liability if, in essence, the provider acts in ignorance of the infringing content and does not benefit directly from the infringement.[12]

• Identification services are seen as so fundamental a part of Internet communication, particularly communications having legal consequences, that they merit an entire chapter – see Chapter 5. Here, too, legislatures have recognised that third party liability is a particular problem, and have enabled providers of these services to limit their liability extensively.

Even in the case of these new services, liability for service failure will generally be determined using the existing principles of national law relating to service provision. The issues which the law will need to address as new services are developed will primarily focus on ways of dealing with potential intermediary liability for third party activities.

4.2 LIABILITY BASED ON INFORMATION CONTENT

The range of laws which impose civil, or in some cases criminal, liability in respect of information content is extremely wide. However, the common feature of all these laws is that they can only be contravened by an intermediary in a limited number of ways. An intermediary's liability for the information content of communications or resources which originate from a third party is derived from one of three things which the intermediary might do:

• copying;
• possession; or
• transmission.

In order to illustrate how liability may arise, this part of the chapter will examine three areas of law: copyright, obscenity and indecency, and defamation. In the case of information protected by copyright, all three of the intermediary's activities are potentially infringing acts. Where the information contravenes laws whose aim is the protection of the public good, such as obscenity or indecency laws or anti-terrorism laws, copying will not normally give rise to liability but possession and transmission may. If the information is defamatory, it is only the act of transmission which raises liability issues.

4.2.1 Copyright

4.2.1.1 *Copying*

Unless we were to analyse an Internet communications transaction in some depth, we would not immediately consider that an intermediary is engaged in copying. If information is sent from user A to user B, we normally say that A has made a copy and sent it to B. If user A places a resource on a host, we consider that A has made the copy which resides on the host, though we might think that when B requests a copy of the resource from that host the copy is made by the host, rather than B. Certainly we think that user A controls all

---

12 Title 17 USC § 512(d) as amended by the US On-Line Copyright Infringement Liability Limitation Act – see extract in 4.3.2.1.

elements of *his* copying, and quite possibly that user B is controlling the copying process when he requests a resource from a host.

In fact, though, an intermediary host can only operate by copying information. If the intermediary is merely part of the communications chain, it copies received packets into memory (and probably onto disk) and then sends fresh copies to the next host in the chain. If it is hosting a resource, it initially makes a copy of that resource onto its disks, and then makes further copies when the resource is requested by a user. If those copies are of a work protected by copyright, the intermediary is in danger of infringing that copyright.

Nowadays, most copyright laws consider even transient copies in computer memory to be sufficient copying for a finding of infringement,[13] and of course many transmission hosts will make further copies on disk, eg when caching a resource. For this reason, the first US case to consider this problem, *Playboy Enterprises v Frena*,[14] held that a bulletin board sysop who encouraged users to use the board to exchange images in which Playboy owned copyright, had infringed Playboy's copyright by the direct copying the system undertook when storing and transmitting images.[15] This approach certainly accords with the language of the various copyright statutes.[16]

However, although the intermediary is, as a matter of technical fact, copying or reproducing the work, it is somewhat metaphysical to say that it is *making* the copies or reproduction. The copying is effected by the intermediary's software, but the instructions to that software to make the copies are in fact given by the user. In other words, the user is operating the resource host's system remotely.[17] This distinction was initially hard to make because the courts had consistently held that lack of intention to infringe was not a defence in copyright actions. It appears, though, that there may be a minimal mental element in copyright infringement – the intention to make a copy. Thus, in *Religious Technology Centre v Netcom On-Line Communications Services Inc*[18] the representatives of the Church of Scientology brought an infringement action against Netcom, an ISP whose customer had posted infringing copies of the works of L Ron Hubbard to a newsgroup. The judge expressly rejected the allegation that the ISP had infringed directly and refused to follow *Playboy v Frena*, on the ground that Netcom could only be guilty of direct infringement if it had *caused* the infringing copies to be made –

13 See eg UK Copyright, Designs and Patents Act 1988, s 17(6); *MAI Systems Corp v Peak Computer Inc* 991 F 2d 511 (9th Cir, 1993).
14 839 F Supp 1552 (MD Fla, 1993).
15 839 F Supp 1552, 1555–1559; see esp [4]–[7] at 1555–1556 (MD Fla, 1993).
16 Berne Convention, art 9(1):
    'Authors of literary and artistic works . . . shall have the exclusive right of authorising reproduction of these works, in any manner or form.'
    UK Copyright, Designs and Patents Act 1988, s 16(1):
    'The owner of the copyright in a work has . . . the exclusive right . . . (a) to copy the work . . .'
    17 USC § 106:
    '. . . the owner of copyright under this title has the exclusive rights . . . (1) to reproduce the copyrighted work . . .'
17 See *Marobie-FL Inc d/b/a Galactic Software v National Association of Fire Equipment Distributors and Northwest Nexus In* 983 F Supp 1167 (ND Ill, 1997).
18 907 F Supp 1361 (ND Cal, 1995).

the mere fact that Netcom's system incidentally makes temporary copies of plaintiff's works does not mean Netcom has caused the copying.[19]

If this argument is accepted in other jurisdictions,[20] an intermediary's liability for copying carried out by its users will be limited to those circumstances where the intermediary is vicariously liable for the users' acts or has authorised or contributed to the copying.

Vicarious liability arises where there is a pre-existing relationship between defendant and infringer, such that the defendant potentially benefits from the infringer's activities.[1] However, there will rarely be a sufficient relationship between a user and a transmission host for such liability to be found.[2] Similarly, although a defendant may authorise infringement by providing the facilities for copying in the knowledge that they will be used to make infringing copies,[3] this will probably not amount to authorisation if the equipment can also be used for non-infringing purposes and the provider cannot control the use made by the copier.[4]

---

19   907 F Supp 1361, 1368 (ND Cal, 1995).
20   In the Netherlands, at least, a similar case brought by the Church of Scientology against an ISP was dismissed on the ground that ISPs 'do no more than give the opportunity of communication to the public, and that, in principle, they can exert no influence over, nor even have knowledge of, what those having access to the Internet through them, will supply' – Decision N 96/160, March 12 1996. See however the UK decision in *Godfrey v Demon Internet Ltd* [1999] 4 All ER 342, which rejects the argument in respect of defamation liability.
 1   The most common such relationship is that of employer and employee, but any relationship in which the defendant expects to benefit from the infringer's acts might give rise to vicarious liability – see eg the cases on liability of an organiser of an entertainment for infringement of performance rights by musicians, *PRS v Bradford Corpn* [1917–1923] Mac CC 309; *Australasian Performing Rights Association v Miles* [1962] NSWR 405.
 2   *Cubby Inc v CompuServe Inc* 776 F Supp 135 (SDNY, 1991).
 3   *Moorhouse and Angus and Robertson (Publishers) Pty v University of New South Wales* [1976] RPC 151.
 4   *CBS Songs Ltd v Amstrad* [1988] RPC 567; *Sony Corp of America v Universal Studios Inc* 464 US 417 (1984). See, however, the contrary argument of Macmillan & Blakeney:
    'It does seem that some ability to control infringement is required before liability for authorisation is required. If, on the basis of the mere supply of a photocopying machine without adequate monitoring or warnings, a library can become liable as for authorising infringement, it is quite unclear why the person who provides the infrastructure for a transmission, including generating the relevant electro-magnetic impulses or other signals, would be in the clear. The argument that the communications carrier would be immune seems to depend upon two assertions: first, the assertion that the carrier does not have the power to prevent infringement; and second, the lack of proximity between the communications carrier and the primary infringer. However, communications carriers do have the power to prevent infringements. It is the same power which university libraries have to prevent infringements on their photocopying machines. This is the power to prevent the equipment being used at all for anything which has the capacity to infringe copyright. As to the issue of proximity between the communications carrier and the actual infringer, it is true that there is not the same possibility of immediate physical proximity. Nevertheless communications carriers might well be regarded as digitally proximate to the broadcasters whose programmes they cause to be diffused through their infrastructure and to the Internet service providers, content providers and billboard services which use the infrastructure to make material available to the public. The point here is not to show conclusively that communications carriers will become liable as authorisers of infringement, it is to show that there is the possibility that they may do so under present law. This possibility ought to be taken seriously by legislators because if it is possible, the desirability of communications providers as defendants means that some plaintiff (probably a collecting society) will try to make it a reality.' F Macmillan et al 'Copyright Liability of Communications Carriers', 1997 (3) The Journal of Information, Law and Technology (JILT). http://elj.warwick.ac.uk/jilt/commsreg/97_3macm/ .

Contributory infringement is a doctrine of US copyright law. For a defendant to be liable for infringing copying by a third party, the defendant must (a) have knowledge of the infringement, and (b) have induced, caused or materially contributed to the third party's infringing conduct.[5] The court in *Netcom* held that there was an issue to be tried on this point. If Netcom had knowledge that infringing material was passing through its servers and failed to take action to prevent the dissemination of that material, it might be liable as a contributory infringer. The deciding factor would be the host's actual knowledge of the infringement:

> [If the host] cannot reasonably verify a claim of infringement, either because of a possible fair use defense, the lack of copyright notices on the copies, or the copyright holder's failure to provide the necessary documentation to show that there is a likely infringement, the operator's lack of knowledge will be found reasonable and there will be no liability for contributory infringement for allowing the continued distribution of the works on its system.[6]

In conclusion, copyright law seems to be moving towards the position that Internet intermediaries will not be strictly liable for the copies they make of information passing through their servers. Liability for carrying infringing copies where the original infringement was carried out by a user will only be imposed:

- where the intermediary actively encourages users to transport infringing material via its facilities;[7] or
- where the intermediary has actual knowledge of the infringement and fails to take reasonable steps to prevent it.[8]

It cannot be stated with certainty that all jurisdictions will follow this trend, however, and for this reason the proposals for granting intermediaries a statutory immunity (see 4.3.2 below) will be important in clarifying the position.

4.2.1.2   Possession

In some jurisdictions, possession of infringing copies made by a third party may itself be an infringement of the copyright owner's rights. In the UK, this is known as secondary infringement. The relevant provision is s 23 of the Copyright, Designs and Patents Act 1988 which states that infringement occurs:

- if the possession is in the course of a business; and
- the defendant knows or has reason to believe that it is an infringing copy.

Most intermediary hosts operate as businesses,[9] so the first element of liability will normally be present. The courts have not yet been required to determine

5   *Gershwin Publishing Corp v Columbia Artists Management Inc* 443 F 2d 1159, 1162 (2d Cir, 1971); *Sega Enterprises Inc v MAPHIA* 857 F Supp. 679 (ND Cal, 1994).
6   *Religious Technology Centre v Netcom On-Line Communications Services Inc.* 907 F Supp 1361, 1374 (ND Cal, 1995). For a detailed analysis of the potential liability of intermediaries as contributory infringers see Eugene A Burcher and Anna M Hughes, Casenote, '*Religious Tech Ctr v Netcom On-Line Communications Inc*: Internet Service Providers: The Knowledge Standard for Contributory Copyright Infringement and The Fair Use Defense' 3 RICH JL TECH 5 (1997), http://www.richmond.edu/~jolt/v3i1/burhugh.html.
7   *Sega Enterprises Inc v MAPHIA* 857 F Supp 679 (ND Cal, 1994).
8   *Religious Technology Centre v Netcom On-Line Communications Services Inc* 907 F Supp 1361 (ND Cal, 1995).
9   Defined to include a trade or profession – UK Copyright, Designs and Patents Act 1988, s 178.

whether the transient possession which occurs when a transmission host is dealing with a packet is sufficient for s 23, or whether more long-term possession is necessary. However, a packet is likely to be in possession of the host for such a short time that it would in practical terms be impossible for the copyright owner to prove the requisite knowledge. It seems probable, therefore, that liability arising from possession will only be relevant for resources which are hosted by the intermediary, or which are cached.

The second element of liability is more problematic. It is notorious that many Internet users are ignorant of or indifferent to copyright, and assume that the fact that a resource is available electronically entitles them to copy it to their own websites.[10] For this reason, almost every intermediary which hosts third party websites or caches resources will have a substantial number of infringing copies on its servers. This is unlikely to amount to sufficient knowledge to give rise to liability under s 23. The cases on the predecessor UK law[11] have held that actual knowledge is required,[12] and that constructive knowledge that some copies may be infringing is insufficient.[13] The *Netcom* case in the US (see 4.2.1.1 above) suggests that the same is true for contributory infringement.

The real problems arise where the copyright owner gives notice to the intermediary that infringing copies are available via the intermediary's server. Where that notice identifies a specific resource, such as a particular file on a user's website or FTP site, few problems arise. Either the intermediary deletes or blocks access to the resource, in which case the copyright owner is unlikely to continue with an action against the intermediary, or it refuses, in which case the copyright owner will be able to prove continued possession with actual knowledge. However, in many cases all that the copyright owner will be able to state in its notice is that the infringing material is being made available via a particular newsgroup or third party website, and that by carrying that newsgroup or by caching resources requested from the website, the intermediary will necessarily be in possession of infringing copies. This is precisely what happened in the *Netcom* case, and there the court held that it was at least arguable that such a notice did give sufficient information to enable the intermediary to attempt to identify the infringing material.[14] However, the court suggested that the notice needed to go further, and provide sufficient information to enable the intermediary to determine whether a particular resource infringed.[15] The UK courts have held under the Copyright Act 1956 that a general notice is insufficient to fix a person with knowledge that a copy infringes.[16]

4.2.1.3   *Transmission*

An intermediary may undertake two types of transmission which have copyright implications:

10 See further Chapter 3.3.
11 Copyright Act 1956, s 5 – infringement by importation, sale etc of copies known to be infringing.
12 See eg *Hoover plc v George Hulme (STO) Ltd* [1982] FSR 565.
13 *Columbia Picture Industries v Robinson* [1987] Ch 38.
14 The court was influenced by the fact that the identified infringing copies all contained the owner's copyright notice.
15 *Religious Technology Centre v Netcom On-Line Communications Services Inc* 907 F Supp 1361, 1374 (ND Cal, 1995).
16 *Hoover plc v George Hulme Ltd* [1982] FSR 565. Note, however, that a non-specific notice may be sufficient under UK defamation law – *Godfrey v Demon Internet Ltd* [1999] 4 All ER 342.

- Forwarding packets received from another host.
- Transmitting a copy of a resource hosted by the intermediary, following a user request (eg where the user follows a link on a Web page).

Transmission of packets takes place by copying, and so the act of transmission may amount to infringement by copying – see the discussion at 4.2.1.1 above. However, this copying is merely transient, with the copies made by the intermediary being in most cases deleted once the packet has been sent. Although this transient copying amounts to infringement in some jurisdictions,[17] in others there is uncertainty whether such copying is an infringement[18] and in some cases it has been held not to infringe.[19]

An alternative ground for holding that the transmission of packets infringes copyright is as a breach of the exclusive right of distribution. Most copyright laws grant the copyright owner some form of exclusive distribution right, but there is substantial doubt whether the statutory formulations of that right extend to packet transmission:

> In legal terms, it is generally accepted that the distribution right, which only applies to the distribution of physical copies does not cover the act of transmission. Also the reproduction right does not cover the act of transmission as such, but only the reproductions which take place in this context.[20]

Uncertainties as to the applicability of distribution right to this type of transmission arise for two reasons:

- the exclusive right may be limited to the distribution of *physical* copies of a work; or
- Distribution to the public may require one-to-many copying, rather than the one-to-one copying (even on multiple occasions) which characterises packet switching.

Additionally, each jurisdiction's law includes exceptions to the right whose applicability in a digital environment is uncertain:

Explanatory Memorandum to the Proposal for a European Parliament and Council Directive on the harmonization of certain aspects of copyright and related rights in the Information Society, COM(97) 628 final, 10 December 1997, p 21[1]

> 2.   . . . Member States' laws provide rather for a number of specific rights, with widely differing characteristics, which form part of the right of communication to the public (right of performance and representation, right of communication to the public by means of sound and visual recordings, right of communication to the public by wire, broadcasting right, right to include a work in a cable programme). The provisions existing in Member States on communication to

---

17 See eg UK Copyright, Designs and Patents Act 1988, s 17(6).

18 '. . . the treatment of temporary acts of reproduction is generally still not addressed, with the result of significant legal uncertainty with respect to the exploitation of protected subject matter in the electronic environment.' *Proposal for a European Parliament and Council Directive on the harmonization of certain aspects of copyright and related rights in the Information Society*, COM (97) 628 final, 10 December 1997, p 15.

19 *Religious Technology Centre v Netcom On-Line Communications Services Inc* 907 F Supp 1361, 1368 (ND Cal, 1995).

20 *Proposal for a European Parliament and Council Directive on the harmonization of certain aspects of copyright and related rights in the Information Society*, COM(97) 628 final, 10 December 1997, p 20.

1 A revised text has been published following scrutiny by the European Parliament, COM (1999) 250 final, 21 June 1999, and that text is referred to hereafter where substantive provisions are discussed.

the public, in particular, do not always protect the same categories of works and other subject matter, which may result in significant legal loopholes when being applied to this new form of 'on-demand' exploitation. First of all, Member States apply different interpretations to the term 'public'; in many Member States, on-demand transmissions, according to the present legal situation, may be considered as non-public communications, not being covered by this right. Furthermore, in the traditional, non-interactive environment, the characteristics and the interpretation of the existing provisions on the right of communication to the public or the rights belonging to this family and their delimitation from one another differ widely, with the potential result of significant legal uncertainty. It should also be noted that the degree of protection for rightholders (exclusive right or right to remuneration) and the management of the relevant rights differ substantially between Member States.

3. Substantial differences between Member States also exist with respect to the limitations and exceptions applied to the exercise of the communication right (or a right belonging to that family), which, for a number of uses (notably for the purposes of education and research, for information purposes, for library and archival use), are the same as those applicable to the reproduction right (see Chapter 3, I.a. above). Some Member States, however, do not provide for exceptions to the communication to the public right at all with respect to library and archival uses (e.g. Austria, Belgium, France, Spain, and Luxembourg). Moreover, it is far from being clear which of the limitations, where they exist, will be applicable in the new digital environment and in particular to 'on-demand' on-line exploitation of protected material. Since the library use exception is in most cases limited to certain forms of copying and physical distribution of protected material, it seems that on-line delivery of protected material to remote users would, in general, not be exempted from the exclusive right of communication to the public by a large number of Member States (Italy, Sweden, Denmark, Greece, Portugal, Austria, Belgium, Finland, France, Luxembourg, and Spain). In other Member States the situation is less clear (Germany, Netherlands, UK, and Ireland).

For these reasons the WIPO Copyright Treaty introduces a new exclusive right of communication to the public:

WIPO Copyright Treaty Art. 8

ARTICLE 8

Right of Communication to the Public

Without prejudice to the provisions of Articles 11(1)(ii), 11*bis*(1)(i) and (ii), 11*ter*(1)(ii), 14(1)(ii) and 14*bis*(1) of the Berne Convention, authors of literary and artistic works shall enjoy the exclusive right of authorizing any communication to the public of their works, by wire or wireless means, including the making available to the public of their works in such a way that members of the public may access these works from a place and at a time individually chosen by them.

The text proposed for implementation of this right in the EU[2] takes the opportunity to clarify the position of intermediaries. Thus, although the wording of art 8 of the WIPO Copyright Treaty is clearly intended to include communication to the public via the Internet, it does not explain precisely what acts will amount to communication. Article 3(1) of the draft Directive

---

2   *Proposal for a European Parliament and Council Directive on the harmonization of certain aspects of copyright and related rights in the Information Society*, COM (1999) 250 final, 21 June 1999.

follows the text of art 8 of the Copyright Treaty very closely, but the meaning of 'communication' is clarified by art 3(4), which reads: 'The mere provision of physical facilities for enabling or making a communication does not in itself amount to communication within the meaning of this Directive'. The intended result is that the creator of a website from which infringing material is available will be covered by art 3, whereas an intermediary which hosts the site or transmits packets emanating from the site will not. In these cases the intermediary is merely providing the facilities which enable the creator of the website to make the communication; in other words, for these purposes communication is an act which requires an intention to communicate.

Proposal for a European Parliament and Council Directive on the harmonization of certain aspects of copyright and related rights in the Information Society, COM(1999) 250 final, 21 June 1999

ARTICLE 3

Right of communication to the public, including the right of making available works or other subject matter

1. Member States shall provide authors with the exclusive right to authorize or prohibit any communication to the public of originals and copies of their works, by wire or wireless means, including the making available to the public of their works in such a way that members of the public may access them from a place and at a time individually chosen by them.[3]

2. Member States shall provide for the exclusive right to authorize or prohibit the making available to the public, by wire or wireless means, in such a way that members of the public may access them from a place and at a time individually chosen by them:
    (a) for performers, of fixations of their performances;
    (b) for phonogram producers, of their phonograms;
    (c) for the producers of the first fixations of films, of the original and copies of their films; and
    (d) for broadcasting organizations, of fixations of their broadcasts, whether these broadcasts are transmitted by wire or over the air, including by cable or satellite.

3. The rights referred to in paragraphs 1 and 2 shall not be exhausted by any act of communication to the public of a work and other subject matter as set out in paragraph 2, including their being made available to the public.

4. The mere provision of physical facilities for enabling or making a communication does not in itself amount to an act of communication to the public within the meaning of this Article.

---

3   The meaning of this provision is clarified by recitals 16 and 17:
    '(16) Whereas the legal uncertainty regarding the nature and the level of protection of acts of on-demand transmission of copyright works and subject matter protected by related rights over networks should be overcome by providing for harmonized protection at Community level; whereas it should provide all rightholders recognized by the Directive with an exclusive right to make available to the public copyright works or any other subject matter by way of interactive on-demand transmissions; whereas such interactive on-demand transmissions are characterized by the fact that members of the public may access them from a place and at a time individually chosen by them; whereas this right does not cover direct representation or performance;
    (17) Whereas the mere provision of physical facilities for enabling or making a communication does not in itself amount to communication within the meaning of this Directive;'

4.2.2   Obscenity and indecency

4.2.2.1   No global consensus

Although there appears to be near-universal agreement that a state should control the possession and dissemination of obscene and indecent material in its territory, there is no consensus on what type of content should be considered as obscene or indecent. The sharpest disagreements lie in the field of nudity and depictions of sexuality. Thus, for example, in Scandinavia there is a general perception that images of naked adults are entirely acceptable,[4] whereas in countries whose law or culture is based on strict orthodox Islamic principles, such as Saudi Arabia[5] depictions of mere nudity may well be unlawful per se, whether those images depict sexual conduct or not. The standards for the determination of obscenity also vary widely. In the UK, for example, the definition of obscenity is based on the potential effects of the material on its readers or viewers. In s 1(1) of the Obscene Publications Act 1959 obscenity is defined as follows –

> an article shall be deemed to be obscene if its effect or the effect of any one of its terms is, if taken as a whole, such as to tend to deprave and corrupt persons who are likely, having regard to all relevant circumstances, to read, see or hear the matter contained or embodied in it.

This definition is not limited to sexually explicit material, and a depiction of violent activity has also been held to tend to deprave or corrupt, and thus to be obscene.[6]

In the US, by contrast, obscenity is limited to sexual material, and requires the material to appeal to the prurient interest, as defined by reference to the standards of the local community, and to depict sexual conduct defined by the applicable State law.[7] The test is therefore not the effects of the material, but whether it contravenes locally determined standards of acceptable sexual depiction. As a result, material which is acceptable in one State may be obscene in another. This was clearly demonstrated in the case of *United States v Thomas*,[8] where a bulletin board operator was extradited from California to Tennessee to face criminal charges. It was stated in argument that the material, which was stored on a computer in California, was not obscene by Californian community standards,[9] but the court determined that the appropriate standards by which to test for obscenity were the standards of Tennessee, the place in which the material was received and viewed.

4   Though of course, the activities depicted might be obscene.
5   Faiza S Ambah 'An Intruder in the Kingdom' (1995) Business Week, 21 August, p 40.
6   *DPP v A and BC Chewing Gum Ltd* [1969] 1 QB 159 (violent picture cards distributed with children's sweets).
7   *Miller v California* 413 US 15 (1973). The three-part test set out by the Supreme Court is:
    '(a) whether the average person, applying contemporary community standards, would find that the work, taken as a whole, appeals to the prurient interest,
    (b) whether the work depicts or describes, in a patently offensive way, sexual conduct specifically defined by the applicable state law, and
    (c) whether the work, taken as a whole, lacks serious literary, artistic, political, or scientific value.' (413 US 15, 425 (1973))
8   74 F 3d 701 (6th Cir), Cert denied, 117 S Ct 74 (1996).
9   Which, according to counsel, do not find that 'bestiality, oral sex, incest, sado-masochistic abuse, and sex scenes involving urination' appeal to the prurient interest.

Where child pornography is concerned, the differences in national standards are equally marked. In general, depictions of minors engaged in sexual conduct are unlawful per se, irrespective of the likely effect of the depictions on viewers or of local community standards. Additionally, depictions of adults who appear to be minors may well be unlawful,[10] as may be depictions which have been modified (eg by computer manipulation of images) to combine depictions of adults with elements of non-obscene images of minors.[11] However, there is no international agreement on the age of sexual consent. Thus, while in the UK a minor for these purposes is a person under 16 years of age, in Tennessee the relevant age is 18 years.[12]

It seems likely that non-US jurisdictions will also adopt the *Thomas* approach of applying their own obscenity laws, provided the acts[13] which are alleged to have contravened the criminal law occurred in the jurisdiction. The questions that need to be answered are therefore:

- what acts which an intermediary might commit in respect of obscene material give rise to liability? and
- where are those acts committed?

4.2.2.2   *Possession*

As a general principle, mere possession of an obscene article is not an offence. However, a distinction is often made between child pornography and other obscene or indecent material, the possession of the former being an offence without more.[14] For other obscene or indecent articles, some further element of intent is required, normally that the possessor intends to distribute or exhibit the article. In some cases that intent alone is sufficient,[15] whereas in other jurisdictions the intent must be to distribute for gain.[16] In the case of child pornography, possession with intent to distribute is normally a more serious offence than mere possession.[17]

Where the basis of liability is possession, an intermediary will only run the risk of liability for third party content if it hosts or caches that content on its servers, and the act of possession will be committed in the jurisdiction where the server is physically located.[18] An additional liability risk may arise if the intermediary controls that server from a different jurisdiction, by drawing an analogy with the principles of data protection law which determines the jurisdiction in which personal data is held by reference to the place of control,

10 See eg 18 USC § 2256(B).
11 See 18 USC § 2256(C); UK Criminal Justice Act 1988, s 160 as amended by Criminal Justice and Public Order Act 1994, s 84(4).
12 UK Protection of Children Act 1978, s 1(1)(a); Tennessee Code § 39-17-901(8).
13 Ie the receipt or transmission of the allegedly obscene article.
14 See UK Criminal Justice Act 1988, s 160 as amended by Criminal Justice and Public Order Act 1994, s 84(4) to cover 'pseudo photographs'; California Penal Code § 311.11(a).
15 See eg California Penal Code § 311.2(a); under § 311.2(b) possession with intent to distribute for gain, where the subject is a minor, is a more serious offence.
16 See eg UK Obscene Publications Act 1964, s 1(2).
17 See California Penal Code § 311.1(a) (possession with intent to distribute), § 311.2(b) (intent to distribute for commercial consideration).
18 For an extensive review of intermediary liability for content, see Sieber *Legal Regulation, Law Enforcement and Self-Regulation: A new alliance for preventing illegal and harmful contents in the Internet* (Bertelsmann Foundation, 1999), p 19 ff, available from http://www.bertelsmann.de.

not the physical location of the data.[19] This point has yet to be raised in reported legal proceedings.

The question then arises whether the intermediary must know that the file held on its server is unlawful. In some cases, the offence requires knowledge on the part of the possessor that the file is obscene.[20] However, it seems that under the UK Obscene Publications Act 1959, s 1(2), the question of knowledge is immaterial, such knowledge being presumed because the essence of the offence is that the possessor intends to distribute the article for gain.[1] This presumption might have had some basis in fact for physical books, pictures and films, where the distributor might reasonably be expected to know his stock. However, where hosted and cached resources are concerned it is commercially infeasible for the intermediary to check files for obscene content. Admittedly under the UK Obscene Publications Act it is a defence for the accused to show that he had not examined the article and had no reasonable grounds for suspicion that his possession of it amount to an offence under the Act,[2] but it is unclear to what extent a criminal court might take the view that a deliberate failure to undertake any checking of content removed any defence of lack of reasonable grounds for suspicion. At the least, the intermediary will have electronic records of the titles of files it is hosting, and the domain names of sites from which information is cached. A hosted website containing a file named 'fellatio.jpeg', or a file cached from a site with the domain name 'hotsex.com' would, at the very least give the intermediary cause to suspect that the file might contain obscene material.

If an intent to distribute is required for liability, the question then arises whether an intermediary, whose primary role is after all the transmission of packets, can be said to have the requisite intention merely because it possesses a copy of the file. This matter has been expressly provided for in UK law by the amendments made to the Obscene Publications legislation by the Criminal Justice and Public Order Act 1994. Schedule 9, para 3 of the 1994 Act amends the definition given to 'publication' in the 1959 Act so as to include 'where the matter is data stored electronically, [transmission of] that data'. This amended definition includes the act of making pornographic material available for electronic transfer or downloading by another party who is thus enabled to access and copy that material.[3] However, because the offence under s 1(2) of the Obscene Publications Act 1964 (publication for gain) is only committed if the intention is to distribute for gain, a website host should only be criminally liable under this section if it has paying subscribers, and possibly only if access to the offending website requires a separate subscription.[4] Where there is no

---

19 See Council Directive on the legal protection of personal data, 95/46/EC OJ L 281, p 31, 23 November 1995, art 3(1).
20 See eg California Penal Code § 311.11(a).
 1 See also Broadcasting Act 1990, Sch 15, para 3, which provides that where an obscene article is in the possession, ownership or control of a person who intends to include the matter recorded on it in a relevant programme, it is to be regarded as an obscene article had or kept by that person for publication for gain.
 2 Obscene Publications Act 1959, s 2(5).
 3 See *R v Fellows and Arnold* (1996) Times, 27 September.
 4 See GJH Smith (ed) *Internet Law and Regulation* (2nd, FT London: Law & Tax, 1997), p 258, which argues that a commercial ISP may be liable as host of the offending material if it receives a subscription fee and in return provides access to, inter alia, material it has stored on its server and has that material in its possession for gain. If, however, the ISP is a 'pass-through' access provider, not hosting the obscene material itself, it should have a valid defence to such charges.

express statutory presumption of intent, the intermediary might attempt to argue that it has no intent to distribute, on the ground that its computer systems are merely the vehicle through which the originator of the file makes it available to others. This argument was accepted in relation to copying by the court in *Religious Technology Centre v Netcom On-Line Communications Services Inc*[5] (see 4.2.1.1 above), but it is unclear whether a criminal court dealing with an obscenity charge would be prepared to adopt a similar approach to the question of intention to distribute.

4.2.2.3   Transmission

It appears from the foregoing that the main mischief which obscenity laws seek to mitigate is the distribution of pornographic material. Mere possession (with the exception of child pornography) is not generally seen as posing a criminal law issue, and even the laws which criminalise mere possession of non-child pornography do so on the basis of an intention to distribute them. This is where the real difficulty for intermediaries lies, as their main business is the transmission of information.

Three basic approaches to the criminal liability of intermediaries are detectable in the law:[6]

- Criminalisation of knowing distribution of obscene material. This is exemplified by the Tennessee Code, § 39-17-902(a) of which provides:

  It is unlawful to knowingly . . . prepare for distribution, publish, print, exhibit, distribute, or offer to distribute, or to possess with intent to distribute or to exhibit or offer to distribute any obscene matter. . .

  This would enable an intermediary to plead ignorance of the content of the material it hosts or re-transmits, provided that it does not monitor the contents of its servers. An intermediary may face difficulties, however, if the statute defines knowledge to include constructive knowledge,[7] as the names or sources of the files retrieved for users might give it reason to believe that they contain obscene material.

- Criminalisation of distribution of obscene material for gain, subject to a defence of lack of knowledge or reasonable suspicion of contents. This is the approach adopted by the UK Obscene Publications Act 1959, s 2(1). The Act has been amended to cover non-physical articles such as electronic transmissions[8] and video distributed via websites.[9]

5   907 F Supp 1361 (ND Cal, 1995).
6   See note 18, p 92.
7   See Tennessee Code § 39-17-901(1):
     "Actual or constructive knowledge': a person is deemed to have constructive knowledge of the contents of material who has knowledge of facts which would put a reasonable and prudent person on notice as to the suspect nature of the material.'
8   See definition of 'article' in s 1(3) as amended by Criminal Justice and Public Order Act 1994.
9   Sections 1(4) and 1(5) extend liability to the inclusion of recorded or live material in a 'programme service', adopting the definition in s 210 of the Broadcasting Act 1990:
     '. . . the sending, by means of a telecommunications system, of sounds or visual images or both . . . for reception at two or more places in the United Kingdom (whether they are so sent for simultaneous reception or at different times in response to requests made by different users of the service).'
     Note that the near-identical wording in the UK Copyright, Designs and Patents Act 1988 has been held to encompass a website – *Shetland Times Ltd v Shetland News* [1997] FSR 604. See further Chapter 3.3.4.

- Criminalisation of knowing distribution of obscene material, but providing a specific exemption from liability for intermediaries who merely provide access to other servers without participating actively in the production or distribution of the material. Californian law adopts this approach,[10] as do some others.[11] However, liability for material distributed from the intermediary's own servers, eg from a hosted website, remains based on knowledge of the intermediary. The effect of this approach is to provide criminal sanctions against an intermediary who knowingly hosts or caches obscene material, but removes the danger of liability from those intermediaries who merely act as transmitters of third party originated packets, whatever the intermediary's state of knowledge.

A similar approach is found in the German Federal Law to Regulate the Conditions for Information and Communications Services 1997 (the luKDG, usually referred to as the 'Multimedia Law'). Under art 5(3) of the Multimedia Law, mere access providers are provided with a blanket immunity from liability except insofar as the access providers knows material is unlawful and fails to comply with a legal duty to block access.[12] Intermediaries who host material, however, are liable under art 5(2) for unlawful content if (a) they know that the content is unlawful, and (b) it is technically possible for the intermediary to block access and it is reasonable to expect such blocking to be effected. It is thought that the language of the Multimedia Law requires actual knowledge, though some doubts still remain.[13]

Additionally, national telecommunications laws often impose criminal liability for the transmission of obscene, indecent or other unlawful material. As Internet communications are in large part carried across telecommunications networks, these laws will also potentially be applicable. Examples of such laws are 18 USC § 1465[14] and the UK Telecommunications Act 1994, s 43.[15] However, the offence is normally committed only by the sender of the material, which suggests that an intermediary which merely transmit packets originating outside its systems

10 California Penal Code § 312.6(a).
     'It does not constitute a violation of this chapter for a person or entity solely to provide access or connection to or from a facility, system, or network over which that person or entity has no control, including related capabilities that are incidental to providing access or connection. This subdivision does not apply to an individual or entity that is owned or controlled by, or a conspirator with, an entity actively involved in the creation, editing, or knowing distribution of communications that violate this chapter.'
11 See eg French Telecommunications Law of July 1996. However, where an intermediary hosts a website it has been held that its acts in providing facilities for users to place files at the disposal of the public is incompatible with treating the intermediary as a mere access provider, and thus it is responsible for the content of its site even in the absence of knowledge – *Hallyday c LaCambre* Cour d'Appel de Paris, 10 February 1999, http://www.legalis.net/legalnet/judiciaire/decisions/ca_100299.htm (civil action for hosting site containing unauthorised nude photographs of plaintiff).
12 German Multimedia Law 1997, art 5(4):
     'any duties to block the use of illegal content according to the general laws remain unaffected, insofar as the service provider gains knowledge of such content . . .'
13 See FW Bulst 'Hear No Evil, See No Evil, Answer for No Evil: Internet Service Providers and Intellectual Property – The New German Teleservices Act' [1997] European Intellectual Property Law Review 32.
14 Offence of using a means of interstate commerce for the purpose of transporting obscene material.
15 Offence of using a public telecommunications system to send grossly offensive, threatening or obscene material.

will not be liable. Less clear is the position of the intermediary who hosts a site – in one sense that intermediary does send the material, in that its software responds to requests for the obscene resource by transmitting it to the requesting user,[16] although it would seem more logical to decide that the true sender is in fact the controller of the resource.

4.2.2.4   External classification

Australia has adopted a markedly different approach to the control of obscene and indecent material available via the Internet, essentially by subjecting it to the same censorship regime as for broadcasting. This regime was introduced by the Broadcasting Services Amendment (Online Services) Act 1999, which inserted a new Sch 5 into the Broadcasting Services Act 1992. The new regime came into operation on 1 January 2000.

Section 10 of the Schedule defines as 'prohibited content' most information[17] made available via the Internet which has either:

- been classified by the Australian Broadcasting Authority (ABA) as X or RC (refused classification), in essence films which depict sexual content in a way which is unsuitable for minors; or
- been classified with an R classification (otherwise unsuitable for minors), if the material is made available other than by a 'restricted access scheme',[18] essentially a control method which restricts children from obtaining access.

Information that has not yet been classified (eg material hosted outside Australia) is 'potential prohibited content'[19] and must, on request from any person, be classified by the ABA. Although the ABA classification system previously applied only to films and computer games, other forms of Internet content including text are to be classified using the same tests as for films and video games.[20]

Where a complaint is made that such content is being hosted in Australia or is accessible via an Australian ISP, once it has been classified:

---

16   This may be the correct interpretation of the UK Indecent Displays (Control) Act 1981, s 1(1), which creates an offence of publicly displaying indecent matter in public or in a manner which permits it to be visible from any public place (s 1(2)). Although s 1(3) exempts places which exclude those under 18 and make a charge for admission, this does not apply to the s 1(1) offence. It has been suggested that this might impose liability for websites, on the grounds that they can be accessed from terminals in public places - see G Smith (ed) *Internet Law and Regulation* (2nd, London: FT Law & Tax, 1997), p 260.

17   'Internet content' is defined in the Australian Broadcasting Services Act 1992, Sch 5, s 3 as 'information that:
(a) is kept on a data storage device; and
(b) is accessed, or available for access, using an Internet carriage service;
but does not include:
(c) ordinary electronic mail; or
(d) information that is transmitted in the form of a broadcasting service.'

18   The ABA is given power to declare a particular access control scheme as compliant with the Act, Australian Broadcasting Services Act 1992, Sch 5, s 4, but as at March 2000 appeared to have made no such declaration.

19   Australian Broadcasting Services Act 1992, Sch 5, s 11.

20   Australian Broadcasting Services Act 1992, Sch 5, s 13.

- the ABA can issue a take-down notice to the Australian content host, who commits an offence if the content is not removed or made inaccessible by the end of the next business day;[1] or
- in the case of content hosted outside Australia, the ABA may give notice to ISPs requiring them to prevent access to that content, which is also an offence if not complied with.[2]

This regime has been criticised extensively on the grounds that it bears no relationship to the reality of Internet activities, and imposes burdens on Australian content hosts and ISPs which are dramatically greater than those imposed elsewhere in the world.[3] It seems to the author unlikely that the regime will achieve its aims, and that it will eventually need to be abandoned for economic and practical reasons as content providers flee the Australian jurisdiction and Australian ISPs cut off access to foreign materials for Australian users.

4.2.3 Defamation

The fundamental basis of defamation liability is the *publication* of untrue information ('transmission' in the terminology of this chapter). Liability is based on damage to the reputation of the person referred to in the information, and that reputation cannot be damaged unless the information is disseminated to others than the author.

Beyond this basic principle, defamation laws differ widely. Thus, for example, English law imposes liability regardless of whether the publisher of a statement knew or ought to have known it was defamatory[4] whereas under Finnish law a distinction is made between intentional and negligent defamation.[5] Under US law a statement referring to a public figure will only be defamatory if malice can be proved on the part of the maker of the statement.[6] These national differences make it difficult for an Internet publisher to assess in advance whether material is likely to give rise to liability.

Because this chapter concentrates on the liability of intermediaries, no attempt will be made to examine the differing provisions of national law in detail. Instead, it will be assumed that the intermediary has transmitted a defamatory statement,[7] either from a website which it hosts or caches, or as one of the hosts in the transmission chain from the offending website. The question which needs to be answered here is whether the intermediary is liable in addition to the author of the statement. The risks to an intermediary of transmitting defamatory information are high, because of the way in which the Internet works and, more importantly, because of the ways in which users communicate using the Internet technologies.[8]

1 Australian Broadcasting Services Act 1992, Sch 5, ss 30–39, 82–3.
2 Australian Broadcasting Services Act 1992, Sch 5, ss 40–51, 82–3.
3 See the extensive set of articles on this topic on the Electronic Frontiers Australia website, http.www.efa.org.au
4 *E Hulton & Co v Jones* [1910] AC 20.
5 Finnish Penal Code.
6 *New York Times Co v Sullivan* 376 US 254 (1964).
7 Ie it will be assumed that the statement is defamatory in the jurisdiction whose laws apply to the action between the plaintiff and the intermediary, which may well not be the law of the country in which the statement originated.
8 See L Edwards 'Defamation and the Internet' in Edwards and Waelde (eds) *Law and the Internet: regulating cyberspace* (Oxford: Hart Publishing, 1997) pp 184–88.

4.2.3.1   *Is the intermediary a publisher or otherwise responsible?*

THE PUBLISHING PROCESS IN A DIGITAL WORLD

In its physical world sense, publishing is seen as a positive activity, ie a publisher will have had to *do* something (such as arranging for the printing of a work, sending out copies, selling copies, etc) to perform his role as a publisher.[9] This accords with those authorities which define publication as the communication[10] of the statement to at least one person other than the plaintiff.[11] In many cases, however, the process whereby a user accesses information held by an intermediary does not require any positive action on the intermediary's part. If the transaction is analysed at the level of the human or legal persons involved, it appears that the user *pulls* the information from the intermediary's server, so that the intermediary plays an entirely passive role. Viewed at the software and hardware level, though, it might be argued that the information is in fact *pushed* out by the software running on the defendant's computer. The process actually carried out is as follows:

- the user (or the user's software) issues a request to the intermediary's computer system;
- software has been set up by the intermediary which automatically responds to such a request with no human intervention;
- that software transmits the information requested from the intermediary's system to the user.

From one perspective, the user is controlling the software running on the intermediary's system, and is thus responsible for the transmission. From a different perspective, the transmission is undertaken by software which is in the possession of and under the overall control of the intermediary, making *him* responsible for the transmission. This second approach was recently adopted by the UK courts in *Godfrey v Demon Internet Lt*,[12] where the defendant ISP was sued for a defamatory statement carried in a newsgroup hosted on its server. Demon argued that it could not be a publisher, as it merely played a passive role by providing the infrastructure necessary for the posters of messages to make their views known. This was rejected by the court, stating that because Demon chose to receive and store the newsgroup, and had the power to delete messages from it, it was at common law a publisher, subject to any specific defences under the Defamation Act 1996 (see below).

FROM TRANSMITTER TO PUBLISHER

Internet intermediaries therefore transmit information, but it is not really accurate to say that they publish it in the physical world sense. Nonetheless, there are circumstances in which they will be treated as if they were publishers.

---

9 See eg the definition of 'publication' in the *Shorter Oxford Dictionary*: 'The action of making publicly known; public notification or pronouncement; promulgation.'

10 Because in each case the method of communication is always known, there has been little discussion on what would be sufficient to constitute communication. A particularly wide definition of publication seems to have been adopted in Australia; 'To publish a libel is to convey by some means to the mind of another the defamatory sense embodied in the vehicle.' *Webb v Bloch* (1928) 41 CLR 331, 363 per Isaacs J.

11 *Halsbury's Laws of England* (4th, London: Butterworths) Vol 28 'Libel and Slander' para 60.

12 [1999] 4 All ER 342.

Although the person primarily responsible for defamation is the author of the defamatory statement, national laws consistently provide that in addition, persons who play an important role in the dissemination of the statement are also liable. In general, publishers and editors are always liable, and in some jurisdictions liability may also be imposed on distributors in certain circumstances.

There are three basic models[13] for deciding whether to impose liability on an intermediary who transmits a defamatory statement. These models are based in part on the nature of the intermediary's activities, and in part on the functions which the law presumes or requires an intermediary of that type to perform.

The first model is that of 'information carrier'. This is a person or enterprise which merely moves information from one place to another, without examining its contents. The argument here is that some organisations so clearly play only an administrative role in the dissemination of statements that they should be immune from defamation claims. US case law has held in *Cubby Inc v CompuServe Inc*[14] that an ISP which merely acts as an information carrier, taking no steps to monitor or control the content of the information it conveys to users, is not liable for third party defamatory statements. It is clear from the judgment that the reason for denying liability was CompuServe's chosen mode of activity in passing on information from third parties unmodified and unexamined.[15] The defamatory statement resided in a discussion forum hosted on CompuServe's computers, and users paid for access to that information, all of which might have provided justification for holding CompuServe liable. Nonetheless, CompuServe was held not to have published it.

The second model is that of the 'information distributor'. This is a person or enterprise whose primary function is the transportation of information, but which is presumed by the law to have the opportunity of examining the content of that information. The difference between this category and the information carrier is solely based on this legal presumption – the actual mode of operation of an information distributor and an information carrier is likely to be the same. However, if the applicable law adopts an information distributor model, there may be additional functions which the intermediary will be expected by the law to perform.

UK defamation law is a clear example of the information distributor model. The position of intermediaries was clarified in 1996:

UK Defamation Act 1996, s 1

(1) In defamation proceedings a person has a defence if he shows that –
  (a) he was not the author, editor or publisher of the statement complained of,
  (b) he took reasonable care in relation to its publication, and
  (c) he did not know, and had no reason to believe, that what he did caused or contributed to the publication of a defamatory statement.

---

13 See also L Edwards 'Defamation and the Internet' in Edwards and Waelde (eds) *Law and the Internet: regulating cyberspace* (Oxford: Hart Publishing, 1997), p 192.
14 776 F Supp 135 (SDNY, 1991).
15 'CompuServe has no more control over such a publication than does a public library, book store, or newsstand, and it would be no more feasible for CompuServe to examine every publication it carries for potentially defamatory statements than it would be for any other distributor to do so.' *Cubby Inc v CompuServe Inc* 776 F Supp 135, 140 (SDNY, 1991).

(3) A person shall not be considered the author, editor or publisher of a statement if he is only involved –

. . .

    (c) in processing, making copies of, distributing or selling any electronic medium in or on which the statement is recorded, or in operating or providing any equipment, system or service by means of which the statement is retrieved, copied, distributed or made available in electronic form;

    (e) as the operator of or provider of access to a communications system by means of which the statement is transmitted, or made available, by a person over whom he has no effective control.

By virtue of s 1(3) most intermediaries will not be publishers. However, to avoid liability they will also need to meet the other s 1(1) conditions, and thus demonstrate that they did not know and had no reason to believe the statement was defamatory, and that they took 'reasonable care in relation to its publication'. It is generally thought that this imposes some minimum obligation to monitor information content, and it has recently been held that as soon as the intermediary learns of the defamatory content of the information available from its servers, it can no longer satisfy the requirements of s 1(1)(c) and thus loses the benefit of the defence.[16] However, as Edwards points out,[17] too much monitoring runs the contrary risk that the intermediary falls outside s 1(3), and is thus treated as a publisher. It is unfortunate that the UK legislature was unable to make its intentions clearer.

The third model is that of 'information controller'. An intermediary will be an information controller if it purports to examine the information content it transmits, and to take action to prevent transmission if the content is unlawful. This is evident from the US case of *Stratton Oakmont Inc v Prodigy Services Co.*[18] In that case the defendant bulletin board claimed in its advertising that it offered a family service, and that all its discussion groups were moderated. In fact, the moderation process had failed, but because Prodigy held itself out as exercising editorial control the New York court held that it was liable for a statement defaming the plaintiff. It is clear that the position would be the same under UK law,[19] and probably under most other countries' laws.

---

16 *Godfrey v Demon Internet Ltd* [1999] 4 All ER 342. There the notice was sufficient to identify the defamatory material, which was contained in a newsgroup posting, and the defendant had the power to remove the material from its newsgroup database but failed to do so. It is not clear whether the defence would have been available if, for example, the complaint was in respect of a Web page hosted on a third party server, but accessible to Demon subscribers via the defendant's services. It is technologically feasible to block access to a website, and possibly to individual pages, but this raises the question of how far a defendant would be required to go in those circumstances. If he did not possess the necessary technology, would he be obliged to purchase and install it?

17 'But [s 1(3)(e)] is problematic in that it seems to require . . . that to get the benefit of the s 1(1) defence, the ISP must *only* provide Internet access, and not do anything else – not, for example, exercise editorial control or spot-check content – for if they do, it would seem they will be exercising "effective control" over the maker of the defamatory statement. Yet it seems unlikely that an ISP which neither monitors nor edits can succeed in proving, as s 1(1)(b) requires, that it took reasonable care to prevent the publication of the defamatory statement. There is thus an inherent catch 22.' L Edwards 'Defamation and the Internet' in Edwards and Waelde (eds) *Law and the Internet: regulating cyberspace* (Oxford: Hart Publishing, 1997), p 194.

18 23 Media L Rep 1794 (NY Sup Ct, May 25 1995).

19 UK Defamation Act 1996, s 1(2): "editor' means a person having editorial or equivalent responsibility for the content of the statement or the decision to publish it'.

ACCIDENTAL DEFAMATION

One interesting side effect of the Internet technologies is that they create the risk of defamation for which the intermediary is directly responsible as publisher. This risk arises where the intermediary produces its own information resources, eg through automated Web searches. A simple example might be a Web page which contains links to information held on other servers.

The reason why a collation of information of this kind might be defamatory in common law systems is through the legal concept of *innuendo*, where words or pictures which are on their face innocent of any defamatory meaning become defamatory because of the inferences drawn by readers or viewers who are in possession of further information. The most commonly cited English example is the case of *Tolley v J S Fry & Sons Ltd*,[20] where a leading amateur golfer was caricatured in an advertisement with the advertiser's chocolate bar displayed prominently in his pocket. At that date, a golfer who accepted money for endorsing a product would lose his amateur status and would be asked to resign from any reputable golf club. The court held that a viewer of the advertisement who understood the rules relating to amateur golf would draw the inference that the plaintiff had endorsed the product, thus forfeiting his amateur status, and was therefore playing in amateur tournaments under false pretences. This innuendo was proved by evidence from witnesses, and the advertisement held to be defamatory.[1]

Many innuendos arise from the juxtaposition of more than one piece of information. For example, a waxwork statue of a man holding a gun is not of itself defamatory of that man. When the statue is placed just outside the Chamber of Horrors at Madame Tussauds, however, the inference drawn by viewers is closer to a defamatory one, and when this is coupled with the information that the man was charged with murder before a Scottish court but the case was found not proven, the defamatory effect is obvious.[2] Thus, a website relating to some criminal activity which contained a link to another site relating to a person who had been suspected, but never convicted, of that criminal activity would give rise to a potentially defamatory innuendo.[3]

In that example the creator of the website would almost certainly have intended to convey the innuendo. An unintended innuendo might arise from the presence on a Web page of links to related sites, the overall effect of which suggested that some of those linked to shared the opinions of the others. A site on the subject of the drug cannabis might contain links to sites maintained by doctors specialising in pain relief (for which cannabis is sometimes used), and to sites advocating the legalisation of the sale of cannabis and its use even before legalisation. These links might have been created by trawling the Internet automatically. If the overall effect of the site suggests to visitors that the doctors in question use cannabis illegally when treating patients, that could give rise to a defamatory innuendo.

---

20 [1931] AC 333.
 1 The court will not find an innuendo unless the plaintiff pleads the precise meaning which is alleged to be attributed to the statement and proves the existence of facts which support that meaning – *Grubb v Bristol United Press Ltd* [1963] 1 QB 309.
 2 *Monson v Tussauds Ltd* [1894] 1 QB 671.
 3 A safe example, because the subject is dead and thus cannot be defamed, would be a website on the subject of American gangster murders with a link to another site containing Al Capone's biography – Capone was only convicted of tax evasion.

Unintended innuendos can also arise, at least under English law, in the case of real people who have the same name as invented characters,[4] juxtapositions of pictures which suggest defamatory things about third persons[5] and statements which are true of one person but defamatory of another with the same name, provided evidence is brought to show that witnesses believed the statement referred to the plaintiff.[6] Because Web pages are accessible world-wide, the risk of such accidental defamations is vastly increased.

4.2.3.2   Where does publication take place?

The question where publication takes place is extremely important, as it defines the theory on which the intermediary is or is not liable for the defamation. As national laws differ so markedly, there may be real value to a plaintiff in being able to choose between jurisdictions.

The technology of the Internet introduces uncertainty as to where publication of a defamatory statement occurs. There are essentially two possibilities:

- the place from which the statement was transmitted; or
- the place where it was received.

At first sight it seems obvious that, because defamation is based on damage to reputation, that damage takes place where the statement is viewed by a user, and that therefore that place is also the place of publication. This, however, depends on whether the courts view the effect of the transmission as the sending of the statement to the user, in which case publication takes place in the user's jurisdiction, or whether the user is 'virtually' collecting the statement from the server on which it is stored, in which case publication occurs there. The discussion in part 4.2.1.1 above of precisely who undertakes the copying involved, indicates that the latter argument is not without some judicial support.

So far as physical world publications are concerned, the courts have taken the view that a publication is made in every jurisdiction in which the publisher ought to have foreseen it would be made available, but excluding copies brought privately into jurisdictions where it was not otherwise foreseeable that the publication would be made available.[7] This distinction can be made because a physical world publisher can be deemed to be aware of the distribution chain for his product, which is limited in extent by the number of physical copies made.

In contrast, an information repository such as a website allows its users to make as many copies as each of them desires, and effects the transport of those copies back to the user's own jurisdiction. If, for example, the website is located in the US, there are two possible ways of treating this issue:

---

4   *E Hulton & Co v Jones* [1910] AC 20.
5   *Cassidy v Daily Mirror Newspapers Ltd* [1929] 2 KB 331, where a picture of the plaintiff's husband with a person stated to be his fiancée suggested that she was not really married.
6   *Newstead v London Express Newspapers Ltd* [1940] 1 KB 377, a newspaper report of a bigamy trial. The defendants would nowadays have a defence in these particular circumstances.
7   *Shevill and others v Presse Alliance SA* [1992] 1 All ER 409, CA, [1995] All ER (EC) 289, [1995] 2 WLR 499, ECJ. The issue which the case decides is whether the UK courts have jurisdiction in these circumstances, which depends on whether publication occurred in the UK and on the applicability of the relevant provisions of the Brussels Convention – the case is discussed further below.

- The publication is made in all those jurisdictions where it is foreseeable that the information may be transported by a user, and where it actually is transported. In practice, this means every jurisdiction in the world. The publisher is potentially liable to an unlimited number of people in an unlimited number of jurisdictions. There are strong policy grounds for rejecting this solution as providing too great a disincentive to electronic publishing, but as yet there is no indication that national laws will take this route.[8]
- Alternatively, the publication may be treated as being made in the location where the information is stored and from which it is received. In this case, a website in the US would publish only in the US, and be subject only to the appropriate US state defamation laws. If the intermediary actively marketed the information service in the UK, however, by eg providing a local access node of his network, it would be appropriate to treat the information as made available in the UK, even if it was in fact located on a computer in the US.

It may be that there is no need to decide where publication takes place. The European Court of Justice in *Shevill and others v Presse Alliance SA*[9] has held that where the Brussels Convention 1988 applies[10] an action may be brought both where the publication occurred and where the plaintiff suffered damage to his reputation. The latter place must surely be where the statement was read, ie the location of the viewer. Thus, intermediaries (and authors) are, indeed, exposed to potential liability in every country of the world. The only small crumb of comfort to be derived from *Shevill* is that the court may only award compensation for the damage to the plaintiff's reputation in that jurisdiction, and not damages for all losses world-wide. In the case of Internet defamation, that will probably be sufficient to make it worthwhile for intermediaries to be sued in a 'plaintiff-friendly' jurisdiction. Indeed, in *Shevill* the Advocate-General of the European Court of Justice expressed this fear succinctly –

> the English courts could even find themselves in danger, by reason of their 'generosity' towards victims of defamation, of becoming the natural choice of forum in such matters.[11]

4.2.4 Common elements of intermediary liability

The analysis above indicates that, in spite of the differences between national laws, there are some common elements to intermediary liability. In general, there is a recognition that intermediaries who transmit information originating

---

8 See Chapter 7.1.3, especially 7.1.3.5.
9 [1995] All ER (EC) 289, [1995] 2 WLR 499, ECJ.
10 Where the Brussels Convention does not apply, the English courts have the power to stay proceedings on the ground that there is insufficient connection with the jurisdiction, eg if the publication in England is *de minimis* in comparison to world-wide publication – *Berezovsky v Forbes Inc* (1998) Times, 19 January (although before the Court of Appeal in that case the plaintiffs adduced sufficient evidence of publication and connection with England and Wales to convince the court that England was a proper forum for trial – The Times, 27 November 1998).
11 Opinion of Advocate General Liger, para 56.

from third parties (including information hosted by the intermediary for such transmission) should not be absolutely liability for the actions of their users. There are two reasons for imposing liability on which most laws seem to be agreed:

- where the intermediary knows or has reason to believe that the information content it transmits is unlawful; and
- where, irrespective of the intermediary's knowledge, it benefits directly[12] from the transmission.

An additional reason for imposing liability, which is not accepted universally, is:

- where the intermediary fails to take reasonable steps to determine if the information content it transmits is unlawful.

It must be recognised, however, that these justifications for imposing liability were developed in respect of physical world transactions. There, an intermediary is more closely connected with the parties to the transaction, and has a greater opportunity to assess the respectability of those for whom it acts and the nature of their activities. Internet intermediaries work in what is effectively an anonymous world. It is theoretically possible to identify the source of transmissions and the nature of the information transmitted, but in practice the volume and speed of transmission makes such identification difficult, if not impossible. For this reason, there is a trend towards granting Internet intermediaries much greater immunities and limitations on their liability for third party content – this is discussed at 4.3.2 below.

4.3   LIMITATIONS ON INTERMEDIARY LIABILITY

From the preceding discussion, it can be seen that a resolution of the Internet intermediary liability issue is of crucial importance. Differing liability models across national boundaries create substantial uncertainty for intermediaries as to the scope and extent of their potential liabilities, which may act as a major disincentive to market entry or the provision of new services.[13]

The liability of intermediaries for the information content and services they supply to users on their own account is a matter which can in most instances be left to existing laws to determine. These intermediaries are usually in a direct relationship with the information source, and can decide whether to provide the information or services as a matter of commercial judgment. Liability questions will play some part in making that judgment, but are not so fundamental as to require international action immediately.

However, there are some areas of intermediary activity where liability issues present real and intractable barriers to that activity:

---

12   This is to be contrasted with the indirect benefit which an intermediary receives through fees for providing access to Internet resources.

13   'The development of electronic commerce could potentially be impeded by illegal and harmful content issues where users fear unwanted content, and where network service providers fear the liability they will take on if they are expected to be responsible for the content that flows across systems.' OECD Policy Brief 'Electronic Commerce' No 1-1997, November 1997.

- New services, such as the identification of Internet actors, where the geographical and jurisdictional diversity of recipients makes the assessment of liability impossible. This is examined further in Chapter 5.
- Liability for third party content – see 4.2 above.

There is a growing international consensus that the way to solve this problem, particularly in respect of third party content liability, is by granting intermediaries some immunity from liability. The questions which remain to be answered, and which are discussed at 4.3.2 below, are the circumstances in which such immunities should arise and their limitations.

Declaration of the Bonn Ministerial Conference on Global Information Networks, 6–8 July 1997

41. Ministers underline the importance of clearly defining the relevant legal rules on responsibility for content of the various actors in the chain between creation and use. They recognise the need to make a clear distinction between the responsibility of those who produce and place content in circulation and that of intermediaries.
42. Ministers stress that the rules on responsibility for content should be based on a set of common principles so as to ensure a level playing field. Therefore, intermediaries like network operators and access providers should, in general, not be responsible for content. This principle should be applied in such a way that intermediaries like network operators and access providers are not subject to unreasonable, disproportionate or discriminatory rules. In any case, third-party content hosting services should not be expected to exercise prior control on content which they have no reason to believe is illegal. Due account should be taken of whether such intermediaries had reasonable grounds to know and reasonable possibility to control content.
43. Ministers consider that rules on responsibility should give effect to the principle of freedom of speech, respect public and private interests and not impose disproportionate burdens on actors.

4.3.1 Intermediary contracts

Until the international consensus results in legislation which defines and limits the responsibility of intermediaries, contracts will be used in an attempt to control the extent of intermediary liability. However, the use of contracts to control liability in multiple jurisdictions is problematic for a number of reasons:

- To be effective these contracts will need to be formed electronically as each user commences dealings with the intermediary. Some types of contract may not be able to be concluded electronically in some jurisdictions, and the effects of contract formation technology such as 'I Agree' buttons on Web pages may differ from state to state.[14]
- In some jurisdictions there is judicial control of unfair or unacceptable contract terms. Thus, in the UK, the Unfair Contract Terms Act 1977 gives

---

14 Commission proposal for a European Parliament and Council directive on certain legal aspects of electronic commerce in the internal market, COM (1998) 586 final, 98/0325 (COD), 18 November 1998, Explanatory Memorandum, pp 11–12.

the courts power to declare most[15] exclusion or limitation terms to be unenforceable on the ground that they are unfair.[16] The differences in national approaches to this issue make drafting a universally applicable limitation of liability almost impossible.

- In almost all jurisdictions, consumer protection laws exist which will render these terms void if the user is a consumer. For example, the EC Directive on Unfair Terms in Consumer Contracts[17] provides that a term is unfair if (a) it has not been individually negotiated and (b) 'contrary to the requirement of good faith, it causes a significant imbalance in the parties' rights and obligations arising under the contract, to the detriment of the consumer'.[18] Unfair terms are not enforceable, although the remainder of the contract remains in force so far as that is feasible. The Annex to the Directive contains an indicative and non-exhaustive list of terms which 'may be regarded as unfair'.[19] Of these, the most important to intermediary contracts are:

  '(b) inappropriately excluding or limiting the legal rights of the consumer . . . in the event of total or partial non-performance . . . ;
  (i)   irrevocably binding the consumer to terms with which he had no real opportunity of becoming acquainted before the conclusion of the contract . . . ;
  (q)   excluding or hindering the consumer's right to take legal action or exercise any other legal remedy, particularly by . . . unduly restricting the evidence available to him or imposing on him a burden of proof which, according to the applicable law, should lie with another party to the contract.'

  Terms which exclude the intermediary's liability to a consumer are likely to fall foul of all three.

- Even if an effective contract can be concluded with the user, it will only be effective to exclude or limit the intermediary's liability to that user. Thus:

  – the contract will not assist the intermediary in any action by a third party based on the information which the intermediary transmits to or from the user, eg a defamation claim; and
  – it will have no effect on any criminal liability of the intermediary for transmitting third party content.

Many of the claims against an intermediary will be made by persons with whom the intermediary has no opportunity of forming a contract, and this method of liability control is clearly inadequate to provide intermediaries with the level of immunity which it is generally accepted that they require.

---

15 The Unfair Contract Terms Act grants these powers in respect of (inter alia) terms excluding contractual or tortious obligations of care (s 2(2)) and terms contained in the written standard terms on the contract is concluded (s 3).
16 As determined in accordance with s 11. For guidance on the assessment of unfairness in relation to software contracts, see *St Albans City and District Council v International Computers Ltd* [1996] 4 All ER 481.
17 Directive 93/13/EEC, OJ L 95, 21 April 1993.
18 Article 3(1).
19 Article 3(3). Note that the UK Department of Trade and Industry in *Implementation of the EC Directive on Unfair Terms in Consumer Contracts* (London: DTI, October 1993), its consultative document on the implementation of the Directive, takes this wording to mean that the terms in the list may be, but are not necessarily, unfair. Other Member States may take a stronger position on this point, perhaps requiring the intermediary to prove that the term is positively fair.

4.3.2   Statutory limitation and immunity

Although the Internet is still a very new phenomenon, governments have been quick to recognise that it presents important issues which require law reform. So far as the liability of intermediaries is concerned, the US has been quick to act by introducing the immunities discussed below, as have some other jurisdictions. The EU undertook a substantial programme of research into the legal differences between European national laws, and the result of that process is Directive on electronic commerce[20] which contains probably the most comprehensive proposal so far for a general scheme for determining intermediary immunities.

4.3.2.1   Specific copyright liability immunity

Because copyright infringement is so obviously a potential danger for internet intermediaries, specific action has been taken in this area in a number of jurisdictions.

The US has recently enacted a detailed set of immunities in the Online Copyright Infringement Liability Limitation Act, part of the Digital Millennium Copyright Act which ratifies the WIPO Copyright Treaty. This Act became law in December 1998. It inserts a new § 512 into the US Copyright Act, Title 17 USC, which in summary provides immunity to intermediaries who:

- merely transmit packets;
- automatically cache information requested by users;
- host third party resources; or
- provide search and location tools for resources located elsewhere.

These immunities are subject to detailed conditions, primarily lack of knowledge, lack of direct financial benefit from the third party activity, and respect for a resource controller's copyright management technologies.

Title 17 USC as amended by the US On-Line Copyright Infringement Liability Limitation Act

§ 512. LIMITATIONS ON LIABILITY RELATING TO MATERIAL ONLINE

(a) Transitory digital network communications –

A service provider shall not be liable for monetary relief, or, except as provided in subsection (j), for injunctive or other equitable relief, for infringement of copyright by reason of the provider's transmitting, routing, or providing connections for, material through a system or network controlled or operated by or for the service provider, or by reason of the intermediate and transient storage of that material in the course of such transmitting, routing, or providing connections, if –

(1) the transmission of the material was initiated by or at the direction of a person other than the service provider;

(2) the transmission, routing, provision of connections, or storage is carried out through an automatic technical process without selection of the material by the service provider;

(3) the service provider does not select the recipients of the material except as an automatic response to the request of another person;

(4) no copy of the material made by the service provider in the course of such intermediate or transient storage is maintained on the system or network in a

---

20 Directive 2000/31/EC, OJ L 178 p. 1, 17 July 2000.

manner ordinarily accessible to anyone other than anticipated recipients, and no such copy is maintained on the system or network in a manner ordinarily accessible to such anticipated recipients for a longer period than is reasonably necessary for the transmission, routing, or provision of connections; and

(5) the material is transmitted through the system or network without modification of its content.

(b) System caching –

(1) Limitation on liability – A service provider shall not be liable for monetary relief, or, except as provided in subsection (j), for injunctive or other equitable relief, for infringement of copyright by reason of the intermediate and temporary storage of material on a system or network controlled or operated by or for the service provider in a case in which –

   (A) the material is made available online by a person other than the service provider;

   (B) the material is transmitted from the person described in subparagraph (A) through the system or network to a person other than the person described in subparagraph (A) at the direction of that other person; and

   (C) the storage is carried out through an automatic technical process for the purpose of making the material available to users of the system or network who, after the material is transmitted as described in subparagraph (B), request access to the material from the person described in subparagraph (A), if the conditions set forth in paragraph (2) are met.

(2) Conditions – The conditions referred to in paragraph (1) are that –

   (A) the material described in paragraph (1) is transmitted to the subsequent users described in paragraph (1)(C) without modification to its content from the manner in which the material was transmitted from the person described in paragraph (1)(A);

   (B) the service provider described in paragraph (1) complies with rules concerning the refreshing, reloading, or other updating of the material when specified by the person making the material available online in accordance with a generally accepted industry standard data communications protocol for the system or network through which that person makes the material available, except that this subparagraph applies only if those rules are not used by the person described in paragraph (1)(A) to prevent or unreasonably impair the intermediate storage to which this subsection applies;

   (C) the service provider does not interfere with the ability of technology associated with the material to return to the person described in paragraph (1)(A) the information that would have been available to that person if the material had been obtained by the subsequent users described in paragraph (1)(C) directly from that person . . .

   (D) if the person described in paragraph (1)(A) has in effect a condition that a person must meet prior to having access to the material, such as a condition based on payment of a fee or provision of a password or other information, the service provider permits access to the stored material in significant part only to users of its system or network that have met those conditions and only in accordance with those conditions; and

   (E) if the person described in paragraph (1)(A) makes that material available online without the authorization of the copyright owner of the material, the service provider responds expeditiously to remove, or disable access to, the material that is claimed to be infringing upon notification of claimed infringement as described in subsection (c)(3) . . .

(c) Information residing on systems or networks at direction of users –

(1) In general – A service provider shall not be liable for monetary relief, or, except as provided in subsection (j), for injunctive or other equitable relief, for infringement of copyright by reason of the storage at the direction of a user of

material that resides on a system or network controlled or operated by or for the service provider, if the service provider –

(A) (i) does not have actual knowledge that the material or an activity using the material on the system or network is infringing;

(ii) in the absence of such actual knowledge, is not aware of facts or circumstances from which infringing activity is apparent; or

(iii) upon obtaining such knowledge or awareness, acts expeditiously to remove, or disable access to, the material;

(B) does not receive a financial benefit directly attributable to the infringing activity, in a case in which the service provider has the right and ability to control such activity; and

(C) upon notification of claimed infringement as described in paragraph (3), responds expeditiously to remove, or disable access to, the material that is claimed to be infringing or to be the subject of infringing activity.

. . .

(d) Information location tools –

A service provider shall not be liable for monetary relief, or, except as provided in subsection (j), for injunctive or other equitable relief, for infringement of copy-right by reason of the provider referring or linking users to an online location containing infringing material or infringing activity, by using information location tools, including a directory, index, reference, pointer, or hypertext link, if the service provider –

(1) (A) does not have actual knowledge that the material or activity is infringing;

(B) in the absence of such actual knowledge, is not aware of facts or circumstances from which infringing activity is apparent; or

(C) upon obtaining such knowledge or awareness, acts expeditiously to remove, or disable access to, the material;

(2) does not receive a financial benefit directly attributable to the infringing activity, in a case in which the service provider has the right and ability to control such activity; and

(3) upon notification of claimed infringement as described in subsection (c)(3), responds expeditiously to remove, or disable access to, the material that is claimed to be infringing or to be the subject of infringing activity, except that, for purposes of this paragraph, the information described in subsection (c)(3)(A)(iii) shall be identification of the reference or link, to material or activity claimed to be infringing, that is to be removed or access to which is to be disabled, and information reasonably sufficient to permit the service provider to locate that reference or link.

The EU has taken a rather simpler approach to this problem in the draft Directive on copyright in the Information Society:

Proposal for a European Parliament and Council Directive on the harmonization of certain aspects of copyright and related rights in the Information Society, COM (97) 628 final, 10 December 1997

COMMENTARY TO ARTICLE 5, P 36

3.   Article 5(1) introduces an obligatory exception to the right of reproduction for certain technical acts of reproductions that are integral to a technological process and made for the sole purpose of executing another act of exploitation of a work. When applying this exception, or any other exception listed in this Article, the 'three step test', as set out in paragraph 4 of this Article, has, of course, also to be met. The purpose of Article 5(1) is to exclude from the scope of the reproduction right certain acts of reproduction which are dictated by technology, but which have no separate economic significance of their own. It applies notably to the on-line environment, but also to acts of reproduction taking place in the context of the use of a protected subject matter in off-line formats. In such cases, it is appropriate to limit the scope of the reproduction right and only protect

those acts of reproduction which are of a separate economic relevance. Such an obligatory exception at Community level is vital as such short lived reproductions ancillary to the final use of a work will take place in most acts of exploitation of protected subject matter, which will often be of a transnational nature. For instance, when transmitting a video on-demand from a database in Germany to a home computer in Portugal, this retrieval will imply a copy of the video, first of all, at the place of the database and afterwards, in average, up to at least a hundred often ephemeral acts of storage along the transmission to Portugal. A divergent situation in Member States with some requiring authorization of such ancillary acts of storage would significantly risk impeding the free movement of works and services, and notably on-line services containing protected subject matter.

ARTICLE 5[1]
Exceptions to the restricted acts set out in Articles 2 and 3
1. Temporary acts of reproduction referred to in Article 2, such as transient and incidental acts of reproduction which are an integral and essential part of a technological process, including those which facilitate effective functioning of transmission systems, whose sole purpose is to enable use to be made of a work or other subject matter, and having no independent economic significance, shall be exempted from the right set out in Article 2 [Reproduction Right].

. . .
4. The exceptions and limitations provided for in paragraphs 1, 2, 3 and 3a shall only be applied to certain specific cases and shall not be interpreted in such a way as to allow their application to be used in a manner which unreasonably prejudices the rightholders' legitimate interests or conflicts with the normal exploitation of their works or other subject matter.

The effect of this provision is that temporary copying by intermediaries, such as packet transmission and caching, do not amount to infringement. Additionally, the more general immunity proposed in the draft Directive on Electronic Commerce (see 4.3.2.2 below) will also apply to copyright actions.

An additional restriction on these immunities in both the US and the EU is that an intermediary must not, when providing access to the resources, strip out technical rights management information, ie information used to prove the copyright ownership of the work or to track licensed users.[2]

4.3.2.2   General immunity

It is now possible to detect a growing international consensus that Internet intermediaries are becoming such a fundamental part of the world communications system that they require protection from liability for the third party information which they carry. This liability must be distinguished from any liability of the intermediary for the provision of its own services or information – although some of these activities may be worthy of legal immunity (see 4.1.2 above), they will not fall within the general immunity provisions which have been proposed.

The first general immunity provisions were introduced by the US, largely by accident, in the Communications Decency Act 1996. The intention of this

---

1   Text from COM (1999) 250 final, 21 June 1999.
2   *Proposal for a European Parliament and Council Directive on the harmonization of certain aspects of copyright and related rights in the Information Society* COM (1999) 250 final, 21 June 1999, arts 6 and 7; 17 USC § 512(i).

legislation was to introduce new criminal offences of knowingly creating, sending, transmitting or displaying obscene or indecent materials to minors, or knowingly permitting the use of one's telecommunications systems for these purposes. As a counterbalancing element of the legislation, § 230 provided protection for 'Good Samaritan' activities on the part of ISPs. The aim was to overrule *Stratton Oakmont Inc v Prodigy Services Co*[3] and thus permit ISPs to introduce blocking or filtering technology without assuming the role of editor or publisher, and thus becoming responsible for the third party content.[4] However, the new criminal offences were struck down in *ACLU v Reno*[5] as infringing the First Amendment protection for freedom of speech, thus leaving the immunity provisions to stand alone:

US Communications Decency Act 1996, 47 USC § 230

SECTION 230. PROTECTION FOR PRIVATE BLOCKING AND SCREENING OF OFFENSIVE MATERIAL[6]

(a) Findings: **The Congress finds the following:**
(1) The rapidly developing array of Internet and other interactive computer services available to individual Americans represent an extraordinary advance in the availability of educational and informational resources to our citizens.
(2) These services offer users a great degree of control over the information that they receive, as well as the potential for even greater control in the future as technology develops.
(3) The Internet and other interactive computer services offer a forum for a true diversity of political discourse, unique opportunities for cultural development, and myriad avenues for intellectual activity.

---

3   23 Media L Rep 1794 (NY Sup Ct, May 25 1995) – see 4.2.3.1 above.
4   The Senate conference report on § 230 states:
    'This section provides "Good Samaritan" protections from civil liability for providers or users of an interactive computer service for actions to restrict or to enable restriction of access to objectionable online material. One of the specific purposes of this section is to overrule *Stratton-Oakmont v Prodigy* and any other similar decisions which have treated such providers and users as publishers or speakers of content that is not their own because they have restricted access to objectionable material. The conferees believe that such decisions create serious obstacles to the important federal policy of empowering parents to determine the content of communications their children receive through interactive computer services.' S Conf Rep No 104-230, at 435 (1996).
5   929 F Supp 824, 830–838 (ED Pa, 1996), *affirmed* 117 S Ct 2329 (1997).
6   The definitions used in this section are:
    '(1) **Internet**: The term Internet means the international computer network of both Federal and non-Federal interoperable packet switched data networks.
    (2) **Interactive computer service**: The term interactive computer service means any information service, system, or access software provider that provides or enables computer access by multiple users to a computer server, including specifically a service or system that provides access to the Internet and such systems operated or services offered by libraries or educational institutions.
    (3) **Information content provider**: The term information content provider means any person or entity that is responsible, in whole or in part, for the creation or development of information provided through the Internet or any other interactive computer service.
    (4) **Access software provider**: The term access software provider means a provider of software (including client or server software), or enabling tools that do any one or more of the following:
       (A) filter, screen, allow, or disallow content;
       (B) pick, choose, analyze, or digest content; or
       (C) transmit, receive, display, forward, cache, search, subset, organize, reorganize, or translate content.'

(4) The Internet and other interactive computer services have flourished, to the benefit of all Americans, with a minimum of government regulation.

(5) Increasingly Americans are relying on interactive media for a variety of political, educational, cultural, and entertainment services.

(b) Policy: **It is the policy of the United States –**

(1) to promote the continued development of the Internet and other interactive computer services and other interactive media;

(2) to preserve the vibrant and competitive free market that presently exists for the Internet and other interactive computer services, unfettered by Federal or State regulation;

(3) to encourage the development of technologies which maximize user control over what information is received by individuals, families, and schools who use the Internet and other interactive computer services;

(4) to remove disincentives for the development and utilization of blocking and filtering technologies that empower parents to restrict their children's access to objectionable or inappropriate online material; and

(5) to ensure vigorous enforcement of Federal criminal laws to deter and punish trafficking in obscenity, stalking, and harassment by means of computer.

(c) Protection for Good Samaritan Blocking and Screening of Offensive Material:

(1) **Treatment of publisher or speaker**: No provider or user of an interactive computer service shall be treated as the publisher or speaker of any information provided by another information content provider.

(2) **Civil liability**: No provider or user of an interactive computer service shall be held liable on account of –

(A) any action voluntarily taken in good faith to restrict access to or availability of material that the provider or user considers to be obscene, lewd, lascivious, filthy, excessively violent, harassing, or otherwise objectionable, whether or not such material is constitutionally protected; or

(B) any action taken to enable or make available to information content providers or others the technical means to restrict access to material described in paragraph (1).

(d) Effect on other laws:

(1) **No effect on criminal law**: Nothing in this section shall be construed to impair the enforcement of section 223 of this Act, chapter 71 (relating to obscenity) or 110 (relating to sexual exploitation of children) of title 18, United States Code, or any other Federal criminal statute.

(2) **No effect on intellectual property law**: Nothing in this section shall be construed to limit or expand any law pertaining to intellectual property.

(3) **State law**: Nothing in this section shall be construed to prevent any State from enforcing any State law that is consistent with this section. No cause of action may be brought and no liability may be imposed under any State or local law that is inconsistent with this section.

(4) **No effect on communications privacy law**: Nothing in this section shall be construed to limit the application of the Electronic Communications Privacy Act of 1986 or any of the amendments made by such Act, or any similar State law.

In subsequent litigation it has been held that § 230 provides a complete immunity from civil actions for defamation,[7] even where the ISP pays the author for the right to provide access to the defamatory material,[8] and from a civil

---

7 *Zeran v America Online, Inc* 129 F 3d 327 (4th Cir, 1997), 1998 US 4047 (cert Denied).

8 *Blumenthal v Drudge and America Online Inc* (1998 District of Columbia Civil Action No 97-1968 (PLF), 22 May 1998).

action alleging negligence in failing to prevent continued solicitations to purchase child pornography made via the ISP's system.[9]

Zeran v. America Online Inc. 129 F.3d 327 (4th Cir. 1997) pp. 330–31

By its plain language, sec. 230 creates a federal immunity to any cause of action that would make service providers liable for information originating with a third-party user of the service. Specifically, sec. 230 precludes courts from entertaining claims that would place a computer service provider in a publisher's role. Thus, lawsuits seeking to hold a service provider liable for its exercise of a publisher's traditional editorial functions – such as deciding whether to publish, withdraw, postpone or alter content – are barred.

The purpose of this statutory immunity is not difficult to discern. Congress recognized the threat that tort-based lawsuits pose to freedom of speech in the new and burgeoning Internet medium. The imposition of tort liability on service providers for the communications of others represented, for Congress, simply another form of intrusive government regulation of speech. Section 230 was enacted, in part, to maintain the robust nature of Internet communication and, accordingly, to keep government interference in the medium to a minimum . . .

None of this means, of course, that the original culpable party who posts defamatory messages would escape accountability . . . Congress made a policy choice, however, not to deter harmful online speech through the separate route of imposing tort liability on companies that serve as intermediaries for other parties' potentially injurious messages.

Blumenthal v. Drudge and America Online Inc. (District of Columbia Civil Action No. 97-1968 (PLF), 22 May 1998)

If it were writing on a clean slate, this Court would agree with plaintiffs. AOL has certain editorial rights with respect to the content provided by Drudge and disseminated by AOL, including the right to require changes in content and to remove it; and it has affirmatively promoted Drudge as a new source of unverified instant gossip on AOL. Yet it takes no responsibility for any damage he may cause. AOL is not a passive conduit like the telephone company, a common carrier with no control and therefore no responsibility for what is said over the telephone wires.[10] Because it has the right to exercise editorial control over those with whom it contracts and whose words it disseminates, it would seem only fair to hold AOL to the liability standards applied to a publisher or, at least, like a book store owner or library, to the liability standards applied to a distributor.[11] But Congress has made a different policy choice by providing immunity even where the interactive service provider has an active, even aggressive role in making available content prepared by others. In some sort of tacit quid pro quo arrangement with the service provider community, Congress has conferred immunity from tort liability as an incentive to Internet service providers to self-police the Internet for obscenity and other offensive material, even where the self-policing is unsuccessful or not even attempted.

. . . While it appears to this Court that AOL in this case has taken advantage of all the benefits conferred by Congress in the Communications Decency Act, and then some, without accepting any of the burdens that Congress intended, the statutory language is clear: AOL is immune from suit, and the Court therefore must grant its motion for summary judgment.

---

9 *Doe v America Online Inc* 718 So 2d 385 (4th Cir, 1999).
10 See David J Goldstone 'A Funny Thing Happened On The Way To the Cyber Forum: Public vs. Private in Cyberspace Speech' (1998) 69 U Colo L Rev 1, 40–48.
11 See Douglas B Luffman 'Defamation Liability For On-Line Services: The Sky Is Not Falling' (1997) 65 Geo Wash L Rev 1071, 1083–35; David R Sheridan 'Zeran v. AOL And The Effect Of Section 230 Of The Communications Decency Act Upon Liability for Defamation On The Internet' 61 (1997) Alb L Rev 147, 167–77.

Although the effects of § 230 appear to have surprised the courts, it is clear from these judgments that the immunity will not be overturned or eroded by the judiciary, and that if the US wishes to reduce the level of immunity fresh legislation will be required.

Such legislation seems unlikely because other jurisdictions, having considered the issues rather more carefully than was the case with the US Communications Decency Act, have introduced or proposed extensive immunities for Internet intermediaries. These immunities extend both to copyright infringement and criminal law, as well as to civil actions for torts such as defamation.

Singapore Electronic Transactions Act 1998

LIABILITY OF NETWORK SERVICE PROVIDERS

10. (1) A network service provider shall not be subject to any civil or criminal liability under any rule of law in respect of third-party material in the form of electronic records to which he merely provides access if such liability is founded on –
   a.   the making, publication, dissemination or distribution of such materials or any statement made in such material; or
   b.   the infringement of any rights subsisting in or in relation to such material.
(2) Nothing in this section shall affect –
   a.   any obligation founded on contract;
   b.   the obligation of a network service provider as such under a licensing or other regulatory regime established under any written law; or
   c.   any obligation imposed under any written law or by a court to remove, block or deny access to any material.
(3) For the purposes of this section –
   •   'provides access', in relation to third-party material, means the provision of the necessary technical means by which third-party material may be accessed and includes the automatic and temporary storage of the third-party material for the purpose of providing access;
   •   'third-party', in relation to a network service provider, means a person over whom the provider has no effective control.

Although this immunity extends to packet transmission and caching, it is clear from the definition of 'provides access' in s 10(3) that the Singapore Electronic Transactions Act does not grant immunity for hosting third party resources, because hosting will not be 'automatic and temporary storage' of those resources.

By contrast, both the German Multimedia Law and the EU Directive on electronic commerce will provide immunity to both transmission and resource hosts as well as to packet transmitters and cache operators:

German Multimedia Law 1998 Art. 5 (trans. Christopher Kuner, www.kuner.com)

RESPONSIBILITY

(1) Service providers are responsible under the general laws for their own content which they make available for use.
(2) Service providers are only responsible for third-party content which they make available for use if they have knowledge of such content and blocking its use is both technically possible and can be reasonably expected.
(3) Service providers are not responsible for third-party content to which they merely provide access for use. The automatic and temporary storage of third-party content because of a user access constitutes the provision of access.
(4) Any duties to block the use of illegal content according to the general laws remains unaffected, insofar as the service provider gains knowledge of such content while complying with the obligation of telecommunications secrecy under Art 85 of

the Telecommunications Law, and blocking is both technically possible and can be reasonably expected.

This law makes a clear distinction between hosting resources, in which case immunity under art 5(2) will be lost where the intermediary knows the nature of the information content and fails to take reasonable steps to block access, and transmission and caching, where according to art 5(3) knowledge appears to be irrelevant.

Directive 2000/31/EC on electronic commerce OJ L 178 p. 1, 17 July 2000
SECTION 4 LIABILITY[12] OF INTERMEDIARY SERVICE PROVIDERS
Article 12
Mere conduit
1. Where an Information Society service is provided that consists of the transmission in a communication network of information provided by a recipient of the service, or the provision of access to a communication network, Member States shall ensure that the service provider is not liable for the information transmitted, on condition that the provider:
   (a) does not initiate the transmission;
   (b) does not select the receiver of the transmission; and
   (c) does not select or modify the information contained in the transmission.
2. The acts of transmission and of provision of access referred to in paragraph 1 include the automatic, intermediate and transient storage of the information transmitted insofar as this takes place for the sole purpose of carrying out the transmission in the communication network, and provided that the information is not stored for any period longer than is reasonably necessary for the transmission.
3. This Article shall not affect the possibility for a court or administrative authority, in accordance with Member States' legal systems, to require the service provider to terminate or prevent an infringement.

Article 13
Caching
1. Where an Information Society service is provided that consists of the transmission in a communication network of information provided by a recipient of the service, Member States shall ensure that the service provider is not liable for the automatic, intermediate and temporary storage of that information, performed for the sole purpose of making more efficient the information's onward transmission to other recipients of the service upon their request, on condition that:
   (a) the provider does not modify the information;
   (b) the provider complies with conditions on access to the information;

---

12 Page 28 of the Explanatory Memorandum for the original proposal (COM (1999) 427 final) stated that the immunities in arts 12 and 14 extended to criminal liability, and the subsequent version of the text (COM (1999) 427 final) clarified that this covered art 13 as well. However, the Common Position text does not mention criminal liability in respect of these immunities, and recital 26 states:
   'Member States, in conformity with conditions established in this Directive, may apply their national rules on criminal law and criminal proceedings with a view to taking all investigative and other measures necessary for the detection and prosecution of criminal offences, without there being a need to notify such measures to the Commission.'
The question whether intermediaries will be granted immunity for criminal prosecutions as well as for civil actions is therefore left to the Member States when implementing the Directive, although the global trend suggests that they will face pressure to cover criminal as well as civil liabilities.

  (c) the provider complies with rules regarding the updating of the information, specified in a manner widely recognised and used by industry;

  (d) the provider does not interfere with the lawful use of technology, widely recognised and used by industry, to obtain data on the use of the information; and

  (e) the provider acts expeditiously to remove or to disable access to the information it has stored upon obtaining actual knowledge of the fact that the information at the initial source of the transmission has been removed from the network, or access to it has been disabled, or that a court or an administrative authority has ordered such removal or disablement.

2. This Article shall not affect the possibility for a court or administrative authority, in accordance with Member States' legal systems, to require the service provider to terminate or prevent an infringement.

Article 14
Hosting
1. Where an Information Society service is provided that consists of the storage of information provided by a recipient of the service, Member States shall ensure that the service provider is not liable for the information stored at the request of a recipient of the service, on condition that:

  (a) the provider does not have actual knowledge of illegal activity or information and, as regards claims for damages, is not aware of facts or circumstances from which the illegal activity or information is apparent; or

  (b) the provider, upon obtaining such knowledge or awareness, acts expeditiously to remove or to disable access to the information.

2. Paragraph 1 shall not apply when the recipient of the service is acting under the authority or the control of the provider.

3. This Article shall not affect the possibility for a court or administrative authority, in accordance with Member States' legal systems, to require the service provider to terminate or prevent an infringement, nor does it affect the possibility for Member States to establish procedures governing the removal or disabling of access to information.

Article 15
No general obligation to monitor
1. Member States shall not impose a general obligation on providers, when providing the services covered by Articles 12, 13 and 14, to monitor the information which they transmit or store, nor a general obligation actively to seek facts or circumstances indicating illegal activity.

2. Member States may establish obligations for Information Society service providers promptly to inform the competent public authorities of alleged illegal activities undertaken or information provided by recipients of their service or obligations to communicate to the competent authorities, at their request, information enabling the identification of recipients of their service with whom they have storage agreements.

Similar principles are set out in Schedule 5 of the Australian Broadcasting Services Act 1992, inserted by the Broadcasting Services Amendment (Online Services) Act 1999 which came into force on 1 January 2000:

Australian Broadcasting Services Amendment (Online Services) Act 1999 Schedule 5[12a]
91 LIABILITY OF INTERNET CONTENT HOSTS AND INTERNET SERVICE PROVIDERS UNDER STATE AND TERRITORY LAWS ETC.
  (1) A law of a State or Territory, or a rule of common law or equity, has no effect to the extent to which it:

13a Commonwealth of Australia Copyright reproduced by permission.

(a) subjects, or would have the effect (whether direct or indirect) of subjecting, an Internet content host to liability (whether criminal or civil) in respect of hosting particular Internet content in a case where the host was not aware of the nature of the Internet content; or

(b) requires, or would have the effect (whether direct or indirect) of requiring, an Internet content host to monitor, make inquiries about, or keep records of, Internet content hosted by the host; or

(c) subjects, or would have the effect (whether direct or indirect) of subjecting, an Internet service provider to liability (whether criminal or civil) in respect of carrying particular Internet content in a case where the service provider was not aware of the nature of the Internet content; or

(d) requires, or would have the effect (whether direct or indirect) of requiring, an Internet service provider to monitor, make inquiries about, or keep records of, Internet content carried by the provider.

However, this immunity is less favourable than at first sight it might appear, as the remainder of Sch 5 introduces a complex and stringent liability regime for both transmission and content host intermediaries – this has been examined in detail at 4.2.2 above.

From these legislative texts we can identify four classes of intermediary activity for which one or more jurisdiction considers immunity to be necessary:

- acting as a transmission host, ie transmitting resources from a third party server to a user (who may or may not be a customer of the intermediary);
- automatically caching user-requested resources, so that future requests for the same resource can be provided from a local server rather than the server where the resource is hosted;
- hosting resources which are under the effective control of a third party user, normally a customer of the intermediary; and
- providing search and directory facilities which enable users to locate and access third party resources.

The immunity granted in respect of these activities is not absolute, however. Although details vary, there seems to be growing consensus that immunity will be lost:

- If the intermediary fails to comply with court orders, such as injunctions to block access or remove unlawful material.
- If the intermediary exercises positive control over the information content, eg by editing it. In this respect the provisions of art 15 of the draft EC Directive are important, as compliance with any obligation to monitor content may make the intermediary an editor or publisher, and thus liable for the content. This was the effect of the UK Defamation Act 1996 (see 4.2.3.1 above), which will need to be modified if the Directive becomes law. Certain non-editorial modifications will also prevent the immunity arising, in particular the removal of copyright management information.
- Where the intermediary hosts a resource, immunity will be lost once the unlawful nature of the resource becomes known to the intermediary and it fails to take reasonable steps to remove access to that resource. Immunity for resource hosts exhibits less consensus than the other immunities – for example, Singapore's Electronic Transactions Act 1998 appears to take the position that the host should be liable, irrespective of knowledge. This would probably also be the position under English law – see the discussion of the respective English law provisions in part 4.2 above. The most obvious justification for such a position is that the host is likely to benefit financially

from its hosting activities, usually through fees charged to its users, and additionally has theoretical control over the resource in that it can remove or block access to it. This argument fails to recognise that in practice the host cannot devote the technical[13] and human resources to monitoring which would enable it to exercise de facto control. The provisions of the German Multimedia Law and the draft EC Directive are much more realistic in this respect.

By contrast, the absolute immunity from civil liability conferred by the Communications Decency Act seems too extreme. For example, in the *Zeran* case[14] an anonymous poster to an AOL bulletin board alleged that the plaintiff was selling T-shirts which referred offensively to the Oklahoma bombing and inviting readers to telephone the plaintiff's home telephone number, which was included in the message. The claim alleged that in spite of numerous requests from the plaintiff, AOL failed to take action for several days to prevent continued postings. Even on the assumption that AOL could have taken action but failed to do so, the court held that the Communications Decency Act provided AOL with absolute immunity from liability. As the judge said in another case, 'Congress has conferred immunity from tort liability as an incentive to Internet service providers to self-police the Internet for obscenity and other offensive material, even where the self-policing is unsuccessful or not even attempted'.[15] It is unclear where, on the scale between the Singapore and US positions, the ultimate consensus will lie. Much depends on whether the international community can agree how far unrestricted free speech is a human right – if that position is taken, there are compelling argument for adopting the US position.[16]

In spite of this last disagreement, the general principle of intermediary immunity seems now to be accepted. Fine tuning will concentrate on matters such as resource hosting liability, but the broad scope of the global consensus is becoming clear. If the Internet is a good thing, then this too must be good. Without the services provided by intermediaries, there would be no Internet.

13 Technical attempts to control information content were undertaken by Prodigy, by scanning information content for unacceptable words. Unfortunately such scanning technology is insufficiently 'intelligent' to recognise the use of such a word in a non-objectionable context, or its fortuitous occurrence as part of another word. Thus, it is rumoured, access to discussions of breast cancer were blocked, as was any material referring to the English seaside town of Scunthorpe.
14 *Zeran v America Online Inc* 129 F 3d 327 (4th Cir, 1997) 1998 US 4047 (cert Denied).
15 *Blumenthal v Drudge and America Online Inc* (District of Columbia Civil Action No 97-1968 (PLF), 22 May 1998).
16 See in particular *Zeran v America Online Inc* 129 F 3d 327 (4th Cir, 1997), p 331
'Interactive computer services have millions of users. See *Reno v ACLU* 117 S Ct at 2334 (noting that at time of district court trial, "commercial online services had almost 12 million individual subscribers"). The amount of information communicated via interactive computer services is therefore staggering. The specter of tort liability in an area of such prolific speech would have an obvious chilling effect. It would be impossible for service providers to screen each of their millions of postings for possible problems. Faced with potential liability for each message republished by their services, interactive computer service providers might choose to severely restrict the number and type of messages posted. Congress considered the weight of the speech interests implicated and chose to immunize service providers to avoid any such restrictive effect.'

Chapter 5

On the Internet, nobody knows you're a dog: identity and identification

A famous cartoon from the *New Yorker* of 5 July 1993, reproduced here, encapsulates one of the best-known features of the Internet. The sender of an Internet communication cannot necessarily be presumed to be who he says he is, nor can the sender always be sure of the recipient's true identity. In other words, a user's digital identity has no necessary connection with his physical world identity.

"On the Internet, nobody knows you're a dog."

Internet users have traditionally selected their own email identities, and that email identity is still the commonest way of identifying Internet users. Staid persons, like lawyers, tend to use their real names as part of their email address.[1]

---

1 Though email host naming conventions may make these real names less apparent – I could appear in an email as reedc, creed, c.reed or chris.reed, in each case @ the relevant host.

Others adopt an identity which they choose for varying and idiosyncratic reasons – for example, in the gliding newsgroup rec.aviation.soaring can be found messages from White Bird, Soarfox, and others who have adopted aviation-related identities. Some Internet actors even use services such as anonymous remailers[2] to hide their identity completely.

Other types of Internet communication also lack clear identification of the communicating parties. For example, when a user requests a Web page, that request is made via a communication which identifies the host through which the user has Internet access, and may possibly identify the user's computer in some way. However, it does not usually identify the person who has made the request. The website controller may also not be easily identifiable – the registered identity of a domain name owner may be checked via the relevant domain name registry, but this simply gives the information provided by the registrant, which may or may not be correct or informative. Additionally, anonymous Web surfing services are available.[3]

5.1   THE PROBLEM OF IDENTITY

In many cases, this uncertainty as to identity raises no problems. If I know through some other means the identity of 'LegalEagle@ccls.edu',[4] the fact that the email address itself does not identify that person is immaterial. However, if I am dealing with someone for the first time, I may have a need to establish their identity before continuing my dealings. This can be particularly important where the dealings have legal consequences, and where the dealings have non-trivial financial effects I may not be satisfied with a mere email address, even if I know (or think I know) the physical world identity of the address's owner.

One method of identifying a correspondent is to use the identity information supplied by that person. This might be included in an email, perhaps as part of the email's 'signature'. Alternatively if a user is viewing a website, a form can be used which requires the user to input identification details. The drawback of this identification method is that is requires the user-provided information to be taken on trust. Even if the user is in fact trustworthy, and provides the correct information, identification in this way may be inadequate for one of two reasons:

- If the result of the communication is some legally binding transaction, such as the formation of a contract, the recipient may need to enforce the terms of that contract at a later stage. Identification through an email or Web page form may not provide sufficient evidence that it was in fact the user who entered into the transaction.
- The recipient of the communication may be under some legal obligation to identify the user with more certainty, eg under financial services or money laundering legislation.

It might be thought that the obvious way of overcoming this problem would be to check the identity of the user with the Internet host identified in the communication. This too is unsatisfactory, however, as:

---

2   See eg http://www.replay.com.
3   See eg http://www.anonymizer.com.
4   This is a fictional email address.

- The host may be unwilling or unable to release that identity information. For example, where host and user are in a jurisdiction where data protection laws apply, it is unlikely that host's data protection registration will permit indiscriminate release of identity details.[5] In other jurisdictions, the host may have adopted a privacy policy which prevents the release of this information.[6]
- Even if the host is willing and able to release the information, the quality of that information will be unknown to the recipient. In general there is no obligation on hosts to take formal identification of their subscribers. Where the host charges for Internet access, it is probable that credit card details will have been taken and checked. However, there is currently a trend towards offering free Internet access, paid for by requiring users to view advertisements which fund the service, and in these cases no identity check is made.[7]

In the physical world identification problems are often overcome by requiring the production of a document or token issued by a reliable third party, who can be relied on to have undertaken identity checks. Typical examples are a passport, identity card, credit card or utility bill. The challenge for the Internet is to develop analogous identification tokens which are effective for digital transactions. This has been achieved by establishing specialised third parties whose function is to take identification evidence and issue electronic identification tokens ('ID Certificates'). However, the provision of identity services raises a number of legal issues which are only now being considered by legislators.

The technologies and infrastructures used to identify Internet users have been developed as part of the search for an effective method of signing electronic documents. However, it has recently become clear that the identification function is quite separate from the question of signature validity. For this reason, identification issues are dealt with in this chapter, while electronic signatures receive separate treatment in Chapter 6.1.2.

5.2   USES OF IDENTIFICATION

In the physical world, taking formal evidence of identity is a cumbersome process, and there are comparatively few transactions where identification is required as a standard procedure. This is likely to change when transactions are undertaken via the Internet. The identification technologies associated with electronic signatures may be technically very sophisticated, but in terms of use they are extremely simple. It is also likely that identification technology will be built in to new software applications, so that the identification process

---

5   See Chapter 9.3.2.
6   See eg AT&T's Privacy Policy, http://www.att.com/privacy:
    'AT&T will not sell, trade, or disclose to third parties any customer identifiable information derived from the registration for or use of an AT&T online service – including customer names and addresses – without the consent of the customer (except as required by subpoena, search warrant, or other legal process or in the case of imminent physical harm to the customer or others).'
7   See eg the UK's Freeserve service, which specifically states: 'You will not be asked to give us any credit card or bank details and we do not ask for any money'. – http://www.freeserve.co.uk/cserve/about.htm

becomes completely transparent[8] to users. For this reason, many recipients of Internet communications are likely to require identification of the sender, even though they would not require such identification in a physical world transaction.

It is thus not possible to produce a definitive list of all the likely uses of identification technology. However, three uses can already be identified with some certainty.

5.2.1   Electronic signatures

Technology which enables the sender of an electronic document to create an electronic signature of that document exists and is in use. This technology uses the mathematics of cryptography to produce a 'signature' which is functionally equivalent to a handwritten signature, though whether it is also legally equivalent is a matter which is dealt with elsewhere – see Chapter 6.1.2 for a discussion of this issue, and also a more detailed description of the technology. A distinction has to be made between communication via closed user groups, such as via an EDI network, in which case the signature's link with the document is independently validated by the network operator, and open communications structures such as the Internet where the connection of signature and document depends solely on the strength of the encryption technology used. Many of the legal issues relating to the former can be managed by contract, but in open communications structures contract law is unlikely to be available to deal with those issues.

In non-technical terms, electronic signature technologies work by linking the information content of a document to some unique information which only the signatory posses. This information might take the form of:

- An encryption key, a large binary number of 56 or more digits. Because humans cannot easily remember such numbers, nor key them in accurately, the encryption key will normally be stored on an information storage device such as a smart card. Alternatively, the key might be stored on the hard disk of the signatory's computer.
- Biometric data, such as the signatory's thumbprint, voiceprint or retina print. Systems also exist which capture the signatory's handwritten signature metrics.[9]

Where, in order to enforce the signatory's legal obligations, the recipient of the document needs to prove the signature, he will do so by producing extrinsic evidence that (a) the signature key or biometric data did in fact originate from the purported signatory, and (b) that the linking of that information to the document could not have been effected by a third party. This is the same process as is used to authenticate a handwritten signature where it is disputed.

Because the signature key or biometric data needs to be kept secret, to prevent third parties from producing messages which are apparently signed by the signatory, the signature information is attached to the message by means of

---

8   Readers should note that computing jargon is often counter-intuitive. In this context, 'transparent' means that the user will be completely unaware that identification data is being added to his Internet communications.

9   See eg http://www.penop.com.

asymmetric cryptography which uses both a public and a private key. Messages signed with the private key can be validated with the public key, but the public key cannot be used to create a signature for a new message. Thus in order to check the validity of an electronic signature, the recipient needs to know both the public key of the signatory and the encryption system used to form the signature.

If the parties have not had previous dealings, however, the recipient will have no knowledge whether the public key does in fact correspond to the purported identity of the signatory. This is where the ID Certificate comes in. It contains:

- a copy of the public key; and
- a statement that the issuer of the certificate has checked the identify of the signatory, that the signatory does in fact possess the signature data which corresponds to the public key, and that the issuer has checked that the public key validates the identified person's electronic signature.

Thus where an electronic signature is made on a document, the accompanying ID Certificate provides evidence from an independent third party that the person named in the certificate did in fact have access to the unique signature data, so long as the public key included in the certificate validates the signature. In the absence of evidence from the alleged signatory that some third party 'forged' his signature, a court should be satisfied by this evidence that the purported signatory was responsible for the electronically signed document.

Electronic signatures are likely to be used for a wide range of transactions which have legal consequences, including:

- the formation of contracts;
- transactions where the recipient of the communication is required to identify its customer, eg funds transfers to which money laundering controls apply; and
- the provision of legally required information to Government agencies where there may be a need to ensure that the information source is correct, or more commonly where there are penalties for supplying incorrect information, eg on tax returns.

Electronic signatures are also likely to be required for identification purposes where the user is requesting information which should not be released to third parties, such as information about the user's bank account.

5.2.2 Information licensing

One of the most important areas of commercial activity which the Internet makes possible is the direct supply of information. Most suppliers will not 'sell'[10]

---

10 Indeed, there must be some uncertainty whether information can be 'sold'. A sale normally predicates the transfer of ownership rights – see eg UK Sale of Goods Act 1979, s 2(1) which defines a sale as 'a contract by which the seller transfers or agrees to transfer the property in the goods to the buyer for a money consideration . . .' The main property rights in information are intellectual property rights, and even where the precise nature of the right transferred is not stated it is hard to imagine a court finding that a supply of information in return for payment was an assignment of those rights, at least in a mass marketing context.

that information – instead, they will seek to licence it to the customer, so as to control use and further copying. Assuming that a licence contract is concluded with the customer, there are two reasons why the supplier would wish to receive proper identification of the customer via an ID Certificate:

- If, at some future date, the supplier needs to enforce the licence terms against the customer (eg the customer is found to be re-selling the information, in breach of the licence), the ID Certificate will assist in proving that it was in fact that customer who purchased the information and agreed to be bound by the licence terms.
- If the supplier requires ID Certificates from all its customers, the fact that a non-customer is found in possession of a copy of the information is strong evidence that the copy is unauthorised, and thus in breach of copyright. This will even more strongly be so if the public key of the original licensee is embedded in the copy supplied by the licensor, and the non-customer's copy is found to contain the same key.[11]

The importance of identification in information transactions has been recognised specifically in the draft US Uniform Computer Information Transactions Act, which proposes specific rules for determining when the person identified should have the transaction attributed to him:

US Uniform Computer Information Transactions Act (October 1999 draft)
SECTION 112. MANIFESTING ASSENT; OPPORTUNITY TO REVIEW.
(a) A person manifests assent to a record or term if the person, acting with knowledge of, or after having an opportunity to review the record or term or a copy of it:
   (1) authenticates the record or term with intent to adopt or accept it; or
   (2) intentionally engages in conduct or makes statements with reason to know that the other party or its electronic agent may infer from the conduct or statement that the person assents to the record or term.
(b) An electronic agent manifests assent to a record or term if, after having an opportunity to review it, the electronic agent:
   (1) authenticates the record or term; or
   (2) engages in operations that in the circumstances indicate acceptance of the record or term.
(c) If this Act or other law requires assent to a specific term, a manifestation of assent must relate specifically to the term.
(d) Conduct or operations manifesting assent may be shown in any manner, including a showing that a person or an electronic agent obtained or used the information or informational rights and that a procedure existed by which a person or an electronic agent must have engaged in the conduct or operations in order to do so. Proof of compliance with subsection (a)(2) is sufficient if there is conduct that assents and subsequent conduct that reaffirms assent by electronic means.
. . .

SECTION 212. EFFICACY AND COMMERCIAL REASONABLENESS OF ATTRIBUTION PROCEDURE.
The efficacy, including the commercial reasonableness, of an attribution procedure is determined by the court. In making this determination, the following rules apply:

---

11 For a discussion of technical copyright protection systems see Tuck 'Electronic Copyright Management Systems' (London: LITC, South Bank University, 1996) parts 2 and 5 – http://136.148.161.14/copyright/ecms.html.

(1) An attribution procedure established by law is effective for transactions within the coverage of the statute or rule.
(2) Except as otherwise provided in paragraph (1), commercial reasonableness and effectiveness is determined in light of the purposes of the procedure and the commercial circumstances at the time the parties agree to or adopt the procedure.
(3) An attribution procedure may use any security device or method that is commercially reasonable under the circumstances.

SECTION 213. DETERMINING ATTRIBUTION.

(a) An electronic authentication, display, message, record, or performance is attributed to a person if it was the act of that person or its electronic agent, or if the person is bound by it under agency or other law. The party relying on attribution of an electronic authentication, display, message, record, or performance to another person has the burden of establishing attribution.
(b) The act of a person may be shown in any manner, including a showing of the efficacy of an attribution procedure.
(c) The effect of an electronic act attributed to a person under subsection (a) is determined from the context at the time of its creation, execution, or adoption, including the parties' agreement, if any, or otherwise as provided by law.
(d) If an attribution procedure exists to detect errors or changes in an electronic authentication, display, message, record, or performance and one party conformed to the procedure but the other party did not, and the nonconforming party would have detected the change or error had that party also conformed, the effect of noncompliance is determined by the agreement but, in the absence of agreement, the conforming party may avoid the effect of the error or change.

Similar attribution provisions are found in the Singapore Electronic Transactions Act 1998, s. 13.

5.2.3 Status information

A third use of ID Certificates is as a way to confirm the status of the user. Examples of the kind of status information which could be incorporated in an ID Certificate are:

• Information about the user's age. A supplier who wishes to enforce a contract with a customer will need to ensure that the customer does not lack capacity to enter into contracts because he is a minor. Age information may also be used to reduce a host's liability risks, particular if the host's site contains material whose supply to a minor might be unlawful. For example, the website www.hotsex.com requires visitors to confirm that 'I am at least 18 years of age and have the legal right to possess adult material in my community' by clicking on a button on the site's home page, but has to take the user's agreement to this on trust. Requiring an ID Certificate which showed the visitor to be 18 or over would enable the website's operators to prove to law enforcement agencies that none of the images on that site had been supplied to minors.
• Information about the user's credit status. This information could be supplied by the issuer of the ID Certificate itself if it is a financial institution which issues certificates to its customers, or the certificate could contain information supplied by a third party credit reference agency.

There is no technical reason why an ID Certificate should not contain a wide range of status information,[12] and because the certificate is controlled by and disclosed by the person to whom it relates, the privacy and data protection issues discussed in Chapter 7.3 become significantly less of a problem.

5.3   CERTIFICATION OF IDENTITY

In order to understand the legal issues arising from the certification of identity, it is not enough simply to examine the technology and processes used to issue ID Certificates. A recipient of a certificate cannot always act on the certificate alone, because he may not know and trust the issuer of the certificate, or may need to check whether the certificate is still valid. Certification of identity therefore also requires a complex infrastructure to be in place, and the legal regulation of this activity concentrates very much on the effectiveness of that infrastructure.

5.3.1 Issue of ID Certificates

ID Certificates are issued by a trusted organisation, generally referred to as a Certification Authority (CA). The precise requirements for issuing an ID Certificate will vary from issuer to issuer, depending on the nature of the service provided and the technical standards used. The most commonly adopted standard is X.509.[13]

The first step in obtaining a certificate is for the user to prove his identity to a CA, so that the CA can link that identity with the user's public signature key (which must also be provided). It is common for CAs to offer different levels of certificate, depending on the quality of identification provided. The lowest level of certificate normally requires only that you produce a valid email address; the highest level may require personal attendance plus the production of physical identity documents.

BelSign Website, http://www.belsign.com/en/products/index.html
BELSIGN OFFERS 3 CLASSES OF DIGITAL CERTIFICATES, DIFFERENTIATED BY WHAT LEVEL OF ASSURANCE THEY PROVIDE:

Class 1
Class 1 Digital Certificates or Demo Certificates provide you with an unambiguous name and e-mail address within the BelSign repository. Class 1 Digital Certificates are free and only used for demo reasons.

---

12 'Certificates can be used for a variety of functions and can contain different pieces of information. The information can include conventional identifiers such as name, address, registration number or social security number, VAT or tax identification number, or specific attributes of the signatory for instance, their authority to act on behalf of a company, their credit worthiness, the existence of payment guarantees, or the holding of specific permits or licenses.' *Proposal for a European Parliament and Council Directive on a common framework for electronic signatures,* COM (1998) 297 final, 13 May 1998, p 6.
13 ITU *Recommendation X.509 (08/97) – Information technology – Open Systems Interconnection – The Directory: Authentication framework.* Additional standards proposals can be found via the Internet Engineering Task Force at http://www.ietf.cnri.reston.va.us/html.charters/pkix-charter.html and the World Wide Web Consortium at http://www.w3.org/DSig/DsigProj.html.

Class 2

Class 2 Digital Certificates or Regular Certificates provide identity assurance by requiring a copy of your identity card/passport/driver's license and your signature. With these personal Digital Certificates for browsers, you can use your certificate for most low-value commercial transactions like online purchases and secure e-mail.

Class 3

Class 3 Digital Certificates provide an even higher level of identity assurance by requiring that you appear before a Local Registration Authority (LRA). You can use such a Digital Certificate for high-value commercial transactions such as electronic banking.

Once the CA has secured evidence of identity and received a copy of the user's public key, an ID Certificate is produced and sent electronically to the user. In order to demonstrate that the certificate does in fact emanate from the CA, it will be signed with the CA's own private key, which can be checked via the CA's public key.

The certificate will contain a number of representations about the person to whom it refers,[14] the most important of which in the X.509 model[15] are:

- Serial number.
- Identity of CA issuer.
- Starting and ending dates of validity for the certificate.
- Identity of holder.
- Public key of holder.
- Electronic signature of issuer, plus a different CA's ID Certificate for issuer.

The inclusion of additional information is also possible under X.509, including restrictions on the uses for which the certificate is valid.

Where the certificate is to be used to back an electronic signature such that the signature has the same legal effect as a traditional signature (see 5.4.2 below), additional minimum contents may be imposed:

Directive 1999/93/EC on a Community framework for electronic signatures, OJ L13 p. 12, 19 January 2000, ANNEX I

REQUIREMENTS FOR QUALIFIED[16] CERTIFICATES

Qualified certificates must contain:

(a) an indication that the certificate is issued as a qualified certificate;
(b) the identification of the certification-service-provider and the State in which it is established;
(c) the name of the signatory or a pseudonym, which shall be identified as such;
(d) provision for a specific attribute of the signatory to be included if relevant, depending on the purpose for which the certificate is intended;
(e) signature-verification data which correspond to signature-creation data under the control of the signatory;
(f) an indication of the beginning and end of the period of validity of the certificate;
(g) the identity code of the certificate;

---

14 See American Bar Association *Digital Signature Guidelines* (Chicago: ABA, 1996) guideline 1.5; German Digital Signature Act (Signaturgesetz) 1997 § 7; Utah Digital Signature Rules (Rule 154-10 of the Utah Commerce, Corporations and Commercial Code), r 301.
15 For a more detailed description of an X.509 certificate see Housley, Ford, Polk and Solo *Internet X.509 Public Key Infrastructure – Certificate and CRL Profile* RFC 2459, available from http://www.ietf.org/rfc.html.
16 In the Directive's terminology a 'qualified' certificate is required if an electronic signature is to have the same effect as a hand written signature – art 5(2).

(h) the advanced electronic signature of the certification-service-provider issuing it;
(i) limitations on the scope of use of the certificate, if applicable; and
(j) limits on the value of transactions for which the certificate can be used, if applicable.

Once the applicant has received this certificate in electronic form and become its holder, the certificate can be stored on his computer ready for presentation to other Internet users who require him to identify himself, or for incorporation into the his electronic signatures. All this will be carried out by the holder's software as required.

5.3.2 Using the certificate to prove identity

Receipt of an ID Certificate demonstrates that the issuing CA has taken identification evidence for its holder, but does not prove that it was in fact the holder who sent the certificate to the recipient. The connection between the sender and holder is made by the electronically signed message which accompanies the certificate. Because the ID Certificate also contains a copy of the holder's public key, this can be used by the recipient to check that the signature of the message matches the signature in the certificate. If they match, this is strong evidence[17] that the holder of the certificate is also the sender of the message.

5.3.3 Certificate checking infrastructure

From the above it should be obvious, however, that a bare certificate will not give the recipient much comfort. It purports to have been issued by a CA, but how is the recipient to discover whether the CA did in fact issue the certificate, or whether it is really a trustworthy CA? This is where the certificate checking infrastructure comes in to play.

5.3.3.1 Checking validity

If the certificate emanates from a CA which is already known to the recipient, and whose public key is thus in the possession of the recipient and known to be correct, that key can be used to check the validity of the certificate. The recipient's software decrypts the certificate's signature with the CA's public key, and if the result is meaningful this will provide strong evidence[18] that the certificate was issued by that CA, and that the level of identification stated in the certificate has been undertaken by the CA.

If the recipient does not already know the CA, he can use the CA's own ID Certificate, which is incorporated in the holder's certificate, to check the CA's true identity with the issuer of that ID certificate. If that issuer is also unknown, *its* identity can be checked via another ID certificate, and so on. Eventually the recipient will find an ID Certificate issued by a CA of whose identity he is certain, and the chain of identity checking then unravels to produce an identification for the user who originally transmitted his certificate to the recipient.[19] This

---

17 See further Chapter 6.1.2.
18 For a discussion of how this evidence derives from the decryption process, see Chapter 6.1.2.3.
19 See American Bar Association *Digital Signature Guidelines* (Chicago: ABA, 1996), p 112, Comment 5.3.5.

process of identification via a chain of trusted persons has been described as 'Certification Path Discovery and Validation'.[20]

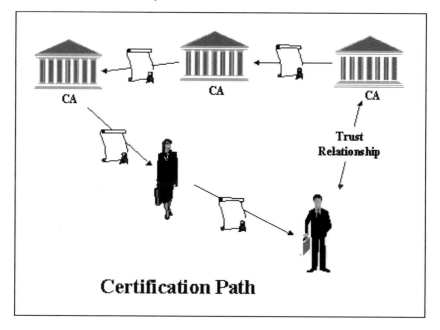

Certification Path

At first sight this process appears to be cumbersome, but in practice whenever a CA is identified that CA's public key is added to the recipient's list of known CAs. Thus when in future an ID Certificate is encountered which has been issued by that CA, the recipient need undertake no additional checking to validate the holder's identity.[1]

In order to reduce the number of separate communications required to validate an ID Certificate, it is envisaged that organisations known as repositories will be set up. These will hold copies of ID Certificates for CAs, and perhaps for users as well. The recipient of a user certificate should thus be able to obtain all the necessary CA certificates from a single source.

It might be thought that a court would be suspicious of identification evidence produced through a long chain of intermediaries, but in fact the concept of authentication of message origin via a train of trusted messages has already been accepted by the English courts. In *Standard Bank London Ltd v Bank of Tokyo Ltd*[2] the defendant communicated with the plaintiff by trusted telexes (telex messages containing secret codes known only to sender and recipient). Because the parties did not have a trusted telex relationship between themselves, the defendant sent its messages to a correspondent with whom it did have such a relationship, and that correspondent forwarded them to another intermediary who passed them on to the plaintiff. The case was decided on the basis that

---

20 Warwick Ford and Michael S Baum 'Secure Electronic Commerce: Building the Infrastructure for Digital Signatures and Encryption' (New Jersey: Prentice Hall, 1997), p 290.
1 Although there is always a need to check that an ID Certificate has not been revoked – this procedure should be undertaken automatically by the receiver's software.
2 [1995] 2 Lloyd's Rep 169.

these messages were properly authenticated as originating from the plaintiff, and the expert evidence (which was accepted by the court) stated that trusted telex messages were treated by banks as if they were signed by the sending party.

5.3.3.2   Validity and revocation

ID Certificates will normally be issued with a limited period of validity, which will be stated within the certificate itself. Once that validity period has expired the certificate is no longer of practical use for proving the holder's identity, as it will be rejected as invalid by the recipient's software.

Additionally, however, the checking infrastructure needs to provide for the situation where a certificate is revoked, eg because control of the private key has been lost. This is achieved by giving notice to the issuing CA, which then produces an electronic notice of revocation and adds it to the Certificate Revocation List (CRL) which it publishes from time to time. A recipient of an ID Certificate may therefore wish to check it against the CA's most recent CRL, obtained either direct from the CA or from a repository. This process should be undertaken automatically by the software which is processing the certificate.

Housley, Ford, Polk and Solo, 'Internet X.509 Public Key Infrastructure – Certificate and CRL Profile' RFC 2459 p. 12[3]

3.3 REVOCATION

When a certificate is issued, it is expected to be in use for its entire validity period. However, various circumstances may cause a certificate to become invalid prior to the expiration of the validity period. Such circumstances include change of name, change of association between subject and CA (e.g., an employee terminates employment with an organization), and compromise or suspected compromise of the corresponding private key. Under such circumstances, the CA needs to revoke the certificate.

X.509 defines one method of certificate revocation. This method involves each CA periodically issuing a signed data structure called a certificate revocation list (CRL). A CRL is a time stamped list identifying revoked certificates which is signed by a CA and made freely available in a public repository. Each revoked certificate is identified in a CRL by its certificate serial number. When a certificate-using system uses a certificate (e.g., for verifying a remote user's digital signature), that system not only checks the certificate signature and validity but also acquires a suitably-recent CRL and checks that the certificate serial number is not on that CRL. The meaning of "suitably-recent" may vary with local policy, but it usually means the most recently-issued CRL. A CA issues a new CRL on a regular periodic basis (e.g., hourly, daily, or weekly). An entry is added to the CRL as part of the next update following notification of revocation. An entry may be removed from the CRL after appearing on one regularly scheduled CRL issued beyond the revoked certificate's validity period.

An advantage of this revocation method is that CRLs may be distributed by exactly the same means as certificates themselves, namely, via untrusted communications and server systems.

One limitation of the CRL revocation method, using untrusted communications and servers, is that the time granularity of revocation is limited to the CRL issue period. For example, if a revocation is reported now, that revocation will not be reliably notified to certificate-using systems until the next periodic CRL is issued – this may be up to one hour, one day, or one week depending on the frequency that the CA issues CRLs.

5.4   ACCREDITATION SCHEMES

5.4.1   Rationale

The rationale for accreditating CAs is simply that persons relying on ID Certificates need to trust and have confidence in the issuing CA,[4] so that the recipient of a certificate can safely undertake dealings with its holder. There are a number of reasons why a certificate might be unreliable as a result of the CA's failure, the most obvious of which are:

* the CA fails to take proper evidence of the holder's identity;
* the encryption technology used to link that identity with the holder's public key and the CA's public key is weak, allowing 'forged' certificates to be produced;
* the CA does not keep proper records, so that revocations are not recorded or the identification process cannot be proved in court; or
* the CA employs incompetent or dishonest staff, thereby compromising the reliability of the information in the certificate.

These matters could be demonstrated to certificate recipients by some independent certification that the CA adhered to appropriate technical and operational standards.[5] However, there is an emerging trend towards dealing with this matter by establishing voluntary accreditation systems, whose effect would be that an accredited CA would be assessed and monitored to ensure continued compliance with the required standards.

An additional rationale for introducing accreditation was, until recently, that it could be linked with key escrow for law enforcement purposes. As a condition of receiving accreditation, CAs would be required to retain a copy of all encryption keys used to ensure message confidentiality and provide them to law enforcement and national security agencies in prescribed circumstances.[6] The linking of key escrow to the provision of CA services has been heavily criticised, and is no longer put forward as a justification for the introduction of accreditation schemes.

---

4   See generally European Commission 'Ensuring Security and Trust in Electronic Communication –Towards a European framework for Digital Signatures and Encryption' COM (97) 157 final, 16 April 1997.
5   Eg adherence to an ITSEC or Common Criteria Certificate, issued by a Certification Body to verify that the certificate has been assessed as meeting certain security assurance criteria.
6   See eg UK Department of Trade and Industry 'Licensing of Trusted Third Parties for the Provision of Encryption Services' (March 1997).

5.4.2 Effects of accreditation

The international consensus is that a CA should be free to choose whether to be accredited or not. The main effects of being accredited are:

- Electronic signatures effected using a certificate from an accredited CA are given greater legal weight than other electronic signatures. Two different approaches to this issue can be discerned:
  - In some schemes[7] only an electronic signature backed by a certificate from an accredited CA is expressly given the same legal effect as a traditional signature. Other electronic signatures act merely as evidence of authentication and approval of a message, but are not specifically stated as complying with the law's formal requirements for signatures.
  - In other schemes,[8] an electronic signature which is backed by a certificate from a CA will be treated as equivalent to a traditional signature if both the certificate and the CA meet objective requirements set out in the law. Under these schemes, the effect of accreditation is to raise a presumption that both the certificate and the CA meet those requirements.

  The question of the legal effectiveness of electronic signatures is discussed further in Chapter 6.1.
- The liability of the CA for losses caused by reliance on a certificate which contains incorrect information is defined and/or limited where the CA is accredited – see 5.5 below.

An additional feature of most accreditation schemes is that they give the accreditation authority power to recognise ID Certificates issued by foreign CAs as having equivalent legal effect to certificates issued by a domestic, accredited CA. It seems likely that in most cases this recognition will be granted on the basis of mutual recognition of accreditation regimes.

Although, therefore, it is possible for a CA to act without being accredited, the incentives to become accredited are substantial. Without accreditation, a CA's certificates will not be useful to an Internet user who wishes to create electronic signatures which have the fullest legal effects. Additionally, the unaccredited CA's liability will be left to the uncertainties of the general law, limited only by the CA's contracts and disclaimers to the extent that they are effective.

5.4.3 Requirements and supervision

The global ID Certificate infrastructure is seen as likely to become a fundamental part of the global communications infrastructure, so that a failure in the system could lead to severe economic disruption. This is very similar to the world banking system, whose main function nowadays is the transport of large volumes of secure, properly identified information. For this reason, the accreditation requirements for CAs and the supervisory arrangements for their operations

---

7   See eg Utah Digital Signature Act 1996 (Utah Code § 46-3) §§ 401, 403; German Digital Signature Act (Signaturgesetz) 1997 § 2(1).
8   See eg Singapore Electronic Transactions Act 1998 ss 18 and 20; *Directive 1999/93/EC on a Community framework for electronic signatures*, OJ L 13, p 12, 19 January 2000, art 5(2).

are very similar to those applicable to banks.[9] Essentially, the questions which are to be asked are:

- whether the CA is a fit and proper person to act;[10]
- whether it is financially well-established so as to be able to continue its operations and meet its obligations;[11]
- whether its staff are properly qualified and adequately trained and supervised;[12]
- whether its technical systems are of sufficient quality and adequately maintained and updated. In particular the CA must demonstrate a high level of competence in:
  - The identification of applicants for a certificate;[13]
  - The secure generation and management of signature keys and maintenance of security and confidentiality in respect of its records;[14] and
  - The maintenance of proper records for the required periods of time.[15]

Legislative proposals ensure that these requirements are met in different ways, ranging from self-regulatory schemes[16] to legislation which specifies the accreditation requirements in detail.

9   See UK Department of Trade and Industry 'Building Confidence in Electronic Commerce – a consultation document' (5 March 1999, URN 99/642), p 18. For the generally accepted requirements for banks, see the Second Banking Directive, 89/646/EEC, 1989 OJ L 386/1 and Council Directive 92/30/EEC on the supervision of credit institutions on a consolidated basis, OJ L 110/53.

10 This is implicit in all accreditation schemes, and is made explicit in German Digital Signature Act (Signaturgesetz) 1997 § 4(2); German Digital Signature Ordinance (Signaturverordnung, made under § 19 Digital Signature Act 1997, in force 1 November 1997) § 3(2).

11 American Bar Association *Digital Signature Guidelines* (Chicago: ABA, 1996), guideline 3.3; *Directive 1999/93/EC on a Community framework for electronic signatures*, OJ L13, p 12, 19 January 2000 Annex II(h); Utah Digital Signature Act 1996 (Utah Code § 46-3) § 201(1)(f); Utah Digital Signature Rules (Rule 154-10 of the Utah Commerce, Corporations and Commercial Code), r 203.

12 American Bar Association *Digital Signature Guidelines* (Chicago: ABA, 1996) guideline 3.4; German Digital Signature Act (Signaturgesetz) 1997 §§ 4(3), 5(5); German Digital Signature Ordinance (Signaturverordnung, made under § 19 Digital Signature Act 1997, in force 1 November 1997) §§ 3(2), 10; Utah Digital Signature Act 1996 (Utah Code § 46-3) § 201(1)(c).

13 German Digital Signature Act (Signaturgesetz) 1997 § 5(1); *Directive 1999/93/EC on a Community framework for electronic signatures*, OJ L13, p 12, 19 January 2000, Annex II(d); Singapore Electronic Transactions Act 1998, s 29; Utah Digital Signature Act 1996 (Utah Code § 46-3) § 302(1)(b); Utah Digital Signature Rules (Rule 154-10 of the Utah Commerce, Corporations and Commercial Code), r 303(1)(a).

14 American Bar Association *Digital Signature Guidelines* (Chicago: ABA, 1996) guideline 3.1; German Digital Signature Act (Signaturgesetz) 1997 §§ 5(4), 14; German Digital Signature Ordinance (Signaturverordnung, made under § 19 Digital Signature Act 1997, in force 1 November 1997) §§ 5(2), 12, 16; *Directive 1999/93/EC on a Community framework for electronic signatures* OJ L13, p 12, 19 January 2000, Annex II(f) & (g); Singapore Electronic Transactions Act 1998, ss 27, 48, 49; Utah Digital Signature Act 1996 (Utah Code § 46-3) §§ 201(1)(e), 301(1).

15 American Bar Association *Digital Signature Guidelines* (Chicago: ABA, 1996) guideline 3.5; German Digital Signature Act (Signaturgesetz) 1997 § 14(3)); German Digital Signature Ordinance (Signaturverordnung, made under § 19 Digital Signature Act 1997, in force 1 November 1997) §§ 8(1), 13; *Directive 1999/93/EC on a Community framework for electronic signatures* OJ L 13, p 12, 19 January 2000, Annex II(i); Singapore Electronic Transactions Act 1998, s 42(2)(h); Utah Digital Signature Rules (Rule 154-10 of the Utah Commerce, Corporations and Commercial Code), r 301.

16 UK Electronic Comunications Act 2000. Although under s 1(1) the Secretary of State has a duty to maintain a register of 'approved providers of cryptography support services' and to make regulations about the requirements for approval (s 2(4)), s 3 gives him power to appoint some other person to carry out these functions, and the current intention is to encourage the establishment of an industry-devised accreditation scheme.

The EC Directive on electronic signatures sets out the general principles under which EU Member States should institute accreditation schemes, but leaves the implementation to national law:

Directive 1999/93/EC on a Community framework for electronic signatures, OJ L13 p. 12, 19 January 2000

ARTICLE 3

Market access

1. Member States shall not make the provision of certification services subject to prior authorization.
2. Without prejudice to the provisions of paragraph 1, Member States may introduce or maintain voluntary accreditation schemes aiming at enhanced levels of certification-service provision. All conditions related to such schemes must be objective, transparent, proportionate and non-discriminatory. Member States may not limit the number of accredited certification-service-providers for reasons which fall within the scope of this Directive.
3. Each Member State shall ensure the establishment of a appropriate system that allows for supervision of certification-service-providers which are established on its territory and issue qualified certificates to the public.
4. The conformity of secure signature-creation-devices with the requirements laid down in Annex III shall be determined by appropriate public or private bodies designated by Member States. The Commission shall, pursuant to the procedure laid down in Article 9, establish criteria for Member States to determine whether a body should be designated.

   A determination of conformity with the requirements laid down in Annex III made by the bodies referred to in the first subparagraph shall be recognised by all Member States.
5. The Commission may, in accordance with the procedure laid down in Article 9, establish and publish reference numbers of generally recognised standards for electronic-signature products in the *Official Journal of the European Communities*. Member States shall presume that there is compliance with the requirements laid down in Annex II, point (f), and Annex III when a electronic signature product meets those standards.
6. Member States and the Commission shall work together to promote the development and use of signature-verification devices in the light of the recommendations for secure signature-verification laid down in Annex IV and in the interests of the consumer.
7. Member States may make the use of electronic signatures in the public sector subject to possible additional requirements. Such requirements shall be objective, transparent, proportionate and non-discriminatory and shall relate only to the specific characteristics of the application concerned. Such requirements may not constitute a obstacle to cross-border services for citizens.

Annex II

REQUIREMENTS FOR CERTIFICATION-SERVICE-PROVIDERS

Certification-service-providers must:
(a) demonstrate the reliability necessary for offering certification services;
(b) ensure the operation of a prompt and secure directory and a secure and immediate revocation service;
(c) ensure that the date and time when a certificate is issued or revoked can be determined precisely;
(c) verify by appropriate means the identity and capacity to act of the person to which a qualified certificate is issued;
(d) verify, by appropriate means in accordance with national law, the identity and, if applicable, any specific attributes of the person to which a qualified certificate is issued;

(e) employ personnel who possess the expert knowledge, experience, and qualifications necessary for the services provided, in particular competence at managerial level, expertise in electronic signature technology and familiarity with proper security procedures; they must also apply administrative and management procedures which are adequate and correspond to recognised standards;

(f) use trustworthy systems and products which are protected against modification and ensure the technical and cryptographic security of the process supported by them;

(g) take measures against forgery of certificates, and, in cases where the certification-service-provider generates signature-creation data, guarantee confidentiality during the process of generating such data;

(h) maintain sufficient financial resources to operate in conformity with the requirements laid down in the Directive, in particular to bear the risk of liability for damages, for example, by obtaining appropriate insurance;

(i) record all relevant information concerning a qualified certificate for an appropriate period of time, in particular for the purpose of providing evidence of certification for the purposes of legal proceedings. Such recording may be done electronically;

(j) not store or copy signature-creation data of the person to whom the certification-service-provider provided key management services;

(k) before entering in to a contractual relationship with a person seeking a certificate to support his electronic signature inform that person by a durable means of communication of the precise terms and conditions regarding the use of the certificate, including any limitations on its use, the existence of a voluntary accreditation scheme and procedures for complaints and dispute settlement. Such information, which may be transmitted electronically, must be in writing and in readily understandable language. Relevant parts of this information must also be made available on request to third-parties relying on the certificate;

(l) use trustworthy systems to store certificates in a verifiable form so that:
- only authorised persons can make entries and changes,
- information can be checked for authenticity,
- certificates are publicly available for retrieval in only those cases for which the certificate-holder's consent has been obtained, and
- any technical changes compromising these security requirements are apparent to the operator.

The Singapore legislation adopts similar principles for accreditation and extends to the supervision of CAs, though it leaves the precise requirements and supervisory arrangements to be determined by later regulations:

Singapore Electronic Transactions Act 1998 s. 42

REGULATION OF CERTIFICATION AUTHORITIES

(1) The Minister may make regulations for the regulation and licensing of certification authorities and to define when a digital signature qualifies as a secure electronic signature.

(2) Without prejudice to the generality of subsection (1), the Minister may make regulations for or with respect to –
   a. applications for licences or renewal of licences of certification authorities and their authorised representatives and matters incidental thereto;
   b. the activities of certification authorities including the manner, method and place of soliciting business, the conduct of such solicitation and the prohibition of such solicitation of members of the public by certification authorities which are not licensed;
   c. the standards to be maintained by certification authorities;
   d. prescribing the appropriate standards with respect to the qualifications, experience and training of applicants for any licence or their employees;

e. prescribing the conditions for the conduct of business by a certification authority;
f. providing for the content and distribution of written, printed or visual material and advertisements that may be distributed or used by a person in respect of a digital certificate or key;
g. prescribing the form and content of a digital certificate or key;
h. prescribing the particulars to be recorded in, or in respect of, accounts kept by certification authorities;
i. providing for the appointment and remuneration of an auditor appointed under the regulations and for the costs of an audit carried out under the regulations;
j. providing for the establishment and regulation of any electronic system by a certification authority, whether by itself or in conjunction with other certification authorities, and for the imposition and variation of such requirements, conditions or restrictions as the Controller may think fit;
k. the manner in which a holder of a licence conducts its dealings with its customers, conflicts of interest involving the holder of a licence and its customers, and the duties of a holder of a licence to its customers with respect to digital certificates;
l. prescribing forms for the purposes of the regulations; and
m. prescribing fees to be paid in respect of any matter or thing required for the purposes of this Act or the regulations.

Some jurisdictions, however, have taken a more detailed approach to accreditation and supervision, and have enacted supplementary legislation which regulates these matters in detail. Probably the best-known examples are the Utah Digital Signature Rules[17] and the German Digital Signature Ordinance.[18] The American Bar Association *Digital Signature Guidelines*,[19] which have influenced much of the US State legislation, are also of interest here. These instruments are too extensive to be extracted in this chapter, but in general they deal with much the same concerns as the EU Directive and the Singapore Act. As well as fleshing out the basic principles of accreditation and supervision, they address additional matters of detail which include:

- the provision by a CA of appropriate guarantees;[20] and
- audits by independent third parties to ensure that the CA is complying with its obligations under the accreditation regime.[1]

5.5   LIABILITY OF CERTIFICATION AUTHORITIES

The identification of what would otherwise be anonymous, or at best indeterminately identified, communicating parties is fundamental to Internet transactions which have legal consequences. As a result, the scope for liability on the part of a CA is obvious. Liability to the holder of an ID Certificate issued

17 Rule 154-10 of the Utah Commerce, Corporations and Commercial Code, effective 1 November 1998.
18 The Signaturverordnung, made under § 19 Digital Signature Act 1997, in force 1 November 1997.
19 American Bar Association *Digital Signature Guidelines* (Chicago: ABA, 1996).
20 Utah Digital Signature Act 1996 (Utah Code § 46-3) §§ 103(34), 201(d); Utah Digital Signature Rules (Rule 154-10 of the Utah Commerce, Corporations and Commercial Code), r 201.
 1 German Digital Signature Ordinance (Signaturverordnung, made under § 19 Digital Signature Act 1997, in force 1 November 1997) § 15; Utah Digital Signature Act 1996 (Utah Code § 46-3) § 202; Utah Digital Signature Rules (Rule 154-10 of the Utah Commerce, Corporations and Commercial Code), r 402.

by the CA will arise if the certificate contains inaccurate information, so that the holder's intended transaction fails, or if the CA enables a third party to have access to the private element of the holder's signature key or discloses other private information about the holder. Because there is likely to be a contractual relationship between the holder and the issuing CA, the liability questions as between CA and holder can be defined and managed in the contract, subject to any consumer protection laws or controls on exclusion clauses[2] from which the holder benefits. However, many of the jurisdictions which have introduced or proposed electronic signature laws have taken the opportunity to clarify these elements of the CA's liability.[3]

The more complex aspect of CA liability is for the losses suffered by a person who relies on an ID Certificate (a 'relying party') which contains incorrect information. This information might be incorrect:

- because the CA has failed to take proper steps to check the information; or
- because the certificate has been revoked by the holder but the CA has not yet publicised that fact.

There is no physical world activity which corresponds to that of a CA, and thus the obligations of CAs and the extent of their liability under existing law are difficult to determine. For this reason, most laws introducing accreditation regimes include provisions defining that liability. However, an unaccredited CA would still be subject to liability under the general law, which therefore requires an initial examination.

5.5.1 General law

Where there is no statutory scheme of liability for CAs, there are two theories under which a relying party might base an action against a CA. The first is that there is a contract between the CA and the relying party, and the CA is in breach of that contract; the second is tortious liability based on the CA's negligence in ascertaining the accuracy of the information in the certificate.

The main difficulty in establishing a contract-based action is that there may have been no direct communications between the CA and the relying party from which an offer and acceptance can be extracted. In most cases the relying party will have received the ID Certificate from its holder, checked the issuing CA's electronic signature with a third party CA (if that signature is not already known to the relying party) and then relied on the certificate by entering into dealings with the holder. There will thus have been no contact between the relying party and the CA through which a contract might have been formed. However, if the relying party checks the certificate direct with the issuing CA, perhaps by interrogating the CA's Certificate Revocation List, it might be possible for the courts to imply a contract from that communication. The relying party's message would be the offer, agreeing to rely on the certificate if in return the CA made promises about the accuracy of the information in the certificate. The CA's response that the certificate was still valid would be the acceptance.

---

2   See eg EC *Directive on Unfair Terms in Consumer Contracts* Directive 93/13/EEC, OJ L 95, 21 April 1993; UK Unfair Contract Terms Act 1977.

3   See eg Utah Digital Signature Act 1996 (Utah Code § 46-3) § 303(1); American Bar Association *Digital Signature Guidelines* (Chicago: ABA, 1996) guideline 3.14(1).

Alternatively, in common law jurisdictions at least, it may be possible for the courts to construct a contract even if the relying party has no direct communications with the issuing CA. This contract would be formed on the basis that the CA had made a unilateral offer to the whole world, promising certain things to any person who accepted its offer by undertaking the conduct required by the offer – in this case, by relying on the certificate. Such an argument was successful in the old English case of *Carlill v Carbolic Smoke Ball Co,*[4] where the defendants advertised that they would pay £100 to any person who contracted influenza after using their product, which was supposed to prevent the disease. The court held that they were contractually obliged to pay the plaintiff, who had fulfilled all the conditions set out in the advertisement, because the advertisement amounted to a unilateral offer which she had accepted by purchasing and using the product.

A further possibility which arises in those jurisdictions which recognise liability to a third party arising out of contracts intended to benefit that third party, is an action based on the contract between the CA and the holder. However, as Froomkin points out, in such an action the third party must clearly demonstrate that the contract was intended to confer a benefit on him, and it is by no means clear that a contract for the issuance of an ID Certificate demonstrates such an intention on the part of either the issuing CA or the holder. He poses a hypothetical example in which Carol (a CA) issues a certificate to Alice (the holder) who uses it to transact with Bob (the relying party):

> Whether the contract between Alice and Carol was for Bob's benefit or for Alice's depends entirely on how one chooses to look at it. Alice procures the certificate in order to induce Bob to transact with her. Alice wants Bob to rely on the certificate; perhaps Carol does also since this enhances the market for her product.[5] But Alice wants Bob to rely because it benefits her, not because it benefits him. The glass is either too empty or too full. Either the holder of the certificate, Alice, is the intended beneficiary because the certificate gives her something to show to Bob, or Bob is the intended beneficiary because without the benefit he will not transact with Alice.[6] Either no third party is intended or they all are.[7]

Even where the courts are able to find a contract which can be enforced by the relying party against the CA, much uncertainty will remain as to the terms of that contract. There are two main issues which the court will need to consider:

- Clearly, the CA is making some promise about the accuracy of the information contained in the certificate, but what exactly is the content of that promise? One possibility is that the CA is warranting that the information is true, and thus accepting strict liability for any inaccuracy.

---

4   [1893] 1 QB 256.

5   Furthermore, the courts are not in agreement as to whether Alice's intent, Carol's intent, or their joint intent should control. See Jean F Powers 'Expanded Liability and the Intent Requirement in Third Party Beneficiary Contracts' (1993) Utah L Rev 67, 73–74.

6   There is great merit to Professor Eisenberg's complaint that: the entire enterprise of finding an intent to benefit the third party as an end is misguided. Except in some cases involving true donee beneficiaries, the intent of the contracting parties is typically to further their own interests, not the interests of a third party. Accordingly, the question whether there is an intent to benefit the third party as an end normally cannot generate a meaningful answer. Eisenberg 'Third-Party Beneficiaries' (1992) 92 Colum L Re 1358, 1381

7   A Michael Froomkin 'The Essential Role of Trusted Third Parties in Electronic Commerce (1996) 75 Oregon L Rev 49 Part III.A.2(a)(iii).

The other possibility is that the CA is warranting no more than that it took reasonable care to ascertain the accuracy of the information, so that liability will only arise if the relying party can prove a failure in that respect.

- What is the status of additional information contained in the certificate which purports to have an effect on liability? The most obvious such information is:
  - Any reliance limit stated in the certificate, eg that it is good for transactions up to US $100. Is the effect of such a statement that no liability arises at all if the transaction is used for a larger transaction, or that this figure is the limit of liability even if the relying party's losses are in fact greater?
  - The cross-reference which is found in some certificates, eg those complying with X.509, to a Certification Policy Statement. This document, which is accessible electronically, sets out the procedures used by the CA to check the information contained in the certificate, and may also contain limitations on liability.

The answer to these conundrums may perhaps be found by noting that the contractual terms are not express but implied,[8] and that the court should therefore take into account any custom and practice in the field of CA activity.[9] Because in some jurisdictions there are statutory rules setting out CA liability, the courts should construe the implied terms to be in accord with any consensus which can be detected in that legislation. As we shall see at 5.5.2 below, some element of consensus can be found, and this suggests that a CA's liability in contract to the relying party should be based on either (a) negligence in ascertaining the accuracy of the information in the certificate, or (b) the liability expressly assumed in the CA's Certification Policy Statement (eg that particular checking procedures had been undertaken). Additionally, the CA's liability should not extend beyond the reliance limit stated in the certificate.

The alternative theory on which a claim might be made against the issuing CA is based on tortious negligence. The argument will be that the CA owes the relying party a duty to take reasonable care in ascertaining the accuracy of the information contained in the certificate, has failed to take such care, and is therefore responsible for the relying party's losses. The question which will need to be answered before liability arises in negligence is whether there is a sufficient relationship between the CA and the relying party so as to give rise to such a duty.[10] In some jurisdictions there is the additional possibility of strict liability, generally under product liability legislation, although in most instances such liability only arises in respect of physical, as opposed to information, products.[11]

---

8 Unless the court finds that there is a contract between CA and relying party whose terms are set out in the Certification Policy Statement.

9 *Trumpet Software Pty Ltd v OzEmail Pty Ltd* [1996] 34 IPR 481.

10 See eg the UK case of *Caparo Industries plc. Dickman* [1990] 2 AC 605 for an extensive discussion of the issues to be considered before finding that a duty exists.

11 See eg the definition of 'product' in EC Council Directive 85/374 on product liability, 1985 OJ L 210/28, art 2.

A. Michael Froomkin, "The Essential Role of Trusted Third Parties in Electronic Commerce", 75 Oregon L. Rev. 49 (1996) Part III.A.2

B. LIABILITY IN TORT FOR NEGLIGENT MISREPRESENTATION[12]

Recovery in tort is generally premised either on the breach of a duty of care, or on strict liability.[13] Unlike their contract claims, the various parties' tort claims will in no way be undermined by any breach of contract Alice may have committed in misrepresenting facts to Carol, except of course for Alice, who may suffer from estoppel, unclean hands, or comparative fault. If Carol has a tort duty to issue accurate statements it exists outside the contract. Nevertheless, the contours of Carol's duty of care will, to a great extent, be defined by the representations she makes about the level of inquiry she promises to make before issuing a certificate. In a sense, therefore, the contract does define the tort;[14] anyone who relies on the certificate can reasonably be expected to take the trouble to read the terms incorporated into the certificate. For example, if Carol says in her certification practice statement, incorporated by reference in the certificate, that she requires applicants to show their passports, but in fact failed to ask Alice to show hers, she is guilty of negligence. Or, if Carol says that she checks passports, and did so, but failed to notice that Alice presented a crude forgery that could have been detected with ordinary care,[15] she is guilty of negligence. Conversely, if Carol did everything she said she would do, but Alice proffered a superbly faked passport, then Carol is not guilty of negligence. Bob and David may still be able to recover in this last case, however, if Carol is strictly liable for the accuracy of her certificates.[16] Even if Carol is not strictly liable, David may be such an attractive plaintiff that he stands to recover if his lawyer can find a way to get him to the jury.[17]

If Carol, the CA, breaches her duty of care in checking the facts about Alice recited in the certificate, she potentially is liable for making a negligent misrepresentation.[18] This liability may run to Bob (Alice's victim), to David (if Alice impersonated him), to Alice's employer (if the certificate was pursuant to a contract with the employer) and perhaps even to Alice, subject to her contributory or comparative negligence or unclean hands if she committed a fraud.[19]

A threshold issue, however, is to whom the negligent misrepresentation in the certificate is addressed. If Bob got his copy of the certificate from Carol's Web site

12 In this article, Froomkin discusses the issues by reference to a hypothetical transaction in which Carol (a CA) issues a certificate to Alice (the holder) who uses it to transact with Bob (the relying party). The certificate falsely states that its holder is David.

13 *See infra* Part III.A.2.b(iv) (discussing imposition of strict liability on CAs).

14 Cf *Restatement (Second) of Torts* (1965) Sec 299A, comment c. (In the ordinary case, the undertaking of one who renders services in the practice of a profession or trade is a matter of contract between the parties . . .).

15 The definition of ordinary care is itself an issue. If there is an industry, trade usages may supply a guide [cross-reference omitted]. Otherwise, judges and juries will have to resort to general principles of ordinary care by reasonable people in like circumstances, whatever those may be.

16 See infra Part III.A.2.b(iv) (discussing applicability of strict liability to CAs).

17 Perhaps David's lawyer might accuse Carol of a privacy tort, or of casting David in a false light by identifying him with the evil Alice.

18 The misrepresentation is clearly of a matter of fact, not opinion, as those terms are used in the *Restatement (Second) of Torts*, Secs 538A, 548A.

In some cases one could also hypothesize other claims against Carol, including false representation under 15 USC Sec 1125(a)(2) (1994) (trademark), which requires neither privity nor negligence, or a privacy tort. If Alice manages to acquire a certificate saying she is David, David may have a tort claim for appropriation of name or likeness, see *Restatement (Second) of Torts* Sec 652C (One who appropriates to his own use or benefit the name or likeness of another is subject to liability to the other for invasion of his privacy.), or a false light claim against Carol, id Sec 652E (publicity placing another in false light that is offensive, based on reasonable person standard, subjects publisher to liability if published with knowledge of or reckless disregard as to falsity), or perhaps even a new tort of impersonation.

19 See Stuart M. Speiser et al *The American Law of Torts* (1992) Sec 32:74, at 367.

where she publishes certificates, Bob has a tort claim for a negligent misrepresentation that Carol made directly to him, although contract privity is absent.[20] David cannot make this claim – he is a third party and his ability to recover depends on how the applicable state's law treats third parties claiming injury from negligent misrepresentation to another. On the other hand, if Carol gives the certificate to Alice and Alice sends a copy of it to Bob, the negligent misrepresentation was made to Alice, and Bob is reduced to a third party.

States differ greatly on when a third party can obtain redress for negligent misrepresentations.[1] Some require only that the third party's reliance be foreseeable; most follow the Restatement (Second) of Torts rule which is an uneasy, and sometimes unclear, compromise between the two views; a few require contract privity.

(I) FORESEEABILITY STATES

A small, but perhaps growing,[2] number of states determine who may bring a third party negligent misrepresentation claim by applying traditional tort analysis focusing on foreseeability. Carol clearly would be liable to Bob in these states, regardless of how he obtained the certificate, since it is completely foreseeable that persons such as Bob would rely on the certificate. Carol should be liable to David as well, since it is foreseeable that a person whose good name is misappropriated in a certificate will be harmed. Both the equities and an economic analysis favor David since he is completely innocent, had no notice, and there is nothing he could have done to protect himself from Alice.

(II) RESTATEMENT STATES

Most states follow the rule set out in section 552 of the Restatement (Second) of Torts[3] and allow a third party to sue if he is within the group of actually foreseen (not all foreseeable) users, the limited group of persons for whose benefit and guidance to whom the author knows the recipient intends to supply the statement.[4] Unfortunately, the Restatement rule is difficult to apply to a CA. The potential class of persons who will be shown a certificate and asked to rely on it is large, much like an appraiser's or accountant's report. Indeed, the potential class is as large or larger than those who might rely on a report regarding a publicly traded security; the possible transactions are more diverse and the reliance by the third party is more likely to be a but for element of the transaction. Furthermore, any CA must be aware of these facts. Because the whole point of having a certificate is to enable the holder to show it to someone who will rely on it, there is no question that the recipient of a valid and

---

20 There may be interesting choice of law problems if Carol and Bob live in different jurisdictions.
1 See generally Jordan H Leibman and Anne S Kelly 'Accountants' Liability to Third Parties for Negligent Misrepresentation: The Search for a New Limiting Principle' (1992) 30 Am Bus LJ 347.
2 James R Adams 'No Privity Required for Negligent Misrepresentation Action' (1993) 60 Def Couns J, 601.
3 See eg *Bily v Arthur Young & Co* 834 P 2d 745, 773 (Cal 1992) (adopting *Restatement (Second) of Torts* Sec 552 approach). The relevant part of s 552 states:
    (1) One who, in the course of his business, profession or employment, or in any other transaction in which he has a pecuniary interest, supplies false information for the guidance of others in their business transactions, is subject to liability for pecuniary loss caused to them by their justifiable reliance upon the information, if he fails to exercise reasonable care or competence in obtaining or communicating the information.
    (2) Except as stated in Subsection (3), the liability stated in Subsection (1) is limited to loss suffered (a) by the person or one of a limited group of persons for whose benefit and guidance he intends to supply the information or knows that the recipient intends to supply it; and (b) through reliance upon it in a transaction that he intends the information to influence or knows that the recipient so intends or in a substantially similar transaction.
  Restatement (Second) of Torts Sec 552.
4 *Restatement (Second) of Torts* Sec 552(2)(a); see eg *Rosenblum Inc v Adler* 461 A 2d 138, 145 (NJ 1983).

verifiable certificate should be within the zone of foreseeable users, that is, among those entitled to justifiable reliance.[5]

The problem with this line of reasoning, however, is that it seems to prove too much. While section 552 of the Restatement (Second) is not a model of clarity, it is a compromise that was not intended to expand the class of potential third-party plaintiffs to the entire world.[6] The class of potential users of a certificate is all users of electronic commerce, indeed all users of e-mail or the World Wide Web, which may equal a good fraction of the world someday; allowing a right of action to this entire group threatens to collapse into the foreseeability test, and thus to exceed the boundaries that section 552 was designed to create. There has been a trend toward allowing third parties to assert negligent misrepresentation claims against professionals, but this trend has not been uniform across states, nor even across professions within individual states.[7] Some have argued that professional opinions such as audits are intended primarily for the benefit of third parties and that accountants should therefore be liable to these essentially foreseeable parties,[8] but many others strongly oppose this idea.[9] Part of this debate concerns the extent to which accountants can foresee the uses to which their clients will put their work product, but commentators have also argued that unfettered liability is disproportionate to the wrong, might discourage socially useful behavior (such as audits of litigation-prone industries), might be expensive to administer, or might otherwise impose greater social costs than benefits.[10]

The CAs' circumstances are materially different from the accountants' in one important respect. If Bob acquires a certificate from Alice, that certificate has almost no value to Bob except as a means of facilitating transactions with other parties.[11] *Every* recipient of a certificate who suffers because of the CA's negligence thus falls squarely within the Restatement (Second) section 552 class of persons who suffer loss through reliance upon [the negligent misrepresentation] in a transaction that [the CA] intends the information to influence or knows that the recipient so intends or in a substantially similar transaction.[12] It may be that the CA's resulting liability is unfairly large or socially detrimental, but it is hardly incidental or unexpected.

(III) PRIVITY STATES

A few states, notably New York, still follow the older rule that if Bob is a third party he can only recover for Carol's negligent misrepresentation to Alice (that Alice then furnished to him) if he is in a relation of privity with Carol, although some of these states slightly relax the qualifications for privity.[13] The policy reason for attempting

5   *Bily v Arthur Young & Co*, 834 P 2d at 772.
6   See *Restatement (Second) of Torts* Sec 552, comment a (noting that liability for negligent misstatement is more restricted than for fraudulent misrepresentation).
7   See Gary Lawson and Tamara Mattison 'A Tale of Two Professions: The Third-Party Liability of Accountants and Attorneys for Negligent Misrepresentation' (1991) 52 *Ohio St LJ*, 1309, 1310.
8   See eg Howard B Wiener 'Common Law Liability of the Certified Public Accountant for Negligent Misrepresentation' (1983) 20 *San Diego L Rev* 233, 250; Richard D Holahan Jr Note '*Security Pacific Business Credit Inc v Peat Marwick Main & Co*: Just in Case You Had Any Doubts There Is No Tort of Negligent Misrepresentation in New York' (1993) 13 *Pace L Rev* 763, 771–76.
9   See eg Victor P Goldberg 'Accountable Accountants: Is Third-Party Liability Necessary?' (1988) 17 J Legal Stud, 295; Thomas L. Gossman 'The Fallacy of Expanding Accountants' Liability' (1988) Colum Bus L Rev 213; John A Siliciano 'Negligent Accounting and the Limits of Instrumental Tort Reform' (1988) 86 Mich L Rev 1929.
10 See eg Siliciano, supra note [9], at 1944.
11 The picture is somewhat more complicated if Alice's employer obtains the certificate for Alice, since the certificate may have uses within the organisation.
12 *Restatement (Second) of Torts* Sec 552(2)(b). Arguably these third parties are thus within the limited group of persons for whose benefit and guidance [Alice] intends to supply the information or knows that the recipient intends to supply it, id Sec 552(2)(a), even if this limited group is in fact limited only to those with computers.
13 See Speiser, supra note [19 p 140], Sec 32:75, at 370.

to limit the class of potential plaintiffs claiming negligent misrepresentation is in deference to what are considered to be legitimate fears of indeterminate liability to third persons. In the infamous words of Justice Cardozo in *Ultramares Corporation v. Touche*, If liability for negligence exists, a thoughtless slip or blunder, the failure to detect a theft or forgery beneath the cover of deceptive entries, may expose accountants to a liability in an indeterminate amount for an indeterminate time to an indeterminate class.[14]

The classic cases about negligent misrepresentation, such as *Ultramares*, involve a common fact pattern in which Bob receives Carol's negligent misrepresentation (regarding, for example, an accountant's report) from Alice. If Bob got the certificate from Alice, his third party negligent misrepresentation claim hews closely to the *Ultramares* facts, giving Bob little hope of recovery against Carol in a privity state.

Bob's position in a privity state such as New York is more complicated if he got Alice's certificate directly from Carol's Web site. It is as if the accountants in *Ultramares* had published the accounts to the world with their client's consent. Yet, Bob still has no contract privity with Carol. As a formal matter, staying squarely within the language of *Ultramares*, Bob's claim is unchanged. Nor does the direct provision of the certificate have any formal effect on Bob's status as a potential third-party beneficiary of the contract a status that would substitute for privity[15] since Carol and Alice's intentions are a necessary element of Bob's third-party beneficiary contract claim,[16] and their intentions are not affected by the mode of delivery.

Carol's claim that she did not foresee Bob's reliance rings particularly hollow if she placed Alice's certificate on the World Wide Web herself rather than giving it to Alice; Bob's claim of justifiable reliance on a certificate published by Carol in this manner seems strong. Nevertheless, since a certificate issued by Carol is used, foreseeably, by the same people in the same way for the same purposes regardless of whether it happens to pass through Alice's hands on the way to Bob, it seems overly formalistic to make a distinction between the legal consequences of the two distribution models. Indeed, with the exception of the case where Alice notifies Carol that she intends to give Bob the certificate, Bob is just as much or as little an intended third party beneficiary whether Alice publishes the certificate or Carol does. Because in practice the two distribution methods are barely distinguishable, especially when one considers that Carol continues to manage the CRL regardless of who distributes the certificate, there is a danger that Bob's tort claim would fail in a strong privity state such as New York even if he got Alice's certificate directly from Carol.[17]

Whatever this result may say about general tort principles applicable in New York, it is not a sensible result in the special context of a CA who issues a certificate at the request of a client, particularly if the CA publishes the certificate. The rule in *Ultramares* was crafted to protect accountants and other professionals from being subjected to unforeseen, arguably unforeseeable, liability by the actions of a client in cases where the person issuing a report could reasonably believe that the report was for the client's own, private, use.[18] A CA issuing a certificate, especially an identifying certificate, knows full well that the client's entire purpose in acquiring the certificate is to show it to third parties who will rely on it. By publishing the certificate itself, the CA removes itself from the *Ultramares* facts. Even if the client publishes the certificate, the CA must logically know that the client intends to do so. The CA cannot, therefore, credibly claim surprise when an unknown third party relies on the certificate in a manner

14   *Ultramares Corp v Touche* 174 NE 441, 444 (NY, 1931).
15   See Lawson and Mattison, supra note [7 p 142], at 1319.
16   [Cross-reference omitted].
17   Cf Holahan, supra note [8 p 142]. A CA that wanted to take on liability in such a state in order to signal that its certificates were reliable would either have to draft a contract that made its intentions very clear, or it might have to adopt a business model in which Carol does not put Alice's certificate on a web page, and does not make it available to all, but instead provides an automated email credential response service in which Carol meters Alice's usage of the certificate, and perhaps charges accordingly.
18   See supra note [14] and accompanying text.

consistent with the CA's representations in that certificate because the certificate exists solely to be relied upon by strangers. The common law should reflect this reality, particularly in the case where the CA itself is the publisher, even in a strong privity state.

(IV) STRICT LIABILITY FOR CAS?

Strict liability is most commonly applied in cases involving goods, such as defective products, and ultrahazardous activities. Furthermore, strict liability traditionally allows recovery for personal injury but not for economic loss. Traditionally, strict liability would thus seem to have had little to do with the issuance of certificates: they are not ultrahazardous in the usual sense of the term,[19] and they are probably not products.[20] However, one commentator suggests that a certificate which used a faulty algorithm to produce the CA's digital signature might be found to have a design defect.[1] Given that some jurisdictions separate hybrid good-service transactions into the part that is a good and the part that is a service,[2] it may be useful to consider briefly the economic principles that might underlie the imposition of strict liability as they apply to certificates as goods. Indeed, there is a policy argument that a regulatory approach to the law of certification authorities might want to take these factors into account in assigning liability, particularly in the absence of the consensus as to what constitutes due care for a CA needed to give teeth to the CA's duty of care.

Imposition of a strict liability regime eliminates the need to find privity: liability follows the good.[3] There is no requirement that plaintiff show fault by defendant; instead, the sole issue is whether the product performed adequately. The Restatement (Second) of Torts section 402A imposes strict liability on products with an unreasonably dangerous defect.[4] Prosser defined this class of products as those which are not safe for such a use that can be expected to be made of [them], and no warning is given.[5]

The Learned Hand test, as reformulated by Dean Calabresi, suggests that courts should impose strict liability on the least-cost avoider.[6] As between Carol and anyone but Alice, Carol will in most cases be the least-cost avoider of the loss caused by an inaccurate certificate. If Alice and Bob are strangers, Bob has no means of testing the validity of the representations in the certificate: his inability to confirm Alice's claims about herself is the precise reason he wants the certificate in the first place.[7] As between Carol and Alice, however, Alice is ordinarily the least-cost avoider of Alice's errors.

The net effect of a policy that makes Alice strictly liable to everyone for her own errors in a certificate, and makes the CA strictly liable to everyone but Alice for the CA's failure to detect Alice's misstatements, would be to turn the CA into an insurer for Alice's veracity in every case where Alice disappears or lacks the assets to satisfy a judgment.[8] There is also a danger that imposing strict liability on Carol removes the incentive for Alice to take care that her statements to Carol are accurate. For Carol to agree to be a CA under these terms would require that Alice provide either extraordinarily strong assurances as to her claims, or that Carol charge prices large enough to pay for a generous insurance cover.

19 [Cross-reference omitted].
20 [Cross-reference omitted].
 1 Michael S Baum *US Department of Commerce National Institute of Standards and Technology, Federal Certification Authority Liability and Policy: Law and Policy of Certificate-Based Public Key and Digital Signatures* (1994) at 130–31.
 2 [Cross-reference omitted].
 3 See *MacPherson v Buick Motor Co* 111 NE 1050 (NY, 1916).
 4 *Restatement (Second) of Torts* Sec 402A, comment i (1977) (discussing definition of unreasonably dangerous).
 5 William L Prosser 'The Fall of the Citadel (Strict Liability to the Consumer)' (1966) 50 Minn L Rev 791, 826.
 6 See Guido Calabresi *The Cost of Accidents: A Legal and Economic Analysis* (1970); Guido Calabresi and Jon T Hirschoff 'Toward a Test for Strict Liability in Torts' (1972) 81 Yale LJ 1055, 1077.
 7 [Cross-reference omitted].
 8 There is also some danger that under a strict liability regime, the fact that Carol was willing to become an insurer for Alice might itself be a signal that Carol was not trustworthy.

Even if tortious liability on the part of the issuing CA can be established under the applicable law, there is still a further issue to be examined. In general, neither contract nor tort imposes liability for *all* the losses suffered by a successful plaintiff – instead, liability is limited to the *foreseeable* losses arising from the defendant's breach.[9] Given that ID Certificates may be used for any type of communication, leading to any possible type of transaction, it is likely that the courts will decide that the losses which a CA can foresee are very limited. The alternative is to take the approach that every kind and extent of loss is foreseeable, and that is a position which the courts have generally refused to adopt. If this reasoning is correct, foreseeable losses are likely to be limited to the following:

- Losses caused by relying on the certificate for transactions up to the reliance limit stated in the certificate. It is not foreseeable that a reasonably prudent relying party would rely on the certificate for transactions in excess of that value.
- Direct loss of transaction value only, ie indirect and consequential losses will be unforeseeably remote and thus irrecoverable.[10]

5.5.2 Statutory liability

Most of the laws and legislative proposals which address the question of CA accreditation also contain some provisions about CA liability to a relying party. In general, the liability regimes apply only to accredited CAs; the liability of unaccredited CAs is left to the general law.

So far, there is no consensus on the basis of CA liability, although the cumulative effect of each liability regime would leave a CA in much the same position. Three different bases of liability can be discerned:

- Liability based on negligence in ascertaining the correctness of the information contained in an ID Certificate. This is the approach adopted by the EC Directive.[11]
- Allowing the CA to define in its Certification Policy Statement the liability which it accepts. This is the approach followed by the ABA Guidelines[12] and the Singapore Act.[13] The introductory text to the UK Electronic Communications Bill 1999 stated: 'The Government has decided that the liability of Trust Service Providers (TSPs), both to their customers and to parties relying on their certificates, is best left to existing law and to providers' and customers' contractual arrangements'.[14]

---

9 See eg *Wagon Mound* [1961] AC 388.
10 See American Bar Association *Digital Signature Guidelines* (Chicago: ABA, 1996) comment 2.3.3, p 78:
'Reliance on a certificate for reasons other than the verification of a digital signature may, however, not be foreseeable.'
11 *Directive 1999/93/EC on a Community framework for electronic signatures* OJ L13, p 12, 19 January 2000, art 6(1). The burden of proving lack of negligence is placed on the certification-service-provider.
12 American Bar Association *Digital Signature Guidelines* (Chicago: ABA, 1996), guideline 3.7, comment 3.7.1.
13 Singapore Electronic Transactions Act 1998, s 30(1).
14 UK Electronic Communications Bill 1999, Introduction, Part I, para 4(e). Now enacted as Electronic Communications Act 2000.

- Making the CA strictly liable for failure to comply with its published procedures for ascertaining the correctness of the information in the certificate[15] or for the accuracy of the information itself.[16]

Additionally, some schemes recognise that the certificate may contain express limitations on its use, eg that it is only valid for communications with a particular Government agency. In those circumstances, there should be no liability for usage outside those limits.[17]

Even where the CA is liable to the relying third party for inaccuracies in an ID Certificate, most accreditation schemes recognise a need to limit the extent of the CA's liability. This is normally done by providing that the CA's liability shall not exceed the reliance limit stated in the certificate itself,[18] although there might still be liability up to that limit even if the value of the transaction were in excess of the limit.[19] The Utah Act also provides specifically that the CA shall have no liability for indirect or consequential losses.[20]

5.6   TOWARDS A GLOBAL SYSTEM?

Because ID Certificates will be used across national boundaries, there is a practical need for national laws to have the same, or at least similar, effects. If the obligations and liabilities of CAs are radically different in other jurisdictions, this will either act as a disincentive to become a CA or lead to their certificates being issued only for domestic use. Fortunately for CAs, a global consensus is beginning to emerge, although the differences in approach identified earlier in this chapter will still present some problems.

One area of consensus is that CAs should be given the opportunity to become accredited. Although accreditation is not theoretically necessary to achieve the objective of a globally consistent system for the identification of Internet actors, once one or more commercially important jurisdictions introduces accreditation (as has already happened) the others will be forced to follow. This is because where accreditation is introduced, it brings with it the important consequences

---

15 Utah Digital Signature Act 1996 (Utah Code § 46-3) § 303(3). Note that if these procedures have been followed, the CA has complete immunity from liability even if the information is in fact inaccurate – § 309(2)(a). On the question of immunity, see also American Bar Association *Digital Signature Guidelines* (Chicago: ABA, 1996), guideline 3.14, which adopts the Utah Act approach.

16 This is the position in Singapore where the CA has no CPS. However, this strict liability is subject to an different liability statement contained in the certificate itself. See Singapore Electronic Transactions Act 1998, s 30(2)(d).

17 *Directive 1999/93/EC on a Community framework for electronic signatures* OJ L 13, p 12, 19 January 2000, art 6(3). Those schemes which allow the CPS to define liability would also have the same effect if the limitation on use were stated in the CPS or the certificate. Note also that although the German law does not define a liability scheme, leaving this matter to the general law, it does refer specifically to use limitations – German Digital Signature Act (Signaturgesetz) 1997 § 7(1). This suggests that use outside those limitations would not give rise to liability in Germany.

18 *Directive 1999/93/EC on a Community framework for electronic signatures* OJ L 13, p 12, 19 January 2000, art 6(4); Singapore Electronic Transactions Act 1998, s 45; Utah Digital Signature Act 1996 (Utah Code § 46-3) § 309(2)(b).

19 Article 6(4) of the Directive specifically provides that there is no liability in these circumstances, whilst the other provisions examined here seem to take the view that there should be liability up to that limit.

20 Utah Digital Signature Act 1996 (Utah Code § 46-3) § 309(2)(c).

for a CA that the legal effectiveness of electronic signatures backed by its certificates is enhanced, and its liability is defined and/or limited. These benefits will only be available to foreign CAs if they, too, are accredited, and their accreditation regime is recognised as equivalent by the domestic law of the country in which the foreign CA's certificates are to be used.[1] If the CA's own jurisdiction does not introduce an accreditation scheme which is recognised in other countries, the CA will be under pressure to become accredited abroad or, in extreme cases, to move its operations to a country where accreditation is available. This will particularly be the case where the CA's own law does not grant limitations on its potential liabilities.

The second area of consensus is on the extent of a CA's liability to a relying party. The laws and proposals examined in this Chapter differ on whether it should be a defence that a CA has taken reasonable care to ensure that its certificates contain accurate information, but most agree that the reliance limits set out in the certificate should be enforced. This will enable CAs to assess the maximum extent of their potential liability, and to obtain insurance against such liability on commercially practicable terms.

---

1   See further Chapter 7.2.2.

Chapter 6

Old wine in new bottles:[1] traditional transactions in the Internet environment

Although, as we have seen, the Internet has produced new actors and new types of transaction, much of the activity taking place via the Internet is still closely analogous to physical world dealings. This is because the Internet is merely a communications mechanism, albeit a highly sophisticated global medium, and can therefore be used to enter into traditional types of transaction. The challenge for the law is to adapt the provisions which currently regulate physical world transactions so as to provide adequate solutions to the new disputes which arise when they are carried out in electronic form.

Difficulties exist because the law has developed over a long period of time during which physical actors and physical media were the only, or at least the primary, mechanisms by which transactions with legal consequences could be effected. When the first elements of communication were dematerialised with the electric telegraph,[2] the result of the communication was still a physical document written by a clerk on a telegram form. This enabled the courts to consider this communication technology as simply a new method of transmitting a physical letter.[3] More recent dematerialisation technology such as the facsimile (fax) machine has been treated in the same way.[4] Similarly, once dematerialised communications methods such as the telephone, radio and telex enabled 'conversations' at a distance, the courts noted that there were human actors at either end and treated these in the same way as face-to-face negotiations.[5]

Now, however, digital communications technologies are making analogies of this type difficult or impossible to draw. A communication with legal consequences may never result in the production of some physical object bearing the information communicated. 'Conversations' may take place between computers, acting (apparently) on their own initiative and with no involvement from human actors.

---

1   With apologies to John Perry Barlow for adapting his title 'Selling Wine Without Bottles: The Economy of Mind on the Global Net' (available from http://www.eff.org).
2   Although earlier dematerialised communications technology existed, eg semaphore and the Napoleonic war signal telegraph, these were used primarily for military purposes. It is thus unsurprising that cases arising from these technologies do not appear in the law reports.
3   See eg cases on contract formation such as *Re London and Northern Bank* [1900] 1 Ch 220 (UK), *Harper v Western Union Telegraph Co* 133 SC 55 (1925) (US). See further Baum and Perritt *Electronic Contracting, Publishing and EDI Law* (New York: John Wiley & Sons, 1991) pp 326–328.
4   See eg *Re a debtor (No 2021 of 1995)* [1996] 2 All ER 345.
5   See the discussion of these concepts in *Entores Ltd v Miles Far East Corpn* [1955] 2 QB 327.

This chapter therefore sets out to re-examine a number of fundamental legal concepts, which have been developed in respect of physical world objects and now need to be extended to the digital world. It also reconsiders some commercial transactions in which physical objects (particularly paper) have played an important part, but which must now be carried out without the comfort of written documents. None of these problems are unique to the Internet, as they arise wherever some form of digital communication is used. However, the Internet is clearly the largest and most important means of digital communication, and this book would be incomplete without a discussion of these issues.

6.1   FUNDAMENTAL CONCEPTS REVISITED

6.1.1   Property rights in information

> Businesses of all sizes use the Internet to create, buy, sell and distribute products and services. Many are realizing substantial productivity improvements as a result, and have been increasing their Internet business activities at dramatic rates. Four companies alone – General Electric, Cisco, Intel, and Dell – were responsible for about $3 billion in Internet commerce in 1997. They plan to exceed $35 billion in online transactions by the year 2000. Instead of Internet commerce totaling 'tens of billions of dollars', it now appears that electronic commerce among businesses alone will total well over $300 billion by early in the next decade.
>
> During the first decade of the next century, virtually all sectors of the economy are being affected. By 2000, nearly 7 percent of all airline tickets purchased in the United States are likely to be sold online. As many as 16 million households may do their banking via the Internet, and over $1 billion of insurance premiums are expected to be generated online. Increasingly, consumers are using the Internet to buy books, music, clothing, electronic goods, and other household items. High-priced items such as automobiles are also being marketed and sold via the Internet – at least 1 out of 5 people will use it to shop for a new car or truck by the turn of the century.[6]

If these predictions are correct (and in general, predictions about the IT industries tend to underestimate growth by a substantial margin) Internet commerce will soon become one of the mainstream methods of doing business.

In addition to using the Internet as a new channel to sell ordinary goods and services, businesses will also use it to sell information products. Already, 'traditional' information products such as software and digitally-recorded music are available via this means. By disintermediating the process of information supply, however, the Internet also opens up the possibility of new types of information product whose sale was previously impossible or uneconomic.

If we examine the way in which information is sold in the physical world, it becomes apparent that the process is very inflexible. Information is recorded on a physical carrier such as paper, bound into a book, and what is actually sold is the book. Similarly, music is recorded on a CD as music information and the CD is sold. In other words, the sale is of the carrier, not the information itself. This sale of physical carriers requires an extensive distribution chain – in the case of books we need publishers, distributors and book shops – which costs

---

6   US Government Working Group on Electronic Commerce *First Annual Report* (November 1998) p 2.

money to run and makes the sale of small amounts of information uneconomic.[7] However, the Internet enables 'pure' information to be supplied, free of the carrier and without the need for a distribution chain. This means that there may be no need to sell a complete book – one could sell a page or half a page or even a single fact or statistic. It seems probable that we will see the rapid development of 'micro' information products, such as stock prices, micro programs, graphics and sound clips.

From the seller's perspective, however, there are drawbacks to selling information products on-line. These products are received by the buyer in a form which permits multiple copying with no degradation of quality, and also permits the product to be made easily available to other Internet users. The creator of an information product therefore requires the right to prevent activities of this kind, which otherwise might quickly destroy the market for the product.

6.1.1.1   *Ownership of information*

Although it is common to refer to owners of information, the concept of ownership in the property sense is almost impossible to apply to information products. Ownership of property is based on two, complementary, rights:

- the right to possession of the property; and
- the right to exclude others from the property.

Exclusive possession is conceptually problematic where information is concerned. For physical property, such as land or goods, exclusive possession by one person precludes the possibility that another person could simultaneously have exclusive possession of it. I cannot use my motor car if someone else is driving it. This is not true of information, which is not *unique* in the same way as physical property. No matter how many other people possess copies of my information, the value of that information to me is not reduced, *except* (and this is the crucial issue) that the more copies there are in existence, the less likely I am to be able to receive payment for supplying copies. For this reason, the law has been very reluctant to treat information in the same way as physical property. Deleting or modifying information is not property damage,[8] and information cannot be stolen[9] unless its value to its 'owner' has been reduced nearly to zero.[10]

There are also two public policy considerations which reduce the scope of ownership rights in information:

---

7 For example, if the reader had been interested only in this particular chapter, or in only this section of this chapter, he still needed to purchase the entire book to read it. It would hardly be economic for Butterworths to print up individual chapters or sections and sell them separately in hard copy form.

8 *Cox v Riley* (1986) 83 Cr App Rep 54. In that case the defendant was convicted of criminal damage when he deleted computer programs stored on a magnetic storage medium, which were used to control cutting equipment. However, the property which was damaged was not the information (the programs) but the storage medium. This decision was felt to be so conceptually problematic that it was later overturned by Computer Misuse Act 1990, s 3, substituting a new offence of unauthorised access to a computer with intent to modify its contents.

9 *Oxford v Moss* (1978) 68 Cr App Rep 183.

10 *R v Lloyd* [1985] QB 829.

- 'Raw' information is considered as somehow pre-existing, or at least as an asset which is free for all to use.[11] Ownership rights can only come into existence if the claimant of those rights has added value, eg through intellectual creativity or effort[12] or through invention.[13]
- Granting ownership rights in information conflicts with the fundamental principles of free speech and freedom of expression, so that all laws limit the scope of these rights to balance the two competing claims in respect of the information.[14]

As a consequence, the law has dealt with property rights in a limited way, concentrating solely on the exclusionary aspects of ownership. Because these intellectual property rights were developed in the physical world, they are not wholly adequate for preserving the position of owners in the Internet world.

6.1.1.2 Basis of intellectual property rights

Intellectual property rights are essentially rights to prevent others from performing certain acts in respect of the protected 'work'.[15] These rights are thus exclusionary in nature, and are of two basic kinds[16]:

- The right to prevent others from copying[17] the 'work' or dealing in copies. These rights are normally conferred by copyright (or author's right) laws.[18]
- The right to prevent others from making use of the 'work' for their own purposes. Effectively, this grants the owner certain rights in know how, and is therefore closely circumscribed. Know how will be protected while it is confidential, but once it becomes public knowledge protection is lost unless the know how is sufficiently inventive for the grant of a patent, in which case complex application and checking procedures must be gone through. These rights will be of limited application in the Internet world, save in those rare cases where an information product is also a patentable invention.

The discussion of copyright issues in Chapters 3 and 4 has already demonstrated that these rights are not easily applicable in the Internet world. As the introduction to this section 6.1.1 has pointed out, in the physical world information is disseminated through copies on physical media. Partial copying is largely a private activity, because there is little commercial future in disseminating 'works' whose information content is worth less than the cost of

---

11 See eg *Feist Publications Inc v Rural Telephone Service Co Inc* 499 US 340 (1990) in relation to copyright in facts; European Patent Convention, art 52(2) excluding from the scope of patentability 'discoveries, scientific theories and mathematical methods'.
12 The basic test for copyright protection.
13 The fundamental requirement for patent protection.
14 See Denicola 'Copyright and Free Speech: Constitutional Limitations on the Protection of Expression' (1979) 67 Calif L Rev 283.
15 'Work' is a term of copyright law, but is used here (in inverted commas) to denote the information asset which receives protection via intellectual property rights. As will become apparent, not all information assets receive such protection.
16 Trade marks are usually classified with intellectual property rights, but their basis is the protection of business reputation, not of rights in information per se. See further Chapter 3.2.2.
17 Including non-literal copying such as adaptation or translation.
18 See Berne Convention, art 9(1) (exclusive right to make copies); UK Copyright, Designs and Patents Act 1988, s 18 (issuing copies to the public); 17 USC § 106(3) (distribution of copies to the public).

production and distribution. In the Internet world, however, partial copying and the dissemination of micro information products begins to make economic sense.

Copyright law does not provide adequate tools for the proprietor of such an information product to protect his market for several reasons:

1. Although Internet distribution takes place through copying, much of that copying will not infringe:
    *   Where the copying is by a non-commercial user, it may be permitted under the fair or private use provisions of national copyright laws.[19] Alternatively, the user may have some implied licence to make the copy,[20] the proprietor's interest being in preventing dissemination by a commercial enterprise.
    *   Where the copying is effected by an intermediary host, either the host may be held not liable on the basis that it only provided the copying mechanism, the actual copying being effected by the sender or recipient,[1] or the intermediary may benefit from the trend towards granting immunities to hosts which has been examined in Chapter 4.3.2.
2. In the case of micro information products, copyright law may provide no protection at all because the product is not sufficiently original,[2] or substantial,[3] to constitute a protected work.
3. Where only a small part of the proprietor's product is copied, that part may be too small to constitute a substantial part, and thus not be an infringement.[4] However, where the copying is for commercial purposes (and particularly for resale) this may not prove a major obstacle.
4. In practice, the proprietor of an information product is unlikely to take action against a non-commercial copier, which means that in those cases where the primary copying was by such a person, the proprietor will need to rely on a claim that the intermediary defendant infringed the distribution right. It is by no means certain that distribution right extends to this activity in many jurisdictions.[5]

If, as seems generally accepted, the proprietors of new information products require economic protection, either copyright law will need substantial amendment or some new form of protection will have to be found.

6.1.1.3   A new bottle?

It seems that once the proprietor of an information product makes it accessible via the Internet, the genie may be out of the bottle of existing copyright laws. Because the fundamental basis of intellectual property laws appears not to

---

19 See eg 17 USC § 107, UK Copyright, Designs and Patents Act 1988, ss 29 and 30.
20 See Chapter 3.3.1.2.
1 See Chapter 4.2.1.1.
2 *Feist Publications Inc v Rural Telephone Service Co Inc* 499 US 340 (1990).
3 *Noah v Shuba* [1991] FSR 14.
4 This issue is addressed in Chapter 3.3.4.2 in relation to Web links.
5 'In legal terms, it is generally accepted that the distribution right, which only applies to the distribution of physical copies does not cover the act of transmission. Also the reproduction right does not cover the act of transmission as such, but only the reproductions which take place in this context.' *Proposal for a European Parliament and Council Directive on the harmonization of certain aspects of copyright and related rights in the Information Society*, COM (97) 628 final, 10 December 1997, p. 20.

provide the mechanisms the proprietor needs to preserve his economic interests, a new bottle has to be constructed and the genie, somehow, squeezed into it.

What is clear is that rights to prevent copying or the distribution of copies are of little use to the proprietor. Instead, he needs powers to control the use that others, and in particular intermediaries, make of his product. There are three ways in which these powers might be granted.

The first is the extension of copyright law to encompass not only copying but also control of dissemination. This is the effect of art 8 of the new WIPO Copyright Treaty,[6] which will grant to authors:

> the exclusive right of authorizing any communication to the public of their works, by wire or wireless means, including the making available to the public of their works in such a way that members of the public may access these works from a place and at a time individually chosen by them.

In the Internet context it is the words 'making available' which provide the proprietor of the information product with a potential remedy. This concept of communication to the public extends beyond dealing with copies of the product – it would be infringed by enabling end users to make their own copies, eg by running a site through which the product could be downloaded via a Web or FTP server. In those circumstances, as we have seen in Chapter 4.2.1, there may be some doubt whether the person making the product available was either copying or distributing it, and we have also noted that it is impractical for the proprietor to take action against the end users, who certainly *do* make copies, even if they can be discovered. The person against whom the proprietor needs to be able to take action is the controller of the resource which is being misused.

Two points need to be considered here, however:

- The right will only subsist in *works* protected by copyright. Some information products will not attract such protection because they are not substantial or original enough – see Chapter 3.3.4.2.
- It is likely that the laws implementing the WIPO Copyright Treaty will take the opportunity to introduce immunities for intermediaries[7] or to define the right in such a way that mere intermediaries are not liable.[8]

The primary defendant in actions for breach of this right will be the resource controller, though because intermediaries are likely to lose immunity once they know they are hosting or caching infringing resources,[9] the proprietor is likely to receive some practical help from that source.

Secondly, we have seen in Chapter 3.3.4.3 that most jurisdictions seem to have some type of unfair competition law which provides remedies for the misappropriation of trade reputation, and some laws also provide remedies for misappropriation of work product. In the latter group of jurisdictions, the proprietor should clearly have a remedy against business activities which result in the dissemination of his information product without payment. In the

---

6   See further Chapter 4.2.1.3.
7   See eg US Online Copyright Infringement Liability Limitation Act, 17 USC § 512, discussed at Chapter 4.3.2.1.
8   See eg *Proposal for a European Parliament and Council Directive on the harmonization of certain aspects of copyright and related rights in the Information Society*, COM (1999) 250 final, 21 June 1999, art 3 as explained by Recitals 16 and 17.
9   See Chapter 4.3.2.

author's view, many of the lacunae in the law relating to commercial Internet activities can only be filled by laws of this kind, based on concepts of wrongful behaviour rather than on property concepts, and he would expect laws of this type to be introduced gradually into other jurisdictions.

Finally, contract law will have an increasing part to play in controlling improper activities with respect to information products. The identification services and infrastructures discussed in Chapter 5 provide the proprietor of an information product with a technological means of identifying his customers. When that identification is embedded into the information product, it enables the proprietor to prove to the courts:

- that the controller of the product is not a licensed user, and thus that the copy of the product infringes under traditional copyright law; or
- that the controller of the product did in fact enter into a licence contract with the proprietor when the product was downloaded, and thus that the proprietor has the right to remedies for any breaches of that licence.

Once these matters can be proved, contracts imposing use restrictions on users will be an effective means of retaining control over resources.

6.1.2 Signatures

The number of transactions which actually require a signature in order to be legally effective is very small, but even where a signature is not strictly necessary the parties to the transaction often want to have signed documentation. Clearly, however, a 'traditional'[10] manuscript signature is not feasible where the parties communicate via the Internet. Digital communications technology requires methods of signature which are very different from the manuscript signature. There are two possibilities so far as Internet communications are concerned:

- The incorporation of a scanned image of a manuscript signature into a word processing file, followed by the sending of that document as an email attachment.
- The 'signature' of an electronic document[11] by means of a mathematical process (an 'electronic signature').[12] For the purposes of this chapter an

10 The physical world concept of 'signature' is the signatory's name, written in his own hand, on a paper document (a 'manuscript signature'). This is so universally understood by lawyers and non-lawyers alike that it generally receives no special treatment in legislation or case reports.

11 The term 'document' is used here in a very broad sense. The definition in the UK Civil Evidence Act 1995, s 13 of a document as 'anything in which information of any description is recorded' would mean that, for evidential purposes, a transmission of data would not consist of a document, but rather that the several recordings on magnetic media during the transmission process would all be documents (or perhaps copies of the same document). Many other UK statutory definitions, however, define 'document' as, *inter alia*, a 'record kept by means of a computer' (see eg s 40 of the Finance Act 1993). For the purposes of this chapter, any discrete set of digital information will be treated as a document provided it performs the essential function of conveying information – see *Grant v Southwestern and County Properties Ltd* [1975] Ch 185. For a more detailed analysis of the concept of 'document' see Reed *Digital Information Law: electronic documents and requirements of form* (London: Centre for Commercial Law Studies, 1996) Chapter 1.

12 The term 'digital signature' is not used here because it has gained a particular technical meaning, viz the use of asymmetric encryption techniques to authenticate the sender of an electronic document and the document's integrity – see part 6.1.2.2. The term is also becoming identified with a particular implementation of encryption technology and signature infrastructure as defined in ANSI X.509 – see Chapter 5.3.

'electronic document' is a set of numbers (normally in ASCII or some proprietary code)[13] which represents text or other information.

These types of signature are effected in ways which are quite different from the affixing of a manuscript signature to a paper document. Drawing analogies with a manuscript signature becomes difficult, perhaps impossible.

One solution available to those who wish to use electronic signatures is to make provision in a contract for the acceptability of the signature method.[14] Even if the use of the technology does not create what the courts would recognise as a valid signature, in some jurisdictions the contractual term would raise an estoppel in favour of the party seeking to rely on the electronic signature.[15] However, the estoppel will not bind a third party, who will be able to plead the lack of signature as a defence and, as a corollary, will not be able to found his own action on the estoppel; and it will be ineffective if the result would be to declare valid a transaction which is in fact *void* according to the law for lack of formalities.[16] Additionally, where one of the parties to the contract is a consumer the term may be invalidated by consumer protection legislation.[17]

---

13 The American Standard Code for Information Interchange is used for most microcomputer communication. Each 8-bit binary word represents a letter of the alphabet or some control or graphics character. For example, in ASCII code A=decimal 65, a=decimal 97, carriage return=decimal 13 etc. EBCDIC (Extended Binary Coded Decimal Interchange Code) is the proprietary format used in IBM mainframes and minicomputers. See Cornwall *Hacker's Handbook III* (London, 1988) pp 10–14 and Appendix IV.

14 See eg American Bar Association *Model Electronic Data Interchange Trading Partner Agreement* (Chicago: American Bar Association, 1990) § 1.5:
    'Each party shall adopt as its signature an electronic identification consisting of symbol(s) or code(s) which are to be affixed to or contained in each Document transmitted by such party ('Signatures'). Each party agrees that any Signature of such party affixed to or contained in any transmitted Document shall be sufficient to verify such party originated such Document.'
    See further Baum and Pettit *Electronic Contracting, Publishing and EDI Law* (New York: John Wiley & Sons Inc, 1991) § 2.16. See also *Trading Partner Agreement to Authorize EDI for Defense Transportation* (Bethesda, Maryland: Logistics Management Institute, 1990) § XIV:
    'Vendor will use a code as specified in each transaction set addendum as its discrete authenticating code in lieu of signature and as the equivalent of a signature.'

15 This estoppel will arise even if the parties know that their agreed electronic signature technology is ineffective as a matter of law:
    'The full facts may be known to both parties; but if, even knowing those facts to the full, they are clearly enough shown to have assumed a different state of facts *as between themselves* for the purposes of a particular transaction, then their assumption will be treated, as between them, as true, in proceedings arising out of the transaction. The claim of the party raising the estoppel is, not that he believed the assumed version of the facts was true, but that he believed (and agreed) that it should be *treated as true.*'
    Spencer Bower and Turner *The Law Relating to Estoppel by Representation* (3rd, London: Butterworths, 1977) p 160, citing *Newis v General Accident Fire and Life Assurance Corpn* (1910) 11 CLR 620 at p 636 per Isaacs J (High Court of Australia). See also *TCB Ltd v Gray* [1986] Ch 621 (estoppel relating to the absence of a seal on a deed).

16 See eg *Swallow and Pearson v Middlesex County Council* [1953] 1 All ER 580 (in respect of the formality of writing). An estoppel can arise, however, if the requirement for a signature is imposed by the law solely to protect the parties to the transaction, as opposed to the public interest – see Spencer Bower and Turner *The Law Relating to Estoppel by Representation* (3rd, London: Butterworths, 1977) p 142.

17 See eg art 6(1) of the Council Directive 93/13/EEC of 5 April 1993 on unfair terms in consumer contracts which provides that unfair terms are not binding on the consumer. A term of this kind might fall within the Annex to the Directive para 1(q) as 'excluding or hindering the consumer's right to take legal action or exercise any other legal remedy . . .' and thus be regarded as *prima facie* unfair.

For these reasons electronic signatures cannot remain creatures of contract. An assessment of the validity and effectiveness of these new types of signature therefore requires a fundamental review of the nature of signatures in law.

6.1.2.1 What is a signature for?

A manuscript signature is accepted without question as legally effective in all jurisdictions, assuming it has not been procured by fraud, and it is rarely asked what effects such a signature is required by law to achieve. However, in those cases where the question has been asked, other methods of signing a document, such as signature by means of a printed or rubber stamp facsimile, have been assessed for validity. The most common approach is to define the functions which a signature must perform, and then to treat signature methods which effect those functions as valid signatures.

The primary function of a physical world signature is to provide evidence of three matters:

- the identity of the signatory;
- that the signatory intended the 'signature' to be his signature; and
- that the signatory approves of and adopts the contents of the document.

Manuscript signatures meet these functional requirements in a number of ways.

Identity is established by comparing the signature on the document with other signatures which can be proved, by extrinsic evidence, to have been written by the signatory. The assumption is that manuscript signatures are unique, and that therefore such a comparison is all that is necessary to provide evidence of identity. In practice, manuscript signatures are usually acknowledged by the signatory once they are shown to him, and extrinsic evidence is only required where it is alleged that the signature has been forged.

Intention to sign is normally presumed also, because the act of affixing a manuscript signature to a document is universally recognised as signing.[18] Intention to sign is normally only disputed where the affixing of the signature has been procured by fraud, and in those cases the signatory bears the burden of displacing the presumption that he intended to sign. Intention to adopt the contents of the document is similarly presumed because it is general knowledge that affixing a manuscript signature to a document has that effect. In both cases, the burden of displacing the presumption is on the signatory.[19]

A difficulty arises, however, if the relevant law imposes specific requirements as to the *form* a signature must take. In the context of Internet communications, the thing to be signed, an electronic document, exists more as a matter of metaphysics[20] than as a physical object. For this reason it is very difficult for an

---

18 See eg *L'Estrange v F Graucob Ltd* [1934] 2 KB 394, 403 per Scrutton LJ.
19 See eg *Saunders v Anglia Building Society* [1971] AC 1004.
20 This is reflected in the jargon of the computer industry which often refers to 'logical' entities, meaning entities which are treated by the technology as a single item even though they may be stored on or transmitted via multiple hardware devices, or may exist in multiple copies.

electronic signature method to meet any physical requirement of form.[1] For example, some of the cases and statutes on physical world signatures appear to state that a signature must take the form of a mark on a document.[2]

A mark, in relation to a hard copy document, has the characteristics of visibility and physical alteration of the thing which is marked. None of the ways in which an electronic document communicated via the Internet may be 'signed' are capable of producing documents which exhibit these characteristics. A distinction must be made between the *information content* of a document and the *carrier* of that information. In the case of a physical signature of a hard copy document, the signature both makes a physical alteration to the carrier (ie ink is placed on the paper) and adds to the information content of the document. By contrast, an electronic signature only alters the information content of the document. Any change to the carrier is merely incidental, and is not linked inextricably to the document in the same way as a hard copy signature is linked to the writing.[3]

For example, the signatory's name or hieroglyph may be added to the document, either as a series of codes, such as ASCII, which represent the letters of the name, or as a digital image of the manuscript signature. In either event, all that is added to the document is a set of 1s and 0s. These can be made visible to the eye if the document is printed out or displayed on a screen, but because the document itself is either the set of binary integers (bits) which comprise it or the carrier on which they are stored,[4] neither the contents of the document nor the attached signature is visible. Furthermore, although attaching this type of 'signature' to the document makes a physical alteration to the storage medium on which the document is held,[5] that alteration takes place at the microscopic level[6] and is conceptually very different from the kind of physical alteration to the document envisaged in the case law – indeed, the bits which make up the document are not altered, merely added to. For this reason, merely adding a scanned image of a manuscript signature to a document will in many case not produce an adequate signature.

1   However, it is perfectly possible for the law to impose *logical* requirements of form. To date, the only requirement of form proposed for electronic signatures is that their validity should depend on compliance with particular technical standards. See e.g. Utah Digital Signature Rules (Rule 154-10 of the Utah Commerce, Corporations and Commercial Code) r. 301(4)(a); German Digital Signature Act (Signaturgesetz) § 14(4), German Digital Signature Ordinance (Signaturverordnung, made under § 19 Digital Signature Act 1997, in force 1 November 1997) § 16(6). Note, however, that logical requirements of form are imposed only in a minority of the current and proposed electronic signature legislation. The majority of that legislation defines the validity of the signature in terms of the functions performed by the signature method.
2   *Morton v Copeland* (1855) 16 CB 517, 535 per Maule J, who stated that signing 'does not necessarily mean writing a person's Christian and surname, but any mark which identifies it as the act of the party.'; *Re Cunningham's Goods* 29 LJPM & A 71. See also UCC § 1-201(39) (1992). For statutes see s. 1(4) UK Law of Property (Miscellaneous Provisions) Act 1989: 'In subsections (2) and (3) above 'sign', in relation to an instrument, includes making one's mark on the instrument and 'signature' is to be construed accordingly.'
3   It is for this reason that the question which is occasionally asked by those unfamiliar with computers, 'Can I place the digital document on a floppy disk and sign the disk's label?', is a nonsense. The digital document can be altered or substituted without any perceptible effect on the disk itself, and thus the *carrier* has been signed, but not the *document* itself.
4   See note 11 p 154.
5   This is true even if the document is contained only in the temporary memory (RAM) of a computer.
6   In the case of magnetic storage media such as disks or tapes, the magnetic polarity of particular areas of the medium is switched by moving electrons into new orbits.

However, if the relevant law defines the validity of a signature in terms of the evidential functions it achieves, an electronic document may be signed by the use of a mathematical function based on the document's data content.[7] This process can meet all the law's evidential requirements for signatures, but can only be considered as a logical (or metaphysical) mark in that it is in many respects functionally equivalent to a mark on paper, primarily because it cannot easily be altered without leaving some trace. The process can be undertaken in a way that will easily produce evidence of the intention to sign and authenticate the signatory and the electronic document's contents, but the result is if anything less visible than and equally as metaphysical as adding text or an image.[8]

6.1.2.2   *Electronic signature technology*

An electronic signature is produced by performing a mathematical function on the document, or part of it, which identifies the signatory and authenticates the contents of the document. To be an effective signature, the modified document must be producible only by the maker, and any attempt to change the content of the document must invalidate the signature. These modifications can be achieved through the use of encryption technology.

Because an electronic document is a string of 1s and 0s it can be treated as a series of numbers.[9] Encryption is carried out by performing a series of mathematical functions (an encryption algorithm) which has two inputs; the series of numbers which represents the document (the plaintext), and a *key*, which is itself a number. The result is a series of different numbers, the ciphertext. There are two distinct types of encryption algorithm:

- single key or symmetric encryption; and
- public key or asymmetric encryption.

Single key encryption uses the same key to encrypt and decrypt, and thus the key needs to be known to both the sender and the recipient of a document. Public key encryption uses two different keys, each of which will decrypt documents encrypted by the other key. This means that one key can be kept secret, while the other is made public. All effective electronic signature

---

7   Or, in some cases, on a mathematical derivative (for example a checksum or hash function) of the document as a whole. For further discussion see 6.1.2.2.

8   Although the document *is* altered (logically but not physically) in that it now consists of a different set of bits.

9   For encryption and decryption, documents are normally broken up into *blocks* of digits, each of which is treated as a number. DES encryption (see below) deals in 64-bit blocks, ie each 64 bits of the documents is encrypted separately. If the first word of a document in 8-bit ASCII were 'Signing' (eight letters including the space), the eight 8-bit ASCII codes:
01010011, 01101001, 01100111, 01101110, 01101001, 01101110, 01100111, 00100000
would be aggregated to produce a single 64-bit number, equivalent to decimal 6,010,448,901,615,530,000.

   Every mathematical encryption system uses this method of breaking up the message into large numbers on which the encryption function is performed, although the block size may differ. In order to speed up calculation for signature purposes, the encryption may be performed on a number derived from the document, in a hash function. If the document is altered its hash will also alter, and this digital signature can thus be used to prove that the current data content of the document is the same as that on which the digital signature function was performed.

techniques require the use of a 'one-way function'. This means that if a document, signed electronically by A, is sent to B, B must be able to decrypt the document or its signature element, but must *not* be able to re-encrypt it with A's key.

All encryption can be broken given sufficient time and computing resources. The effectiveness of encryption as a method of signing electronic documents relies on the fact that it is *computationally infeasible*[10] to break the encryption method, and thus become able to forge the signature, within a reasonable period of time.

SINGLE KEY ENCRYPTION

The most commonly used single key encryption system is the Data Encryption Standard (DES).[11] DES is a complicated form of encryption which is normally effected in hardware, but in essence it requires a 56-bit key which is common to sender and recipient and kept secret from all others. This key is used to scramble the document to such a degree that it is computationally infeasible to unscramble it without knowing the key. The fact that a document is DES encrypted is therefore extremely strong evidence that it could have emanated only from one or other of the keyholders. This, however, does not authenticate it fully as both parties have the key. Either could alter the contents of the document and then re-encrypt it. The alteration would be undetectable, and the court would still be left with two documents, each claimed to be authentic. However, techniques have been invented which enable one-way functions, encryption which can only have been performed by *one* of the parties, to be performed using DES and thus to create a digital signature of the electronic document.[12]

10 Computational infeasibility means that although the message can in theory be decoded, the amount of time this would take is so large that for practical purposes the encryption can be regarded as secure. For DES the average time required to break the code using a computer that checks one potential key per microsecond, operating 24 hours a day, is on average over 1,000 years, and for RSA encryption (see below) using a 200 digit key the average time required is longer than the expected lifetime of the universe – see Beckett *Introduction to Cryptology* (Oxford: Blackwell Scientific Publications, 1988) Chapter 9. Modern computers can process encryption keys much faster than this, so an evidentially effective electronic signature requires the use of a key length which will convince the court, on the balance of probabilities or beyond reasonable doubt as appropriate, that the encryption is unlikely to have been broken. Note that an increase of one digit in the key length doubles the average time required to break the encryption.
11 US National Bureau of Standards FIPS Publication 64 (1977), ANSI X3.92-1981. All the details of the algorithm are public, but because the key is kept secret it is computationally infeasible to discover that key within a realistic time, even with samples of plaintext and its equivalent encrypted text – see Longley and Shain *Data and Computer Security – dictionary of standard concepts and terms* (New York, 1987) p 94; Beckett *Introduction to Cryptology* (Oxford: Blackwell Scientific Publications, 1988) Chapter 16.
    A more recent single key encryption system which is gaining increased acceptance is IDEA, the International Data Encryption Algorithm, which addresses some of the weaknesses of DES – see Schneier *Applied Cryptography* (London: John Wiley & Sons, 1994) 11.9.
12 See the explanations of the Lamport-Diffie and the Rabin signatures in Longley and Shain *Data and Computer Security – dictionary of standard concepts and terms* (New York: Macmillan, 1987); Man Young Rhee *Cryptography and Secure Communication* (New York: McGraw Hill, 1994) section 10.

PUBLIC KEY ENCRYPTION

One of the best known public key encryption methods is RSA.[13] The two keys are formed of pairs of integers: k_s and n for the secret key, and k_p and n for the public key. The key pair k_p and n is made public. A document is encrypted by breaking its digital form into blocks, each of which is treated as a single number, raising each number to the power of k_s or k_p (depending on whether the secret or public key is being used) and then calculating the result modulus n.[14] The document is decrypted using the same algorithm with the other key pair.[15]

Thus:

(plaintext)^{ks} mod n Þ ciphertext
(ciphertext)^{kp} mod n Þ plaintext

The effective security of the RSA algorithm depends on mathematical proof of the fact that, because of the way k_p, k_s and n are derived, it is computationally infeasible to calculate k_s knowing only k_p and n.[16]

The RSA algorithm was originally devised to allow encrypted messages to be sent to the holder of the secret key, which only he would be able to decipher. However, because the algorithm is symmetrical it is also possible to encrypt a document using the sender's secret key k_s and decrypt it with the public key k_p. This is the method used to effect a digital signature.[17]

13 Named after its inventors – see RL Rivest, A Shamir and L Adleman 'A method of obtaining digital signatures and public key cryptosystems' (1978) 21 Communications of the ACM 120.
14 The remainder when n is successively subtracted from the result of the calculation as many times as is possible. The simplest example of modulus arithmetic is the clock: 14 = 2 mod 12, or 14.00 = 2 o'clock.
15 An algorithm of this kind is based on trapdoor one-way functions, so-called because once the data has passed through the 'trapdoor' of the algorithm it is not practically possible (ie computationally infeasible) to reverse the algorithm to recover the original data:
     'Trapdoor one-way functions, which are one way computable functions, provide the basis for public-key encryption. Easy to calculate in one direction, they are virtually impossible to reverse calculate without knowing the trapdoor or secret. One of the keys provides the forward direction of the function and the corresponding key provides the trapdoor to facilitate the reverse calculation.'
     (Davies, 'Encryption techniques' appendix to Reed & Davies *Digital Cash – the legal implications* (London: Centre for Commercial Law Studies, 1995)).
     See further Schneier *Applied Cryptography* (London: John Wiley & Sons, 1994) 12.4.
16 n is an extremely large number (200 digits or more) that is the product of two primes P1 and P2. To produce kp and ks the first step is to calculate f[n] = (P1-1)x(P2-1). kp is then chosen (conforming to certain specified criteria) and ks is calculated from the formula: kpxks = 1 mod f[n].
     To discover ks from the public information (n and kp) f[n] must be known. To find f[n] P1 and P2 must be discovered, but as these are both prime numbers, the only method is 'brute force', ie dividing n by every prime less than the square root of n.
     As a simple example, if P1=13 and P2=7 then n=91. f[n] is found by (13–1) x (7–1) = 72. If we choose kp=5, then ks=29 (5 x 29 = 145 = 1 mod 72). Encryption is thus plaintext5 mod 91, and decryption is ciphertext29 mod 91. This example is not secure because n can easily be factorised using pencil and paper as there are only five prime numbers less than the square root of 91.
17 The sender begins his document with some form of identification which he leaves unencrypted, and then encrypts the rest of the document using ks. When it is received, the recipient uses the identification to discover the sender's identity and decrypts the document using the sender's public key, kp. As only the sender could have encrypted the document, if both encrypted and plaintext versions are produced in court the judge can check the identity of the sender by decrypting the document and checking it against the plaintext version. This also authenticates the contents of the document, as if the recipient alters the contents he will not be able to re-encrypt the document so that it decrypts with kp.

In practice, encrypting an entire document using RSA is computationally expensive, and so a single key encryption system such as DES or IDEA is used to ensure that transmission of the document remains private, while RSA is used to make a digital signature by encrypting a smaller file which derives from the original document. Many encryption products which can be used to create digital signatures are now available, the best known of which is probably PGP.[18]

BIOMETRIC RECORDING

A method of signing an electronic document which, at first sight, appears very different from the encryption techniques described above, uses a pen attached to a digitising pad to record the physical signature of the maker of the document. This signature is normally displayed in a window on the screen of the computer to which the digitising pad is connected, and looks just like a traditional hard copy signature. However, the way in which this signature is attached to the document is very different from a physical signature.[19]

The data captured by the digitising pad is not merely the appearance of the signature but, more importantly, its biometric characteristics. These are, primarily, the speed and acceleration rates of the pen strokes used to make the signature and the occasions on which the pen is lifted from the digitising pad, together with the time taken to make each pen stroke. This biometric data is recorded,[20] and can be checked against the signatory's known biometric signature data, either in the possession of the recipient of a document or held by a trusted third party. If the biometric data matches sufficiently closely, the extremely low probability that some other person could have created the same signature data can be given in evidence to prove the identity of the signatory.

Additionally, it is necessary to attach the signature to the document. This is achieved by deriving a numerical identifier from the document, using a function such that the identifier is very unlikely to match any other document, and encrypting that number together with the biometric signature data. The evidential value of this process can be assessed by calculating:

- the probability that some person other than the alleged signatory could have created the biometric signature data, and some document other than that alleged to be signed could have produced the same numerical identifier; and
- the probability that the encryption algorithm could have been 'cracked', thus allowing a genuine set of biometric data from one document to be linked to a numerical identifier from another.

Signature metrics are not the only form of biometric data which can be used to effect a signature. Other data such as fingerprints or retina prints can be collected in digital form and attached to the document in identical ways.[1]

18 For more information on PGP see Zimmerman *PGP™ User's Guide* (Boston: MIT Press, 1995); Garfinkel *PGP: Pretty Good Privacy* (New York: O'Reilly & Associates, 1994).
19 The description of the technology in this section is based on the published details of the PenOp system, but other systems of biometric recording are likely to operate in a similar manner. See Wright 'Alternatives for Signing Electronic Documents' [1995] 11 Computer Law & Security Report 136.
20 The physical appearance of the signature is the least important element in authentication, as it can be reproduced by scanning or copying, and to reduce the quantity of information stored and processed this part of the data may be discarded.
 1 The collection of biometric data raises many additional issues, in particular issues relating to human rights. See Prins 'Biometric Technology Law' [1998] 14 Computer Law & Security Report 159.

USING ENCRYPTION TO MAKE AN ELECTRONIC SIGNATURE

American Bar Association *Digital Signature Guidelines* **(ABA: Chicago 1996) p. 9, reprinted by permission.**

HOW DIGITAL SIGNATURE TECHNOLOGY WORKS

Digital signatures are created and verified by cryptography, the branch of applied mathematics that concerns itself with transforming messages into seemingly unintelligible forms and back again. Digital signatures use what is known as 'public key cryptography', which employs an algorithm using two different but mathematically related 'keys'; one for creating a digital signature or transforming data into a seemingly unintelligible form, and another key for verifying a digital signature or returning the message to its original form.[2] Computer equipment and software utilizing two such keys are often collectively termed an 'asymmetric cryptosystem'.

The complementary keys of an asymmetric cryptosystem for digital signatures are arbitrarily termed the private key, which is known only to the signer[3] and used to create the digital signature, and the public key, which is ordinarily more widely known and is used by a relying party to verify the digital signature. If many people need to verify the signer's digital signatures, the public key must be available or distributed to all of them, perhaps by publication in an on-line repository or directory where it is easily accessible. Although the keys[4] of the pair are mathematically related, if the asymmetric cryptosystem has been designed and implemented securely[5] it is 'computationally infeasible'[6] to derive the private key from knowledge of the public key. Thus, although many people may know the public key of a given signer and use it to verify that signer's signatures, they cannot discover that signer's private key and use it to forge digital signatures. This is sometimes referred to as the principle of 'irreversibility'.

Another fundamental process, termed a 'hash function', is used in both creating and verifying a digital signature. A hash function is an algorithm which creates a digital representation or 'fingerprint' in the form of a 'hash value' or 'hash result' of a standard

2   In contrast with public key cryptography, 'conventional', 'single key' or 'symmetric cryptography' uses the same single key to 'encrypt' 'plaintext' into 'ciphertext,' and to 'decrypt' it from ciphertext back to plaintext.

3   Of course, the holder of the private key may choose to divulge it, or may lose control of it (often called 'compromise'), and thereby make forgery possible. The Guidelines seek to address this problem in two ways, (1) by requiring a subscriber, who holds the private key, to use a degree of care in its safekeeping, and (2) enabling the subscriber to disassociate himself from the key by temporarily suspending or permanently revoking his certificate and publishing these actions in a 'certificate revocation list', or 'CRL'. A variety of methods are available for securing the private key.

   The safer methods store the private key in a 'cryptographic token' (one example is a 'smart card') which executes the signature program within an internal microprocessing chip, so that the private key is never divulged outside the token and does not pass into the main memory or processor of the signer's computer. The signer must typically present to the token some authenticating information, such as a password, pass phrase, or personal identification number, for the token to run a process requiring access to the private key. In addition, this token must be physically produced, and biometric authentication such as fingerprints or retinal scan can assure the physical presence of the token's authorized holder. There are also software-based schemes for protecting the security of the private key, generally less secure than hardware schemes, but providing adequate security for many types of applications. *See generally* Schneier 'Applied Cryptography' (1994), at § 2.7, 41–44.

4   Many cryptographic systems will function securely only if the keys are lengthy and complex, too lengthy and complex for a person to easily remember or use.

5   *See generally* Warwick Ford 'Computer Communications Security: principles, standard protocols & techniques' 29-30 (1994), at 71–75; Charlie Kaufman, Radia Perlman and Mike Speciner 'Network Security: private communication in a public world' 48-56 (1995).

6   'Computationally infeasible' is a relative concept based on the value of the data protected, the computing overhead required to protect it, the length of time it needs to be protected, and the cost and time required to attack the data, with such factors assessed both currently and in the light of future technological advance. *See generally* Schneier 'Applied Cryptography' (1994), at § 7.5, 166–167.

length which is usually much smaller than the message but nevertheless substantially unique to it.[7] Any change to the message invariably produces a different hash result when the same hash function is used. In the case of a secure hash function, sometimes termed a 'one-way hash function', it is computationally infeasible[8] to derive the original message from knowledge of its hash value. Hash functions therefore enable the software for creating digital signatures to operate on smaller and predictable amounts of data, while still providing robust evidentiary correlation to the original message content, thereby efficiently providing assurance that there has been no modification of the message since it was digitally signed.

Thus, use of digital signatures usually involves two processes, one performed by the signer and the other by the receiver of the digital signature:

- Digital signature creation uses a hash result derived from and unique to both the signed message and a given private key. For the hash result to be secure, there must be only a negligible possibility that the same digital signature could be created by the combination of any other message or private key.
- Digital signature verification is the process of checking the digital signature by reference to the original message and a given public key, thereby determining whether the digital signature was created for that same message using the private key that corresponds to the referenced public key . . .

Verification of a digital signature . . . is accomplished by computing a new hash result of the original message by means of the same hash function used to create the digital signature. Then, using the public key and the new hash result, the verifier checks: (1) whether the digital signature was created using the corresponding private key; and (2) whether the newly computed hash result matches the original hash result which was transformed into the digital signature during the signing process. The verification software will confirm the digital signature as 'verified' if: (1) the signer's private key was used to digitally sign the message, which is known to be the case if the signer's public key was used to verify the signature because the signer's public key will verify only a digital signature created with the signer's private key;[9] and (2) the message was unaltered, which is known to be the case if the hash result computed by the verifier is identical to the hash result extracted from the digital signature during the verification process.

Various asymmetric cryptosystems create and verify digital signatures using different algorithms and procedures, but share this overall operational pattern.

The processes of creating a digital signature and verifying it accomplish the essential effects desired of a signature for many legal purposes:

- Signer authentication: If a public and private key pair is associated with an identified signer, the digital signature attributes the message to the signer. The digital signature cannot be forged, unless the signer loses control of the private key (a 'compromise' of the private key), such as by divulging it or losing the media or device in which it is contained.
- Message authentication: The digital signature also identifies the signed message, typically with far greater certainty and precision than paper signatures. Verification reveals any tampering, since the comparison of the hash results (one made at signing and the other made at verifying) shows whether the message is the same as when signed.

7   *See generally* Warwick Ford 'Computer Communications Security: principles, standard protocols & techniques' 29–30 (1994) at 75–84; Charlie Kaufman, Radia Perlman and Mike Speciner 'Network Security: private communication in a public world' 48–56, at 101–127; Nechvatal 'Public Key Cryptography' in Gustavas Simmons (ed.) *Comtemporary Cryptology: the science of information integrity* (1991) 179, 199–202; Schneier 'Applied Cryptography' (1994), §§ 18.1–18.14, 429–459.

8   'Because hash functions are typically many-to-one, we cannot use them to determine with certainty that the two [input] strings are equal, but we can use them to get a reasonable assurance of accuracy.' Schneier 'Applied Cryptography' (1994) at § 2.4, 30–31. It is extremely improbable that two messages will produce the same hash result. *See* Charlie Kaufman, Radia Perlman and Mike Speciner 'Network Security: private communication in a public world' 48-56, at 102.

9   Because of the mathematical relationship between the public and private keys which correspond to each other as a key pair. Schneier 'Applied Cryptography' (1994) at § 2.6, 34–41.

- Affirmative act: Creating a digital signature requires the signer to use the signer's private key. This act can perform the 'ceremonial' function of alerting the signer to the fact that the signer is consummating a transaction with legal consequences.[10]
- Efficiency: The processes of creating and verifying a digital signature provide a high level of assurance that the digital signature is genuinely the signer's. As with the case of modern electronic data interchange ('EDI') the creation and verification processes are capable of complete automation (sometimes referred to as 'machinable'), with human interaction required on an exception basis only. Compared to paper methods such as checking specimen signature cards – methods so tedious and labor-intensive that they are rarely actually used in practice – digital signatures yield a high degree of assurance without adding greatly to the resources required for processing.

6.1.2.3   How electronic signatures meet the law's functional requirements

EVIDENCE OF THE SIGNATORY'S IDENTITY

An electronic signature of the kind described above cannot, by itself, provide sufficient evidence of the signatory's identity. To establish this matter, further evidence is required which links the signature key or other signature device to the signatory himself. There is no theoretical reason why this link should not be proved, if the electronic signature is disputed, by extrinsic evidence of the kind used to establish identity for manuscript signatures.[11]

However, in practice the recipient of an electronically signed document wishes to be able to rely on the signature without needing to collect such evidence for use in the unlikely event that the signature is disputed. For this reason, most electronic signatures used for Internet communications are likely to be accompanied by an ID Certificate issued by a Certification Authority. The Certification Authority takes traditional evidence of identity, eg by examining passports, and (in the case of public key encryption signatures) checks that signatures effected with the signatory's secret key are verifiable using the public key. Once the Certification Authority is satisfied as to the signatory's identity, it issues an ID Certificate which includes, inter alia, a certification of the signatory's identity and of his public key.[12] This certificate may be used by the recipient to

---

10 If the person 'signing' the message is not a human being but a device under the control of a human being as permitted by these Guidelines, this ceremonial function may be undermined.
11 In the case of electronic signatures, the extrinsic evidence required would be: (a) that the signature key or its equivalent was in the possession of the alleged signatory or his authorised agent; (b) that the use of that signature key produces the electronic signature affixed to the document in question; and (c) that the mathematical probability that some alternative key in the possession of a third party could have created the same signature is sufficiently low to convince the court that the signature was in fact affixed by the signatory.
    In the case of the public key encryption systems discussed at 6.1.2.2, proof that the signature decrypts with the signatory's public key should be sufficient if that public key can reliably be attributed to the signatory.
12 Of course, to operate effectively this certificate must be processable automatically without human intervention. Thus, the certificate is authenticated not in a traditional paper-based way but by the Certification Authority's electronic signature. This signature will be certified by a different Certification Authority, and that certificate will also be signed electronically. The theoretical circularity of this process is obviated in practice because a recipient will have identified some Certification Authority (eg his bank) whose electronic signature has been authenticated by some other means, and which is therefore trustworthy. Any other Certification Authority certified by *that* Certification Authority is also trustworthy, at least as to its identity, and so on. The user gradually builds up a database of authenticated electronic signatures, which reduces the amount of checking required. See further Chapter 5.3.3.

prove the signatory's identity. These issues have been examined in depth in Chapter 5.

EVIDENCE OF INTENTION TO SIGN AND ADOPTION OF CONTENTS

Once identity has been proved, the very fact that an electronic signature has been affixed to a document should raise the same presumptions as for manuscript signatures, ie that the signatory intended to sign the document and thereby adopt its contents. There is one difference, however. In the case of a manuscript signature, the signatory has to be present in person and must have the document to be signed in front of him. Electronic signature technology is a little different. There are essentially two options:[13]

- the signature is effected by selecting from an on-screen menu or button, with the signature key stored on the signatory's computer; or
- the signature key is stored on a physical token, such as a smart card, which needs to be present before the signature software can affix the signature.

In either case, a third party who had access to the computer or to the storage device would be able to make the signature. For this reason, an electronic signature should be considered as more closely analogous to a rubber stamp signature. The party who is seeking to rely on the validity of the signature may need to adduce extrinsic evidence that the signature was applied with the authority of the signatory[14] until the use of electronic signatures becomes so common that the courts are prepared to presume that a third party who is given access to the signature technology has been authorised by the signatory to sign on his behalf, or unless a statute introduces a presumption as to the identity of the signatory.[15] In cases where an electronic signature which has previously been acknowledged by the signatory is effected by an unauthorised third party, however, the apparent signatory will be estopped from denying that it was his signature.[16]

The objection that an electronic signature fails to meet the evidential requirements because a successful forgery cannot be detected is easily dismissed by pointing out that no such requirement is imposed for manuscript signatures. Indeed, signatures in pencil have been held valid for such important commercial documents as bills of exchange[17] and guarantees.[18] In fact, as the discussion of electronic signature technologies in part 6.1.2.2 above demonstrates, electronic signatures are normally many orders of magnitude harder to forge than manuscript signatures. Thus, the only function which electronic signatures cannot provide is that of making a mark on a document, a function which is unnecessary in the digital environment.

---

13 A third option, that the signatory remembers the key and types it in to the software application which produces the signature, is not practicable. Signature keys are too lengthy to be remembered reliably or keyed in without errors.

14 See eg *Jenkins v Gaisford and Thring, Re Jenkins' Goods* (1863) 3 Sw & Tr 93.

15 See 6.1.2.4.

16 *Brown v Westminster Bank Ltd* [1964] 2 Lloyd's Rep. 187.

17 *Geary v Physic* (1826) 5 B & C 234.

18 *Lucas v James* (1849) 7 Hare 410.

SEALS AS SIGNATURES

An interesting side-effect of the challenge posed by electronic signatures is that the question of whether a seal can function as a signature becomes relevant. The reason for this is that many of the electronic signature technologies require the signatory to use a numerical key to produce the signature (see 6.1.2.2 above). The smallest useful keys are a minimum of 56 bits in length, offering a range of numbers between approximately 563,000,000,000,000 and 72,000,000,000,000,000 in decimal notation. These keys are too small for adequate security, however, and 128 bit or larger keys are more desirable. Numbers of this size are not easily memorable nor easily keyed in without error, and so the keys are normally stored on some physical device, such as a magnetic disk or a smart card.

Signature is therefore performed by application of the physical device to the electronic document. This is a close, perhaps an exact, analogy to the application of a personal seal to a paper document. Indeed, the German Digital Signatures Act provides:

> For the purposes of this Act 'digital signature' shall mean a seal affixed to digital data which is generated by a private signature key and establishes the owner of the signature key and the integrity of the data with the help of an associated public key provided with a signature key certificate of a certification authority . . .[19]

In England, it has been held that seals are not acceptable on wills because they are too easy to forge:

> For any one may put a seal; no particular evidence arises from that seal: common seals are alike, and one man's may be like another's; no certainty or guard therefor arises from thence.[20]

There do not appear to be any cases, however, which deny the validity of seals as signature methods for documents which are not deeds.[1] It seems probable, therefore, that the courts will recognise electronic seals as producing valid signatures if the particular use of the technology achieves the necessary evidential functions.

6.1.2.4   *Legislative recognition of electronic signatures*

Because of the uncertainties as to whether courts would apply the principles outlined above in a consistent manner, there have been a number of legislative initiatives designed to validate the use of electronic signatures. The first of these was the Utah Digital Signatures Act of 1996, which was influenced by the discussions leading to the UNCITRAL Model Law on Electronic Commerce, also of 1996. At the time of writing there are over 100 laws or proposals for laws on this topic.

At present, three clear divisions can be seen in these instruments:[2]

---

19   German Digital Signature Act (Signaturgesetz) 1997 §2(1).
20   *Grayson v Atkinson* (1752) 2 Ves Sen 454, 459 per Hardwicke LC, reversing his previous opinion in *Gryle v Gryle* (1741) 2 Atk 176. See also *Smith v Evans* (1751) 1 Wils 313; *Ellis v Smith* (1754) 1 Ves 11 at p 13 per Willes CJ and p 15 per Sir John Strange MR.
  1   The execution of a deed requires both sealing and a signature or mark – *Halsbury's Laws of England* (4th) Vol 12, para 1328.
  2   Credit for identifying this classification is due to Mr Juan Avellan, PhD researcher at the Information Technology Law Unit, Centre for Commercial Law Studies, Queen Mary and Westfield College London.

- Laws which validate the use of electronic signatures in a closed group of users, such as systems for transferring medical data between doctors, hospitals and insurers.[3] These laws are of no relevance to open Internet communications, and will not be considered further. This category includes EDI transactions, for which contract is often a potentially suitable mechanism for dealing with signature issues.[4]
- Laws which define validity solely in terms of the functions achieved by an electronic signature method.
- Laws which define validity by reference to the use of ID Certificates within the electronic signature method. These laws may be technology-neutral, in the sense that they do not prescribe a particular technical standard which must be adopted but merely describe the requirements which a certificate and its issuing Certification Authority must meet. Some laws, however, mandate the use of particular technical standards.[5]

FUNCTIONAL DEFINITIONS OF VALIDITY

The starting point for most electronic signature laws is art 7(1) of the UNCITRAL Model Law on Electronic Commerce 1996, which provides:

> Where the law requires a signature of a person, that requirement is met in relation to a data message if:
>
> (a) a method is used to identify that person and to indicate that person's approval of the information contained in the data message; and
>
> (b) that method is as reliable as was appropriate for the purpose for which the data message was generated or communicated, in the light of all the circumstances, including any relevant agreement.

Further work is being undertaken by UNCITRAL with the aim of producing Uniform Rules on Electronic Signatures, but at the time of writing the working party has not determined whether to maintain the functional approach of the Model Law or to adopt Rules based on ID Certificates.[6]

In the meantime, a number of jurisdictions have introduced legislation. A few have taken a purist attitude, defining the functional requirements for an electronic signature but leaving it to the courts to determine whether those requirements are met on a case-by-case basis.[7] More recently, however, the trend has been towards a two-tier approach to this issue; electronic signatures which meet the functional requirements are validated, but the law also makes provision for a greater level of legal acceptability for those signatures which are based on

3   Eg Connecticut Regulations for Electronic Signatures on Medical Records. Connecticut General Statutes 1995 Title-19a Chapter-368a, Sec 19a-25a.
4   See European Commission Recommendation of 19 October 1994 relating to the legal aspects of electronic data interchange (94/820/EC) OJ L 338 1994, ANNEX 1: European Model EDI Agreement art 3(1).
5   Eg Utah Digital Signature Rules (Rule 154-10 of the Utah Commerce, Corporations and Commercial Code) r 301(4)(a); German Digital Signature Act (Signaturgesetz) § 14(4), German Digital Signature Ordinance (Signaturverordnung, made under § 19 Digital Signature Act 1997, in force 1 November 1997) § 16(6).
6   See 'Draft Uniform Rules on Electronic Signatures – Note by the Secretariat', A/CN.9/WG.IV/WP.79, 23 November 1998 prepared for the Thirty-fourth session of the Working Group on Electronic Commerce, Vienna, 8–19 February 1999.
7   Australian Electronic Transactions Act 1999, s 10(1); UK Electronic Communications Bill 1999, cl 7; Massachusetts Electronic Records and Signatures Bill (April 14 1998 draft) § 4; Oklahoma Electronic Records and Signature Act 1998, Oklahoma Statutes Title 15 §§ 962(4), 965.

ID Certificates. This two-tier approach is demonstrated particularly clearly in the Singapore Electronic Transactions Act 1998 and the EU Directive on electronic signatures.

Singapore Electronic Transactions Act 1998
ELECTRONIC SIGNATURES

8. (1) Where a rule of law requires a signature, or provides for certain consequences if a document is not signed, an electronic signature[8] satisfies that rule of law.
    (2) An electronic signature may be proved in any manner, including by showing that a procedure existed by which it is necessary for a party, in order to proceed further with a transaction, to have executed a symbol or security procedure for the purpose of verifying that an electronic record is that of such party.

SECURE ELECTRONIC SIGNATURE

17. If, through the application of a prescribed security procedure or a commercially reasonable security procedure agreed to by the parties involved, it can be verified that an electronic signature was, at the time it was made –
    a. unique to the person using it;
    b. capable of identifying such person;
    c. created in a manner or using a means under the sole control of the person using it; and
    d. linked to the electronic record to which it relates in a manner such that if the record was changed the electronic signature would be invalidated,
    such signature shall be treated as a secure electronic signature.

Secure electronic signatures benefit from a number of legal presumptions which are examined below.

The EU Directive[9] takes a somewhat more rigorous approach, imposing requirements similar to those for secure electronic signatures under the Singapore legislation as its basic test for validity. Electronic signatures are defined by art 2 as follows:

1. 'electronic signature' means data in electronic form which are attached to or logically associated with other electronic data and which serve as a method of authentication;
2. 'advanced electronic signature' means an electronic signature which meets the following requirements:
    (a) it is uniquely linked to the signatory;
    (b) it is capable of identifying the signatory;
    (c) it is created using means that the signatory can maintain under his sole control; and
    (d) it is linked to the data to which it relates in such a manner that any subsequent change of the data is detectable.

The draft Directive proposes a two-tier system of electronic signatures:[10]

*   simple electronic signatures, which have merely to meet the definition in art 2(1); and

---

8 Defined in s 2: '"electronic signature" means any letters, characters, numbers or other symbols in digital form attached to or logically associated with an electronic record, and executed or adopted with the intention of authenticating or approving the electronic record'.
9 *Directive 1999/93/EC on a Community framework for electronic signatures* OJ L 13 p 12, 19 January 2000.
10 The terminology of 'simple' and 'certified' signatures is not found in the Directive, but is adopted here for ease of reference.

- certified advanced electronic signatures, where the identity of the signatory is confirmed by a certificate issued by an appropriate third party[11] and complying with other provisions of the Directive (a 'qualified certificate')[12] and the certificate is created by means of a secure-signature-creation device.[13]

The distinction is important because the main purpose of the draft Directive is not to make provision for the validity of electronic signatures, but to ensure that national laws do not impose barriers to the free flow of certification services in the European Community.

Article 5 lays down the circumstances in which electronic signatures are to be valid, enforceable and legally effective. For simple electronic signatures its provisions are entirely negative – Member States are to ensure that signatures of this type are not denied validity, enforceability and effectiveness solely on the grounds that they are in electronic form or are not certified.[14] However, Member States are free to refuse to recognise electronic signatures for any other reason. Certified advanced electronic signatures receive more favourable treatment, as explained in the next section.

VALIDITY BASED ON IDENTITY CERTIFICATION

Other legislative initiatives make validity conditional on the use of an ID Certificate in the electronic signature method or, in the case of two-tier systems, grant additional advantages to certified electronic signatures. The Utah Act was the first example of such legislation:

Utah Digital Signature Act 1996 (Utah Code § 46-3)

46-3-401. SATISFACTION OF SIGNATURE REQUIREMENTS.

(1) Where a rule of law requires a signature, or provides for certain consequences in the absence of a signature, that rule is satisfied by a digital signature if:
  (a) that digital signature is verified by reference to the public key listed in a valid certificate issued by a licensed certification authority;
  (b) that digital signature was affixed by the signer with the intention of signing the message; and
  (c) the recipient has no knowledge or notice that the signer either:
    (i) breached a duty as a subscriber; or
    (ii) does not rightfully hold the private key used to affix the digital signature.
(2) Nothing in this chapter precludes any symbol from being valid as a signature under other applicable law, including Uniform Commercial Code, Subsection 70A-1-201(39).

It should be noted that under the Utah system, licensing of the Certification Authority is a prerequisite for signature validity. However, the essential point is the use of the ID Certificate, not the licensing per se, and many laws of this

11 A 'certification service provider', defined in art 2(11), ie a Certification Authority (see Chapter 5).
12 Article 2(10). The certificate must fulfil the requirements of Annex I, and it must be issued by a certification-service-provider who meets the requirements of Annex II.
13 Under art 2(6) such a device must meet the requirements of Annex III.
14 Article 5(2).

type are based on the American Bar Association Guidelines[15] which do not mandate licensing.[16]

The Singapore Electronic Transactions Act introduces a further concept of 'secure digital signature', which is by definition a secure electronic signature and thus receives the benefit of the presumptions explained below. It does not mandate licensing of the Certification Authority per se, but the wording of s 20(b) clearly indicates that in most cases licensing will be required.

Singapore Electronic Transactions Act 1998
SECURE DIGITAL SIGNATURE

20. When any portion of an electronic record is signed with a digital signature, the digital signature shall be treated as a secure electronic signature with respect to such portion of the record, if –
   a. the digital signature was created during the operational period of a valid certificate and is verified by reference to the public key listed in such certificate; and
   b. the certificate is considered trustworthy, in that it is an accurate binding of a public key to a person's identity because –
      i. the certificate was issued by a licensed certification authority operating in compliance with the regulations made under section 42;
      ii. the certificate was issued by a certification authority outside Singapore recognised for this purpose by the Controller pursuant to regulations made under section 46;
      iii. the certificate was issued by a department or ministry of the Government, an organ of State or a statutory corporation approved by the Minister to act as a certification authority on such conditions as he may by regulations impose or specify; or
      iv. the parties have expressly agreed between themselves (sender and recipient) to use digital signatures as a security procedure, and the digital signature was properly verified by reference to the sender's public key.

By contrast, the EU Directive is specifically drafted in such a way that ID Certificates from unlicensed Certification Authorities can still be capable of producing a certificated signature. Under art 5(1) an electronic signature will receive the benefit of a higher level of validity if it is based on a qualified certificate which was created using a secure-signature-creation device. To be a qualified certificate, the certificate must link the signature verification data[17] used to the signatory and confirm his identity,[18] and be issued by a certification-

---

15 American Bar Association Digital Signature Guidelines (Chicago: ABA, 1996).
16 American Bar Association Digital Signature Guidelines (Chicago: ABA, 1996) guideline 5.2: 'Satisfaction of signature requirements. Where a rule of law requires a signature, or provides for certain consequences in the absence of a signature, that rule is satisfied by a digital signature which is (1) affixed by the signer with the intention of signing the message, and (2) verified by reference to the public key listed in a valid certificate.'
17 Defined in art 2(7). This definition would encompass any of the electronic signature methods discussed in this chapter.
18 Article 2(9).

service-provider who meets the requirements of Annex II.[19] Additionally, the certificate itself must comply with Annex I.[20]

To fulfill the requirements of Annex II, the certification-service-provider must, in essence, be a fit and proper person to provide such services. The relevant criteria are that the provider should operate a secure, efficient and properly run business; take appropriate steps to identify signatories to whom a certificate is issued; employ suitably qualified personnel and use trustworthy computer systems and products; take measures against forgery and to preserve the confidentiality of signature keys; have sufficient financial resources; maintain proper records; not store the signatory's signature-creation data; provide proper information about the terms and conditions on which certificates are issued; and use trustworthy systems to store certificates.[1] In practice, compliance with Annex II is likely to be demonstrated by acquiring a licence from a European accreditation authority or one recognised[2] by the relevant EU body.

The effect of meeting these requirements is that the electronic signature is treated as equivalent to a manuscript signature. Article 5(1) provides that such signatures:

(a) satisfy the legal requirements of a signature in relation to data in electronic form in the same manner as a hand-written signature satisfies those requirements in relation to paper-based data; and
(b) are admissible as evidence in legal proceedings.

LEGAL PRESUMPTIONS

The purpose of laws validating electronic signatures would be defeated if the person relying on an electronic signature needed to produce technical evidence from which the court could make its own assessment of validity. For this reason, most laws introduce a number of presumptions about an electronic signature which meets the law's requirements. It will always be possible for the other party to adduce evidence to displace these presumptions if there has in fact been some technical failure resulting in a 'forgery' or other defect in the signature. The most important of these presumptions are:

•   that the apparent signatory did in fact make the electronic signature;[3]

---

19 Article 2(10).
20 Which states: 'Qualified certificates must contain: (a) an indication that the certificate is issued as a qualified certificate; (b) the identification of the certification-service-provider and the State in which it is established; (c) the name of the signatory or a pseudonym, which shall be identified as such; (d) provision for a specific attribute of the signatory to be included if relevant, depending on the purpose for which the certificate is intended; (e) signature-verification data which correspond to signature-creation data under the control of the signatory; (f) an indication of the beginning and end of the period of validity of the certificate; (g) the identity code of the certificate; (h) the advanced electronic signature of the certification-service-provider issuing it; (i) limitations on the scope of use of the certificate, if applicable; and (j) limits on the value of transactions for which the certificate can be used, if applicable.'
1   These requirements, with minor differences to reflect the difference nature of the services provided, are very similar to those used to determine whether a banking licence should be granted – see Banking Act 1987, Sch 3 and *Statement of Principles: Banking Act 1987, Banking Co-ordination (Second Council Directive) Regulations 1992* (London: Bank of England, 1993), made under s 16 of the Banking Act.
2   The principles and procedures for recognition are set out in Directive 1999/93/EC on a Community framework for electronic signatures, OJ L 13 p 12, 19 January 2000, art 7.
3   Singapore Electronic Transactions Act 1998, s 18(2)(a).

- that the apparent signatory intended to sign and adopt the contents of the document;[4]
- that the signed document has not been altered since the time of signature;[5]
- that the information in the ID Certificate is accurate[6] and the holder's public key in fact belongs to that holder;[7] and
- that the ID Certificate was issued by the Certification Authority whose electronic signature is contained in the certificate.[8]

The Australian Electronic Transactions Act 1999 simply provides that a signature which complies with s 10 meets any Commonwealth requirement for a signature, while the UK Electronic Communications Act 2000, s 7 simply states that such a signature is admissible in evidence as to the authenticity or integrity of a communication.[9]

6.1.2.5　*The future of electronic signature law*

The current trend in laws and legislative proposals is to link the question of signature validity with certification of identity. It seems likely that, as commercial activity on the Internet increases, businesses will increasingly require their customers to identify themselves through ID Certificates, and will demand electronic signatures which are validated by those certificates. Use of uncertificated electronic signatures will probably be confined to non-commercial transactions; as these will rarely have legal consequences, the evidential issues of proving signatory identity will be unlikely to trouble the courts excessively.

There is also a clear trend towards introducing accreditation schemes for certification authorities, for the reasons explained in Chapter 5. This trend will be supported by the advantages of electronic signatures supported by a certificate from an accredited Certification Authority. Such signatures will avoid the difficulties inherent in proving the effectiveness of the signature method in achieving the required evidential functions, and will also benefit from reciprocal recognition in those jurisdictions which make the use of accredited Certification Authorities compulsory as a condition of electronic signature validation.

4　Singapore Electronic Transactions Act 1998, s 18(2)(b); Utah Digital Signature Act 1996 (Utah Code § 46-3) § 406(3)(b).

5　American Bar Association Digital Signature Guidelines (Chicago: ABA, 1996) guideline 5.6(3); Singapore Electronic Transactions Act 1998, s 18(1).

6　American Bar Association Digital Signature Guidelines (Chicago: ABA, 1996) guideline 5.6(1); Singapore Electronic Transactions Act 1998, s 21; Utah Digital Signature Act 1996 (Utah Code § 46-3) § 406(2).

7　American Bar Association Digital Signature Guidelines (Chicago: ABA, 1996) guideline 5.6(2); Utah Digital Signature Act 1996 (Utah Code § 46-3) § 406(3)(a).

Association Digital Signature Guidelines (Chicago: ABA, 1996) guideline 5.6(4); Signature Act 1996 (Utah Code § 46-3) § 406(1).

h law this makes it de facto equivalent to a manuscript signature, as a signature h law is primarily an evidential matter only – see Reed *Digital Information Law: ments and requirements of form* (London: Centre for Commercial Law Studies, 1996)

6.1.3   Writing

It is quite common for the law to provide that a particular transaction must be undertaken in written form or evidenced in writing. Normally the additional requirement that the writing be signed is imposed. The reasons why the formality of writing is required appear, in general, to be intended to secure particularly strong evidence of the agreement of the parties. Thus, a signed writing is commonly required for transactions in land,[10] negotiable instruments which, in addition to their existence as documents, also represent property rights in goods or money,[11] and transactions which impose onerous obligations on a consumer.[12] Additionally, signed writings are often required to validate administrative action, particularly where that action affects a person's liberty or property rights.[13]

It seems generally to be agreed that there is, at best, uncertainty whether an electronic record is not capable of amounting to writing:

> some *formal requirements* prevent contracts from being concluded electronically, or result in a considerable lack of legal certainty as to their lawfulness or validity. This may take the form of requirements which obviously rule out electronic contracts, (for example, a requirement that a contract be drawn up on paper), or more frequently, difficulty arising from the interpretation to be given to requirements such as 'in writing' (i.e. on paper), 'in a durable medium', 'an original'.[14]

For this reason, the position has been clarified in some jurisdictions. Two approaches seem to be adopted:

- Electronic records may simply be declared to be writings for certain purposes. This may apply to all electronic records,[15] or only to those which allow their information content to be retrieved with some degree of reliability.[16]
- Alternatively, only those electronic records whose unaltered state is guaranteed via a digital signature may be treated as writing. Thus, the Utah Digital Signature Act 1996 § 403 provides:

---

10   See eg UK Law of Property (Miscellaneous Provisions) Act 1989, s 2.

11   See eg UN Convention on International Bills of Exchange and International Promissory Notes (1988) art 3.

12   In these cases, the signed writing is evidence that the consumer received actual notice of the onerous terms and agreed to them – see Slawson 'Standard Form Contracts and Democratic Control of Lawmaking Power' (1971) 84 Harv L Rev 529. Typical examples which might be applicable in the Internet environment are consumer credit transactions (eg SA law?) and mail order sales (eg Portuguese Mail Order Act, art 10(3) for transactions exceeding PTE 20,000 in value).

13   Eg arrest warrants and summonses (eg UK Magistrates' Court Rules 1968, rr 78, 81); warrants to enter land (eg UK Food Safety Act 1990, s 32).

14   *Commission proposal for a European Parliament and Council directive on certain legal aspects of electronic commerce in the internal market* COM (1998) 586 final, 98/0325 (COD), 18 November 1998, p 11.

15   US Federal Rules of Evidence rule 1001: '(1) Writings and recordings. 'Writings' and 'recordings' consist of letters, words, or numbers, or their equivalent, set down by handwriting, typewriting, printing, photostating, photographing, magnetic impulse, mechanical or electronic recording, or other form of data compilation.'

16   Singapore Electronic Transactions Act 1998, s 7: 'Where a rule of law requires information to be written, in writing, to be presented in writing or provides for certain consequences if it is not, an electronic record satisfies that rule of law if the information contained therein is accessible so as to be usable for subsequent reference.'

(1) A message is as valid, enforceable, and effective as if it had been written on paper, if it:
   (a) bears in its entirety a digital signature; and
   (b) that digital signature is verified by the public key listed in a certificate which:
      (i) was issued by a licensed certification authority; and
      (ii) was valid at the time the digital signature was created.
(2) Nothing in this chapter precludes any message, document, or record from being considered written or in writing under other applicable state law.

Digital (electronic) signatures are discussed at 6.1.2 above, and Certification Authorities in Chapter 5.

The difference between these two approaches appears to reside in differing views of the nature of hard copy writing. If that type of writing is seen as permanent and unalterable, and for this reason the primary method of evidencing a transaction, the second approach is adopted. Where physical writing is seen merely as one of several ways in which information can be recorded, the first approach makes more sense.

What is clear is that, as the Internet comes to play a greater part in formal as well as informal communications, there will be a need to make electronic records as legally acceptable as physical writing. How this is achieved will depend very much on the reliability of the technology and how it is perceived by its users. If electronic records are seen as inherently insecure, so that electronic signature technology becomes widely used as a method of ensuring accuracy and attributability, it is probable that only signed electronic records will be equated with writing. If security is not perceived as a particular problem, unsigned records will be equated with writing and their reliability as evidence evaluated on a case-by-case basis. Whichever approach is adopted it seems likely that the whole question of requiring formalities for certain transactions will need to be revisited, either to abolish them where unnecessary[17] or to impose new formal requirements which make sense in the Internet world.

6.2   CONTRACTS REVISITED

In many places in the preceding chapters it has been asserted that the Internet is fundamentally no more than a means of communication, and that the new issues of Internet law arise from the differences between Internet and physical world communications methods, particularly communicating via intermediaries (see Chapter 4). A contract is not a communication, however, but the result of a series of communications which create a legally binding agreement. It would therefore be entirely reasonable to ask what, if anything, is the difference between on-line contracts and those made by traditional methods.

17 This approach has been taken by the EU Directive 2000/31/EC on electronic commerce, OJ L 178 p. 1, 17 July 2000, art 9(1) of which provides: 'Member States shall ensure that their legal system allows contracts to be concluded by electronic means. Member States shall in particular ensure that the legal requirements applicable to the contractual process neither create obstacles for the use of electronic contracts nor result in such contracts being deprived of legal effectiveness and validity on account of their having been made by electronic means.' See also UK Electronic Communications Act 2000, s 8(1), which gives the appropriate Minister power to alter legislation or schemes, licences or approvals 'for the purpose of authorising or facilitating the use of electronic communications or electronic storage' if the aim of the alteration falls within s 8(2), which includes modification of requirements for writing and signature.

The answer to this question is that the contracts themselves are not fundamentally different. What *is* different is the method by which those contracts are formed, using indirect communications via packet switching hosts. When we add to this the fact that a seller may not be communicating directly with the customer but instead form part of a virtual marketplace or Internet shopping mall, and that the customer may not be making purchasing decisions directly but acting through an automated agent, it becomes obvious that the process of contract formation is not so straightforward as in the physical world.

The basic principles of contract formation are still the same, however, so that the existence of a contract and its terms are discovered by identifying the communications which pass between the parties, identifying one of them as an offer, and then determining whether that offer has been accepted. The difficulties arise when one attempts to apply the existing legal rules to Internet communications methods. In particular, it may not be easy to analogise Internet messages to the types of physical document exchange for which the contract formation rules were developed.

If an analysis of the parties' communications reveals that a contract has been formed, there are a number of additional issues which do not normally arise in physical world contracts:

- How is the contract affected by communication through intermediaries (eg a virtual marketplace)?
- What is the legal consequence of concluding a contract through electronic agents?
- Where the contract is for the on-line supply of information rather than a physical product or a service, what are the terms implied by law into such a contract?
- Are there consumer protection rights which apply irrespective of the contract terms, and if so how can they be enforced?[18]

6.2.1 Contracting via intermediaries

6.2.1.1 Basic contract formation

A contract is an agreement between the parties which exhibits the characteristics required by law to make it legally binding on them.[19] Most legal systems identify the moment of agreement by analysing the parties' communications to find an offer (which contains, explicitly or by reference, the terms of the agreement) and a corresponding acceptance. This process is identical for on-line contract formation.

Some complexity is introduced by the fact that there have as yet been no judicial decisions which clarify precisely when these communications become effective – in the case of an email, for example, there are four possibilities:

- when it leaves the sender's mailbox, as it cannot be recalled after that moment;[20]

---

18 The issue is examined later in Chapters 7.1, 7.2.2 and 9.2.
19 Eg consideration (in the common law system) or cause (in the civil law system), contractual capacity, compliance with formalities, etc.
20 This would be the position if the postal rule applies and the communication is an acceptance. The postal rule is not unique to the common law; for example, in Spain the postal rule applies to acceptances in commercial transactions – art 54 of the Spanish Commercial Code.

- when it reaches the recipient's mailbox, because from that moment it is accessible to the recipient;[1]
- when the recipient collects his email from his mailbox; or
- when the recipient actually reads the email.[2]

Where the contract is entered into via a form on a Web page the possibilities are similarly numerous. Additionally, because the result of submitting the form is that the data it contains is processed automatically on behalf of the recipient, there will have been no meeting of minds, a traditional element of contract formation. If this transaction is to be treated as forming a contract, knowledge by the recipient of the form's contents will need to be imputed by the law on the same basis as for contracts made via physical world automated machinery.[3]

Once it has been determined which rule decides when the message becomes effective, however, it is then merely a matter of tracing the (often complex) route that particular message has taken in order to determine whether a contract has been formed.[4] Provided the parties have communicated directly, in the sense that any intermediaries have merely been involved in the transmission of messages, the problems which arise are the technical difficulties in determining message paths and arrival, and not problems arising from the contract formation rules.

Clearly, though, a commercial vendor via the Internet will wish for greater certainty than the law currently provides. Assuming that the contracting process begins with a Web page advertisement, which will be an invitation to treat (an invitation to make offers) rather than an offer itself, that certainty can be achieved by imposing conditions as to the technical format of offers which the Web vendor will consider and specifying the acts which will amount to the formation of a contract. This approach is certainly valid under English law,[5] and the TEDIS research[6] which resulted in the European Model EDI Agreement[7] suggests that it will also be valid under the laws of the other EU Member States.

In the longer term, legislation is likely to address some of these issues. The EU directive on electronic commerce[8] provides in art 11 that:

1. Member States shall ensure, except when otherwise agreed by parties who are not consumers, that in cases where the recipient of the service places his order through technological means, the following principles apply:

---

1   This might be the position for an acceptance under art of the 1335 Italian Civil Code, which states that an acceptance is effective once it reaches the offeror's premises, provided he is then likely to receive it. See also the US decisions of *United Leasing* 656 P.2d 1250 and *Kendel v Pontious* 261 So 2d 167 (Fla, 1972), which hold that an offer is accepted if reasonable efforts were used to communicate the acceptance, and *Restatement (2nd) of Contracts* § 56 comments a & b.
2   These last two possibilities are relevant if an approach like the common law receipt rule is adopted by the relevant law.
3   See eg the English case of *Thornton v Shoe Lane Parking Ltd* [1971] 2 QB 163 (contract for car parking).
4   For a more detailed examination of the complexities of contract formation see Davies 'Contract Formation on the Internet: Shattering a Few Myths' in Edwards and Waelde (eds) *Law & the Internet: regulating cyberspace* (Oxford: Hart Publishing, 1997).
5   *Manchester Diocesan Council for Education v Commercial and General Investments Ltd* [1969] 3 All ER 1593; *Holwell Securities Ltd v Hughes* [1974] 1 WLR 155.
6   *Trade Electronic Data Interchange Systems* OJ L 285, 8 October 1987.
7   Commission Recommendation of 19 October 1994 relating to the legal aspects of electronic data interchange, 94/820/EC, OJ L 338, 28 December 1994. Annex 1 contains the European Model EDI Agreement, arts 3, 12 and 13 of which deal with these issues.
8   Directive 2000/31/EC, OJ L 178 p. 1, 17 July 2000.

- the service provider has to acknowledge the receipt of the recipient's order without undue delay and by electronic means;
- the order and the acknowledgement of receipt are deemed to be received when the parties to whom they are addressed are able to access them.

2. Member States shall ensure that, except when otherwise agreed by parties who are not consumers, the service provider makes available to the recipient of the service appropriate, effective and accessible technical means allowing him to identify and correct input errors, prior to the placing of the order.

3. Paragraph 1, first indent, and paragraph 2 shall not apply to contracts concluded exclusively by exchange of electronic mail or by equivalent individual communications.

Earlier drafts of art 11 attempted to define the moment at which the contract was concluded,[9] but the text quoted above now merely imposes acknowledgement obligations on the trader which will make it more likely that the customer's final communication with the trader amounts to the offer.

An similar approach has been adopted by the drafters of the US Uniform Electronic Transactions Act, which leaves most of these issues to be clarified by the courts but makes specific provision for aspects of contract formation in cases where the contracting technology renders the existing legal approach difficult or impossible to apply.[10]

6.2.1.2 The legal relationship between buyer and intermediary

Because the Internet allows the distribution of an activity across multiple servers, many of the functions which a physical world business would perform itself may be outsourced to third parties (see Chapter 1.4). These third parties will all intermediate in some way between the business and its customers, but only some of them will be of legal relevance to the contracting process.

Legally insignificant intermediaries are those who provide services to the Internet vendor, but in such a way that the vendor retains control over the processing of communications to form a contract. An obvious example is the hosting of a website. Although here the technical process of delivering Web pages to the customer is controlled by the host, the *content* of those pages is controlled by the site owner. Less obvious, but still within this category, is the intermediary which provides electronic commerce technology to a vendor, for example allowing the vendor to use the intermediary's software to process orders. Provided the vendor controls the use of that software, by defining what actions it is to take when processing the order, that fact that the software is owned by the intermediary[11] and operates on its servers should not change the legal consequences of the contracting process.

The position may be different where the intermediary plays an active part in forming the contract between the business and its customer. In the physical world, such a person is an agent, whose powers to bind the principal depend

---

9 See *Commission proposal for a European Parliament and Council directive on certain legal aspects of electronic commerce in the internal market* COM (1998) 586 final, 98/0325 (COD), 18 November 1998, art 11(1).

10 US Uniform Electronic Transactions Act 1999, § 14 (use of electronic agents – see further 6.2.2) and § 15 (time and place of receipt of communications).

11 Or more likely, licensed to it.

on the authority which has actually, or ostensibly, been granted by the principal. On the Internet, however, it is difficult to find intermediaries who act as agents in the normally understood sense.

This is because the reason for the use of agents in the physical world, that it is difficult for the customer to communicate and negotiate directly with the vendor, no longer applies on the Internet. Geographical location of vendor and customer becomes irrelevant, and the technologies used for electronic commerce allow the vendor to deal with multiple customers simultaneously. For these reasons, most intermediaries act merely to enable the customer to locate the vendor, and the contracting process takes place directly without any involvement of the intermediary. Examples of such intermediaries include:

- Product location services, such as bottomdollar.com.[12] They act in a similar manner to insurance brokers in the physical world, identifying the best price for the customer's requirements. Unlike insurance brokers, however, these intermediaries do not deal with any part of the contracting process itself, but merely direct the customer to the vendor's website. These services are funded by advertising, or by 'click-through' payments from vendors for each customer referred to their site.
- Passive shopping malls, websites which merely contain links to vendors' sites. Again, the customer is directed via the link to the vendor's site and makes the contract directly. The only legal significance of these intermediaries is the extent to which they may have some liability for false statements about a particular vendor which induce the customer to enter into the contract.

However, there are some instances where the intermediary does more than merely directing the customer to the vendor's website. Here there is a real possibility that the intermediary's actions will either modify the legal relationship between seller and buyer, or even that a legal relationship will be created between the intermediary and the seller's customer. This is particularly apparent where the intermediary operates an *active* shopping mall, in which the intermediary controls the presentation of the vendor's information and, perhaps, makes certain express or implied promises to potential customers.

A useful example of such an active shopping mall is the BarclaySquare website.[13] This website contains links to a number of online stores, and at first sight appears identical to a passive shopping mall. However, when the link to a store is selected, it becomes apparent from the address box of the viewer's browser[14] that the website for that store is hosted on the BarclaySquare server.[15] This immediately raises in the lawyer's mind the question, with whom is the customer contracting if he orders a product from that store?

Discovering the answer to this question is not always easy. For example, suppose the customer visits the T3 Go!Gadget store. This is hosted on the BarclaySquare site, as its URL demonstrates. However, the 'T3' symbol links the user to the independent site for the T3 magazine, owned by Future

12 http://www9.bottomdollar.com/.
13 http://www.barclaysquare.com.
14 Apparent, though, only if the user is displaying that address window – most browser software allows the user to turn off selected toolbars, including the toolbar where the address box is displayed.
15 Thus, the URL displayed for the T3 Go!Gadget store is http://www.cafe.barclaysquare.com/gadget/index.html.

Publishing. Is the user buying from Future Publishing? Not according to a link on the Go!Gadget page, titled 'Customer Services', which leads to a page which reads as follows:

> The individual manufacturer/distributor of each individual product on sale in T3 Go!Gadget is responsible for your order acceptance, credit card authorisation and order shipment.
> Prices quoted include delivery within the UK only.
> The contact details of each manufacturer/distributor are contained at the top of each product review. Should you need any after sales service, please contact the manufacturer or distributor directly, quoting your Barclaysquare order reference number.
> For your ease, we have included a list below of all manufacturer contact details . . .
> T3 and Future Publishing are not responsible for any element of the placement, acceptance or shipment of products sold within Go!Gadget. T3's activity in Go!Gadget is limited to the supply of product reviews.

Many customers will not read this page, but will simply elect to buy the product. This takes the customer to a standardised credit-card entry page, which from its copyright notice appears to be under the control of Barclays Bank plc.

The intention of the parties involved (with the exception of the customer) becomes clear at this point. BarclaySquare hosts on-line stores, and processes card payments on their behalf. T3 merely operates an intermediary facility which introduces customers to the sellers of advertised products. The customer contracts directly with the manufacturer or distributor of that product.

However, this intention may not correspond with the legal reality. Because T3 (ie Future Publishing, as the legal entity which owns the magazine) does not give the customer notice of its intended limited role in the transaction, the customer is led to believe that he is purchasing the product from T3. There are two possible analyses of this transaction, both of which impose liability on T3:

- T3 is acting as agent for an undisclosed principal, ie the distributor or manufacturer. Under English agency law, the contract is binding as between the customer and the undisclosed principal, but in addition the customer can enforce the contract against the agent directly.[16]
- T3 is not an agent for the true seller, because it has no actual or ostensible authority to make the contract.[17] In this case, the contract would be between the customer and the distributor or agent, but if the customer sued T3, T3 would be estopped from denying that it was the actual seller (or the seller's agent), and would thus be liable.

It must also be borne in mind that the doctrine of agency for an undisclosed principal, and the doctrine of estoppel, are both largely confined to the common law jurisdictions. If the customer were from a civil law jurisdiction whose law applied to the transaction, this might produce an entirely different answer as to the identity of the seller.

Furthermore, it appears that when the customer purchases a product from a BarclaySquare merchant an additional legal relationship is created between the customer and BarclaySquare itself. The 'BarclaySquare Promise' Web page[18] contains a number of promises to the customer, and it would seem that by

16 *Bowstead & Reynolds on Agency* (16th, London: Sweet & Maxwell, 1996) paras. 8-069 ff, 9-012.
17 *Bowstead & Reynolds on Agency* (16th, London: Sweet & Maxwell, 1996) paras 8-001, 8-069.
18 http://www.barclaysquare/promise.html, accessible from a link on the home page.

purchasing from a merchant these promises become contractually binding via a collateral contract[19] between the customer and BarclaySquare:

- to reimburse holder of UK-issued credit cards for fraudulent misuse arising from purchases via the site;
- that product prices include taxes and carriage costs;
- that security measures on the site will prevent misuse of personal information; and
- that delivery will be made on time, and refunds given on a 'no quibble' basis.

While the precise nature of these promises is not completely clear (for example, the drafting does not make it absolutely clear whether BarclaySquare undertakes that delivery times *will* be met, subject to *force majeure*, or merely that it obliges merchants to give it such an undertaking), in many cases the customer will have an additional avenue for redress via BarclaySquare if the merchant defaults.

It is not only virtual shopping mall intermediaries who enter into legal relationships with purchasers. The Which? Webtrader[20] certification scheme[1] includes a promise by Which? to reimburse customers whose credit card is misused when shopping with a certified trader,[2] and because the scheme seal appears on a trader's website that promise should be enforceable against Which? as a collateral contract.

The above analysis indicates that the legal status of an Internet intermediary in electronic commerce is far less clear-cut than in the physical world. It may be liable as principal if it fails to disclose its intermediary role, or it may undertake collateral responsibilities (intentionally or unintentionally). All this depends on the way in which it presents vendor information to on-line customers, and how effectively it brings its own terms and conditions to the attention of shoppers.[3]

6.2.2   Concluding a contract through electronic agents

Research into electronic agents, which search the Internet for offers, conclude contracts and (potentially) negotiate with human parties or even each other, has been under way for some years.[4] Examples include the IntelliTrip[5] site which searches for the best air fares for a user's route, the BIDnASK site which provides offer matching for sellers and buyers of financial instruments[6] and the GE

---

19 *Shanklin Pier Ltd v Detel Products Ltd* [1951] 2 KB 854.
20 http://www.which.net/webtrader/index.html
 1 See further Chapter 9.3.3.
 2 http://www.which.net/webtrader/consumer-guide.html
 3 For the BarclaySquare site, these are not hyperlinked to directly but form a section at the end of the BarclaySquare Promise page. The fact that it is possible to order from a merchant without being directed to these terms raises serious doubt whether they are always enforceable.
 4 For a helpful listing of links to electronic agent research and projects see http://haas.berkeley.edu/~citm/OFFER/Ressources.html. An interesting example of an application of wireless Internet access to electronic agents is the Andersen Consulting Pocket BargainFinder project – see Adam B Brody and Edward J Gottsman 'Pocket BargainFinder: A Handheld Device for Augmented Commerce' (1999) First International Symposium on Handheld and Ubiquitous Computing (HUC '99), 27–29 September, Karlsruhe, Germany, available from http://www.ac.com/services/cstar/Projects/PocketBargainFinder.html.
 5 http://www.thetrip.com/it/
 6 http://stocks.bidnask.com

TPN (Trading Process Network) Post system[7] which provides tools for automating the sales and bidding process for business-to-business electronic commerce. As electronic agents are perfected and come into widespread use, the legal issues which arise from their contracts will need to be clarified.

The main uncertainty arises because traditional contract theory works on the basis of a 'meeting of minds', so that if the contracting parties' minds never reached agreement there is no contract.[8] In the case of contracts concluded by electronic agents, such a meeting of minds is impossible to detect, particularly if the electronic agents have been given negotiating powers.[9] However, once the use of electronic agents becomes widespread the law will need to adapt itself to the fact that, for all practical purposes, these agreements *are* contracts, and a model has been developed by the US National Conference of Commissioners on Uniform State Laws through the Electronic Transactions Act 1999:

US Uniform Electronic Transactions Act 1999

SECTION 2. DEFINITIONS.

In this Act:

(2) 'Automated transaction' means a transaction conducted or performed, in whole or in part, by electronic means or electronic records, in which the acts or records of one or both parties are not reviewed by an individual in the ordinary course in forming a contract, performing under an existing contract, or fulfilling an obligation required by the transaction.

. . .

(6) 'Electronic agent' means a computer program or an electronic or other automated means used independently to initiate an action or respond to electronic records or performances in whole or in part, without review or action by an individual.

SECTION 14. AUTOMATED TRANSACTION.

In an automated transaction, the following rules apply:

(1) A contract may be formed by the interaction of electronic agents of the parties, even if no individual was aware of or reviewed the electronic agents' actions or the resulting terms and agreements.

(2) A contract may be formed by the interaction of an electronic agent and an individual, acting on the individual's own behalf or for another person, including by an interaction in which the individual performs actions that the individual is free to refuse to perform and which the individual knows or has reason to know will cause the electronic agent to complete the transaction or performance.

(3) The terms of the contract are determined by the substantive law applicable to it.

This model law validates contracts made by automated agents, and if adopted by US states and used as a model for legislation elsewhere, will resolve the meeting of minds issue.[10]

---

7 http://www.tpn.geis.com/tpn/getting_started/index.html

8 Although in fact the law works on the apparent manifestation of assent, so that a contract may be formed even if, subjectively, one or other party did not intend it – see eg US Restatement of Contracts (2nd, 1979) § 3.

9 In the existing cases on physical world automated machines, such as *Thornton v Shoe Lane Parking Ltd* [1971] 2 QB 163, the machine has no negotiating authority and so can be seen as a standing offer by its operator, who clearly knows what dealings that machine is able to conclude with the human.

10 See also US Uniform Computer Information Transactions Act (October 1999 draft) §§ 202, 206.

The other question which then arises is how the law should approach the situation where the interaction between electronic agents produces unintended results, because of some incompatibility in their programming or interfacing. The obvious way to deal with problems of this kind is by extending the doctrine of apparent or ostensible authority[11] to cover non-human agents. The effect would be that the offers or agreements made by that electronic agent would be construed objectively; if another 'reasonable'[12] electronic agent would have been led to believe that it was contracting within the parameters to be expected of such an agent, the contract would be binding on the human principal. However, initially at least, it is likely that the range of freedom of electronic agents will be so constrained by their programming that problems of the electronic agent's apparent authority are unlikely to arise in practice. More likely, the electronic agent may misunderstand a human or electronic counterparty's intentions, and the US Uniform Computer Information Transactions Act 1999, § 206 attempts to deal with those issues:

(a) A contract may be formed by the interaction of electronic agents. If the interaction results in the electronic agents' engaging in operations that under the circumstances indicate acceptance, a contract is formed, but a court may grant appropriate relief if the operations resulted from fraud, electronic mistake, or the like.

(b) A contract may be formed by the interaction of an electronic agent and an individual acting on the individual's own behalf or for another person. A contract is formed if the individual takes an action or makes a statement that the individual can refuse to take or say and that the individual has reason to know will:

  (1) cause the electronic agent to perform, provide benefits, or allow the use or access that is the subject of the contract, or send instructions to do so; or

  (2) indicate acceptance, regardless of other expressions or actions by the individual to which the individual has reason to know the electronic agent cannot react.

Although this discussion may seem highly theoretical, as business-to-business electronic commerce grows in volume and the purchasing process becomes increasingly automated, high-value transactions are likely to be effected with little or no human intervention. A purchaser who has made a bad bargain electronically will have a substantial incentive to reopen the fundamental question whether contracts can be made other than by human-to-human agreement.

6.2.3   Implied terms in on-line supplies of information

In the physical world most objects of commerce are classifiable either as goods or services. In either case, a developed legal system will have, over time, identified the terms which should be implied into contracts for the provision of goods or services. These implied terms are largely standard across most jurisdictions, and have often been codified in international instruments such as the UN Convention on the International Sale of Goods 1980 and the Uniform Law on the International Sale of Goods 1964.

By contrast, information products which are supplied as discrete packages and without being embodied in some physical carrier are not easily classifiable as either goods or services. Thus, the English courts, faced with a question

---

11 See *Bowstead & Reynolds on Agency* (16th, London: Sweet & Maxwell, 1996) para 3-005.
12 Or perhaps reasonably programmed?

about the quality terms to be implied into a contract to provide customised package software via download from a disk pack, have expressed the opinion that there is no statutorily implied term as to quality for such a contract because the subject matter is neither goods nor services.[13]

If other jurisdictions adopt this approach, the result will be that there are no pre-determined implied terms. Clearly such terms will need to be developed, but what should they be? The existing international conventions suggest that, at a minimum, implied terms should cover delivery, ownership and use rights, and description and quality. However, in the case of information products the content of these terms is likely to be very different from their physical world analogues.

Implied terms as to delivery of goods or performance of services tend to be simple, requiring delivery or performance within a reasonable time, unless a specific time is agreed.[14] For Internet-supplied information products, however, this is unlikely to be specific enough. In the author's opinion the likely content of such an implied term might be:

- if the information is transmitted by the supplier, eg via an http download or an email attachment, it should be transmitted[15] within a reasonable time of payment – as cases come before the courts, the length of this period (which is likely to be minutes rather than hours)[16] will be clarified. Internet commerce in such products will require payment before delivery, and thus the completion of the payment process should trigger the time period;[17]
- if the information is to be collected by the purchaser, eg by providing him with an ftp password or creating a customised Web site with password-protected http download, it should be made available for collection within a reasonable time of payment (for the same reasons) and remain available for collection for a reasonable time.[18]

---

13 See the judgment of Sir Ian Glidewell LJ in *St Albans City and District Council v International Computers Ltd* [1995] FSR 686. There the court implied a term that the software would be 'be reasonably fit for, i.e., reasonably capable of achieving, the intended purpose'.

14 UN Convention on the International Sale of Goods 1980, art 33; Uniform Law on the International Sale of Goods 1964, arts 20–22.

15 US Uniform Computer Information Transactions Act (October 1999 draft) § 606(a)(2): 'The place for electronic delivery of a copy is an information processing system designated or used by the licensor.'

16 The California State legislature has addressed the maximum permissible time for delivery in § 17538 of the California Business and Professions Code, which makes it a criminal offence to fail to provide goods or services ordered by distance selling means (and expressly including the Internet) within 30 days.

17 See US Uniform Computer Information Transactions Act (October 1999 draft) § 607.

18 US Uniform Computer Information Transactions Act (October 1999 draft) § 606(b): 'Tender of delivery of a copy requires the tendering party to put and hold a conforming copy at the other party's disposition and give the other party any notice reasonably necessary to enable it to obtain access to, control, or possession of the copy. Tender must be at a reasonable hour and, if applicable, requires tender of access material and other documents required by the agreement. The party receiving tender shall furnish facilities reasonably suited to receive tender. In addition, the following rules apply: (1) . . . (2) If the tendering party is required or authorized to send a copy to the other party and the contract does not require the tendering party to deliver the copy at a particular destination, the following rules apply: . . . (B) In tendering electronic delivery of a copy, the tendering party shall initiate or cause to have initiated a transmission that is reasonable in light of the nature of the information and other circumstances, with expenses of transmission to be borne by the receiving party.'

Additional implied terms will also be necessary to deal with communications failures in the file transfer process:

- that the seller will provide for redelivery if delivery fails; and
- that the seller will make refund if delivery is impossible, and in a similar form to the payment method used to purchase the information.

Implied terms as to ownership and use rights are at first sight simpler. By analogy to the provisions for goods,[19] the purchaser should receive the information free of third party intellectual property (and other) rights which prevent or limit the purchaser's use of the information. The difficulty here is to determine what uses by the purchaser should be protected – he will not be the owner but a licensee of the information and should therefore receive limited protection against interferences by the rightholder with his use of the product. Should that protection cover common uses of the information, extend to expected uses, or even to the purchaser's subjectively intended use? In many cases this question will be answered by express licence terms, and in others the courts may well decide to determine the scope of use rights by constructing an implied licence. The Australian case of *Trumpet Software Pty Ltd* v *OzEmail Pty Ltd*[20] suggests that such an implied licence might allow those uses which do not adversely affect the 'owner's' ability to exploit the information product commercially. The US Uniform Computer Information Transactions Act defines the purchaser's use rights as follows:

SECTION 602. LICENSOR'S OBLIGATIONS TO ENABLE USE.

(a) In this section, 'enable use' means to grant a contractual right or permission with respect to information or informational rights and to complete the acts, if any, required under the agreement to make the information available to the licensee.

(b) A licensor shall enable use by the licensee pursuant to the contract. The following rules apply to enabling use:
   (1) If nothing other than the grant of a contractual right or permission is required to enable use, the licensor enables use when the contract becomes enforceable.
   (2) If the agreement requires delivery of a copy, enabling use occurs when the copy is tendered to the licensee.
   (3) If the agreement requires delivery of a copy and steps authorizing the licensee's use, enabling use occurs when the last of those acts occurs.
   (4) In an access contract, enabling use requires tendering all access material necessary to enable the agreed access.
   (5) If the agreement requires a transfer of ownership of informational rights and a filing or recording is allowed by law to establish priority of the transferred ownership, on request by the licensee, the licensor shall execute and tender a record appropriate for that purpose.

Quality terms will also be needed, and will be important for liability purposes as more and more reliance is placed on commercially purchased information products. These terms are likely to be based on conformity with description and fitness for purpose,[1] but the latter will prove problematical. For supplies of

---

19 UN Convention on the International Sale of Goods 1980, arts 41–42; Uniform Law on the International Sale of Goods 1964, art 52.
20 [1996] 34 IPR 481 (Federal Court of Australia).
 1 See eg UK Sale of Goods Act 1979, ss 13–14; UCC art 2 §§ 2-314, 2-315.

goods, the English courts have been able to identify a limited range of 'common' purposes for which they must be fit,[2] but digital information is so versatile that this may prove difficult for information products. Purchasers of physical-world services tend to specify their precise purpose, but this is unlikely to be possible in a mass-market supply of on-line information. The US Uniform Computer Information Transactions Act 1999 has made a first attempt at defining the necessary implied quality terms in supplies of information products:

SECTION 403. IMPLIED WARRANTY: MERCHANTABILITY OF COMPUTER PROGRAM.

(a) Unless the warranty is disclaimed or modified, a licensor that is a merchant with respect to computer programs of the kind, warrants:
  (1) to the end user that the computer program is fit for the ordinary purposes for which such computer programs are used;
  . . .
  (3) that the program conforms to any promises or affirmations of fact made on the container or label.
  . . .

SECTION 404. IMPLIED WARRANTY: INFORMATIONAL CONTENT.

(a) Unless the warranty is disclaimed or modified, a merchant that, in a special relationship of reliance with a licensee, collects, compiles, processes, provides, or transmits informational content, warrants to that licensee that there is no inaccuracy in the informational content caused by the merchant's failure to perform with reasonable care.
(b) A warranty does not arise under subsection (a) with respect to:
  (1) published informational content; or
  (2) a person that acts as a conduit or provides no more that editorial services in collecting, compiling, distributing, processing, providing or transmitting informational content that under the circumstances can be identified as that of a third person.
. . .

SECTION 405. IMPLIED WARRANTY: LICENSEE'S PURPOSE; SYSTEM INTEGRATION.

(a) Unless the warranty is disclaimed or modified, if a licensor at the time of contracting has reason to know any particular purpose for which the computer information is required and that the licensee is relying on the licensor's skill or judgment to select, develop, or furnish suitable information, the following rules apply:
  (1) Except as otherwise provided in paragraph (2), there is an implied warranty that the information is fit for that purpose.
  (2) If from all the circumstances it appears that the licensor was to be paid for the amount of its time or effort regardless of the fitness of the resulting information, the warranty under paragraph (1) is that the information will not fail to achieve the licensee's particular purpose as a result of the licensor's lack of reasonable effort.
(b) There is no warranty under subsection (a) with regard to:
  (1) the aesthetics, appeal, suitability to taste, or subjective quality of informational content; or
  (2) published informational content, but there may be a warranty with regard to the licensor's selection among published informational content from different providers.

2   Codified in UK Sale of Goods Act 1979, s 14(2B).

(c) If an agreement requires a licensor to provide or select a system consisting of computer programs and goods, and the licensor has reason to know that the licensee is relying on the skill or judgment of the licensor to select the components of the system, there is an implied warranty that the components provided or selected will function together as a system.

It remains to be seen whether the Act will be adopted in the US, and only time and litigation will reveal how this issue can be resolved on a global scale.

Chapter 7

The long arm of the law: cross-border law and jurisdiction

It is a general principle in the physical world that the laws of a particular jurisdiction normally only have effect within the boundaries of that jurisdiction. The application of this principle to physical world activities is comparatively straightforward; the geographical location of an actor or an object at the relevant time is objectively determinable,[1] and on that basis the application of local law and the appropriate jurisdiction can be decided.

The geography of the Internet, however, is purely virtual. In operation it pays no heed to geographical or political boundaries. Furthermore, the physical world location of those parts of the Internet infrastructure via which a communication is carried may be purely fortuitous. The result in many cases is that the parties to an Internet transaction are faced with overlapping and often contradictory claims that national law applies to some part of their activities. In the physical world such overlaps are comparatively rare and, except in private law actions, are often ignored as being too trivial to require legal action.[2] In the Internet world these overlaps are pervasive, and have the potential to stifle legitimate activity or even to encourage deliberate law-breaking.

This issue of overlap raises three detailed questions which are discussed in this chapter:

- Where an Internet activity has a cross-border element, on what principles can we decide which country's law applies and which court has jurisdiction?
- On what basis can a national government claim to apply its laws and regulations to Internet activities which originate in a different jurisdiction?
- How far, if at all, is it possible to resolve the conflict between differing national laws where the only effective means of compliance is to limit information flows across national boundaries?

7.1 WHERE DO INTERNET TRANSACTIONS TAKE PLACE?

The principles for establishing applicable law and jurisdiction in cross-border transactions were established many years ago, well before the invention of

---

1   In theory at least. In practice, the distributed structure of the Internet may make discovery of the physical location of any electronic 'object' almost impossible.
2   For example, financial services advertisements are strictly controlled under most national laws, but action is almost never taken against an advertiser in a magazine which is not intentionally distributed in that country.

computers and digital communications networks. Private international law, or conflict of laws, determines these matters by deciding whether a relevant element of the transaction can be *localised* in the jurisdiction in question. We therefore need to ask where an Internet transaction occurs or, more pertinently, where each element of that transaction takes place.

7.1.1   The 'cyberspace' fallacy

As has already been pointed out in the Introduction, it is easy to be seduced by the cyberspace fallacy. This concept, particularly attractive to technologists and idealists, states that the Internet is a new and separate jurisdiction in which the rules and regulations of the physical world do not apply – 'a seamless global-economic zone, borderless and unregulatable'.[3] Internet activities, so the argument goes, do not take place anywhere in the physical world, but occur solely in this new place called 'cyberspace'.

If this conception of cyberspace as a separate jurisdiction were well-founded, the problems outlined above would not exist. Competing claims of national law would be denied on the ground that the transaction occurred exclusively within the jurisdiction of cyberspace, and is thus governed by its laws, customs and practices.[4]

The problem with cyberspace is that its constituent elements, the human and corporate actors and the computing and communications equipment through which the transaction is effected, all have a real-world existence and are located in one or more physical world legal jurisdictions. These corporeal elements of cyberspace are sufficient to give national jurisdictions a justification for claiming jurisdiction over, and the applicability of their laws to, an Internet transaction.

7.1.2   Localisation in the physical world

The principles used to localise activities for private international law purposes are comparatively simple. In the physical world, localisation is most commonly achieved by examining the geographical location where a human actor was situated when that person performed a relevant act. For legal persons such as corporations, which may be 'present' in multiple jurisdictions simultaneously, the rules of private international law make various presumptions based on the location of the corporate seat, head office, or a branch or trading office.

3   John Perry Barlow 'Thinking Globally, Acting Locally' (1966) Time 15 January. Barlow has written elsewhere that 'digital technology is also erasing the legal jurisdictions of the physical world, and replacing them with the unbounded and perhaps permanently lawless seas of Cyberspace. In Cyberspace, there are not only no national or local boundaries to contain the scene of a crime and determine the method of its prosecution, there are no clear cultural agreements on what a crime might be'. (John Perry Barlow 'Selling Wine Without Bottles: The Economy of Mind on the Global Net' http://www.eff.org/pub/Intellectual_property/ idea_economy.article).

   Barlow is not, however, a subscriber to the Cyberspace fallacy, recognising that the competing claims of national law to control the Internet will raise the kinds of problems discussed in this chapter, although he takes the view that a separate law of Cyberspace should, and perhaps will, be developed. Barlow's collected writings on the subject of law and the Internet, archived at www.eff.org, are well worth examination.

4   For an illuminating discussion of the advantages of establishing cyberspace as a separate jurisdiction, see Johnston & Post 'Law And Borders – The Rise of Law in Cyberspace' (1996) 48 Stanford Law Review 1367.

For contracts, the normal rule is that the applicable law and jurisdiction are those agreed in the contract.[5] However, this is subject to various exceptions, the most important of which are:

- different rules often apply where one of the parties is a consumer;[6] and
- irrespective of any choice of law, mandatory rules of the otherwise applicable national law will still apply.[7]

Where there is no agreement on applicable law and/or jurisdiction, localisation is achieved on the basis of apparently objective factors, which include:

- the habitual residence of the person who is to make characteristic performance;[8]
- the principal place of business of the person who is to make characteristic performance;[9]
- the place where the contract is to be performed;[10]
- the place where the steps necessary for the conclusion of the contract were taken;[11]
- the place where an advertisement or invitation to enter into the contract was received;[12]
- the place where a branch, agency or other establishment is situated.[13]

For tortious claims the rules are much simpler. Jurisdiction is normally available in every jurisdiction where damage occurred as a result of the tort,[14] although it is often only possible to sue in that jurisdiction for the losses suffered there,[15] and the applicable law will normally be that of the jurisdiction in which the tort was committed.[16]

5 See eg Rome Convention on the Law Applicable to Contractual Obligations, art 3; Hague Convention on the Law Applicable to Contracts for the International Sale of Goods, art 7; European Communities Convention on Jurisdiction and Enforcement of Judgments in Civil and Commercial Matters (EEC Judgments Convention or Brussels Convention), art 17 (requiring the agreement to be, or to be evidenced in, writing).

6 See eg European Communities Convention on Jurisdiction and Enforcement of Judgments in Civil and Commercial Matters (EEC Judgments Convention or Brussels Convention), art 15.

7 Eg Rome Convention on the Law Applicable to Contractual Obligations, art 5(2).

8 Rome Convention on the Law Applicable to Contractual Obligations, art 4(2).

9 Rome Convention on the Law Applicable to Contractual Obligations, art 4(2); Hague Convention on the Law Applicable to Contracts for the International Sale of Goods, art 8(1).

10 Hague Convention on the Law Applicable to Contracts for the International Sale of Goods, art 8(2)(b); European Communities Convention on Jurisdiction and Enforcement of Judgments in Civil and Commercial Matters (EEC Judgments Convention or Brussels Convention), art 5(1).

11 Rome Convention on the Law Applicable to Contractual Obligations, art 5(2); European Communities Convention on Jurisdiction and Enforcement of Judgments in Civil and Commercial Matters (EEC Judgments Convention or Brussels Convention), art 13(3)(b); Hague Convention on the Law Applicable to Contracts for the International Sale of Goods, art 8(2)(a).

12 Rome Convention on the Law Applicable to Contractual Obligations, art 5(2); European Communities Convention on Jurisdiction and Enforcement of Judgments in Civil and Commercial Matters (EEC Judgments Convention or Brussels Convention), art 13(3)(a).

13 European Communities Convention on Jurisdiction and Enforcement of Judgments in Civil and Commercial Matters (EEC Judgments Convention or Brussels Convention), art 5(5).

14 Eg European Communities Convention on Jurisdiction and Enforcement of Judgments in Civil and Commercial Matters (EEC Judgments Convention or Brussels Convention), art 5(2).

15 *Shevill v Presse Alliance* (ECJ Case C-68/93) [1995] 2 AC 18.

16 This is approximately correct for Civil law jurisdictions and for the UK if the Brussels or Lugano Conventions apply – Dicey & Morris *The Conflict of Laws* (13th, Sweet & Maxwell, 2000) 11-002 and 11-003. See also *Berezovsky v Forbes Inc* (1998) Times, 27 November.

17 See note 10 p 189.

Rome Convention on the Law Applicable to Contractual Obligations

ARTICLE 4

Applicable law in the absence of choice

1. To the extent that the law applicable to the contract has not been chosen in accordance with Article 3, the contract shall be governed by the law of the country with which it is most closely connected. Nevertheless, a severable part of the contract which has a closer connection with another country may by way of exception be governed by the law of that other country.
2. Subject to the provisions of paragraph 5 of this Article, it shall be presumed that the contract is most closely connected with the country where the party who is to effect the performance which is characteristic of the contract has, at the time of conclusion of the contract, his habitual residence, or, in the case of a body corporate or unincorporate, its central administration.
    However, if the contract is entered into in the course of that party's trade or profession, that country shall be the country in which the principal place of business is situated or, where under the terms of the contract the performance is to be effected through a place of business other than the principal place of business, the country in which that other place of business is situated.
3. Notwithstanding the provisions of paragraph 2 of this Article, to the extent that the subject matter of the contract is a right in immovable property or a right to use immovable property it shall be presumed that the contract is most closely connected with the country where the immovable property is situated.
4. A contract for the carriage of goods shall not be subject to the presumption in paragraph 2. In such a contract if the country in which, at the time the contract is concluded, the carrier has his principal place of business is also the country in which the place of loading or the place of discharge or the principal place of business of the consignor is situated, it shall be presumed that the contract is most closely connected with that country. In applying this paragraph single voyage charter-parties and other contracts the main purpose of which is the carriage of goods shall be treated as contracts for the carriage of goods.
5. Paragraph 2 shall not apply if the characteristic performance cannot be determined, and the presumptions in paragraphs 2, 3 and 4 shall be disregarded if it appears from the circumstances as a whole that the contract is more closely connected with another country.

ARTICLE 5

Certain consumer contracts

1. This Article applies to a contract the object of which is the supply of goods or services to a person ('the consumer') for a purpose which can be regarded as being outside his trade or profession, or a contract for the provision of credit for that object.
2. Notwithstanding the provisions of Article 3, a choice of law made by the parties shall not have the result of depriving the consumer of the protection afforded to him by the mandatory rules of the law of the country in which he has his habitual residence:
    – if in that country the conclusion of the contract was preceded by a specific invitation addressed to him or by advertising, and he had taken in that country all the steps necessary on his part for the conclusion of the contract, or
    – if the other party or his agent received the consumer's order in that country, or
    – if the contract is for the sale of goods and the consumer travelled from that country to another country and there gave his order, provided that the consumer's journey was arranged by the seller for the purpose of inducing the consumer to buy.
3. Notwithstanding the provisions of Article 4, a contract to which this Article applies shall, in the absence of choice in accordance with Article 3, be governed by the

law of the country in which the consumer has his habitual residence if it is entered into in the circumstances described in paragraph 2 of this Article.

4. This Article shall not apply to:
    (a) a contract of carriage;
    (b) a contract for the supply of services where the services are to be supplied to the consumer exclusively in a country other than that in which he has his habitual residence.

5. Notwithstanding the provisions of paragraph 4, this Article shall apply to a contract which, for an inclusive price, provides for a combination of travel and accommodation.

European Communities Convention on Jurisdiction and Enforcement of Judgments in Civil and Commercial Matters (EEC Judgments Convention or Brussels Convention)

ARTICLE 2

Subject to the provisions of this Convention, persons domiciled in a Contracting State shall, whatever their nationality, be sued in the courts of that State.

Persons who are not nationals of the State in which they are domiciled shall be governed by the rules of jurisdiction applicable to nationals of that State . . .

ARTICLE 3

Persons domiciled in a Contracting State may be sued in the courts of another Contracting State only by virtue of the rules set out in Sections 2 to 6 of this Title . . .

ARTICLE 5

A person domiciled in a Contracting State may, in another Contracting State, be sued:

(1) in matters relating to a contract, in the courts for the place of performance of the obligation in question;

. . .

(3) in matters relating to tort, delict or quasi-delict, in the courts for the place where the harmful event occurred;

. . .

(5) as regards a dispute arising out of the operations of a branch, agency or other establishment, in the courts for the place in which the branch, agency or other establishment is situated;

. . .

ARTICLE 13

In proceedings concerning a contract concluded by a person for a purpose which can be regarded as being outside his trade or profession, hereinafter called 'the consumer', jurisdiction shall be determined by this Section, without prejudice to the provisions of point 5 of Articles 4 and 5, if it is:

(1) a contract for the sale of goods on instalment credit terms, or

(2) a contract for a loan repayable by instalments, or for any other form of credit, made to finance the sale of goods, or

(3) any other contract for the supply of goods or a contract for the supply of services, and
    (a) in the State of the consumer's domicile the conclusion of the contract was preceded by a specific invitation addressed to him or by advertising, and
    (b) the consumer took in that State the steps necessary for the conclusion of the contract.

Where a consumer enters into a contract with a party who is not domiciled in a Contracting State but has a branch, agency or other establishment in one of the Contracting States, that party shall, in disputes arising out of the operations of the branch, agency or establishment, be deemed to be domiciled in that State.

This Section shall not apply to contracts of transport.

ARTICLE 14

A consumer may bring proceedings against the other party to a contract either in the courts of the Contracting State in which that party is domiciled or in the courts of the Contracting State in which he is himself domiciled.

Proceedings may be brought against a consumer by the other party to the contract only in the courts of the Contracting State in which the consumer is domiciled.

These provisions shall not affect the right to bring a counter-claim in the court in which, in accordance with this Section, the original claim is pending.

ARTICLE 15

The provisions of this Section may be departed from only by an agreement:
(1) which is entered into after the dispute has arisen, or
(2) which allows the consumer to bring proceedings in courts other than those indicated in this Section, or
(3) which is entered into by the consumer and the other party to the contract, both of whom are at the time of conclusion of the contract domiciled or habitually resident in the same Contracting State, and which confers jurisdiction on the courts of that State, provided that such an agreement is not contrary to the law of that State.

7.1.3   Localisation in the Internet world – chasing packets

There are fundamental difficulties in applying traditional localisation principles to a transaction which is effected via the Internet. Doing so requires an identification of the physical place where the appropriate element of the transaction occurred, as a consequence of which jurisdiction is awarded to the state in whose territory that place is located, or its law is applied.

This produces workable answers for most physical world transactions. As we shall see, however, the likely result of applying the concept of localisation to an electronic commerce or Internet transaction is either:

- the applicable law or jurisdiction is potentially that of every country in the world; or
- the applicable law or jurisdiction is purely fortuitous, and has no obvious connection with the parties or the substantive transaction.

This can be demonstrated by applying the localisation principles of the various international conventions on private international law to examples from real-life electronic commerce or Internet transactions.

7.1.3.1   Place of supply of goods, services or performance of principal obligation

There are numerous provisions in the conventions relating to the applicable law or jurisdiction for contracts which specify the place of supply as a localisation trigger.[17] Whether a sensible result is produced depends on the subject-matter of the contract. Thus where the contract is to supply physical goods (ie the electronic commerce transaction is simply an equivalent channel to mail or telephone ordering) the localisation of the contract presents no special problems; the relevant place is the address for delivery of the goods.

18 So far as the author is aware, there is as yet no judicial decision in any jurisdiction which has

However, the position is quite different if the contract is for a 'product' which is to be delivered electronically. The most obvious of such products are on-line services, and information products (eg software, images, music, video or games). For these, the place of supply is hard to define. The options are as follows:

1. The place of electronic 'delivery'. Delivery of information products and services is an elastic concept, which depends very much on the supply technology used. For example:
    *   If the product is sent as an email attachment, its place of receipt will probably[18] be determined in the same way in which the courts would decide where a contractual acceptance was received. Taking the example of a purchaser who is employed in London by a multinational corporation whose domain name points initially to a server in the US,[19] there are at least three possible places of receipt:
        −   If the place of receipt is the moment the message enters the corporation's systems (as would probably be the case under eg art 1335 of the Italian Civil Code), the relevant location would be the US, ie the physical location of the server to which the corporation's domain name points. We must also note that this server could at any time be moved to a different physical location, in any jurisdiction, without affecting the operation of the email process[20] and without the sender or recipient realising the fact.
        −   If the place of receipt is at the purchaser's mailbox, this would probably be located on a UK-based server to which the email is routed by the corporation's internal network. However, there is no technical reason why the corporation might not, without this being apparent to the purchaser or the vendor, physically relocate that server to eg Guatemala. The system would perform in an apparently identical way so far as both parties are concerned.
        −   If the place of receipt is where the purchaser actually downloads and/or reads the email, that could occur in whichever jurisdiction he or she happened to be located when the email was collected from the mailbox. The place of downloading and the place of reading could also be different, eg if the purchaser downloads email to a laptop in London but does not read it until arrival in Paris.
    The Australian Electronic Communications Act 1999 does not deal with this issue directly, but offers two possible analogies by making provision in s 14 for the time and place of receipt of an electronic communication.[1] Time of acceptance is either the entry of the communication into the system denoted by the recipient (eg the email host) or, if none is

had to decide this point. However, courts tend to look for analogous situations, and in most jurisdictions the question of place and time of receipt of contractual communications has received extensive judicial attention, and some states have enacted legislation which clarifies the law for electronic communications – see below.

19 Most multinationals operate their email systems in a similar way, pointing their domain names at their primary IT centre and then routing received emails internally to the various countries of receipt, and users may use the system to contract in their employee capacity and possibly also their consumer capacity, subject to their employer's rules on use of the system.

20 Provided, of course, that the DNS record for that domain name were updated to map the domain name to the new IP address of that server.

1   See also the US Uniform Electronic Transactions Act 1999, § 15(b) & (d), which contains almost identical provisions.

designated, the time when the communication actually comes to the attention of the recipient. In the context of the Internet the second option will rarely apply, as it is usually impossible to communicate with a person without knowing the address of the relevant system.[2]

Australian Electronic Communications Act 1999, s 14[2a]

(3) For the purposes of a law of the Commonwealth, if the addressee of an electronic communication has designated an information system for the purpose of receiving electronic communications, then, unless otherwise agreed between the originator and the addressee of the electronic communication, the time of receipt of the electronic communication is the time when the electronic communication enters that information system.

(4) For the purposes of a law of the Commonwealth, if the addressee of an electronic communication has not designated an information system for the purpose of receiving electronic communications, then, unless otherwise agreed between the originator and the addressee of the electronic communication, the time of receipt of the electronic communication is the time when the electronic communication comes to the attention of the addressee.

These rules appear to be based on the existing principles for contractual communications. However, the Act's rules on *place* of receipt adopt quite different principles, based on a presumption as to the recipient's location:

Australian Electronic Communications Act 1999, s 14

(5) For the purposes of a law of the Commonwealth, unless otherwise agreed between the originator and the addressee of an electronic communication:
   (a) the electronic communication is taken to have been dispatched at the place where the originator has its place of business; and
   (b) the electronic communication is taken to have been received at the place where the addressee has its place of business.

(6) For the purposes of the application of subsection (5) to an electronic communication:
   (a) if the originator or addressee has more than one place of business, and one of those places has a closer relationship to the underlying transaction – it is to be assumed that that place of business is the originator's or addressee's only place of business; and
   (b) if the originator or addressee has more than one place of business, but paragraph (a) does not apply – it is to be assumed that the originator's or addressee's principal place of business is the originator's or addressee's only place of business; and
   (c) if the originator or addressee does not have a place of business – it is to be assumed that the originator's or addressee's place of business is the place where the originator or addressee ordinarily resides.

2   Presumably, however, it would apply to an unsolicited communication (irrelevant in the context of delivery of electronic products or services) and to a person communicating via an anonymous remailer or surfing the World Wide Web via an anonymising service (see further Chapter 2.3.3.3).
2a Commonwealth of Australia Copyright reproduced by permission.

These rules produce a slightly odd result when applied to our example. The email is received at the moment when it arrives at the corporation's primary IT centre in the US, but is received at a different place, ie London.[3]

- If the product is 'collected' by the purchaser from the supplier's website, there is a strong argument that delivery occurs at that website.[4] This may not be in the supplier's jurisdiction of establishment; many electronic commerce enterprises adopt a distributed mode of operation, locating eg the advertising website in one jurisdiction, the stock catalogue in another, the payment processing system in a third and the server from which information products are delivered in a fourth.

2. The place where the service is performed, in the case of on-line services. Such services include eg database access, professional advice[5] and technical services.[6] This will normally be in the supplier's own jurisdiction, unless a distributed electronic commerce model has been adopted. Certainly, for VAT purposes a special 'reverse charge' rule has needed to be introduced to overcome the normal presumption that services which take the form of information or advice are provided where the service provider is located.[7] In many cases adopting the place of performance for localisation will produce odd results, particularly where the service is performed by software, operating automatically. In such a case, performance might occur on an entirely different server from the website through which the customer requests the service and thus in an unexpected third jurisdiction.

7.1.3.2   *Place where purchaser took steps towards contract formation*

The place where the purchaser took these steps may be one of the jurisdictions in which an action can be brought, though often only if the purchaser is habitually resident there.[8] At first sight this presents fewer difficulties, as the physical location of the purchaser can usually be determined with some certainty. Even here, however, problems can arise:

- The purchaser begins the transaction in one jurisdiction and completes it in another. Some electronic commerce suppliers allow customers to store partial orders and return to them at a later date to complete the order.

---

3   This oddness is intentional; because the questions when and where an electronic communication is received are somewhat metaphysical, the law sets out bright line rules which have no necessary connection with the actual message path. This point is specifically acknowledged in US Uniform Electronic Transactions Act 1999, § 15(c), which provides: 'Subsection (b) applies even if the place the information processing system is located is different from the place the electronic record is deemed to be received under subsection (d)'.

4   The purchaser makes his own arrangements for collection, using the Internet technologies to do so. This is analogous to the free on board contract used for international shipping trade.

5   For example, a network of UK lawyers currently provides on-line will writing services, and on-line drafting of simple commercial documents – see http://www.desktoplawyer.co.uk.

6   Examples include foreign language translation, route planning for pilots, calculation of tax returns.

7   Sixth Council Directive of 17 May 1977 on the harmonisation of the laws of the Member States relating to turnover taxes (Directive 77/388/EEC) arts 9(2)(e) and 21(1)(b).

8   See note 11 p 189.

- The purchaser is 'visiting' a website in a different location, and the applicable law (an equally difficult question) determines that the contract-forming actions took place on that website, and not at the user's computer.

7.1.3.3   *State where supplier's branch, agency etc. is established*

In the field of regulated services, such as banking and financial services,[9] some commentators have suggested that whenever a person accesses the supplier's website, a temporary, virtual, branch is created. If this argument is accepted, it means that each electronic commerce business has, at some time or other, established a branch in every jurisdiction of the world where Internet access is possible. All that would be necessary to establish jurisdiction in a particular state under art 9 would be to prove a single access to the website from that state.

The European Commission has rejected this argument in a consultation document relating to the Second Banking Directive,[10] but the document is merely explanatory and does not establish the legal position even in respect of banking services. It is not possible to predict whether a court would find this argument attractive. However, it may be worth noting that in a criminal action based on obscene content, a Tennessee court found that it had jurisdiction over a Californian bulletin board on the basis of a proved access to the board from Tennessee.[11]

7.1.3.4   *'Targeting'*

An approach which at first sight seems attractive is to grant jurisdiction to those jurisdiction whose residents are targeted by the supplier. The justification for this approach is that the supplier is seeking customers in that jurisdiction, and can thus hardly complain if its courts claim jurisdiction over his activities. This has similarities to the US 'minimum contacts' doctrine, which was explained in *CompuServe v Patterson*[12] as follows:

> As always in this context, the crucial federal constitutional inquiry is whether, given the facts of the case, the nonresident defendant has sufficient contacts with the forum state that the district court's exercise of jurisdiction would comport with 'traditional notions of fair play and substantial justice'. *International Shoe Co. v. Washington*, 326 U.S. 310, 316 (1945) (quoting *Milliken v Meyer*, 311 US 457, 463 (1940)); *Reynolds*, 23 F.3d at 1116; *Theunissen*, 935 F 2d at 1459. This court has repeatedly employed three criteria to make this determination: First, the defendant must purposefully avail himself of the privilege of acting in the forum state or causing a consequence in the forum state. Second, the cause of action must arise from the defendant's activities there. Finally, the acts of the defendant or consequences caused by the defendant must have a substantial enough connection with the forum to make the exercise of jurisdiction over the defendant reasonable.

In *CompuServe v Patterson* the defendant used the CompuServe system, located in Ohio, from which to sell software, and for this reason was held subject to Ohio jurisdiction.

9 See 7.2 below
10 *Freedom to provide services and the interest of the general good in the second banking directive* Commission interpretative communication SEC(97) 1193 final, 20 June 1997.
11 *United States v Thomas* 74 F.3d 701, 706-07 (6th Cir, 1996).
12 89 F 3d 1257 (6th Cir, 1996).

This immediately raises the question whether a website, which by definition can be accessed world-wide, amounts to 'activities' in those jurisdictions in which it is accessible. The US courts appear to have answered this question by making a distinction between an 'active' website, which solicits those outside the jurisdiction to undertake a commercial transaction with the website owner, and a 'passive' website which merely provides information. The former is sufficient to satisfy the minimum contacts doctrine[13] whereas the latter is not.[14]

The European Commission has proposed the targeting approach in its draft regulation to implement the Brussels Convention as part of EU law.[15] The proposed regulation provides:

ARTICLE 15

In matters relating to a contract concluded by a person, the consumer, for a purpose which can be regarded as being outside his trade or profession, jurisdiction shall be determined by this Section, without prejudice to Article 4 and Article 5(5), if:

. . .

(3) in all other cases, the contract has been concluded with a person who pursues commercial or professional activities in the Member State of the consumer's domicile or, by any means, directs such activities to that Member State or to several countries including that Member State, and the contract falls within the scope of such activities.

. . .

ARTICLE 16

A consumer may bring proceedings against the other party to a contract either in the courts of the Member State in which that party is domiciled or in the courts for the place where the consumer is domiciled.

Proceedings may be brought against a consumer by the other party to the contract only in the courts of the Member State in which the consumer is domiciled.

This proposal has been criticised on the ground that art 15 is based on an unrealistic view of electronic commerce, ie that websites can easily be classified into 'active' and 'passive'. In practice, an electronic commerce supplier will wish to sell to customers in some jurisdictions, but not others, and to do this from the same website. The result is likely to be that *all* jurisdictions are targeted, unless complicated and costly steps are taken to partition the website into purely national elements. Simple disclaimers that the site is not open to dealings with consumers in a particular country will probably be insufficient[16] unless steps

---

13 *Maritz Inc v Cybergold Inc* 947 F Supp 1328 (ED Mo, 1996); *Zippo Mfg Co v Zippo Dot Com Inc* 952 F, Supp 1119.

14 *Bensusan Restaurant Corp v King* 937 F Supp 295 (SDNY, 1996) aff'd 126 F 3d 25 (2nd Cir, 1997). 'The mere fact that a person can gain information on the allegedly infringing product is not the equivalent of a person advertising, promoting, selling or otherwise making an effort to target its product in New York.' See also *Cybersell Inc v Cybersell Inc* 130 F 3d 414 (9th Cir, 1997); *Hornell Brewing Co v Rosebud Sioux Tribal Ct* 133 F 3d 1087 (8th Cir, 1998). However, in *Inset Sys Inc v Instruction Set Inc* 937 F Supp 161 (D Conn, 1996) the court held that Internet advertising coupled with a toll-free telephone number was sufficient targeting of the court's state to give it jurisdiction. This case appears to be anomalous, though, and numerous other cases have followed the *Bensusan* approach.

15 *Proposal for a Council Regulation (EC) on jurisdiction and the recognition and enforcement of judgments in civil and commercial matters* COM (1999) 348 final.

16 See Mike Pullen 'On The Proposals To Adopt The Amended Brussels Convention And The Draft Rome II Convention As EU Regulations Pursuant To Article 65 Of The Amsterdam Treaty' *EU Version* – Position Paper Prepared For The Advertising Association (http://www.ilpf.org/confer/present99/pullen_posit.htm) paras 1.9–1.12.

are also taken to prevent consumers from viewing the advertising without certifying that they are not from the disclaimed jurisdiction.

7.1.3.5   *Place of commission of a tort, or place of injury resulting from the tort*

The normal rule is that both these states (if different) have jurisdiction over an action in respect of the tort, though the applicable law will normally be the place where the tort is committed.[17] For torts committed via the Internet, this often produces the answer that the place of commission and/or the injury occurs everywhere.

To take defamation as an example, suppose that a defamatory message is posted to a newsgroup as occurred in the UK case of *Godfrey v Demon Internet Ltd.*[18] Each ISP which hosts that newsgroup has a copy of the database containing the newsgroup postings on its servers. Several times a day, that copy is collated with the database of the newsgroup held on another ISP's server, each passing over and receiving postings which are not contained in the other copy. As a result, any posting propagates across the Internet until, within a few hours, it appears in every copy of the newsgroup database.

Because the tort occurs, and the injury is suffered, in every jurisdiction in which the posting is published, and the defendant who posted the message is responsible for the expected further transmission of his initial publication, localisation for this tort occurs:

- in every jurisdiction where an ISP hosts the newsgroup; and
- in every jurisdiction where a subscriber reads the defamatory posting. It is technically possible for a subscriber in one jurisdiction to access a newsgroup hosted on a server in another jurisdiction, although in practice some (but by no means all) ISPs only allow their own subscribers to access the news server.

In this example, the tort is probably committed almost everywhere in the world, and injury suffered everywhere also.

Similar results can be found for other torts based on 'broadcast' information, such as torts of property damage arising from computer viruses (assuming that the applicable law recognises damage to information as falling within the tort).[19]

7.3.1.6   *Alternative approaches*

These examples demonstrate that localisation is often a meaningless concept in relation to electronic commerce and the Internet. This is because the communications infrastructure is intentionally flexible – every Internet resource is available from everywhere. Each individual transaction via the communications network potentially uses a different part of the fixed

---

17 See notes 14–16 p 189. The position in Civil law jurisdictions is examined in Law Commission Working Paper no 87 *Private International law: Choice of law in Tort and Delict* (1984), Appendix. The US adopts a different approach, applying the law of the jurisdiction with the closest connection to the tort – Restatement, Second on the Conflict of Laws (1972) § 145.

18 [1999] 4 All ER 342. See further Chapter 4.2.3.1.

19 Eg the UK Computer Misuse Act 1990, s 3 creates a criminal offence of unauthorised modification of data, and most criminal offences of this type also amount to torts.

infrastructure (the servers and their communications links), and that fixed infrastructure is often neither owned nor operated by its commercial users.

Some suggestions have been made that a different form of localisation should be considered, based on the physical location of the server used in the transaction or the physical place from which a person (eg a tortfeasor) accessed a server (usually described as the place of 'uploading'). This attempt at localisation is equally likely to fail for the reasons described above. Two simple examples may suffice:

- An information resource may be delivered from a choice of servers, determined purely automatically. For example, if a file is requested from ibm.com, it is quite likely that it exists in multiple copies on servers in different jurisdictions, and the delivery server is determined by software which is conducting load balancing on IBM's network. To add further complication, the user's ISP may already have a copy of the file, stored in a cache own its on server, and may use that copy to deliver the file.
- The place of uploading has no necessary connection with any contract or tort. For example, X might 'upload' a computer virus to a server, but not make it accessible to others. Y might then change the access permissions to the file containing the virus. In this case, X commits no tort (unless he is a co-conspirator with Y). Y commits the tort, but never uploads the virus file.

There are no obvious solutions to this problem. One possibility, whose only virtue is its workability, is a bright line rule that jurisdiction exists only in the places of habitual residence of the parties to the action. There are many objections to this rule on other grounds, the most cogent being that the solution has no theoretical basis but is merely expedient. In addition, such a rule would not satisfy the US Constitution's requirement for due process in asserting jurisdiction, which has led to the 'minimum contacts' doctrine discussed in 7.1.3.4 above. As yet, it is not possible to predict how the law in this area will develop.

7.2 JURISDICTIONAL AND REGULATORY COMPETENCE

In theory there is no limit on the circumstances in which a national Government might claim to apply its laws and regulations to Internet activities which originate in a different jurisdiction, although practical enforcement of those laws against a foreign enterprise is a different matter. In practice, however, governments attempt to limit the extraterritorial effect of their laws by applying the principle of comity,[20] thus reducing the risk of legislative 'arms races'. In essence, comity requires that a state should not claim to apply its legislation to persons within another state unless it is reasonable to do so, which normally means that legislation should be undertaken by the state which has the greater interest in so doing.[1]

The most common way in which legislators attempt to maintain comity is to apply their laws only to *activities* undertaken within the state. This is a form of localisation, a concept which we have already seen (see 7.1.3 above) to be

---

20 The US Supreme Court has defined comity as 'the recognition which one nation allows within its territory to the legislative, executive, or judicial acts of another nation, having due regard both to international duty and convenience, and to the rights of its own citizens or of other persons who are under the protections of its law'. *Hilton v Guyot* 115 US 113, 163–64 (1995).

1 See eg Restatement (Third) of Foreign Relations Law of the United States, § 403(1) (1987).

extremely difficult to apply to the Internet. However, localisation for the purposes of applying local law and regulation uses some different localisation triggers from those already examined, and so merits further discussion.

Increasingly, there is a recognition that localisation on the basis of Internet activities is inappropriate, and that some alternative basis for maintaining comity must be found. The most promising alternative seems to be that of accepting 'country of origin' regulation, coupled with an appropriate degree of harmonisation or convergence of national laws.

7.2.1   Activities undertaken in the jurisdiction

One of the most heavily regulated areas of commercial activity is financial services (including banking), and because this is an activity which consists almost exclusively in the transfer and management of information it is ideally suited to electronic commerce via the Internet. As a consequence, many of the problematic issues of regulatory competence have already become apparent, and suggestions have been made for resolving them. Similarly, the implications of electronic commerce for the collection of income and sales taxes have also been investigated by national and international bodies. For this reason, most of the examples examined in this part of the chapter will be drawn from financial services and income tax regulation.

In the field of financial services and taxation law, there are three main localisation triggers used to determine whether national law applies:

- whether the enterprise has an establishment in the national territory;
- whether it is doing business by offering services in or deriving income from transactions in that territory; or
- whether it is advertising its services to potential customers in that territory.

7.2.1.1   *Establishment*

Having a permanent establishment in the relevant jurisdiction is the primary trigger for the application of financial services regulation to,[2] and the imposition

---

2   See eg UK Financial Services and Markets Act 2000, s 418: '(1) In the four cases described in this section, a person who- (a) is carrying on a regulated activity, but (b) would not otherwise be regarded as carrying it on in the United Kingdom, is, for the purposes of this Act, to be regarded as carrying it on in the United Kingdom. (2) The first case is where—(a) his registered office (or if he does not have a registered office his head office) is in the United Kingdom; (b) he is entitled to exercise rights under a single market directive as a UK firm; and (c) he is carrying on in another EEA State a regulated activity to which that directive applies. (3) The second case is where—(a) his registered office (or if he does not have a registered office his head office) is in the United Kingdom; (b) he is the manager of a scheme which is entitled to enjoy the rights conferred by an instrument which is a relevant Community instrument for the purposes of section 264; and (c) persons in another EEA State are invited to become participants in the scheme. (4) The third case is where- (a) his registered office (or if he does not have a registered office his head office) is in the United Kingdom; (b) the day-to-day management of the carrying on of the regulated activity is the responsibility of- (i) his registered office (or head office); or (ii) another establishment maintained by him in the United Kingdom. (5) The fourth case is where—(a) his head office is not in the United Kingdom; but (b) the activity is carried on from an establishment maintained by him in the United Kingdom. (6) For the purposes of subsections (2) to (5) it is irrelevant where the person with whom the activity is carried on is situated.'

of income tax liability on,[3] a commercial enterprise. Establishment is a somewhat elastic concept, however. Even in the physical world, it is possible to undertake trading activities in another state through the means of agents, or through distance selling techniques such as telephone marketing which do not require the business to occupy premises or possess business equipment located in that state.

In the context of banking services, the European Court of Justice has attempted a definition of establishment in the *Somafer* case:[4]

> The concept of branch, agency or other establishment implies a place of business which has the appearance of permanency, such as the extension of a parent body, has a management and is materially equipped to negotiate business with third parties, so that the latter, although knowing that there will if necessary be a legal link with the parent body, the head office of which is abroad, do not have to deal directly with such parent body but may transact business at the place of business constituting the extension.

In essence this ruling sets out three requirements, which are also reflected in other areas of regulation:[5]

- the use of fixed premises or equipment in the state;
- the presence of staff (which may include some intermediaries who act as agents for the enterprise); and
- the ability of those staff to undertake business transactions with customers in the state.

Immediately, it can be seen that if this interpretation of the concept of establishment is applied to Internet activities from a foreign jurisdiction, the fact that the supplier's website appears (temporarily) on the customer's computer will not be sufficient to create a virtual branch. The supplier has no premises or staff in the jurisdiction, and the computer equipment is used only temporarily and in any event belongs to the customer.

A more difficult issue arises, however, if the supplier's website is stored on a server in the jurisdiction.[6] Even if the website runs from a server owned by the supplier, located in premises owned or rented by him, and maintained by his employees, not all the requirements of a permanent establishment are met.

3   Draft OECD Model Tax Convention on Income and on Capital (30 June 1998) art 7(1). See also *Tax and the Internet* Discussion report of the Australian Taxation Office Electronic Commerce Project Team on the challenges of electronic commerce for tax administration (Canberra: Australian Government Publishing Service, August 1997) paras 7.2.2 and 7.2.3:
    'The legal basis of tax jurisdiction is premised on taxation concepts such as residency, source and permanent establishment. . . . All of these concepts have an important element of physical or territorial nexus with Australia. In simple terms, the primary test for individual residents is that they physically reside in Australia. For companies the tests are that they are incorporated in Australia or carry on business in Australia and are centrally managed and controlled from Australia. Australian sourced income often includes income that is derived from a physical place in Australia and a non-resident business is considered to have a permanent establishment in Australia if it has a "fixed place of business" in Australia (in terms of both timing and geography).'
4   Case 33/78 [1978] ECR 2183.
5   See eg *Electronic Commerce and Canada's Tax Administration* Minister of National Revenue's Advisory Committee on Electronic Commerce (April 1998) s 4.2.2.4.
6   Operating from multiple websites can be a sensible electronic commerce strategy because of the communication bottlenecks which arise as Internet traffic crosses difficult geographic boundaries, such as oceans. A global electronic commerce supplier might well choose to operate websites in each of the major continents for precisely this reason.

There are still no staff in that jurisdiction who have authority to contract with customers – that function is performed by software running on the server.

So far as banking services are concerned, the European Commission appears to have accepted this argument:[7]

Freedom to provide services and the interest of the general good in the second banking directive, **Commission interpretative communication SEC(97) 1193 final 20 June 1997**

Unlike other services, where the place of supply can give rise to no doubts (legal defence, construction of a building, etc.), the banking services listed in the Annex to the Second Directive are difficult to pin down to a specific location. The are also very different from one another and are increasingly provided in an intangible form. The growth of distance services, particularly those using electronic means (Internet, home banking, etc.), will undoubtedly soon result in excessively strict criteria on location becoming obsolete.

It is not always easy to draw the line between the concepts of provision of services and establishment, particularly since, as the case-law of the Court indicates, one may be considered in certain circumstances to be operating in a Member State under the freedom to provide services despite having some kind of infrastructure in that Member State.

Some situations are particularly difficult to classify. This is especially true of:

- recourse to independent intermediaries; and
- electronic machines (ATMs) carrying out banking activities.

. . .

(b) Electronic machines
This means fixed, ATM-type electronic machines capable of performing the banking activities listed in the Annex to the Second Directive.[8]

Such machines may be covered by the right of establishment if they fulfil the criteria laid down by the Court of Justice (see above).

For such a machine to be capable of being treated as an establishment, therefore, it would have to have a management, which is by definition impossible unless the Court acknowledges that the concept can encompass not only human management but also electronic management.

. . .

The presence in the host country of a person or company responsible simply for maintaining the machine, equipping it and dealing with any technical problems encountered by users cannot rank as an establishment and does not deprive the credit institution of the right to operate under the freedom to provide services.

The Commission considers, however, that technological developments could, in the future, induce it to review its position.

If such developments were to make it possible for an institution to have only a machine in a given country which could 'act' as a branch, taking actual decisions which would completely obviate the need for the customer to have contact with the parent company, the Commission would be forced to consider an appropriate Community legal framework. The present legal framework in fact rests on mechanisms

7   See also *Commission proposal for a European Parliament and Council directive on certain legal aspects of electronic commerce in the internal market* COM (1998) 586 final, 98/0325 (COD), 18 November 1998, explanatory memorandum p 20: 'Thus, the following, for example, do not amount to an establishment on the territory of a Member State: – *the location of the technology used*, e.g. the hosting of web pages or of a site; – *the ability to access an internet site* in a Member State (any other approach would mean that an operator would be considered to be established in several or indeed fifteen Member States); – the fact that a service provider established in another Member State offers *services targeted* at the territory of another Member State (in fact, the internal market enables businesses, particularly SMEs, to tailor their offers to specific niche markets in other Member States).'

8   It does not mean individual, mobile data-processing equipment which can provide or receive distance banking services, eg through the Internet.

which are still based on a 'human' concept of a branch (for example, the programme of operations must contain the names of those responsible for the management of the branch). It is therefore not possible, under the existing rules, to consider machines as constituting a branch.

The last paragraph of this extract recognises that Internet banking websites can act autonomously, as replacements for physical branches. However, there is no urgent need for legislation to preserve the regulatory competence of national regulators because this is based on *either* establishment or offering banking services in the jurisdiction (see further 7.2.1.2 below).

The concept of establishment is more critical for income tax purposes, however. Tax laws commonly provide that a business is only liable to income-related[9] taxes in a foreign jurisdiction if it is resident or has a permanent establishment there,[10] or that if it has no establishment it is only liable to tax on profits from business activities undertaken in (not *with*) the jurisdiction.[11] For this reason, it is likely that the tax authorities will wish to take a more restrictive view of website hosting.

The definition of permanent establishment for tax purposes, so far as physical world activities is concerned, is very similar to that discussed above; it requires premises or equipment, or employed staff acting on behalf of the enterprise in its transactions with customers.[12] Working Party No 1 on Tax Conventions and Related Questions of the OECD Committee on Fiscal Affairs has proposed that for income tax purposes, a website hosted on a server where the server is a

---

9   Including corporation taxes.

10 Draft OECD Model Tax Convention on Income and on Capital (30 June 1998), art 7(1): 'The profits of an enterprise of a Contracting State shall be taxable only in that State unless the enterprise carries on business in the other Contracting State through a permanent establishment situated therein. If the enterprise carries on business as aforesaid, the profits of the enterprise may be taxed in the other State but only so much of them as is attributable to that permanent establishment.'

11 This is the current position under UK law – see further Chissick and Kelman *Electronic Commerce: Law and Practice* (London: Sweet & Maxwell, 1999) Chapter 9.15-9.17.

12 See eg Draft OECD Model Tax Convention on Income and on Capital (30 June 1998) art 5: '1. For the purposes of this Convention, the term 'permanent establishment' means a fixed place of business through which the business of an enterprise is wholly or partly carried on. 2. The term 'permanent establishment' includes especially: a) a place of management; b) a branch; c) an office; . . . 4. Notwithstanding the preceding provisions of this Article, the term 'permanent establishment' shall be deemed not to include: a) the use of facilities solely for the purpose of storage, display or delivery of goods or merchandise belonging to the enterprise; b) the maintenance of a stock of goods or merchandise belonging to the enterprise solely for the purpose of storage, display or delivery; c) the maintenance of a stock of goods or merchandise belonging to the enterprise solely for the purpose of processing by another enterprise; d) the maintenance of a fixed place of business solely for the purpose of purchasing goods or merchandise or of collecting information, for the enterprise; e) the maintenance of a fixed place of business solely for the purpose of carrying on, for the enterprise, any other activity of a preparatory or auxiliary character; f) the maintenance of a fixed place of business solely for any combination of activities mentioned in sub-paragraphs a) to e), provided that the overall activity of the fixed place of business resulting from this combination is of a preparatory or auxiliary character. 5. Notwithstanding the provisions of paragraphs 1 and 2, where a person — other than an agent of an independent status to whom paragraph 6 applies — is acting on behalf of an enterprise and has, and habitually exercises, in a Contracting State an authority to conclude contracts in the name of the enterprise, that enterprise shall be deemed to have a permanent establishment in that State in respect of any activities which that person undertakes for the enterprise, unless the activities of such person are limited to those mentioned in paragraph 4 which, if exercised through a fixed place of business, would not make this fixed place of business a permanent establishment under the provisions of that paragraph.'

business asset of the enterprise should be treated as a permanent establishment of the enterprise. However, if the website is merely hosted by an independent ISP, because there is no equipment or premises controlled exclusively by the enterprise it would have no permanent establishment in the jurisdiction.

***The Application of the Permanent Establishment Definition in the Context of Electronic Commerce: Proposed Clarification of the Commentary on Article 5 of the OECD Model Tax Convention* (Revised Draft For Comments), Working Party No. 1 on Tax Conventions and Related Questions, OECD Committee on Fiscal Affairs (March 2000).**

. . .

5.   The Working Party also wishes to repeat that this revised draft is concerned solely with the issue of the application to electronic commerce of the permanent establishment definition as it currently appears in Article 5 of the OECD Model Tax Convention and does not, therefore, address the broader and ultimately more important issue of whether any changes should be made to that definition or whether the permanent establishment concept should be abandoned. The Committee on Fiscal Affairs has indicated that it 'believes that the principles which underlie the OECD Model Tax Convention are capable of being applied to electronic commerce'.[13] It has set up a Technical Advisory Group to monitor the application of existing treaty norms for the taxation of business profits in the context of electronic commerce. The general mandate of that Group is 'to examine how the current treaty rules for the taxation of business profits apply in the context of electronic commerce and examine proposals for alternative rules'. The work of that group will therefore assist the Working Party in deciding whether changes need to made to the Model Tax Convention to address this broader issue. Also, as was already mentioned in the previous proposal, the draft below does not address the issue of how much income should be attributed to electronic commerce operations carried on through computer equipment in circumstances where there would be a permanent establishment.

. . .

THE APPLICATION OF ARTICLE 5 IN THE CONTEXT OF ELECTRONIC COMMERCE:

Revised draft

1.   There has been some discussion as to whether the mere use in electronic commerce operations of computer equipment in a country could constitute a permanent establishment. That question raises a number of issues in relation to the provisions of the Article.

2.   Whilst fixed automated equipment operated by an enterprise may constitute a permanent establishment in the country where the equipment is located (see paragraph 10 [of the existing Commentary]), a distinction needs to be made between computer equipment, which could constitute a permanent establishment under certain circumstances, and the data and software which is used by, or stored on, that equipment. For instance, an Internet web site is a combination of software and electronic data that does not, in itself, involve any tangible property. It therefore cannot itself constitute a 'place of business' ('installation d'affaires' in the French version) as there is 'no facility such as premises or, in certain circumstances, machinery or equipment' (see paragraph 2 [of the existing Commentary] above) as far as the software and data constituting that web site is concerned. On the other hand, the server on which the web site is stored and used is a piece of equipment having a physical location and may thus constitute a 'fixed place of business' of the enterprise that operates it.

---

13   *Electronic Commerce: A Discussion Paper on Taxation Issues* p 23.

3. The distinction between a web site and the server on which the web site is stored and used is important since the enterprise that operates the server may be different from the enterprise that carries on business through the web site. For example, it is common for the web site through which an enterprise carries on its business to be hosted on the server of an Internet Service Provider (ISP). Although the fees paid to the ISP under such arrangements may be based on the amount of disk space used to store the software and data required by the web site, these contracts typically do not give to the enterprise to which the web site belongs any right to particular space or control over the operation of the server (as opposed to the operation of the web site software itself). In such case, the server and its location are not at the disposal of the enterprise (see paragraph 4 [of the existing Commentary]), even if the enterprise has been able to determine that its web site should be hosted on a particular server at a particular location; in fact, the enterprise does not even have a physical presence at that location since the web site does not involve tangible assets. In these cases, the enterprise cannot be considered to have acquired a place of business by virtue of that hosting arrangement. However, if the enterprise carrying on business through a web site also owns (or leases) and operates the server on which the web site is stored and used, the enterprise could constitute a permanent establishment of the enterprise if the other requirements of the Article [5] are met.

4. Computer equipment may only constitute a permanent establishment if it meets the requirement of being fixed. In the case of a server, what is relevant is not the possibility of the server being moved around, but whether it is in fact so moved. In order to constitute a fixed place of business, a server will need to be located at a certain place for a sufficient period of time so as to become fixed within the meaning of paragraph 1 [of Article 5].

5. Another issue is whether the business of an enterprise may be said to be wholly or partly carried on through equipment such as a server that it controls and operates. Some countries believe that the issue is already dealt with in paragraph 10 [of the existing Commentary], which expressly recognizes that the business of an enterprise may be carried on through automatic equipment. Other countries, however, draw a distinction between the example, given in that paragraph, of a gaming or vending machine and the servers used in electronic commerce operations. These countries consider that in the case of a gaming or vending machine, the machines are in a fixed place and enter into completed transactions with customers to provide goods or services. They note that a vendor who changes locations each week would quickly lose its customers. The location of a server is, however, irrelevant to the customer of an e-commerce operation, since the customer has access to the business' goods or services wherever the customer has an Internet connections. Thus, the e-tailer's business is carried on, not through the server, but through the enterprise's offices, warehouses, research facilities and other locations in which its income-generating activities take place. According to these countries, the requirement that the e-tailer have a 'fixed place of business' is therefore not met by the server in these circumstances.

6. A further issue is to what extent human intervention is necessary for automatic equipment to be considered to constitute a permanent establishment of an enterprise.

7. Under one view, automated equipment that does not require human intervention for its operation may constitute a permanent establishment. For these countries, the relevant question is the nature of the business and whether the activities performed through the equipment are the core income-generating activities of that business. In this respect, electronic commerce activities can be compared to other activities in which equipment operates automatically, e.g. automatic pumping equipment used in the exploitation of natural resources. It seems illogical to these countries to conclude that personnel are necessary to have a permanent establishment when no personnel are in fact necessary to generate

income. These countries cannot find any explicit reference to a requirement of human intervention in the definition of 'fixed place of business' and note that paragraph 10 [of the existing Commentary] already recognizes that automatic equipment may constitute a permanent establishment.

8.   Another view is that some human intervention is indeed necessary for a permanent establishment to exist. There are different views, however, as to the exact parameters of that requirement. Those differences relate to the following questions:
     –   whether the intervention must necessarily take place in the country or can be done from abroad;
     –   whether the intervention needs to be that of employees of the enterprise or of any person, whether or not employed by the enterprise;
     –   what level of human intervention is required.

9.   On the first question, some members consider that the intervention must be that of persons who are present for that purpose in the country where the equipment is located. According to that view, it is only under these circumstances that the enterprise can be regarded as participating in the economic life of that country like domestic enterprises that also employ capital and labour there. This requirement can also be inferred from a comparison with income from employment that can also only be taxed in the country of source if the employer is physically present there to exercise his activities. Others believe that this is the case if, as a matter of fact, it would not be possible to operate and maintain the equipment from a remote location.

10. On the second question, some Member countries consider that an enterprise may only be said to carry on, wholly or partly, business activities in a country through equipment located in that country if the equipment is operated by persons, whether or not employed by the enterprise. Others believe that there is a requirement that this input be made by persons who are employees or dependent agents, though not necessarily authorised to conclude contracts, of the enterprise and note the references to 'personnel' in paragraph 2 and 10 of the Commentary on Article 5 as support for that view. They conclude that, at least in the case of automatic equipment, where the operation and control of the equipment is done by non-enterprise personnel, this requirement is not satisfied.

11. On the third question, there are different views as to which activities would require human intervention for a permanent establishment to exist. While some members consider that what matters is whether or not the equipment is operated, and not merely set up and maintained, by persons, others think that it may be difficult to distinguish the operation from the maintenance of computer equipment, especially when databases are updated or software upgraded.

12. Another issue relates to the fact that no permanent establishment may be considered to exist where the electronic commerce operations carried on through computer equipment located in a country are restricted to the preparatory or auxiliary activities covered by paragraph 4 [of Article 5]. The question of whether particular activities performed through computer equipment fall within paragraph 4 needs to be examined on a case-by-case basis having regard to the various functions performed by the enterprise through that equipment. Examples of activities which, by themselves, would generally be regarded as preparatory or auxiliary include:
     –   providing a communications link – much like a telephone line – between suppliers and customers;
     –   advertising of goods or services;
     –   relaying information through a mirror server for security and efficiency purposes;
     –   gathering market data for the enterprise;
     –   supplying information.

13. All countries agreed that, where such functions form in themselves an essential and significant part of the commercial activity of the enterprise as a whole, or

where other core functions of the enterprise are carried on through the computer equipment, these would go beyond the activities covered by paragraph 4 and if the equipment constituted a fixed place of business of the enterprise (as discussed in paragraphs 2 to 11 above), there would be a permanent establishment.

14. There were, however, different views as to what constitutes core functions of the enterprise. Some countries took the view that where sales functions are performed through the computer equipment, whether the product is delivered on-line or by traditional methods, the equipment would constitute a 'place of business' and may be a permanent establishment. Other countries draw a parallel with the use of other communication facilities, such as the use of telephone lines to conclude a transaction. These countries are of the opinion that the essential business activity of an enterprise that sells certain products –physical or in the form of software – is the selling of the product itself. The communication tools used in the selling process should make no difference, whether the transaction is concluded by mail order, by telephone or through a server connecting the computer (web site) of the selling enterprise with the computer of the customer. They see this view as in line with the recently adopted changes to the part of the Commentary on Article 12 dealing with software payments, which put forward the view that the form in which a product is delivered (physically or electronically) should make no difference for the way in which it is taxed. Thus, only in exceptional cases do these countries see a possible permanent establishment for this category, for example if the relevant transaction (the conclusion of a contract, the payment and the delivery of the goods) is handled fully (automatically) by the server itself.

15. A last issue is whether paragraph 5 [of Article 5] may apply to deem an ISP to constitute a permanent establishment. As already noted, it is common for ISPs to provide the service of hosting the web sites of other enterprises on their own servers. The issue may then arise as to whether paragraph 5 [of Article 5] may apply to deem such ISPs to constitute permanent establishments of the enterprises that carry on electronic commerce through web sites operated through the servers owned and operated by these ISP. While this could be the case in very unusual circumstances, paragraph 5 will generally not be applicable because the ISPs will not constitute an agent of the enterprises to which the web sites belong, because they will not have authority to conclude contracts in the name of these enterprises and will not regularly conclude such contracts or because they will constitute independent agents acting in the ordinary course of their business, as evidenced by the fact that they host the web sites of many different enterprises. It is also clear that since the web site through which an enterprise carries on its business is not itself a 'person' as defined in Article 3, paragraph 5 cannot apply to deem a permanent establishment to exist by virtue of the web site being an agent of the enterprise for purposes of that paragraph.

What is clear, however, is that unless the concept of permanent establishment is modified radically, an enterprise whose website is not located in the jurisdiction will not be subject to the regulation of that jurisdiction via the 'virtual branch' theory. More likely, local regulation will apply (if at all) because the enterprise does business there.

7.2.1.2   *Doing business in the jurisdiction*

Most financial services regulations apply not only to activities from a permanent establishment in the jurisdiction, but also to specified activities carried out there by other means. The difficulty lies in deciding where precisely these activities take place when they are effected through electronic communications.

A similar problem can arise for sales of physical goods via the Internet, as in many instances those contracts may be formed outside the buyer's jurisdiction,[14] although the problem is less intractable because the fundamental performance, delivery of the goods, takes place within the jurisdiction.

The core element of all financial services activities, with the exception of giving financial advice,[15] is the manipulation of account data. This is true for eg bank account transactions, share dealings[16] and dealings in investment funds. Although there may be underlying 'real' assets,[17] the service consists in transmitting messages and modifying account data. Thus if a bank customer uses the Internet to instruct his bank to pay a bill, the required service is the transmission by the bank of an appropriate payment message and the consequential amendment of the customer's account data. Both of these activities take place on the bank's computers, in the bank's jurisdiction.[18]

From a regulator's perspective this might appear undesirable, as such an approach would permit a business which could operate purely via electronic communications to establish itself abroad, but sell its services within the regulator's jurisdiction without being subject to the regulator's control. For this reason, some national laws have been structured in such a way as to extend the regulator's jurisdiction.

Thus, for example, the UK Financial Services and Markets Act 2000 deals with this problem of deciding where a business activity takes place by extending the range of business activities covered. The basic prohibition is set out in s 19(1) of the Bill, which provides that 'No person may carry on a regulated activity in the United Kingdom, or purport to do so, unless he is – (a) an

---

14 See Chapter 6.2.1.1.

15 It is arguable that advice is given where it is received, as until that point it is merely potential advice. However, we have already noted that for VAT purposes advice would be treated as a service provided in the advisor's jurisdiction, were it not for the reverse charge provisions of VAT law – see note 7 p 195 above. The UK courts have established that the giving of advice by means of software, running without further intervention on the part of the author, is nonetheless given by the author – *Re Market Wizard Systems (UK) Ltd* [1998] 2 BCLC 282 – and it has been suggested that the same reasoning should apply to make the operator of a website liable for advice given via automated means from that website – Lars Davies 'From uncertainty to uncertainty: Developments in securities law and the Internet in the United Kingdom' (1999) Compliance Monitor, 12(5), p 71.

16 At least on modern dematerialised securities exchanges, where the dealings are in undifferentiated quantities of shares from nominee accounts rather than numbered shares identified by physical certificates – see eg UK Uncertificated Securities Regulations 1995 SI 3272.

17 Though even in terms of assets, most are 'unreal' in the sense that they are merely debts, evidenced by data relating to another account. Typical examples for a bank include loans made to its customers (eg mortgages) and Certificates of Deposit with the central bank.

18 See *Freedom to provide services and the interest of the general good in the second banking directive* Commission interpretative communication SEC(97) 1193 final, 20 June 1997, pp 6–7: 'The growth of distance services, particularly those using electronic means (Internet, home banking, etc.), will undoubtedly soon result in excessively strict criteria on location becoming obsolete. The Commission has examined certain possibilities for locating the service (originator of the initiative, customer's place of residence, supplier's place of establishment, place where contracts are signed, etc.) and considers that none could satisfactorily apply to all the activities listed in the Annex. It considers it necessary to adhere to a simple and flexible interpretation of Article 20 of the Second Directive. Accordingly, in its opinion, only activities carried on *within the territory* of another Member State should be the subject of prior notification. In order to determine where an activity was carried on, the place of provision of what may be termed the 'characteristic performance' of the service, i.e. the essential supply for which payment is due must be determined. . . . the provision of distance banking services, for example through the Internet, should not, in the Commission's view, require prior notification, since the supplier cannot be deemed to be pursuing its activities in the customer's territory.'

authorised person; or (b) an exempt person'. Schedule 2 of the Act sets out a list of eight regulated activities:

- Dealing in investments.
- Arranging deals in investments.
- Deposit taking.
- Safekeeping and administration of assets.
- Managing investments.
- Giving investment advice.
- Establishing collective investment schemes.
- Using computer-based systems for giving investment instructions.

If the prohibition merely covered performing these activities, then in most cases performance would occur on the seller's server and thus potentially outside the UK. However, Sch 2 expressly states that, with the exception of deposit taking, performance of all these activities includes offering or agreeing in the UK to undertake the activity. Thus unless the seller can structure his operations so that no offer or agreement takes place in the UK, the UK regulator will have jurisdiction over an Internet supplier of financial services.

Tax law takes a different approach. As we have seen, income-related taxes are normally only payable if business is undertaken through a permanent establishment. However, the position is different for indirect taxes. To avoid the migration of service business to low-tax jurisdictions, the EU has made specific provision in its Value Added Tax laws which deems the service to have been supplied in the recipient's jurisdiction, and thus at the recipient's VAT rate.

Sixth Council Directive of 17 May 1977 on the harmonization of the laws of the Member States relating to turnover taxes (Directive 77/388/EEC) art. 9(2):

(e) the place where the following services are supplied when performed for customers established outside the Community or for taxable persons established in the Community but not in the same country as the supplier, shall be the place where the customer has established his business or has a fixed establishment to which the service is supplied or, in the absence of such a place, the place where he has his permanent address or usually resides:

  – transfers and assignments of copyrights, patents, licences, trade marks and similar rights,
  – advertising services,
  – services of consultants, engineers, consultancy bureaux, lawyers, accountants and other similar services, as well as data processing and the supplying of information,
  – obligations to refrain from pursuing or exercising, in whole or in part, a business activity or a right referred to in this point (e),
  – banking, financial and insurance transactions including reinsurance, with the exception of the hire of safes,
  – the supply of staff,
  – the services of agents who act in the name and for the account of another, when they procure for their principal the services referred to in this point (e).

Further provisions, known as the 'reverse charge' principle, deal with the problem of tax collection by deeming the recipient to have made a taxable supply of services to himself,[19] although as we shall see in Chapter 8.1.1.1 this creates further, intractable difficulties.

19 Sixth Council Directive of 17 May 1977 on the harmonization of the laws of the Member States relating to turnover taxes (Directive 77/388/EEC) art 21(1)(b).

Either of these techniques can be used by national legislators to grant jurisdictional competence to their national regulators over Internet businesses which attract customers from the jurisdiction. However, there is a clear and important distinction to be made between the *applicability* of a law and its *enforcement*. Enforcement is normally only practicable where the defendant has personnel or assets within the jurisdiction. These issues are considered further in Chapter 9.

7.2.1.3   *Advertising*

Advertising controls are extensive in most jurisdictions,[20] and present a real problem for commercial users of the Internet. By definition, an intended commercial communication will not become an advertisement until it is read (or at least readable) by potential customers. It is this act of communication which constitutes advertising, and the only logical conclusion is that the advertising takes place where the potential customer sees the communication. In the case of a Web page advertisement, that place is the reader's computer, and thus the jurisdiction where the reader is physically located. The law which regulates that particular instance of the advertisement will therefore be the law of the place of reading.

For comparatively uncontroversial products, such as books on Internet law, it may be possible to produce a Web advertisement which is likely to comply with most, if not all, the applicable advertising laws[1] by being truthful and accurate. However, in highly regulated sectors such as financial services it is usually a criminal offence to issue an advertisement, irrespective of its truth and accuracy, unless the issuer is authorised by the national regulatory body.[2]

The UK consolidation of financial services regulation in the Financial Services and Markets Act 2000 makes this clear in s 21, which provides:

(1) A person ('A') must not, in the course of business, communicate an invitation or inducement to engage in investment activity.

---

20 For examples see Chissick and Kelman *Electronic Commerce: Law and Practice* (London: Sweet & Maxwell, 1999) Chapter 8.
1   Although where national law requires the advertisement to be in the national language, as in eg France and Portugal, this may prove expensive.
2   See eg UK Financial Services Authority, *Treatment of material on overseas Internet World Wide Web sites accessible in the UK but not intended for investors in the UK* Guidance 2/98: '10. . . . It is the FSA's view that, for the purposes of the Act, an advertisement which can be accessed on a computer screen by a person in the UK, will have been issued in the UK, but there is an important qualification to this for material issued outside the UK. The qualification appears in section 207(3) [of the Financial Services Act 1986] which sets out particular circumstances in which an investment advertisement issued outside the UK is to be treated as issued in the UK. This is particularly relevant to the operation of the Internet. 11. Broadly speaking, section 207(3) provides that an advertisement issued outside the UK will be treated as having been issued in the UK if it is either "directed at" people in the UK or "made available" to them other than by way of a periodical publication published and circulating principally outside the UK (or in a sound or television broadcast transmitted principally for reception outside the UK). It is possible that an electronic publication could fall within the definition of a "periodical publication" (this will depend on the precise facts in each case) but the FSA considers that Internet material is not "a sound or television broadcast". So, much of the information on the Internet may be viewed, for the purposes of determining whether section 57(1) applies, as having been issued in the UK as it is "made available" to persons in the UK.'

unless that person is authorised by the regulator or the advertisement is approved by an authorised person.[3] The US legislation is more diverse, but produces the same overall effect:

Securities and Exchange Commission, *Statement of the Commission Regarding Use of Internet Web Sites to Offer Securities, Solicit Securities Transactions or Advertise Investment Services Offshore,* **(Release Nos. 33-7516, 34-39779, IA-1710, IC-23071, International Series Release No. 1125) 23 March 1998**

B.   Regulation of Offers

Many registration requirements under the U.S. securities laws are triggered when an offer of securities or financial services, such as brokerage or investment advisory services, is made to the general public.

- Under the Securities Act, absent an exemption, an issuer that offers or sells securities in the United States through use of the mails or other means of interstate commerce must register the offering with the Commission.[4] An offering of securities may be exempt from registration if it is conducted as a 'private placement,' without any general solicitation of investors.[5]
- Under the Investment Company Act, a foreign investment company may not use the mails or other means of interstate commerce to publicly offer its securities in the United States or to U.S. persons unless the investment company receives an order from the Commission permitting it to register under the Investment Company Act.[6] A foreign investment company may, however, make a private offer of its securities in the United States or to U.S. persons in reliance on one of the exclusions from the definition of 'investment company' under the Investment Company Act.[7]
- Under the Advisers Act, an adviser is prohibited from using the mails or other means of interstate commerce in connection with its business as an investment adviser, unless the adviser is registered with the Commission, or is exempted or excluded from the requirement to register.[8]
- Under the Exchange Act, a broker or dealer generally must register with the Commission if it uses the mails or any means of interstate commerce to effect transactions in, or to induce or attempt to induce the purchase or sale of, any security.[9]
- Under the Exchange Act, an exchange generally must register with the Commission if it uses the mails or any means of interstate commerce for the purpose of using its facilities to effect any transaction in a security or to report any such transaction.[10]

The posting of information on a Web site may constitute an offer of securities or investment services for purposes of the U.S. securities laws.[11] Our discussion of these issues will proceed on the assumption that the Web site contains information that constitutes an 'offer' of securities or investment services under the U.S. securities

3   UK Financial Services and Markets Act 2000, s 21(2)(b).
4   Section 5 of the Securities Act, 15 USC 77e.
5   See eg s 4(2) of the Securities Act, 15 USC 77d(2); Regulation D (17 CFR 230.501-508).
6   Section 7(d) of the Investment Company Act, 15 USC 80a-7(d).
7   See s 3(c)(1) and s 3(c)(7) of the Investment Company Act, 15 USC 80a-3(c)(1), 15 USC 80a-3(c)(7). See also Staff no-action letter, Goodwin, Procter and Hoar (available February 28 1997) ('Goodwin Procter').
8   Section 203(a) of the Advisers Act, 15 USC 80b-3(a).
9   Section 15(a) of the Exchange Act, 15 USC 78o(a).
10 Section 6 of the Exchange Act, 15 USC 78f.
11 See eg Securities Act Release No 7233, Question 20 (6 October 1995) (60 FR 53458) ('The placing of the offering materials on the Internet would not be consistent with the prohibition against general solicitation or advertising in Rule 502(c) of Regulation D.').

laws.[12] Because anyone who has access to the Internet can obtain access to a Web site unless the Web site sponsor adopts special procedures to restrict access, the pertinent legal issue is whether those Web site postings are offers *in the United States* that must be registered.

The difficulty which provisions such as these presents to Internet financial services suppliers is that, to be 'legal', they in theory need to register with every supervisory authority in the world! The consequences of failure to register usually include criminal sanctions, and any transaction entered into with customers in that jurisdiction may be unenforceable.[13]

Even regulators recognise that world-wide registration is impracticable, although there are as yet no proposals to limit radically the application of the relevant laws. Some regulators have, however, attempted to mitigate the impossibility of the current situation by issuing statements about their *enforcement* policy, stating that in practice they will not take action against an advertisement unless it is targeted at customers in their jurisdiction.

The question which remains to be answered is what 'targeting' consists of. Here there are two possible approaches:

- an advertiser will not be targeting a jurisdiction if the advertisement is not made available to customers in that jurisdiction; or
- even though the advertisement is available, targeting will not have taken place if there are adequate measures to prevent customers from that jurisdiction from purchasing the financial products or services.

The UK Financial Services Authority initially adopted the first approach[14] but this was widely criticised as unworkable – in effect, a financial services company would have been required to prevent readers from viewing any part of their website which constituted an investment advertisement under the Financial Services Act 1986 unless the reader certified that he or she was not viewing the site from the UK. The current policy mixes the two approaches, although it still appears to believe that access restriction is a practicable matter:[15]

Financial Services Authority, Treatment of material on overseas Internet World Wide Web sites accessible in the UK but not intended for investors in the UK, Guidance 2/98

(II) FSA ENFORCEMENT IN RESPECT OF INVESTMENT ADVERTISEMENTS

a) General considerations
15. The FSA's main concern will be whether or not, in respect of the potential breach of the advertising provisions of the Act, any UK financial services investor protection issues are involved. A decision to take enforcement action against persons claimed to be responsible for the content of an Internet World Wide Web site[16] or those who are the sponsors or advisers to such persons (or otherwise

---

12 We also assume that the Internet is an instrument of interstate commerce and that its use satisfies the 'jurisdictional means' requirements of the federal securities laws. See *American Library Association v Pataki* 969 F Supp 160, 161 (SDNY, 1997).
13 See eg UK Financial Services and Markets Act 2000, s 28.
14 FSA Guidance Letter 'Advertising over the Internet' June 1996 – see http://www.fsa.gov.uk.
15 See particularly note 19 p 213 below.
16 By 'those claimed to be responsible for the content of an Internet World Wide Web site' the FSA means those who originate and arrange for material to appear on a site – not the provider of the technological infrastructure (eg the person providing capacity on a server or access to the World Wide Web) has no commercial interest or control over the content of the investment advertisement.

knowingly concerned with a breach of the Act) will depend upon the facts of the particular case. The FSA will consider the steps which a person has taken to avoid 'issuing', or 'causing the issue' of, an investment advertisement in the UK as indicated in this statement.

16. The FSA's policy is to ascertain first whether there has been a contravention of the provisions in section 57 of the Act. Not all material on the Internet will fall within the definition of an 'investment advertisement'. Relevant here will also be the question whether there are any other apparent infringements of the Act such as misleading statements made in breach of section 47 of the Act or the carrying on of unauthorised investment business in contravention of section 3 of the Act. Then the FSA will consider what enforcement action, if any, to take. In enforcement decisions on possible advertising contraventions the FSA will judge each case on its merits and take into account the particular circumstances and all relevant factors including, in particular, the following:

(a) whether the Internet World Wide Web site was located on a server outside the UK;[17]

(b) the extent to which the underlying investment or investment service to which the advertisement on the site related was available to UK investors who may respond to the advertisement, including the question whether the underlying investment or investment service is available to UK investors through other media;

(c) the extent to which positive steps had been taken to ensure that UK investors did not obtain the investment service as a result of an advertisement having been issued over the Internet. This would include whether the person issuing or causing the investment advertisement to be issued had systems in place to ensure that the service could be received only by persons who may lawfully receive it (which would include, for example, an effective system[18] for ascertaining the country of origin of an individual who attempts to open an account to purchase or to request further information regarding investment services on the site);

(d) the extent to which any advertisement was directed at persons in the UK (see below);

(e) the extent to which positive steps had been taken to limit access to the site[19] (see also paragraph 6 above);

b)   The extent to which investment advertisements are directed at persons in the UK

17. As regards 'directed at persons in the UK' (see (d) above) the FSA would take account of the following factors in considering any particular case:

Factors relating to the content of the site

i.   whether the site contained disclaimers and warnings, present on the home page and/or pages where investment services could be ordered/purchased (eg an application form), as well as hypertext links[20] to the disclaimer/ warning from other pages, which either stated:-

17 In the FSA's view the existence of a web site on a UK server would not be conclusive evidence that material on that site was aimed at the UK.

18 An example of an ineffective system would be one which permits a visitor to the site to purchase products or services simply by 'clicking' a box to state that he was not from the UK.

19 The 'positive steps' might include requiring pre-registration (and the issuing of passwords) to ensure that only those to whom the material was aimed had access. However, if it was in fact possible to circumvent the pre-registration process or if the pre-registration did not form a substantive check to access (for instance if you only had to 'click here' to confirm you were not from the UK), then clearly it would be difficult to argue that the material had not been 'made available' for the purposes of s 207(3) of the Act.

20 Text or a picture which provides an electronic link to another area of text/picture which may be on the same site or on another Internet site.

- that the investment services were, as a matter of fact, available only in certain countries (and if so stating which ones), or
- (where the investment services were not restricted by their nature to specific countries) that the investment services were not available in those jurisdictions where the firm was not authorised or permitted by local laws to promote or sell the product, or stating the countries where the services were, or were not, available legally;

ii. whether the warnings/disclaimers could be viewed by visitors to the site in the same browser format as the rest of the site;[1]

iii. whether the content of the site was written in a manner which made it clear that it was not aimed at UK investors (eg financial projections given in a currency other than pounds sterling; the UK not listed in a country of origin 'drop down box' option; a 'postcode', as well as a 'zipcode' option; and the material was not of specific relevance to potential UK investors – this is not an exhaustive list).

Factors relating to the promotion of the site

iv. whether those responsible for the content of the site and/or sponsors or advisers to those providing the investment services appear to have notified the existence of the site to a UK search engine or to the 'UK section' of a search engine or to any other UK orientated compendium of World Wide Web sites or listing of investment opportunities;

v. whether those responsible for the content of the site and/or the sponsors or advisers to those providing the investment services appear to have established any e-mail, or newsgroup, or bulletin board, or chat room facility associated with the site (eg which made mention of it or was (hypertext) linked to it), and that associated facility appeared to have been used actively to promote the investment in the UK (eg by sending out unsolicited e-mails or posting material to a newsgroup or chat room or through any other unsolicited approach);

vi. whether those responsible for the content of the World Wide Web site and/ or the sponsors or advisers to those providing the investment services appear to have advertised the site in the UK whether in a printed publication (eg newspaper or journal – unless the printed publication was principally for circulation outside the UK) or by broadcasting (eg TV or satellite or sound), though advertisements contained within a TV or satellite or sound broadcast which was principally for reception outside the UK would be less relevant here.

18. The above is not an exhaustive list – there may be other factors involved in a particular case which would need to be taken into account.

When the UK Financial Services and Markets Act 2000 comes into force, this advice may change, as s 21(3) provides that 'In the case of a communication originating outside the United Kingdom, subsection (1) [the prohibition] applies only if the communication is capable of having an effect in the United Kingdom'. On the assumption that mere communication of information without the possibility of any transaction taking place (because of other controls) is not capable of having an effect in the UK, it is possible that the FSA will move closer the US position.[2]

---

1 Thus ensuring that the warnings and disclaimers are visible to visitors to the site.
2 For a more detailed discussion of targeting under the UK legislation see Lars Davies 'From uncertainty to uncertainty: Developments in securities law and the Internet in the United Kingdom' (1999) Compliance Monitor, 12(5), p 71.

In the US the Securities and Exchange Commission (SEC) is responsible for authorising financial services advertisements, and its statement on enforcement policy adopts the second approach. The most important factor in deciding whether to enforce the relevant law is whether the advertiser has taken reasonable steps to prevent US persons from purchasing products or services:

Securities and Exchange Commission, *Statement of the Commission Regarding Use of Internet Web Sites to Offer Securities, Solicit Securities Transactions or Advertise Investment Services Offshore,* **(Release Nos. 33-7516, 34-39779, IA-1710, IC-23071, International Series Release No. 1125) 23 March 1998**

III. OFFSHORE OFFERS AND SOLICITATIONS ON THE INTERNET

A. General approach

Some may argue that regulators could best protect investors by requiring registration or licensing for any Internet offer of securities or investment services that their residents could access. As a practical matter, however, the adoption of such an approach by securities regulators could preclude some of the most promising Internet applications by investors, issuers, and financial service providers.

The regulation of offers is a fundamental element of federal and some U.S. state securities regulatory schemes. Absent the transaction of business in the United States or with U.S. persons, however, our interest in regulating solicitation activity is less compelling.[3] We believe that our investor protection concerns are best addressed through the implementation by issuers and financial service providers of precautionary measures that are reasonably designed to ensure that offshore Internet offers are not targeted to persons in the United States or to U.S. persons.[4]

B. Procedures Reasonably Designed to Avoid Targeting the United States

When offerors implement adequate measures to prevent U.S. persons from participating in an offshore Internet offer, we would not view the offer as targeted at the United States and thus would not treat it as occurring in the United States for registration purposes. What constitutes adequate measures will depend on all the facts and circumstances of any particular situation. We generally would not consider an offshore Internet offer made by a non-U.S. offeror as targeted at the United States, however, if:

3   Under a resolution adopted by the North American Securities Administrators Association ('NASAA'), states are encouraged to take appropriate steps to exempt Internet offers from the registration provisions of their securities laws when the offers indicate that the securities are not being offered to residents of their state and the offers are not otherwise specifically made to any persons in their state. Sales of the securities that were the subject of the Internet offer could be made in that state after the offering has been registered and the final prospectus has been delivered to investors, or where the sales are exempt from registration. NASAA, Resolution Regarding Securities Offered on the Internet (adopted 7 January 1996), 1996 CCH Par 7040 (January 1996). According to NASAA, 32 states have implemented the resolution and 15 states have indicated an intent to do so. Several foreign authorities have provided guidance on Internet and securities related issues. See eg Policy Statement 107 on Electronic Prospectuses (September 1996) http://www.asc.gov.au (Australia); Notice and Interpretation Note, Trading Securities and Providing Advice Respecting Securities on the Internet (3 March 1997) NIN #97/9 (British Columbia, Canada).
4   We use the term 'U.S. person' as it is defined in r 902(k) of Regulation S under the Securities Act (17 CFR 230.902(k)), which is premised on residence in the United States, regardless of any temporary presence outside the United States. See Securities Act Release No 7505 (18 February 1998) (63 FR 9632 (25 February 1998)) (renumbering CFR sections). 'U.S. person' generally has the same meaning for purposes of s 7(d) of the Investment Company Act as under r 902(k) of Regulation S under the Securities Act. See Goodwin Procter, supra note 13. For purposes of this release, we deem Internet offers 'targeted at the United States' to include Internet offers targeted to US persons. Cf r 902(h)(2) of Regulation S (17 CFR 230.902(h)(2)) (offers targeting identifiable groups of US persons offshore are not offshore transactions).

- The Web site includes a prominent disclaimer making it clear that the offer is directed only to countries other than the United States. For example, the Web site could state that the securities or services are not being offered in the United States or to U.S. persons, or it could specify those jurisdictions (other than the United States) in which the offer is being made;[5] and
- The Web site offeror implements procedures that are reasonably designed to guard against sales to U.S. persons in the offshore offering. For example, the offeror could ascertain the purchaser's residence by obtaining such information as mailing addresses or telephone numbers (or area code) prior to the sale. This measure will allow the offeror to avoid sending or delivering securities, offering materials, services or products to a person at a U.S. address or telephone number.

These procedures are not exclusive; other procedures that suffice to guard against sales to U.S. persons also can be used to demonstrate that the offer is not targeted at the United States. Regardless of the precautions adopted, however, we would view solicitations that appear by their content to be targeted at U.S. persons as made in the United States. Examples of this type of solicitation include purportedly offshore offers that emphasize the investor's ability to avoid U.S. income taxes on the investments.[6] We are concerned that the advice that we provide to assist those who attempt to comply with both the letter and spirit of the securities laws will be used by others as a pretext to violate those laws. Sham offshore offerings or procedures, or other schemes will not allow issuers or promoters to escape their registration obligations under the U.S. securities laws.

C.   Effect of Attempts by U.S. Persons to Evade Restrictions

We recognize that U.S. persons may respond falsely to residence questions, disguise their country of residence by using non-resident addresses, or use other devices, such as offshore nominees, in order to participate in offshore offerings of securities or investment services. Thus, even if the foreign market participant has taken measures reasonably designed to guard against sales to U.S. persons, a U.S. person nevertheless could circumvent those measures.

In our view, if a U.S. person purchases securities or investment services notwithstanding adequate procedures reasonably designed to prevent the purchase, we would not view the Internet offer after the fact as having been targeted at the United States, absent indications that would put the issuer on notice that the purchaser was a U.S. person. This information might include (but is not limited to): receipt of payment drawn on a U.S. bank; provision of a U.S. taxpayer identification or social security number; or, statements by the purchaser indicating that, notwithstanding a foreign address, he or she is a U.S. resident. Confronted with such information, we would expect offerors to take steps to verify that the purchaser is not a U.S. person before selling to that person.[7] Additionally, if despite its use of measures that appear to be reasonably designed to prevent sales to U.S. persons, the offeror discovers that it has sold to U.S. persons, it may need to evaluate whether other measures may be necessary to provide reasonable assurance against future sales to U.S. persons.

5   The disclaimer would have to be meaningful. For example, the disclaimer could state 'This offering is intended only to be available to residents of countries within the European Union'. Because of the global reach of the Internet, a disclaimer that simply states 'The offer is not being made in any jurisdiction in which the offer would or could be illegal', however, would not be meaningful. In addition, if the disclaimer is not on the same screen as the offering material, or is not on a screen that must be viewed before a person can view the offering materials, it would not be meaningful.
6   In our view, while a relevant factor, the fact that an Internet offeror posts offering materials in English even though it is based in a non-English speaking country will not, by itself, demonstrate that the offer is targeted at the United States.
7   These additional steps could include a request for further evidence (eg a copy of a passport or driver's licence).

D. Third-Party Web Services

An issuer, underwriter or other type of offshore Internet offeror may seek to have its offering materials posted on a third-party's Web site. In that event, if the offeror uses a third-party Web service that employs at least the same level of precautions against sales to U.S. persons as would be adequate for the offshore Internet offeror to employ, we would not view the third-party's Web site as an offer that is targeted to the United States.[8]

When an offeror, or those acting on its behalf, uses a third-party's Web site to generate interest in the Internet offer, more stringent precautions by the offeror than those outlined in Section III.B. may be warranted. These precautions may include limiting access to its Internet offering materials to persons who can demonstrate that they are not U.S. persons. For example, additional precautions may be called for when the Internet offeror:

- Posts offering or solicitation material or otherwise causes the offer to be listed on an investment-oriented Web site that has a significant number of U.S. clients or subscribers, or where U.S. investors could be expected to search for information about investment opportunities or services; or
- Arranges for direct or indirect hyperlinks from a third-party investment-oriented page to its own Web page containing the offering material.

Enforcement policies of this kind can provide some short-term comfort to Internet businesses. In the long term, however, they are likely to prove unworkable. The fundamental assumption behind these documents is that a financial services company will wish to retain the present geographical partitioning of the market, and will thus be prepared to register with the local supervisor each time it enters a new geographical market. However, the only structural reason why financial services products might be unattractive to customers in a foreign country is the risk of currency fluctuation, and there are comparatively simple ways of reducing this risk to an acceptable level. This means that the potential market is world-wide, and it will not be long before global financial services enterprises start to target that market. Multiple, and often contradictory, regulation will then be unrealistic. The long-term trend will have to be towards reliance on country of origin regulation.

7.2.2 Country of origin regulation

Country of origin regulation (also known as home country regulation) is the only regulatory model so far attempted which, at least in the author's opinion, is capable of resolving the conflicts between the multifarious and overlapping claims by national jurisdictions to regulate particular Internet activities. The principles of country of origin regulation are simple:

- by mutual agreement two states, or a group of states collectively, provide that activities of an organisation which is established and regulated in one state (the home state) may be carried out in another (the host state) without any requirement for prior authorisation from or supervision by the appropriate regulatory body in the host state;

---

8   Governmental authorities or securities exchanges could post issuer information that is required by law to be filed with them, including prospectuses, on their Web sites without restriction. Securities exchanges, however, should consider the US registration implications of their Web sites as a whole. See infra Section VII.B.

- the basis of this agreement is an assessment by all participating states that the others operate systems of authorisation and/or supervision which are adequate to achieve the aims of the home state's regulatory system;
- the laws of the host state will still apply:
  - to the appropriate aspects of individual transactions undertaken in the state, eg the law of contract or consumer protection law; and
  - where the host state's law or regulation has overriding effect, eg the protection of national security.

One of the first, and still the most extensive and well-developed, multilateral schemes of country of origin regulation is the EU 'single passport' for banking services. All the states making up the EEA have implemented national legislation which transposes the First and Second Banking Directives, and other related legislation,[9] the net effect of which is to provide a pan-European system under which a credit institution which is established in and regulated by one country is free to provide banking services in all the others. The essence of the system is described in the Recitals to the Second Banking Directive:

Second Council Directive 89/646/EEC of 15 December 1989 on the coordination of laws, regulations and administrative provisions relating to the taking up and pursuit of the business of credit institutions, Recitals (numbering added)

4. Whereas the approach which has been adopted is to achieve only the essential harmonization necessary and sufficient to secure the mutual recognition of authorization and of prudential supervision systems, making possible the granting of a single licence recognized throughout the Community and the application of the principle of home Member State prudential supervision;

. . .

8. Whereas the principles of mutual recognition and of home Member State control require the competent authorities of each Member State not to grant authorization or to withdraw it where factors such as the activities programme, the geographical distribution or the activities actually carried on make it quite clear that a credit institution has opted for the legal system of one Member State for the purpose of evading the stricter standards in force in another Member State in which it intends to carry on or carries on the greater part of its activities; whereas, for the purposes of this Directive, a credit institution shall be deemed to be situated in the Member State in which it has its registered office; whereas the Member States must require that the head office be situated in the same Member State as the registered office;

. . .

10. Whereas responsibility for supervising the financial soundness of a credit institution, and in particular its solvency, will rest with the competent authorities of its home Member State; whereas the host Member State's competent authorities will retain responsibility for the supervision of liquidity and monetary policy; whereas the supervision of market risk must be the subject of close cooperation between the competent authorities of the home and host Member States;

. . .

12. Whereas, by virtue of mutual recognition, the approach chosen permits credit institutions authorized in their home Member States to carry on, throughout

---

9   Eg Council Directive 89/299/EEC of 17 April 1989 on the own funds of credit institutions, OJ L 124 05.05.89, p 16; Council Directive 89/647/EEC of 18 December 1989 on a solvency ratio for credit institutions OJ L 386 30.12.89, p 14 (as amended); Council Directive 92/30/ EEC of 6 April 1992 on the supervision of credit institutions on a consolidated basis, OJ L 110 28.04.92, p 52; Council Directive 92/121/EEC of 21 December 1992 on the monitoring and control of large exposures of credit institutions, OJ L 029 05.02.93, p 1.

the Community, any or all of the activities listed in the Annex by establishing branches or by providing services;

...

16. Whereas the Member States must ensure that there are no obstacles to carrying on activities receiving mutual recognition in the same manner as in the home Member State, as long as the latter do not conflict with legal provisions protecting the general good in the host Member State;

...

20. Whereas the authorizations granted to credit institutions by the competent national authorities pursuant to this Directive will have Community-wide, and no longer merely nationwide, application, and whereas existing reciprocity clauses will henceforth have no effect; whereas a flexible procedure is therefore needed to make it possible to assess reciprocity on a Community basis; whereas the aim of this procedure is not to close the Community's financial markets but rather, as the Community intends to keep its financial markets open to the rest of the world, to improve the liberalization of the global financial markets in other third countries; whereas, to that end, this Directive provides for procedures for negotiating with third countries and, as a last resort, for the possibility of taking measures involving the suspension of new applications for authorization or the restriction of new authorizations;

Similar EU initiatives in the related fields of financial services[10] and insurance[11] are creating comparable schemes for those fields of activity.

However, banking and financial services is not the only field of activity where country of origin regulation is being adopted. The developing global infrastructure for electronic signatures, examined in detail in Chapter 5, recognises that a Certification Authority will find it unrealistically burdensome to become accredited in each jurisdiction where certificate holders might wish to use electronic signature based on its certificates. Most digital signature laws therefore contain provision for mutual recognition of foreign accreditation schemes, with the result that certificates emanating from a Certification Authority accredited under such a scheme will be given equivalent legal effect to certificates from a locally accredited issuer. Thus the Singapore Electronic Transactions Act 1998 s. 20 provides:

When any portion of an electronic record is signed with a digital signature, the digital signature shall be treated as a secure electronic signature with respect to such portion of the record, if –

a. the digital signature was created during the operational period of a valid certificate and is verified by reference to the public key listed in such certificate; and

b. the certificate is considered trustworthy, in that it is an accurate binding of a public key to a person's identity because . . .

   ii. the certificate was issued by a certification authority outside Singapore recognised for this purpose by the Controller pursuant to regulations made under section 43 . . .

10 See eg Council Directive 93/22/EEC of 10 May 1993 on investment services in the securities field OJ L 141 11.06.93, p 27.
11 See eg Council Directive 92/49/EEC of 18 June 1992 on the coordination of laws, regulations and administrative provisions relating to direct insurance other than life assurance and amending Directives 73/239/EEC and 88/357/EEC (third non-life insurance Directive) OJ L 228 11.08.92, p 1; Council Directive 92/96/EEC of 10 November 1992 on the coordination of laws, regulations and administrative provisions relating to direct life assurance and amending Directives 79/267/EEC and 90/619/EEC (third life assurance Directive) OJ L 360 09.12.92, p 1.

Similarly, the EU Directive on electronic signatures[12] art 7(1) provides:

> Member States shall ensure that certificates which are issued as qualified certificates to the public by a certification-service-provider established in a third country are recognised as legally equivalent to certificates issued by a certification-service-provider established within the Community if . . .
>
> (c) the certificate or the certification-service-provider is recognised under a bilateral or multilateral agreement between the Community and third countries or international organisations.

and arts 7(2) and 7(3) give the European Commission powers to make proposals for achieving the effective implementation of standards and international agreements, and to propose the negotiation of bilateral and multilateral agreements with third countries and international organisations.

It seems likely that as new types of Internet commercial activity are devised which require supervisory regulation, these precedents will lead to similar systems of country of origin regulation. EC Directive 2000/31/EC on electronic commerce has already adopted the rinciple, in arts 3 and 4, as standard for most electronic commerce activities.

Because the essence of country of origin regulation is the acceptance by the host country that the home country provides an adequate and broadly equivalent level of regulatory oversight, there are two fundamental issues which any scheme needs to address:

- What are the minimum standards for authorisation and supervision?
- What exceptions to country of origin regulation are permitted? This is particularly important, as there is otherwise a tendency for states to maintain or impose regulatory requirements whose indirect effect is to reserve the home market to those established in and regulated by the home country.

7.2.2.1   Minimum standards for authorisation and supervision

Both the banking and electronic signatures implementations of home country regulation recognise four factors as the basis for a set of minimum standards:

- the enterprise must be a fit and proper person to undertake the regulated activity;[13]
- it must be financially sound so as to ensure continued, solvent operation;[14]
- its staff must be properly qualified, adequately trained and well-supervised;[15]
- its operational and technical systems must be of appropriate quality and adequately maintained and updated.[16]

---

12 Directive 1999/93/EC OJ L13 19.1.2000, p 12.

13 See eg Second Council Directive 89/646/EEC of 15 December 1989 on the coordination of laws, regulations and administrative provisions relating to the taking up and pursuit of the business of credit institutions, art 5; German Digital Signature Act (Signaturgesetz) 1997 § 4(2); German Digital Signature Ordinance (Signaturverordnung) § 3(2).

14 See eg Second Council Directive 89/646/EEC of 15 December 1989 on the coordination of laws, regulations and administrative provisions relating to the taking up and pursuit of the business of credit institutions, art 4; American Bar Association *Digital Signature Guidelines* (Chicago: ABA, 1996) guideline 3.3.

15 See eg Council Directive 92/30/EEC of 6 April 1992 on the supervision of credit institutions on a consolidated basis, OJ L 110 28.04.92, p 52; Utah Digital Signature Act 1996 (Utah Code § 46-3) § 201(1)(c).

16 See eg Second Council Directive 89/646/EEC of 15 December 1989 on the coordination of laws, regulations and administrative provisions relating to the taking up and pursuit of the business of credit institutions, art 13(2); for electronic signatures see Chapter 5.4.3.

Because acting as a bank is, in operational terms, quite different from acting as a certification authority, in each case it has proved necessary to expand on these fundamental principles in detail.[17] However, the principles are only intended to set out the minimum requirements for an international business which is one element of an interconnected infrastructure that is fundamental to the continuance of commercial and private life, rather than to address any particular technology or type of business activity. It thus seems likely that they will prove to be applicable to new Internet activities as they develop.

7.2.2.2 *Exceptions to country of origin regulation*

The basis of country of origin regulation is not that the regulation by home and host country is the same, but that it is broadly equivalent. It is therefore tempting for a host country to wish to apply certain elements of its own regulatory system to foreign providers of services, notwithstanding multilateral or bilateral agreement establishing the country of origin principle. An essential element of such agreements is therefore the establishment of the limits on the host country's ability to apply its national regulations. In the EU, whose single market project has resulted in extensive jurisprudence on the topic,[18] departure from the country of origin principle is normally only justified if it is for 'the general good'.[19]

In the context of the Second Banking directive, this issue caused so many problems that the European Commission found it necessary to issue a consultation document on the topic, setting out the circumstances in which it would be legitimate to derogate from the principle. An important element in assessing legitimacy is whether the derogation is proportionate, in other words whether there is a less restrictive measure which would achieve the general good objective. The Commission's reasoning is likely to influence future schemes for country of origin regulation.

> **Freedom to provide services and the interest of the general good in the second banking directive, Commission interpretative communication SEC(97) 1193 final 20 June 1997**
>
> An assessment of the proportionality of a restriction may in fact differ depending on the mode of operation.
>
> Accordingly, a restriction could more readily be considered to be proportionate in the case of an operator working permanently within a territory than in the case of the same operator working only temporarily.

---

17 See eg references in note 9 p 218; Singapore Electronic Transactions (Certification Authority) Regulations 1999, Parts III and V.
18 See eg *Säger v Dennemeyer* Case C-76/90 [1991] ECR I-4221; *Commission v Germany* Case 205/84 [1986] ECR 3755; *Commission v Belgium* Case C-11/95 [1996] ECR I-4115.
19 The general good encompasses a wide range of interests; those so far recognised by the European Court of Justice are:
'protection of the recipient of services, protection of workers, including social protection, consumer protection, preservation of the good reputation of the national financial sector, prevention of fraud, social order, protection of intellectual property, cultural policy, preservation of the national historical and artistic heritage, cohesion of the tax system, road safety, protection of creditors and protection of the proper administration of justice.'
Freedom to provide services and the interest of the general good in the second banking directive, Commission interpretative communication SEC(97) 1193 final, 20 June 1997.

The Court has recognized this difference by imposing a less restrictive and more 'lightweight' legal framework for suppliers of services operating in a temporary capacity than for established suppliers.

It has consistently held that a Member State:

'may not make the provision of services in its territory subject to compliance with all the conditions required for establishment and thereby deprive of all practical effectiveness the provisions of the Treaty whose object is, precisely, to guarantee the freedom to provide services'.[20]

The Court has also held that restrictions on the freedom to provide services are even less acceptable in cases where the service is supplied 'without its being necessary for the person providing it to visit the territory of the Member State where it is provided'.[1] This clarification is particularly relevant to banking services, which are increasingly supplied without physical movement on the part of the supplier.

The Court has likewise consistently held that it does not follow from the third paragraph of Article 60 of the Treaty that:

'all national legislation applicable to nationals of that State and usually applied to the permanent activities of undertakings established therein may be similarly applied in its entirety to the temporary activities of undertakings which are established in other Member States'.[2]

Thus, depending on the circumstances, the same restriction applied in the interest of the general good could be adjudged proportionate in respect of a branch but disproportionate in respect of a temporary provider of services. The Commission considers, for example, that a Member State which imposes certain formalities on credit institutions (controls, registration, costs, communication of information, etc.) for reasons that purport to be in the general good should take account of the mode of operation chosen by the credit institution carrying on activities within its territory under mutual-recognition arrangements.

However, this distinction cannot be applied to consumer-protection rules (provided, of course, that they have satisfied the other tests). The level of consumer protection required must be identical, whether the service is supplied under the freedom to provide services or by way of establishment. It would be unacceptable for a consumer to be less well protected according to whether he received a service from a non-established undertaking or an established undertaking.

It may be necessary, however, to take account of the circumstances in which the service was requested. There may be situations in which the consumer has deliberately avoided the protection afforded him by his national law, particularly where he requests a service from a non-established bank without having first been canvassed in any way by that bank.

7.3   HUMAN RIGHTS AND TRANSBORDER COMMUNICATION

It is not at first sight obvious that there is a potential clash between laws protecting human rights and the principle on which the Internet works, unrestricted flow of information across national boundaries. However, even a cursory examination of the two human rights which are most affected by Internet communications – privacy and free speech – reveals that these rights themselves are potentially conflicting.

---

20 Case C-76/90 *Säger;* [1991] ECR I-4221. See also Case C-198/89 *Commission v Greece* [1991] ECR I-727.

1 Case C-76/90 *Säger* [1991] ECR I-4221.

2 Case 205/84 *Commission v Germany* [1991] ECR I-727. See also the judgment of 17 December 1981, Case 279/80 *Webb* [1981] ECR 3305.

United Nations Convention on Human Rights 1948

Article 12. No one shall be subjected to arbitrary interference with his privacy, family, home or correspondence, nor to attacks upon his honour and reputation. Everyone has the right to the protection of the law against such interference or attacks.

Article 19. Everyone has the right to freedom of opinion and expression; this right includes freedom to hold opinions without interference and to seek, receive and impart information and ideas through any media and regardless of frontiers.

An absolute right to free speech means that those whose privacy is infringed by that speech have no remedy. An absolute right to privacy prevents free speech about others. Even within a single jurisdiction, the law must balance these two rights by placing restrictions on each.

Once information crosses national borders, as is almost inevitable with Internet communications, additional conflicts arise. Because the rights of privacy and free speech are not absolute most states impose limitations on them, either for the protection of other citizens or to preserve elements of the national and economic interest.[3] These limitations vary widely from state to state, as legislators and courts take differing views of the necessary balance to be struck.[4] Because, say, a Web page is accessible from all jurisdictions, an author will only be able to comply with the differing national limitations by complying with the most stringent limitations on his freedom of speech, and similarly may need to observe the highest privacy standards.

In practice those limitations which protect individual interests by giving the affected person a right of action will rarely have substantially restrictive effects. The normal remedy is one of damages,[5] and cross-border litigation is likely only for the most serious infringements. More serious are the limitations which are enforced by national authorities, whose actions will in many cases have an

---

3 See eg European Convention For Protection Of Human Rights And Fundamental Freedoms 1950, art 8 (right to respect for private life): '2. There shall be no interference by a public authority with the exercise of this right except such as is in accordance with the law and is necessary in a democratic society in the interests of national security, public safety or the economic well-being of the country, for the prevention of disorder or crime, for the protection of health or morals, or for the protection of the rights and freedoms of others.' and art 10 (freedom of expression): '2. The exercise of these freedoms, since it carries with it duties and responsibilities, may be subject to such formalities, conditions, restrictions or penalties as are prescribed by law and are necessary in a democratic society, in the interests of national security, territorial integrity or public safety, for the prevention of disorder or crime, for the protection of health or morals, for the protection of the reputation or rights of others, for preventing the disclosure of information received in confidence, or for maintaining the authority and impartiality of the judiciary.'

4 See Chapter 4.2.2 and 4.2.3 for an examination of the differing standards for defamation and obscenity.

5 Though note the recent practice of the Dutch Courts of issuing a world-wide mandatory injunction against further publication, deriving from the Supreme Court (*Hooge Raad*) decision in *Interlas v Lincoln* (1989) NJ No 404, p 1597. Although that case concerned trade mark infringement, it is recognised that the principle applies at a minimum to other intellectual property rights – Wolfgang Meibom and Hohann Pitz 'Cross-border Injunctions in International Patent Infringement Proceedings' [1997] 8 EIPR 469 – and might in the future be extended to other rights infringed by publication. Even though the UK courts, for example, do not grant such wide-ranging injunctions, a Dutch world-wide injunction would be enforceable in the UK under the Brussels Convention on Jurisdiction and the Enforcement of Judgments in Civil and Commercial Matters 1968, art 25 of which defines 'judgment' to include judgments which are not final and which are interlocutory or provisional in nature.

extraterritorial effect, and this part of the chapter will concentrate on that aspect of the issue.

7.3.1   Free speech

The First Amendment to the US Constitution provides one of the most powerful protections for freedom of speech. Although it is possible for Congress to enact restrictions on freedom of speech, particularly for forms of expression such as defamation and obscenity which 'are no essential part of any exposition of ideas, and are of such slight social value as a step to truth that any benefit that may be derived from them is clearly outweighed by the social interest in order and morality',[6] the US courts are highly suspicious of any limitations on the right. In *ACLU v Reno*[7] the Supreme Court struck down the criminal provisions of the Communications Decency Act 1996[8] on the grounds that it did not define its offences adequately, provided no defence that the communication had socially redeeming value, and was more restrictive than necessary to achieve its legitimate aims. The courts have also recognised the risk that operators of Internet services will exercise self-censorship because of the difficulties in complying with access control obligations and the costs of implementing them, and that this is a factor to be taken into account when determining whether a statute contravenes the First Amendment.[9]

Other countries protect freedom of speech less strongly than the US, giving greater weight to the interests of social order and the public good. We have already seen in Chapter 4.2.3 how UK law provides a low level of free speech protection to makers of defamatory statements, and particularly to on-line intermediaries who transmit those statements. Similarly large differences are also found in laws prohibiting the dissemination of obscene material.[10] Thus many disputes arise concerning material which is hosted by US ISPs, and is lawful in the US, but which contravenes the laws of another country in which is it equally accessible.

Some of the most prominently publicised disputes have arisen in Germany:

European Commission Communication, *Illegal and harmful content on the Internet* **(http://www2.echo.lu/legal/en/internet/communic.html [footnotes omitted])**[11]

[An] approach which involves requiring access providers to block their subscribers' access to illegal content on a case-by-case basis has been followed recently by law enforcement authorities in Germany.

In the CompuServe case the public prosecutors considered that certain items available on newsgroups were illegal, and requested CompuServe to block access to these newsgroups. Since CompuServe's software did not initially make it possible to differentiate between German subscribers and others for access to newsgroups,

---

6   *Chaplinsky v New Hampshire* 315 U.S. 568, 572 (1942).

7   929 F Supp 824, 830–838 (ED Pa, 1996), *affirmed* 117 S Ct 2329 (1997).

8   See Chapter 4.3.2.2 for a discussion of the surviving parts of the Act, which provide immunity to communications intermediaries.

9   *American Civil Liberties Union v Reno (II)* No. 98-5591(ED Pa, 1 February 1999), granting a preliminary injunction prohibiting enforcement of the 'material harmful to minors' provisions of the Child Online Protection Act 1998, 47 USC 231.

10   See Chapter 4.2.2.1.

11   See also Decision No 276/1999/EC of the European Parliament and of the Council of 25 January 1999 adopting a multiannual Community action plan on promoting safer use of the Internet by combating illegal and harmful content on global networks, OJ L 33/1 6.2.1999.

CompuServe suspended access to a number of newsgroups to all its subscribers world-wide, which created wide-spread protests that German standards of morality were being exported. Subsequently, CompuServe restored access to most of these newsgroups except to its German subscribers. No action was apparently taken against other access providers based in Germany, so their subscribers could continue to consult this content, if the access provider chose to carry the newsgroup in question.

In a recent case, the German public prosecutors threatened to prosecute the German Internet access providers unless they blocked access to a magazine published on a Web site on a server in the Netherlands which allegedly promoted terrorist violence. Under protest, the access providers did so. However, this meant blocking access to all content on the Dutch server, including harmless content, while the document continues to be available to Internet users outside Germany. A number of anti-blocking tactics were also immediately put in place. It is not clear whether the content is contrary to Dutch law – at all events the Dutch authorities have not intervened. The Dutch host service provider has complained that the action of the German authorities constitutes an interference with the free movement of services within the EU.

Further actions by German prosecutors have included investigations of AOL in respect of distributing Neo-Nazi material,[12] the prosecution of a leading politician for including on her Web page a link to an underground magazine dedicated to the overthrow of the German government by force,[13] forcing the blocking of German access to the alt.sex hierarchy of usenet newsgroups[14] and the conviction of the managing Director of CompuServe Germany for transmission of images of bestiality, child pornography and sexual violence which could have been blocked.[15]

Interestingly, none of these actions appear to have been successful in preventing German residents from gaining access to material concerned. In the case of the Dutch website referred to above, the material immediately became available from other sources.[16] It seems that, in practical terms, the Internet overcomes constraints on free speech through the relocation of materials:

Viktor Mayer-Schönberger and Teree E. Foster, *Free Speech and the Global Information Infrastructure*, **56 Michigan Telecommunications and Technology Law Review [Vol. 3:45 1996–1997] 45, 54**

B. NATIONAL ENFORCEMENT AND INTERNATIONAL STRUCTURES

As we have established, the Internet, even if global in scope, is not an absolutist free speech domain, but is instead subject to innumerable national restrictions. At the same time, the very structure of the Net substantially diminishes the chances for enforcement of national regulations.[17]

12 An offence under art 86 of the German Criminal Code (Strafgesetzbuch).
13 Although she was acquitted on the ground that she did not have actual knowledge of the site linked to – see KL Rappaport 'In the Wake of *Reno v ACLU*: The Continued Struggle in Western Constitutional Democracies with Internet Censorship and Freedom of Speech Online' [1998] American University Int Law Review, 13(3), 765, 789.
14 A Kennedy *Net Censorship: Fighting for Free Speech* http://www.netfreedom.org/uk/angus.html (1997).
15 (1998) Independent, 25 June. The conviction was overturned on appeal in 1999.
16 European Commission Communication *Illegal and harmful content on the Internet* http://www2.echo.lu/legal/en/internet/communic.html notes that 'At the latest count, the document is mirrored on 43 WWW sites and 2 newsgroups and is available from an e-mail listserver'.
17 'The on-line world's lack of respect for state and national borders is making a mockery of outdated laws.' Attempts to erect national barriers against subversive or culturally-polluting information are readily circumvented. 'On-Line Boundaries Unclear: Internet Tramples Legal Jurisdictions' (1995) Computerworld, June 5, News, at 1.

National speech restrictions can be enforced directly only within the territory to which they apply.[18] But the Net is global, and so is the flow of information. People who disseminate information through the Net that is illegal in one country can easily transfer their operations to a country with no similar prohibitions and effectively reorganize their disseminating action in matters of hours.

For the recipients of such information, redeployment is hardly noticeable in an environment dominated by the World Wide Web where information is accessed and retrieved by simply clicking on information links. Because distance from or location of information sources within the World Wide Web is irrelevant to the recipient, access to the relocated information sources is easy and straightforward. Already there exist numerous examples of exiled political groups taking advantage of information infrastructure networks located in countries with regulatory environments more sympathetic to their cause to widely disseminate political information to countries with more restrictive speech and information regulations. Chinese human rights activists use the World Wide Web to advocate for their cause,[19] and Tibetan women in exile castigate the Chinese government for its treatment of their sisters still in Tibet.[20] CAPA, an organization that supports Cubans fleeing their country and delivers accounts on their rescue and survival can be found on the Web, as well as solidarity pages for the Tupac Amaru hostage takers in Peru,[1] while German Nazis use American and Canadian Web sites to discuss fascism and to issue denials of the Holocaust, a crime under the German Penal Code.[2]

Information sources need not necessarily be redeployed for information to be disseminated across porous national borders. Other tools are available on the global Net to channel information in order to obscure its source and place of origin. Anonymous remailers allow electronic information to be stripped of all its identifying bits and sent without attribution to any recipient.[3] Together with widely available tools of public key encryption,[4] remailers allow worldwide electronic communication on a totally anonymous level, thus circumventing any national attempts at speech regulation.

18 However, the United States has occasionally, and with some degree of success, extended its territorial reach. For example, in *United States v Alvarez-Machain* 504 US 655 (1992), the Supreme Court upheld the United States' assertion of jurisdiction over a Mexican national who had been forcibly kidnapped and brought to the United States to stand trial for the murder of a Drug Enforcement Agent in Mexico.

19 *Support Democracy in China* <http://christusrex.org/wwwl/sdc/ sdchome.html>.

20 *Statement of the Tibetan Women's Delegation Fourth World Conference on Women, NGO Forum 95 Huairou, China—September 2, 1995* <http:// www.grannyg.bc.ca/tibet/ tibetpr3.html>.

 1 See eg The official Tupac Amaru Homepage can be found at <http://www.cybercity.dk/users/ ccc17427>, for an US Tupac Amaru Solidarity Page, see <http://burn.ucsd.edu/~ats/ mrta.htm>. For an Italian one see <http://vivaldi.nexus.it/commerce/tmcrew/news/mrtal.htm>.

 2 The Institute for Historical Review, an organization denying the Holocaust, is present on the WWW through a server in the United States. Its internet offerings include 'Auschwitz myths and facts' and 'What is a Holocaust denial?' and include outrageous quotes presented in a quasi-scientific context. The Stormfront magazine is a fascist publication operating servers in the United States and Canada. It maintains the White Nationalist Resource Page and contains explicit references to notorious Nazi Gary Lauck. Lauck has used electronic and conventional mail to massively disseminate Nazi propaganda in Germany. He was arrested in Denmark while on a lecture tour and later extradited to Germany, where he is currently awaiting trial for violation of the German Penal Code prohibiting national socialist propaganda. Other web sites include The White Nationalist Page and the Counter-Revolutionary Resource Page. Electronic mailing lists are available a well. For extensive information, see Burkhard Schröder *Neonazis und Computernetze* (Reinbek: Rowohlt, 1995) at 41 and see also Ursula Maier-Rabler, Viktor Mayer-Schönberger, Gabriele Schmölzer and Georg Nening-Schöfbänker *Net Without Qualities* (1995) http://www.komdat.sbg.ac.at/nikt., at 72.

 3 The most well-known anonymous remailer is operated without charge by Johan Helsingius in Finland. His remailer can be reached at anon.penet.fi. A Usenet discussion group on remailers can be found at alt.privacy.anon-server; *see* Andre Bacard *Anonymous Remailer FAQ* <http:// www.well.com/ user/abacard/remail.html>.

 4 David Chaum *Achieving Electronic Privacy* (1992) Sci Am, August, at 96–101.

Continued information redeployment will eventually shape and reshape the global information infrastructure. Nations with little speech regulation or inefficient enforcement structures will attract vast quantities of data and information illegal in other countries. The global infrastructure will experience sustained economic pressures similar to those experienced on the high seas by the 'flags of convenience' phenomenon. By redeploying their fleets under 'flags of convenience', shipping companies essentially forced countries to deregulate.[5] A similar phenomenon could materialize on the Net. Some countries might evolve into booming 'data havens', while others might face a choice between economic hardship and relinquishing their speech constraints, thus compromising their national or civic values.

7.3.2 Privacy

Probably the best-known description of privacy is as the 'right to be let alone'.[6] This, by itself, is an inadequate statement of the right. With the exception of hermits and recluses, it is not possible to live in human society without interacting with others, and this requires the sharing of personal information.[7] A privacy law thus consists of two elements:

- a definition of the circumstances in which third parties have the right to collect, use and disseminate personal information about others; and
- a mechanism for preventing collection, use and dissemination outside those limits.

The first of these is largely culturally-determined, with nation states taking very different views of what information should be treated as private. For example, in Sweden tax returns are publicly available information, and the initial text of the EU telecommunications privacy Directive[8] contained a provision drafted at the behest of France that itemised telephone bills should not display the last few digits of the numbers called.[9]

The second also reflects cultural differences, and in particular the national view as to what role the state should play in protecting privacy. At one extreme, the US tends to leave the question of privacy to be dealt with by State legislation and common law, although there are some laws which apply to particular sectors of industry or the administration.[10] The majority of US privacy protection, however, is provided by industry self-regulation and enforcement is left to action

---

5 'Flags of convenience' defines a situation where registration of foreign-owned and foreign-controlled vessels is permitted by certain countries under conditions that are convenient and opportune for the registrant. Flags of convenience have been variously referred to as 'flags of necessity', 'cheap flags', and 'free flags'. R Tali Epstein 'Should the Fair Labor Standards Act Enjoy Extraterritorial Application? A Look At the Unique Case of Flags of Convenience' (1993) 13 U Pa J Int'l Bus L, 653, 655.
6 Warren and Brandeis 'The Right to Privacy' (1890) Harvard Law Review, IV(5), p 193.
7 A concept recognised well before the Information Age – see eg John Donne Meditation 17 from *Devotions Upon Emergent Occasions* (1624) 'No man is an island, entire of itself'.
8 Now enacted without those provisions as Directive 97/66/EC of the European Parliament and of the Council concerning the processing of personal data and the protection of privacy in the telecommunications sector, OJ L 24, 30 January 1998, p 1.
9 This was widely rumoured to have been designed to prevent the wives of French politicians from discovering the telephone number of their husband's mistress.
10 See eg US Electronic Communications Privacy Act 1986, applying to the Federal sector; US Children's Online Privacy Protection Act 1998.

by the individual concerned.[11] For these reasons, US privacy law has little practical transborder effect.

The position is quite different in those countries which take the view that the state should play the primary role in protecting privacy. The clearest example is the European system of data protection, which initially covered only personal information held in computerised form[12] but has recently been extended to cover organised collections of manually accessible information.[13] The structure of the regime is set out in Directive 95/46/EC on the protection of individuals with regard to the processing of personal data and on the free movement of such data[14] which harmonises the law of the Member States and is implemented by national law.[15]

- 'controllers'[16] of personal data[17], and those who merely process data on behalf of controllers ('processors')[18] are normally required to register with the appropriate national supervisory authority,[19] stating the purposes for which personal data will be processed, the categories of data subject on whom data will be collected, the categories of recipient to whom disclosure will be made and any proposed transfers of data to non-EU countries;[20]
- controllers must then comply with the basic principles of the Directive, set out in art 6(1):

   Member States shall provide that personal data must be:

   (a) processed fairly and lawfully;
   (b) collected for specified, explicit and legitimate purposes and not further processed in a way incompatible with those purposes. Further processing of data for historical, statistical or scientific purposes shall not be considered as incompatible provided that Member States provide appropriate safeguards;
   (c) adequate, relevant and not excessive in relation to the purposes for which they are collected and/or further processed;
   (d) accurate and, where necessary, kept up to date; every reasonable step must be taken to ensure that data which are inaccurate or incomplete, having regard to the purposes for which they were collected or for which they are further processed, are erased or rectified;

11 For a review of US privacy law, see Eric J Sinrod and Barak D Jolish 'Controlling Chaos: The Emerging Law of Privacy and Speech in Cyberspace' (1999) Stan Tech L Rev 1 http://stlr.stanford.edu/STLR/Articles/99_STLR_1/.
12 Reflecting its origins in the Council of Europe *Convention for the Protection of Individuals with regard to Automatic Processing of Personal Data* (Strasbourg, 1981). See also the OECD Guidelines on the Protection of Privacy and Transborder Flows of Personal Data (1981).
13 Directive 95/46/EC on the protection of individuals with regard to the processing of personal data and on the free movement of such data, OJ No. L 281, 23.11.1995, art 2(b) (defining 'filing system').
14 OJ No. L 281, 23.11.1995.
15 Eg UK Data Protection Act 1998.
16 Directive 95/46/EC, art 2(d).
17 Defined in Directive 95/46/EC, art 2(a) as 'any information relating to an identified or identifiable natural person ("data subject"); an identifiable person is one who can be identified, directly or indirectly, in particular by reference to an identification number or to one or more factors specific to his physical, physiological, mental, economic, cultural or social identity'.
18 Directive 95/46/EC, art 2(e).
19 The permissible exemptions to the registration requirement are set out in Directive 95/46/EC, art 18(2)–(4).
20 Directive 95/46/EC, arts 18 and 19.

(e) kept in a form which permits identification of data subjects for no longer than is necessary for the purposes for which the data were collected or for which they are further processed. Member States shall lay down appropriate safeguards for personal data stored for longer periods for historical, statistical or scientific use.

- enforcement of the controller's obligations is primarily through action by the supervising authority,[1] although affected individuals who suffer damage as a result of a controller's breach of the relevant national law are also entitled to claim compensation from the controller.[2]

To decide whether a particular controller is subject to the regime, art 4 provides as follows:

- the controller is subject to the law of each Member State where it has an establishment and undertakes processing;[3]
- a controller who is established outside the EU will nonetheless be subject to the law of each Member State where he makes use of data processing equipment (other than solely for transmitting data through that country);[4]
- a controller is also subject to a Member State's law if it is 'not established on the Member State's territory, but in a place where its national law applies by virtue of international public law'.[5]

It is clear that the second and third parts of art 4 have the potential for extraterritorial effect, subjecting an Internet user outside the EU to the data protection laws of one or more Member States.

The Directive also contains provisions designed to prevent personal data whose privacy is protected under the regime from losing that protection by being exported to a third country, unless the data subject has consented to the transfer or there is some legitimate justification for it.[6] Article 25 states:

---

1   Directive 95/46/EC, art 28.
2   Directive 95/46/EC, art 23.
3   Directive 95/46/EC, art 4(1); for a discussion of establishment see 7.2.1.1 above.
4   Directive 95/46/EC, art 4(3).
5   Directive 95/46/EC, art. 4(2); the work of the Hague Conference on Private International Law may incorporate provisions on this point in its forthcoming Convention on jurisdiction and the effects of judgments in civil and commercial matters – see http://www.hcch.net.
6   Directive 95/46/EC, art 26(1): 'By way of derogation from Article 25 and save where otherwise provided by domestic law governing particular cases, Member States shall provide that a transfer or a set of transfers of personal data to a third country which does not ensure an adequate level of protection within the meaning of Article 25(2) may take place on condition that: (a) the data subject has given his consent unambiguously to the proposed transfer; or (b) the transfer is necessary for the performance of a contract between the data subject and the controller or the implementation of precontractual measures taken in response to the data subject's request; or (c) the transfer is necessary for the conclusion or performance of a contract concluded in the interest of the data subject between the controller and a third party; or (d) the transfer is necessary or legally required on important public interest grounds, or for the establishment, exercise or defence of legal claims; or (e) the transfer is necessary in order to protect the vital interests of the data subject; or (f) the transfer is made from a register which according to laws or regulations is intended to provide information to the public and which is open to consultation either by the public in general or by any person who can demonstrate legitimate interest, to the extent that the conditions laid down in law for consultation are fulfilled in the particular case.'

1. The Member States shall provide that the transfer to a third country of personal data which are undergoing processing or are intended for processing after transfer may take place only if, without prejudice to compliance with the national provisions adopted pursuant to the other provisions of this Directive, the third country in question ensures an adequate level of protection,

2. The adequacy of the level of protection afforded by a third country shall be assessed in the light of all the circumstances surrounding a data transfer operation or set of data transfer operations; particular consideration shall be given to the nature of the data, the purpose and duration of the proposed processing operation or operations, the country of origin and country of final destination, the rules of law, both general and sectoral, in force in the third country in question and the professional rules and security measures which are complied with in that country.

It is clear that adequate protection can be provided through codes of conduct and contractual arrangements, as well as via legislation, and negotiations are currently under way between the European Commission and the US Department of Commerce to establish a 'safe harbor' system of self-regulation which will allow transfer of data to US organisation which are part of that safe harbor:

US Department of Commerce draft Safe Harbor Principles, 15 November 1999 http://www.ita.doc.gov/td/ecom/Principles1199.htm (footnotes omitted)

NOTICE: An organization must inform individuals about the purposes for which it collects and uses information about them, how to contact the organization with any inquiries or complaints, the types of third parties to which it discloses the information, and the choices and means the organization offers individuals for limiting its use and disclosure, where the organization is using or disclosing it for a purpose other than that for which it was originally collected or for a purpose which it was processed by the transferring organization. This notice must be provided in clear and conspicuous language when individuals are first asked to provide personal information to the organization or as soon as is practicable, but in any event before the organization uses or discloses such information for a purpose other than that specified above.

CHOICE: An organization must offer individuals the opportunity to choose (opt out) whether and how personal information they provide is used or disclosed to third parties, where such use or disclosure is incompatible with the purpose(s) for which it was originally collected, or subsequently authorized by the individual.

For sensitive information, (i.e. personal information specifying medical or health conditions, racial or ethnic origin, political opinions, religious or philosophical beliefs, trade union membership or information specifying the sex life of the individual) they must be given affirmative or explicit (opt in) choice if the information is to be used for a purpose other than those for which it was originally collected or disclosed to any type of third party other than those already notified to the individual, or used or disclosed in a manner other than as subsequently authorized by the individual through the exercise of opt in choice. Individuals must be provided with clear and conspicuous, readily available, and affordable mechanisms to exercise choice.

ONWARD TRANSFER: An organization may only disclose personal information to third parties consistent with the principles of notice and choice. Where an organization has not provided choice (because a use is not incompatible with a purpose for which the data was originally collected or which was subsequently authorized by the individual) and the organization wishes to transfer the data to a third party, it may do so if it first either ascertains that the third party subscribes to the principles or is subject to the Directive or another adequacy finding or enters into a written agreement with such third party requiring that the third party provide at least the same level of privacy protection as is required by the relevant principles. If the organization complies with these requirements, it shall not be held responsible when a third party to which it transfers such information processes it in a way contrary to any restrictions or representations.

SECURITY: Organizations creating, maintaining, using or disseminating personal information must take reasonable precautions to protect it from loss, misuse and unauthorized access, disclosure, alteration and destruction.

DATA INTEGRITY: Consistent with the principles, an organization may not process personal information in a way that is incompatible with the purposes for which it has been collected or subsequently authorized by the individual. To the extent necessary for those purposes, an organization should take reasonable steps to ensure that data is reliable for its intended use, accurate, complete, and current.

ACCESS: Individuals must have access to personal information about them that an organization holds and be able to correct, amend, or delete that information where it is inaccurate, except where the burden or expense of providing access would be disproportionate to the risks to the individual's privacy in the case in question, or where the rights of persons other than the individual would be violated.

ENFORCEMENT: Effective privacy protection must include mechanisms for assuring compliance with the principles, recourse for individuals to whom the data relate affected by non-compliance with the principles, and consequences for the organization when the principles are not followed. At a minimum, such mechanisms must include (a) readily available and affordable independent recourse mechanisms by which each individual's complaints and disputes are investigated and resolved by reference to the principles and damages awarded where the applicable law or private sector initiatives so provide; (b) follow up procedures for verifying that the attestations and assertions businesses make about their privacy practices are true and that privacy practices have been implemented as presented; and (c) obligations to remedy problems arising out of failure to comply with the principles by organizations announcing their adherence to them and consequences for such organizations. Sanctions must be sufficiently rigorous to ensure compliance by organizations.

7.3.3 Home country regulation as a solution?

Is it then possible to resolve these conflicts through adopting the principle that free speech and privacy are to be regulated only in the home country (the country of origin, to use the terminology of 7.2.2 above) of the Internet user who publishes information or controls personal data?

So far as privacy is concerned, the answer is a qualified 'yes'. The EU data protection regime is specifically based on home country regulation, as the text of art 25 demonstrates. All the countries which implement the Directive have, by definition, an 'adequate' level of privacy protection, and the privacy of the data subject in respect of the transferred data is then a matter for the law of the new controller's jurisdiction. The same applies to non-EU countries to which data transfer is permitted under art 25 on the basis that an adequate level of protection is provided, and the Directive contains provisions under which the European Commission can declare that particular countries provide adequate protection.[7] The same is true of other data protection laws.[8] Provided there is international consensus on the basic principles under which privacy is to be protected, a home country system of regulation is workable.

The reason the answer 'yes' is qualified is because there are political and philosophical objections in some countries to establishing state agencies to

---

7 Directive 95/46/EC, art 25(6).
8 See eg Australian Privacy Act 1988; Canadian Privacy Act 1983, Personal Information Protection and Electronic Documents Bill (Bill C-6 of 1999); Hong Kong Personal Data (Privacy) Ordinance 1996.

regulate privacy. Even there, however, the experience of the US safe harbor scheme suggests that workable solutions are likely to be found.

Home country regulation is far less likely to provide a workable mechanism for reconciling the conflicts between national laws which impose restrictions on free speech because, as noted at 7.3.1 above, there are wide variations in the restrictions which different countries deem appropriate. It seems unlikely that, in the medium term future at least, an international consensus on the minimum levels of free speech restriction will emerge,[9] and without such a consensus home country regulation is impossible.

This, of course, will not prevent Internet users from publishing information which contravenes the laws of foreign countries. US neo-Nazi organisations will not be deterred from operating websites which are hosted on US servers merely because they are committing offences under German law, as it is not possible in practice for the German authorities to take effective action against foreign website operators. The danger, as the discussion at 7.3.1 above illustrates, is that action taken against ISPs might lead to excessive self-censorship of their systems. However, the emerging trend towards granting immunities to intermediaries will mitigate this risk (see Chapter 4.3.2.2). It may well be that the differences in national free speech laws are justified and should be maintained – it is at least arguable that, for example, a neo-Nazi website hosted in the US and operated by a US resident is less dangerous than one hosted or operated in a country which has a comparatively recent history of Nazi control, and that the latter state's laws are beneficial even if they can only be enforced against its own residents.

---

[9] For a contrary argument see Viktor Mayer-Schönberger and Teree E Foster *Free Speech and the Global Information Infrastructure* (1996–1997) 56 Michigan Telecommunications and Technology Law Review, 3(45) 45, 56–60, arguing that such a consensus can be built on the basis of the International law principle of *jus cogens*, defined in the Vienna Convention on the Law of Treaties (1969) art 53 as: '[A] norm accepted and recognized by the international community of States as a whole as a norm from which no derogation is permitted and which can be modified only by a subsequent norm of general International law having the same character.' However, it is apparent from their analysis that such a consensus would impose few restrictions on free speech, and would be far closer to the US First Amendment model than e.g. the German or the Saudi Arabian model. In the author's view, it will be many years before there is sufficient cultural convergence to produce a *jus cogens* consensus, if indeed it ever happens.

Chapter 8

Legislative and regulatory arbitrage

Arbitrage, in the financial markets, is the process of finding a difference in pricing between two counterparties and exploiting the differential for profit. Arbitrage in terms of law and regulation is a very similar process, and consists of locating a commercial activity (or part of it) in a jurisdiction which confers advantages, while continuing to do business in other jurisdictions without being subject to the burdens which those jurisdictions impose on local businesses. This phenomenon is well-known already in the field of taxation, and many corporations locate their head offices in tax havens (usually small islands with favourable climates).

However, the opportunities for legislative and regulatory arbitrage are limited for physical world businesses. The need for a sales force and physical distribution infrastructure usually subjects the business to the laws and regulations of the jurisdictions in which it has customers. This is not true for Internet activities.[1] In particular, where the business is dealing in information products it will often be able to adopt a distributed business model (see Chapter 2.4) and locate the different elements in multiple jurisdictions. This can create two main types of arbitrage advantage:

- Decreased overheads, eg because lower taxes are payable or a reduction in the cost of complying with supervisory regimes.
- Avoidance of restrictions on, or in extreme cases prohibition of, certain activities.

8.1   DECREASING OVERHEADS

If an Internet business can reduce its overheads by taking advantage of differences between national laws, it is engaging in legal or regulatory arbitrage. The most obvious way to lower overheads is to reduce the tax burden on the business, and using the Internet for taking orders and delivering products and services offers substantial scope for such reductions. An equally effective way of reducing overheads is to reduce the regulatory and supervisory burden on the business's operations, for example by structuring operations so that only one country's regulatory regime applies. This second issue will be examined in

---

1   For an early discussion of arbitrage in Internet activities, see Michael J Froomkin 'The Internet as a Source of Legal Arbitrage' in Brian Kahin and Charles Nesson (ed) *Borders In Cyberspace* (Boston: MIT Press, 1996), discussing the issue in relation to free speech, gambling, transborder data flows and taxation.

relation to financial services, where the rules on transborder activity are most clearly established. However, there are many other regulated sectors, such as medical and pharmaceutical products and services, where similar problems and solutions will arise. Additionally, use of the Internet for commercial activities can be a way of avoiding national non-sectoral regulation which imposes costly burdens on the enterprise.[2]

8.1.1   Reducing the impact of taxation

There are two ways in which an Internet business could reduce the impact of a particular country's tax laws on its activities:

- it could structure the business so that all, or particular categories of, its business activities are not subject to tax in the jurisdiction; or
- it could distribute the business across multiple jurisdictions in such a way that the bulk of profits is only taxable in the jurisdiction with the lowest tax rates.

8.1.1.1   Non-taxable activities

If a business activity conducted via the Internet is to escape taxation in a jurisdiction which might hope to tax it, the activity will need to fall outside the definitions of taxable activity in at least the two main classes of taxation: income-based taxes, such as income or corporation tax; and consumption taxes, such as Value Added Tax (VAT) or Goods and Services Tax (GST). There may also be particular national forms of taxation on certain classes of activity[3] which also need to be considered, but these will not be examined here as they vary widely from country to country.

In order to analyse these issues we will need a simple concrete example:

> NetCorp Inc,[4] a Delaware corporation, sells music CDs via the Internet, taking payment via credit card and delivering the CDs world-wide by mail. NetCorp also sells the individual tracks of some artists as MP3 files,[5] taking payment in the same way, and the purchaser downloads these files direct to his computer. The whole of NetCorp's website and other systems are located on a server in Delaware.

The question is whether these transactions attract tax in the jurisdiction of a particular customer.

INCOME-BASED TAXES

As we have already seen in Chapter 7.2.1, a corporation is in general only subject to tax in a jurisdiction if it has a permanent establishment there or, as is the

---

2   Perhaps the best-known example of such laws is the German Act Against Unfair Competition, which imposes quite stringent restrictions on commercial activities, in particular advertising and promotion. Article 3(2) of Directive 2000/31/EC will prevent the application of this law to most electronic commerce activities which originate in an EU Member State.

3   For example, the UK levies Stamp Duty on share dealings and other classes of instrument. Interestingly, although the Stamp Duty regime has been modified to cover dematerialised share dealings, the remaining provisions of the Stamp Act 1891 arguably apply only to physical, written instruments – see Reed *Digital Information Law: electronic documents and requirements of form* (London: Centre for Commercial Law Studies, 1996) Chapter 4.

4   An imaginary company, with no connection to the numerous Netcorps discoverable via an AltaVista search.

5   For further information on the MP3 technology see http://www.mp3.com.

case under the laws of some countries such as the UK, derives income from business activities *in* (not merely with) the jurisdiction.[6] So far as permanent establishment is concerned, it is clear that NetCorp only has a permanent establishment in Delaware; it is a Delaware corporation with a registered head office in that jurisdiction, and all the computing technology used to contract with customer is also in Delaware. The only reason why NetCorp might be taxable in some other jurisdiction on the basis of its establishment is if its central management and control is in fact in another jurisdiction, eg if all the executive directors are UK residents and the board meets in the UK.[7] A place of management outside Delaware could constitute residence or a permanent establishment in that jurisdiction.[8]

However, if NetCorp sells CDs or MP3 files to, say, a UK customer, the profit on that transaction might be taxable if it amounted to doing business in the UK. The test appears to be where the contract of sale between NetCorp and the UK customer was made.[9] In the current state of English law it is possible for the vendor to define in advance the acts which complete the formation of the contract[10] and thus ensure that these occur on the server in Delaware.

An interesting point which arises in relation to the on-line supply of MP3 files is whether the profits from sale contracts concluded in a jurisdiction which would otherwise tax those profits should be excluded from taxation on the ground that they are royalties. Article 12(1) of the Draft OECD Model Tax Convention on Income and on Capital provides that royalties[11] paid in one state to the beneficial owner in another shall only be taxable in the beneficial owner's state, ie in Delaware in our example. Clearly, the main element of the transaction between NetCorp and the purchaser of an MP3 file is a licence to copy that file, both onto permanent storage and into RAM for the purposes of listening to the music. However, the revised commentary on art 12 states that when assessing the taxation of software supplies, a distinction must be made between a licence which allows the licensee to undertake further exploitation of the software and a licence which only permits copying and other restricted acts to the extent necessary for use of the software.[12] Only the former will amount to a royalty; the latter is a normal supply for the purposes of assessing income taxes. Although the commentary does not discuss the tax position for information

6 See eg US Internal Revenue Code §§ 871, 881 and 882.
7 *De Beers Consolidated Mines Ltd v Howe* [1905] 2 KB 612.
8 Draft OECD Model Tax Convention on Income and on Capital (30 June 1998) arts 4(1) and 5(2)(a).
9 Chissick and Kelman *Electronic Commerce: Law and Practice* (London: Sweet & Maxwell, 1999) Chapter 9.15, citing *Grainger & Son v Gough* [1896] AC 325.
10 See Chapter 6.2.1.1.
11 Defined in draft OECD Model Tax Convention on Income and on Capital (30 June 1998) art 12: '2. The term "royalties" as used in this Article means payments of any kind received as a consideration for the use of, or the right to use, any copyright of literary, artistic or scientific work including cinematograph films, any patent, trade mark, design or model, plan, secret formula or process, or for information concerning industrial, commercial or scientific experience. 3. The provisions of paragraph 1 shall not apply if the beneficial owner of the royalties, being a resident of a Contracting State, carries on business in the other Contracting State in which the royalties arise, through a permanent establishment situated therein, or performs in that other State independent personal services from a fixed base situated therein, and the right or property in respect of which the royalties are paid is effectively connected with such permanent establishment or fixed base. In such case the provisions of Article 7 or Article 14, as the case may be, shall apply.'
12 OECD *Revision of the Commentary on Article 12 Concerning Software Payments* 29 September 1998.

products other than software, the contracts under which on-line supplies of packaged information (such as MP3 files) are made are so similar to package software licences that it is difficult to argue they should be treated differently.

CONSUMPTION TAXES

Consumption taxes such as GST and VAT operate on a completely different basis to income-related taxes. In the case of GST the tax is levied on the supplier of a product or service to its final consumer, while for VAT each commercial supplier of goods or services charges the tax to its purchaser, reclaiming any VAT paid on the goods or services the supplier has purchased.[13] Each is in effect a tax on the consumer of the product or service, but collected by the supplier.

Where the product or service is supplied to a customer in the same jurisdiction as the supplier, tax is collected in the normal way. However, the underlying basis of consumption taxes is that they should be paid in the country of consumption. Thus, where goods or services are exported, the normal rule is that this occurs free of consumption tax. The justification is fairly obvious – were the rule that exports carried consumption tax in their country of origin, a sensible purchaser would buy from a supplier in the country with the lowest rate of consumption tax,[14] thus eroding the tax base of the purchaser's country.

So far as supplies of physical goods are concerned, the theory is simple. The goods are exported free of consumption tax, and the Customs authorities in the purchaser's jurisdiction collect the appropriate local consumption taxes and import duties when the goods enter the country.[15] In practice, Customs authorities are unable to identify which small mail-order purchases are taxable, and so (except for supplies from one EU Member State to a consumer in another)[16] the majority of consumer cross-border purchases are effectively made free of consumption tax. Because electronic commerce reduces the transaction costs of cross-border supply to consumers, the volume of such transactions is likely to grow substantially.

Under the EU VAT regime commercial supplies which are not of goods are treated as services.[17] This includes supplies of information products. Where information products or information services are supplied electronically, the rules produce interesting effects:

- If the supply is of an information product such as software, the place of supply is deemed to be the purchaser's place of business, establishment or

13 This explanation of VAT is grossly simplistic, but is not too inaccurate for the simple case of a supplier who produces only one type of product or service.
14 Rates of consumption tax vary widely. For example, at the time of writing the UK's standard rate of VAT is 17.5% while the Danish rate is 25%. US State sales taxes are set at even lower rates.
15 For the EU VAT system the theory is rather different. Where the supply is from a VAT-liable person in one Member State to a VAT-liable person in another, the supply is deemed to have been made on arrival and subject to the purchaser's tax rates. The practical effect is similar, except that the VAT-registered purchaser collects the tax and accounts for it to the tax authorities. See Sixth Council Directive of 17 May 1977 on the harmonization of the laws of the Member States relating to turnover taxes (Directive 77/388/EEC) art 28. Additionally, if the supplier sells more than 100,000 euros worth of goods in another Member State in any one year, he is obliged to register and account for VAT in respect of transactions with purchasers in that state – art 28b(B)(2). However, if the purchaser is not VAT-liable, the supplier of goods will charge VAT at his home country rate, which under the Directive must be at least 15%.
16 See note 15 above.
17 Sixth Council Directive of 17 May 1977 on the harmonization of the laws of the Member States relating to turnover taxes (Directive 77/388/EEC) art 6(1).

residence.[18] If the purchaser is VAT-liable he is deemed to have supplied the product to himself,[19] and must therefore account for VAT at his local rate, even if the product was purchased from outside the EU. However, a consumer purchaser from a non-EU supplier will legitimately purchase the product free of VAT. Thus, in our example, no consumption tax will be payable on the MP3 files unless the UK purchaser is a business.

- An information service will normally be subject to the same rules, unless it is a service relating to 'cultural, artistic, sporting, scientific, educational, entertainment or similar activities', in which case it is deemed to have been supplied at the supplier's location and thus, if the supplier is outside the EU, no VAT will be payable. Thus, a supply for payment of a Webcast of a concert would not be taxable, irrespective of whether the purchaser was a consumer or a business.

It is clear from this analysis that a supplier of information products and services to EU customers would be well-advised to locate his business outside the EU, and similarly a US supplier should not supply within his state of establishment. The consumption tax regimes positively encourage export sales of information products, because these can often be made tax-free and even where, as in the case of sales of goods, tax is theoretically chargeable, this is the responsibility of the purchaser rather than the supplier and will rarely be collected.[20]

However, no tax authority will be satisfied with a system which allows consumption taxes to be avoided so simply. The first detailed attempt to apply local consumption taxes to on-line information supplies has been set out by the European Commission in its recent proposal to amend the Sixth VAT Directive.[1] Although technically complex, in summary its effect would be to make a non-EU supplier of services[2] to consumers nonetheless liable to charge VAT on those supplies. This is to be achieved by deeming the supplier to have a fixed establishment in a Member State[3], thus creating a liability to register for VAT, and then deeming the supply to have been made from that fixed establishment.[4] This proposal will be at least partially effective if non-EU electronic commerce businesses do indeed register – however, the discussion in the Explanatory Memorandum[5] of this issue strikes a rather forlorn note on this topic:

> From the perspective of the non tax compliant business, failure to meet legitimate obligations carries several direct and serious risks. Not the least of these is that an incurred liability for VAT does not resolve itself simply by its concealment or failing to report it to the correct tax administration. Failure to comply with self-assessment obligations does nothing to reduce or remove a debt owing in respect of taxation. Rather, it exposes the business to additional penalty and interest charges which only serve to cause the liability to escalate further.

18 Article 9(2)(e). The same applies to professional services such as legal advice.
19 Article 21(1)(b).
20 In a totally unscientific survey of the author's Internet law class, most students would not declare a small tax liability on imported goods purchased via the Internet. The exception was the Danish students, reinforcing their country's reputation as Europe's most law-abiding, but even they felt that at a de minimis level of about US $5 they would not bother to declare the tax liability.
 1 Proposal for a Council Directive amending Directive 77/388/EEC as regards the value added tax arrangements applicable to certain services supplied by electronic means, COM(2000) 349 final, 7 June 2000.
 2 See note 17, p 236.
 3 Article 1(5)(b).
 4 Article 1(1).
 5 Page 9 ff.

For an operator, even one located outside the EU, to risk exposure to significant and unresolved tax debts in the world's largest marketplace cannot be considered prudent business practice. Neither does the debt lapse over time but continues to hover over the business and even, in certain circumstances, passes on to a subsequent purchaser of the operation. The presence of such a liability is furthermore hardly likely to assist in access to legitimate capital or funding sources. Normal accepted standards of statutory auditing or due diligence examinations would be expected to detect failure to comply with tax obligations in a significant jurisdiction such as the EU. The risk of punitive tax assessments is also high.

Moreover, in certain cases, sanctions under civil or criminal law may attach to the managers or owners of the business. Moreover, existing Community provisions in relation to mutual assistance and recovery ensure that a tax debt in one Member State is effectively enforceable anywhere in the Community.

Legitimate operators will moreover wish to ensure that they have access to legal protection and remedies in respect of infringements of copyright or other intellectual property rights. To this end, they will also wish to ensure that they respect their own legal and regulatory obligations.

Although all of the foregoing are strong forces in favour of opting for compliance, they are however not enough in themselves and, particularly for remote suppliers, there is a need to develop tools of direct enforcement on which tax administrations can call ... Developing the necessary tools and procedures is a part of the maturing process for e-commerce and there are good indications that this will be achieved.

These disincentives to non-compliance may be influential for well-established, multinational businesses, but will carry less weight with smaller and newer dot.com enterprises. In practice it will be difficult to identify whether such a business is making taxable supplies to the EU at all, let alone the volume of such supplies. Additionally, dot.com businesses are likely to restructure and reinvent themselves on a regular basis, which will have the effect that the entity liable for VAT has ceased to exist by the time the liability is discovered.

From the point of view of a non-EU electronic commerce business, the proposal is effectively a scheme for voluntary submission to taxation. It is likely that some businesses at least will take a conscious decision not to comply with the scheme, particularly because compliance will put them at a competitive advantage as against competitors who decline to comply, or who are ignorant about their legal obligations under foreign tax law. Additionally, the costs of collecting VAT are not insignificant, and the proposal would require the business to bear these additional costs itself. These practical difficulties, coupled with the generally recognised undesirability of extraterritorial taxation based on deemed presence in the jurisdiction, must raise doubts whether the proposal will be enacted in anything resembling its current form.

8.1.1.2   *The distributed enterprise*

From the point of view of the customer, there is no practical difference between an electronic commerce enterprise which operates all parts of its business from a single jurisdiction, and an enterprise which distributes the various functions across multiple jurisdictions.[6] At first sight, this seems to offer substantial scope for tax arbitrage.

---

6   Except for any delays caused by the distribution, which are the result of bandwidth restrictions at different parts of the Internet. As more bandwidth becomes available, delays of this kind should reduce to a level which is indistinguishable by the customer.

For example, suppose that NetCorp discovers that jurisdiction A offers very favourable tax treatment for royalty income, while jurisdiction B similarly favours on-line distribution activities. It therefore restructures its business to set up a holding company in jurisdiction A (A-Corp), which will own the rights to distribute the MP3 files. Actual sales are made from a wholly-owned subsidiary in Delaware (D-Corp), which pays a royalty to the holding company on each sale under a contract between D-Corp and A-Corp. Delivery of MP3 files to customers is made from a wholly owned subsidiary in jurisdiction B (B-Corp), under a contract between A-Corp and B-Corp. This produces the following structure:

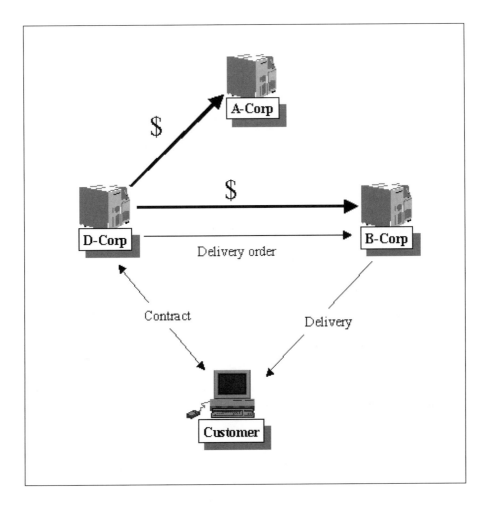

It should be immediately obvious that by increasing the royalty rate, a larger proportion of the overall profits of the group can be made to arise in jurisdiction A, while by increasing the charge for delivery of the MP3 files the proportion arising in jurisdiction B can be increased.

Not surprisingly, most countries' tax laws have rules to counter such schemes. The basic principle is set out in the OECD Model Tax Convention, art 9(1) which provides:

> Where
> (a) an enterprise of a Contracting State participates directly or indirectly in the management, control or capital of an enterprise of the other Contracting State, or
> (b) the same persons participate directly or indirectly in the management, control or capital of an enterprise of a Contracting State and an enterprise of the other Contracting State,
> and in either case conditions are made or imposed between the two enterprises in their commercial or financial relations which differ from those which would be made between independent enterprises, then any profits which would, but for those conditions, have accrued to one of the enterprises, but, by reason of those conditions, have not so accrued, may be included in the profits of that enterprise and taxed accordingly.

This process is known as transfer pricing. The basis on which the notional profits to be taxed are to be determined is set out in art 7(2) as, 'the profits which [the enterprise] might be expected to make if it were a distinct and separate enterprise engaged in the same or similar activities under the same or similar conditions and dealing wholly independently with the enterprise of which it is a permanent establishment', and further guidance is provided in the OECD Transfer Pricing Guidelines.[7]

This is what is described as the 'arm's length principle'; in assessing the taxable profits of, say, D-Corp, the aim is to compare the actual profits declared by A-Corp from an MP3 file sale with the profits which would have been recorded had the contracts with A-Corp and B-Corp been negotiated with independently-owned entities. Various methods of achieving this comparison[8] have been proposed, which fall into two main groups:

- Methods which attempt to ascertain comparable costs of goods, services etc. provided by the associated company if provided by an independent enterprise – in our example, the comparable royalty rates for MP3 files and charges for distribution – and then using those figures to adjust the taxable profits of D-Corp.
- Methods which aggregate the profits of a group, and then attempt to allocate them between group members on the basis of work and skill input, resource use and risks taken, although use of these methods other than as a last resort has been described as 'not acceptable in theory, implementation or practice'.[9] As a general rule profit splitting should not be used unless transactions are so closely integrated across a group that it is not possible to evaluate transactions on a separate basis.[10]

The problem is that the existing techniques for transfer pricing were developed for groups of companies undertaking physical world activities, and are thus

---

7   OECD Committee on Fiscal Affairs *Transfer Pricing Guidelines for Multinational Enterprises and Tax Administrations* (OECD, 1995).

8   See Kaminski and Strunk 'Transfer Pricing Features of Transactions over the Internet' (1999) 1.1 Tax Planning International – E-Commerce, p 3.

9   OECD Committee on Fiscal Affairs *Transfer Pricing Guidelines for Multinational Enterprises and Tax Administrations* (OECD, 1995) para 1.14.

10 OECD *The Taxation of Global Trading of Financial Instruments: a Discussion Draft* OCDE/GD(97)29 paras 108 ff. For an explanation of calculations of profit splits see OECD Committee on Fiscal Affairs *Transfer Pricing Guidelines for Multinational Enterprises and Tax Administrations* (OECD, 1995) paras 3.5 and 3.6.

based on a model of production processes rather than one which identifies the sources of value for networked information.[11] Electronic commerce is such a new activity that appropriate techniques for transfer pricing have not yet been developed; the closest analogy is thought to be the global trade in financial instruments,[12] and even though this field of commerce has been studied extensively there are, as yet, no commonly agreed principles for transfer pricing:

OECD, The Taxation Of Global Trading Of Financial Instruments: A Discussion Draft, OCDE/GD(97)29

151. Countries seem to share the view that trading, marketing, management, and major supporting activities should share in the profits to the extent that they are integral to the realization of the global trading profits. For example, marketers who actively co-operate with traders (as opposed to general salespeople who do not) should be entitled to a share of the global trading profit.

152. Some countries, however, argue that activities that are less integrated into the global business should be compensated using an acceptable method following the Transfer Pricing Guidelines other than a profit split. The question is at what threshold does an activity become so integral that it should instead be rewarded by a share of global profits? They believe that this determination must be made on a case-by-case basis because the same activity may perform different functions when global trading is conducted under different organizational models so that a single rule to apply in all cases could easily produce arbitrary results.

153. Other countries disagree, because of the limitations of the service fee approach discussed earlier and/or because of the practical difficulty of distinguishing those activities that are 'integrated' from those that are not. For example, most countries believe that systems and product development could be categorized as performing integral parts of global trading which should be rewarded with a share of the global profits. Countries disagree, however, as to whether certain back office functions such as product control are such an integral part of a global trading business as to be appropriately rewarded by a share of the global trading profits. The issue of whether or not an activity is integral to global trading is factual in nature and so can only be resolved on a case-by-case basis. However, reference to the comparability standard in the Guidelines, i.e. what would have happened between independent enterprises in a similar situation, may be helpful.

An interesting development which might eventually lead to greater clarity in tax laws is the establishment of safe harbour schemes for particular types of activity. Under these schemes, the tax system establishes bright line rules for determining the taxable profits of the local subsidiaries of a global, integrated trading activity.[13] Although these might result in some erosion of the local tax base, because notional income which might otherwise have been taxable is foregone, it is arguable that this will be outweighed by the attraction to global enterprises of locating parts of the distributed activity in a jurisdiction where there is tax certainty.

8.1.2 Internet banking and finance

Because of the heavy regulatory regime which most countries apply to banking and financial services businesses, an Internet provider of banking and finance

11 Kaminski and Strunk 'Transfer Pricing Features of Transactions over the Internet' (1999) 1.1 Tax Planning International – E-Commerce, p 6.
12 Doernberg and Hinneken *Electronic Commerce and International Taxation* (Kluwer Law International, 1999) p 204.
13 See eg the Belgian tax authority's Circular Letter of 26 July 1996, introducing such a system for call centres located in Belgium, discussed in Doernberg and Hinneken *Electronic Commerce and International Taxation* (Kluwer Law International, 1999) pp 209–212.

is faced with serious difficulties. One possible strategy is to establish branches in every country (or more realistically most countries where there is a potential market) and work under a system of multiple regulation. This is only an option for the very largest financial institutions, and immediately removes many of the advantages of providing services via the Internet.

A more interesting strategy is to set up the on-line financial institution in a way which uses regulatory arbitrage to avoid the extra costs and difficulties of multiple regulation. This is possible because it is rare for a jurisdiction to regulate financial institutions per se; instead, they regulate particular financial *activities* when carried out in that country. Thus, effective arbitrage consists of structuring the institution so that the regulated activities take place only in one country or a small number of countries, where the institution can comply with the legal and supervisory regime.

8.1.2.1   *Deposit taking*

Most countries require banks to be licensed or authorised by a regulatory body. The determining factor in deciding whether a financial institution falls under national banking law is normally whether it accepts deposits in that country.[14] Thus, the definition of 'credit institution' for the purposes of EU banking law is 'an undertaking whose business is to receive deposits or other repayable funds from the public and to grant credits for its own account'.[15]

Definitions of 'deposit' vary, but that in the UK Banking Act 1987, s 5(1) is fairly typical:[16]

> 'deposit' means a sum of money . . . paid on terms –
> (a) under which it will be repaid, with or without interest or a premium, and either on demand or at a time or in circumstances agreed by or on behalf of the person making the payment and the person receiving it; and
> (b) which are not referable to the provision of property or services or the giving of security.

In deciding whether an Internet bank is subject to the UK Banking Act, the question is therefore whether it accepts such monies in the UK. Clearly, if the Internet bank acquires premises in the UK and engages staff to take money from customers, it will have established a branch[17] and thus be subject to UK law so far as deposits accepted by that branch are concerned. However, this is not a commercially realistic scenario. Instead, the Internet bank would normally enter into arrangements with a third party in each country where it wished to accept deposits. Would this mean that the Internet bank was accepting deposits in the jurisdiction (ie through its agent), and thus obliged to register?

An analysis of the EU jurisprudence indicates that the use of an independent intermediary to deal with customers does not amount to the establishment of a branch in that jurisdiction, even if the intermediary works solely for the foreign

---

14 See eg German Banking Act (Kreditwegengesetz) art 32(1); Luxembourg Law of 5 April 1993; Swedish Banking Business Act 1987, Chapter 2, s 2; Swiss Banking Act *SR* 952.0, art 2(1); UK Banking Act 1987, s 3(1).

15 First Council Directive 77/780/EEC of 12 December 1977 on the coordination of the laws, regulations and administrative provisions relating to the taking up and pursuit of the business of credit institutions OJ L 322, 17 December 1977, p 30, art 1.

16 Interestingly, the Financial Services and Markets Act 2000, which will replace this part of the Banking Act, does not define deposit taking.

17 See Chapter 7.2.1.1 for further discussion of the concept of permanent establishment.

enterprise, provided the intermediary is truly independent.[18] Of course, in our example the intermediary might well be a deposit taker and so would need to be registered as a bank, but this would probably be commercially desirable to ensure customer confidence. The answer to the question posed above seems, therefore, to depend on the way in which the transaction is structured:

- If the Internet bank's UK intermediary accepts cash or cheques for payment into the customer's account with the bank, it would appear that the bank is accepting deposits in the UK through its agent.
- However, if the Internet bank's customer effects a funds transfer from an existing account with a UK bank to its account with the Internet bank, either directly or via the Internet bank's UK intermediary, this should not amount to deposit taking by the Internet bank. Although there is no authority on this point, if it were not so it would be unlawful for a bank to accept funds transfers from a foreign bank if the transferor were also a customer of the bank. The argument is that the transfer takes place in the receiver's jurisdiction, not the sender's, even if it is effected via an intermediary,[19] and therefore the deposit is taken in the country where the customer's account with the Internet bank is held.

8.1.2.2   *Payment services*

Most jurisdictions do not regulate the provision of electronic payment services per se,[20] although some aspects of payment transactions may be regulated.[21] This is because normal interbank electronic funds transfer systems work by moving funds from one account to another, adjusting the sending and receiving account balances and settling through a Central Bank or a correspondent account. An institution which provides such an account will be a deposit taker, and thus fall under normal banking regulation. Similarly, on-line credit card payments are regulated not on the basis that they are payment services, but because of the credit facilities provided to cardholders.

However, new forms of payment service are developing which do not necessarily require the manipulation of bank accounts or credit facilities, and therefore may be provided by enterprises which do not have authorisation as banks. These are generally known as digital cash or electronic money systems, and fall into three main types:[22]

- Systems which effect transfers between accounts, although the accounts are not general bank accounts but specifically limited to electronic money transactions. Examples of such systems include Proton and the various eCash

---

18 See the discussion in *Freedom to provide services and the interest of the general good in the second banking directive* Commission interpretative communication SEC (97) 1193 final 20 June 1997, p 10 ff.

19 This is precisely what happens in normal bank transfers where the sending and receiving banks do not have a correspondent relationship.

20 Although the report 'Competition in UK Banking' (London: HMSO, March 2000) has proposed a licensing scheme for payment system operators and participants, designed to remove the de facto monopoly of the banks in this area – paras 3.183–3.204.

21 See eg US Electronic Funds Transfers Act 1978 15 USC §1693 and Regulation E 12 CFR part 205.

22 For an explanation of the workings of these systems, see Sutter 'Law and Technology Convergence: Electronic Payment Systems' ECLIP Research Paper (1999) http://www.jura.uni-muenster.de/eclip/.

systems. Because these systems require an account with the electronic money service provider, they can only be provided by authorised banks.

- Systems where value is purchased from the electronic money service provider and stored on a smartcard, eg the Mondex system. Although the value may be deposited in a bank when the holder decides to do so, while it is held on the smartcard there is no account in the holder's name which would attract the application of banking regulation.

- Systems where the electronic money service provider pays the recipient on behalf of the payer and is then reimbursed by debiting the payer's credit card account or via an interbank transfer initiated as a 'pull' transaction[23] CyberCash is probably the best-known example. Again, banking regulation does not apply because the service provider does not hold an account in the payer's name, and credit regulation is equally inapplicable where credit cards are involved because the service provider is selling a service and collecting payment as a credit card merchant, rather than providing credit to the payer.

Although no court has yet ruled on the point, there is an extremely compelling argument that where the requirement to be authorised as a bank is based on deposit taking[24] an enterprise which adopts the second or third method of operation is free to issue and deal in electronic money without restriction. The mere fact that the enterprise accepts money from payers will not amount to taking a deposit if the payment is consideration for providing a service, and the enterprise has no obligation to return it unless the service is not provided.[25] Most electronic money systems operate by treating the issue of digital cash as a *withdrawal* from the customer's deposit. Admittedly the issuer normally undertakes to accept that digital cash for re-deposit, but this undertaking will not be sufficient to allow the transaction to be classified as the transformation of a deposit from one form into another. The defining factor is *repayment*, which by definition requires the funds to be in the custody and control of the depository. True digital cash gives custody and control to the customer. The result is that institutions which provide the new Internet payment services do not need to be licensed as banks or to comply with bank supervision rules.[1] Similarly, they also fall outside credit licensing regulations.

Laura Edgar, 'Electronic Payment Systems' ECLIP Research Paper (1999), http://www.jura.uni-muenster.de/eclip/ p. 17

Whether or not a system requires authorisation therefore depends on how it actually works. Systems which operate through the use of credit cards, such as Cybercash, provide a service and accept money from their customers as consideration for the service. They are not therefore under any obligation to repay the money unless they fail to provide the service and so are not accepting deposits. Other systems provide services such as manipulating the user's bank account[2] or holding funds which are to

23 Ie in terms of UK banking practice a direct debit.
24 This requirement is not universal, and some European jurisdictions adopt a more extensive definition of banking which can encompass some forms of electronic money issuing – see Edgar 'Electronic Money' ECLIP Research Paper (1999) http://www.jura.uni-muenster.de/eclip/ p 3.
25 This is specifically stated in UK Banking Act 1987, s 5(2)(a) to preclude such a payment from being a deposit.
1 See d'Alelio and Collins 'Electronic Cash under Current Banking Laws' in Ruh (ed) *The Internet and Business: A Lawyer's Guide to the Emerging Legal Issues* (Washington: Computer Law Association, 1996) p 91 at p 98, who suggest that US banking regulation will apply when the system operator 'holds funds received from the customer to be transferred and delivered to a third party', but not where the operator does not hold any such funds.

be delivered to the seller on receipt of a notice from the buyer. The actions of the third party do not amount to deposit taking because they are not repaying the money to the original lodger of the funds. Rather they act as a payment intermediary by issuing the funds to someone else.[3]

Furthermore if someone buys tokens or coins by credit card without any provision for repayment then this constitutes a sale rather than taking a deposit as the money is paid as consideration for the provision of the service, in this case tokens.[4] However, according to the definition above, it is likely that a system which requires users to lodge repayable funds in an account will constitute deposit taking thus obliging the institution to obtain authorisation. It is the repayable account which would bring the activities of the issuer within the scope of the regulations and not the actual issuing of the digital money itself. However the mere taking of deposits is not sufficient to fall into the scope of banking regulations, this must be carried out by a deposit taking business. Regarding the definition of deposit taking businesses, if businesses lend the funds received or finance any activity out of the capital or interest on the deposit, for example by using the interest earned from placing the deposit in a bank or building society account, then this would fall within the scope of the definition. Therefore the majority of the systems described [earlier] do not fall within the definition and so the issuer would not be defined as a credit or banking institution.

However, this opportunity for arbitrage is not likely to continue much longer. Central banks are concerned that widespread use of electronic money which is issued by unlicensed and unsupervised enterprises might have effects on the money supply and pose a threat to the stability of the global financial system. For these reasons, the EU is proposing to introduce a regulatory and supervisory scheme for electronic money issuers.

First, these institutions are to be brought within the definition of 'credit institution' in the Second Banking Directive, with some exemptions from its provisions.[5] This will allow authorised issuers to do business throughout the EU by taking benefit of the 'single passport' provisions of the Directive. Second, 'electronic money institutions' are to be subject to a limited system of supervision, covering matters such as prior authorisation, minimum capital requirements, fit and proper management, sound and prudent operation and owner control.[6]

An electronic money institution is one which issues means of payment in the form of electronic money or invests the proceeds from such activities. Electronic money is defined by the draft Directive as value which is:

(i) stored electronically on an electronic device such as a chip card or a computer memory;
(ii) accepted as a means of payment by undertakings other than the issuing institution;
(iii) generated in order to be put at the disposal of users to serve as an electronic surrogate for coins and bank notes; and
(iv) generated for the purpose of effecting electronic transfers of limited value payments.[7]

2 For example, the Cybercash system for cash transactions involves this method.
3 See Nicholson Graham and Jones *Report to the European Commission (DG XV) on the Legal and Regulatory Aspects of the Issue and Use of Pre-Paid Cards*.
4 An example of this is the sale of foreign currency.
5 Commission proposal for a European Parliament and Council Directive amending Directive 77/780/EEC on the co-ordination of laws, regulations and administrative provisions relating to the taking up and pursuit of the business of credit institutions COM (1998) 461 final.
6 Proposal for a European Parliament and Council Directive on the taking up, the pursuit and the prudential supervision of the business of electronic money institutions COM (1998) 461 final.
7 Proposal for a European Parliament and Council Directive on the taking up, the pursuit and the prudential supervision of the business of electronic money institutions COM (1998) 461 final, art 1(3)(b).

Issuance of electronic money will not be treated as deposit taking if the contract with the receiver establishes that the electronic money is a surrogate for coins and notes and does not require advance payment against the later withdrawal of electronic money.[8]

The most important restrictions which the draft Directive will place on electronic money issuers are:

- the other business activities of the enterprise are limited to 'closely related financial and non-financial services . . . and . . . the provision of non-financial services that are delivered through the electronic device';[9]
- it must meet capital adequacy and own funds requirements, though at a substantially lower level than is required for banks;[10] and
- an amount equivalent to the outstanding electronic money liabilities of the institution must be held in specified types of investment.[11]

Until this regime comes into operation, however, there is still scope for electronic money institutions to take advantage of the arbitrage opportunity to set up free of regulation. Those institutions which are already lawfully doing business as an electronic money issuer when the Directive is implemented in the relevant jurisdiction are given grandfathering rights[12] by being presumed to be authorised, although they will need to comply with the legislation within a reasonable time.

8.2   RESTRICTED AND PROHIBITED ACTIVITIES

The Internet is an obvious communications mechanism for criminals, as it enables them to remain outside jurisdictions where they would be at risk of arrest. A particularly striking example of the way in which use of the Internet can evade legal prohibitions is found in the UK news report[13] that cannabis dealers are avoiding the application of the UK's anti-drugs laws by selling from Dutch websites.[14] Even if the dealers are breaking UK law by operating these websites, there is no method of enforcing it against them. UK buyers of cannabis are committing an offence, but in practice this is unlikely to be detected and prosecuted.

Of more interest to commercial lawyers, however, are those commercial activities which can be lawfully be undertaken in one country but are restricted or prohibited in another. Assuming that there is a market for that commercial activity in the second jurisdiction, it is tempting for an enterprise in the country where the activity is lawful to use the Internet to sell its services or products to those customers who cannot obtain them in their own jurisdiction.

An activity which is particularly well-suited to attracting customers of this type is gambling. All the elements which are necessary for gambling – transfer of funds, information about the game or lottery, and information about who has won or lost – can easily be transmitted via the Internet. Gambling also presents an arbitrage opportunity for governments of small countries because

---

 8 Article 2(4).
 9 Article 1(4).
10 Article 3.
11 Article 4.
12 Article 8.
13 'Police foiled by internet dope dealers' (2000) Independent on Sunday, 6 February.
14 See also *Report of the International Narcotics Control Board for 1999* E/INCB/1999/1, paras 271, 424 and 455, reporting growth in Internet sales of cannabis seeds and growing equipment – http://www.incb.org/e/ar/1999/index.htm.

unlicensed gambling is unlawful in most large jurisdictions, and the restrictions placed on licensees are generally designed to discourage gambling. If the small country licenses on-line gambling operations without these kinds of restriction, it will be able to attract high-value gambling corporations to its territory and thus generate tax revenues and employment. This is already happening, with the establishment of on-line casinos and lotteries in countries such as Antigua, the Dominican Republic and Liechtenstein.

There are two options for such an on-line gambling operation so far as legal compliance is concerned:

- it can make a conscious decision to commit crimes in foreign jurisdictions, and structure its operations so that it has no assets or management personnel in the countries where its operations are unlawful; or
- it can attempt to structure its activities so that it does not infringe the laws of those countries.

The second option may be preferable, as it allows management personnel to travel to those countries, reduces the likelihood of political pressure being placed on its host jurisdiction to change the law, and improves the chances of raising capital financing from other countries. The remainder of this section examines how an on-line gambling operation might avoid Great Britain's[15] prohibitions on gaming and lotteries. Although the details of other countries' laws will differ, the basic principles and techniques are likely to be comparable.

In summary, British law prohibits most unlicensed gaming[16] under the Gaming Act 1968, and unlicensed lotteries[17] (with minor exceptions) under the Lotteries and Amusements Act 1976. Clearly, an on-line casino or lottery which is operated by a foreign corporation from a server situated outside Britain will not be committing the primary offences under these Acts. However, they also create a number of ancillary criminal offences which might endanger the lawfulness of the operation under British law. These fall into four main groups.

8.2.1 Charging for admission to the game or lottery

Under the Gaming Act 1968, s 8 it is an offence to charge persons for taking part in unlawful gaming. Thus, an entry fee to an Internet casino levied on a British player would seem at first sight to be unlawful. However, the offence of gaming other than on licensed premises under ss 1 and 2 can only be committed if the gaming takes place in the UK. Where does the gaming occur in the case of an Internet casino?

As gaming is the determination by chance whether a player wins or loses,[18] the gaming must occur where that determination takes place. This happens on the casino's server, which decides the run of cards in eg blackjack or the winning number for a spin of the virtual roulette wheel. Because that server is located

---

15 The discussion here focuses on Great Britain rather than the UK, as Northern Ireland's laws differ.

16 Defined as '. . . the playing of a game of chance for winnings in money or money's worth', Gaming Act 1968, s 52(1).

17 Not defined by statute, but in essence any activity in which prizes are distributed by chance and payment is made for entry – *Reader's Digest Association Ltd v Williams* [1976] 3 All ER 737.

18 See note 16 above.

outside Britain, it would seem that simple charging of British residents for entry is not an offence.[19]

The offences for lotteries are a little different, consisting of the sale or distribution of tickets or chances in a lottery.[20] To be an offence, the sale or distribution must take place in Britain. The first is easy to overcome; we have seen in Chapter 6.2.1 that it is possible to define in an offer the acts which will amount to the formation of a contract, and thus the on-line lottery must define entry in such a way that the contract is formed in its home country, not the player's country. Distribution is a more difficult concept. Because a chance is an intangible thing, it almost certainly cannot be distributed. The question therefore is whether the on-line lottery produces tickets for its players. A 'ticket' under s 23(1) 'includes any document evidencing the claim of a person to participate in the chances of the lottery'. All that a player will see, however, is a Web page acknowledging the numbers the player has chosen. It is straining the principles of legislative interpretation to treat that Web page as a ticket, particularly if the lottery rules provide that the sole evidence of participation is the database of entries on the lottery's server in its home country.

8.2.2 Advertising

Advertising is unlawful under British law for both gaming and lotteries if it is aimed at inducing the British public to participate in the unlawful game or lottery. The phrasing of the offence under the two Acts is slightly different. Under the Gaming Act 1968 it is an offence to issue or cause to be issued an advertisement which invites the public to subscribe money or money's worth to be used in gaming, even if the gaming takes place outside Great Britain.[1] For lotteries it is a defence to prove that the person charged believed and had reasonable grounds to believe that the lottery would not be promoted in Great Britain or tickets or advertisements issued there.[2]

This suggests that a prosecution could be avoided by taking the kinds of anti-targeting measures discussed in Chapter 7.2.1.3, which might include refusing to accept bets or other payment from a person in the relevant jurisdiction and refusing to pay prizes there. Even measures of this kind might be insufficient to persuade a court that the casino or lottery was not operating in the relevant jurisdiction – in *People v World Interactive Gambling Corp and Others*[3] a New York court suggested that an on-line casino whose software rejected bets by those who identified themselves as residents of (inter alia) New York had not taken sufficient steps to show a good faith attempt to avoid engaging in

---

19 But note that this depends very much on the wording of the statute. In *People v World Interactive Gambling Corp* (1999) QDS 22310325 (Supreme Court of New York) 24th July 1999, Justice Ramos held 'However, under New York Penal Law, if the person engaged in gambling is located in New York, then New York is the location where the gambling occurred [See, Penal Law §225.00(2)]. Here, some or all of those funds in an Antiguan bank account are staked every time the New York user enters betting information into the computer. It is irrelevant that Internet gambling is legal in Antigua. The act of entering the bet and transmitting the information from New York via the Internet is adequate to constitute gambling activity within the New York state.'

20 Lotteries and Amusements Act 1976, s 2(1)(b).

 1 Gaming Act 1968, s 42(1).

 2 Lotteries and Amusements Act 1976, s 2(1), 2(2A).

 3 (1999) QDS 22310325 (Supreme Court of New York) 24th July 1999.

gambling in New York, because these safeguards could be overcome by entering a false State as part of the player's address.[4]

An examination of the terms and conditions of on-line casinos indicates some attempt to avoid liability on this basis by the use of terms such as:

> *Void Where Prohibited.* Game is subject to any and all applicable laws. Game is void wherever prohibited, regulated or taxed.[5]

> *Void Where Prohibited.* The game is void wherever prohibited, regulated, or taxed. It is the sole responsibility of the player to comply with all country, state, and/or local laws and regulations having jurisdiction.[6]

> *Legality.* Globe Casino's games are played over the Internet which reaches virtually every country in the world. Some of these jurisdictions have not addressed the legality of Internet gaming, while some have specifically made Internet gaming illegal. In practical terms, it is impossible for Globe Casino to determine the state of the law in every country around the world on an ongoing basis. Therefore, by clicking the 'I agree' button, you are acknowledging that you have determined what the laws are in your jurisdiction, and that it is legal for you to place a bet via the Internet, and for Globe Casino to receive your bet via the Internet.[7]

It seems unlikely that these terms are sufficient to avoid liability for advertising the casino in those jurisdictions where advertising constitutes an offence, particular as the terms are not displayed on the home page of the casino but required a few minutes searching to discover.

8.2.3 Use of premises

Use of premises for purposes connected with the promotion or conduct of an unlicensed lottery is an offence under British law.[8] Independent ISPs whose systems cache the lottery site will not be guilty of the offence, as it requires knowledge on the defendant's part. However, if the on-line lottery operators make use of UK servers for some part of the operation (eg processing credit card payments), this might constitute an offence. Similarly, any person in Great Britain who was involved in designing the lottery website or writing software specifically for the operation of the lottery would probably be guilty of the offence.

8.2.4 Procurement

Under the Lotteries and Amusements Act 1976, s 2(1)(g) there is a general offence of procuring any person to undertake the acts made unlawful by s 2(1).

---

4 'Although a user which entered a state such as New York, which does not permit land-based gambling, was denied permission to gamble, because the software does not verify the user's actual location, a user initially denied access, could easily circumvent the denial by changing the state entered to that of Nevada, while remaining physically in New York State. The user could then log onto the GCC casino and play virtual slots, blackjack or roulette. This raises the question if this constitutes a good faith effort not to engage in gambling in New York.' per Justice Ramos. The judge did not consider whether there was any feasible way in which the user's actual location could in fact be determined. However, it should be noted that in this case the on-line casino was wholly owned and managed by New York residents, and targeted mailings were sent from a New York location – these were the primary reasons for holding the defendant liable.
5 MegaPlay Casino, Dominican Republic – http://www.MegaPlay.com.
6 Show Girls Casino, Dominican Republic – http://www.showgirlscasino.com.
7 Globe Casino, Venezuela – http://www.globecasino.com.
8 Lotteries and Amusements Act 1976, s 2(1)(f).

Thus, if the on-line lottery entered into contracts with British service providers there would be a risk that this offence was committed by so doing. Because the offence requires the procuring of the unlawful acts discussed in 8.2.1 to 8.2.3 above, it is probably lawful to procure services which are not specific to the lottery's activities – thus off-site backup services, for example, do not require the service provider to undertake the acts prohibited by s 2(1). On the other hand, a disaster recovery service might well fall within s 2(1)(g), as were the disaster to happen the British service provider would be required under the contract to provide s 2(1) services.

8.2.5   Is gambling arbitrage possible?

It is clear from the discussion above that on-line gaming and lotteries will inevitably operate close to the edge of legality outside their home jurisdictions. Whether arbitrage is possible depends so much on the specific drafting of a country's anti-gambling laws that no general conclusion is possible. It seems likely that an on-line gambling enterprise will only find it economic to engage in arbitrage of this kind if it is at particular risk in some jurisdiction – eg if a major shareholder or senior manager has a home in or is a regular visitor to that jurisdiction. However, the safeguarding techniques discussed above suggest that, for commercial activities which are less strongly disapproved of by the law, legal and regulatory arbitrage may offer an effective way of escaping overly restrictive regulation.

8.3   THE APPLICATION OF GRESHAM'S LAW?

Gresham's law, as applied to precious metal coinage, states simply that 'Bad money drives out good'.[9] Could legal and regulatory arbitrage have the same effect, driving out good law and replacing it with bad?

The answer depends very much on the values used to determine goodness. If a law is 'good' for a particular state[10] but bad for electronic commerce and other Internet activities, it is likely to come under severe pressure. This pressure will take two forms.

The first is economic pressure, as business activities restructure their electronic operations to minimise the impact of the law. For example, although national Governments have collectively agreed as a basic principle of consumption tax law that 'Rules for the consumption taxation of cross-border trade should result in taxation in the jurisdiction where consumption takes place and an international consensus should be sought on the circumstances under which supplies are held to be consumed in a jurisdiction',[11] there are as

---

9   In other words, as the precious metal content of coins decreases the real value of the coins also decreases. Thus, the 'good' (high precious metal content) coins are taken out of circulation and melted down because their metal content is worth more than their face value, while the proportion of 'bad' coins in circulation increases.
10   For the purposes of argument, the fact that the state has enacted it is taken as sufficient evidence of goodness.
11   OECD Committee on Fiscal Affairs 'Electronic Commerce: Taxation Framework Conditions' p 7, report adopted at the OECD Ministerial Conference: 'A Borderless World –Realising the potential of Electronic Commerce' 8 October 1998.

yet few[11a] suggestions how this principle might be implemented. As the discussion of consumption taxes at 8.1.1.1 above demonstrates, the benefits of using tax arbitrage are so large, and the difficulties of collecting consumption tax on information products so great, that there may indeed be no way in which the principle can be complied with. If so, 'bad' law will indeed drive out good, as countries are forced to reduce their consumption tax rates (at least for information products) to prevent their national electronic commerce businesses from migrating to low-tax jurisdictions.

The second is what might be described as 'legitimacy' pressure. A law which is either unenforceable, or unenforced, falls into disrepute and loses its normative effect as law.[12] Laws restricting free speech,[13] pornography[14] and gambling[15] are likely to be unenforceable against persons outside the jurisdiction who use the Internet to disseminate information and services to persons inside. This may ultimately result in pressure to reduce laws of this type to the 'lowest common denominator'.

Reversing the perspective, laws which are good for Internet activities seem likely to drive out those which are, by the same test, bad. By this standard, Gresham's law will not apply. What, then, does 'goodness' mean from this viewpoint. The answer is very simple, at least from the perspective of commercial activities via the Internet – a 'good' law is one which imposes similar requirements to other laws, whereas a 'bad' law is one that is more restrictive or whose terms are unclear. Thus, if all laws impose similar restrictions, all are equally good. Electronic commerce has little moral content, and is more concerned with the compliance costs of operating under widely differing laws than with the actual content of those laws. This means that the economic pressures can be reduced or eliminated through the convergence of national laws on common principles discussed further in Chapter 10.

This is not so for non-commercial activities. Freedom of communication, irrespective of the moral content communicated, is such a fundamental consequence of the Internet technologies that even convergence of national laws seems unlikely to curtail that freedom to any great extent. Ultimately restrictions of this kind, no matter how strong the argument in their favour, may be driven out of national law and replaced by filtering technology which, set to the user's preferences, prevents the receipt of communications on unwanted topics.

11a See 8.1.1 above for the European Commission's proposals on this issue.
12 See Fuller *The Morality of Law* (Yale University Press, 1964) Chapter II.
13 See Chapter 7.3.1.
14 See Chapter 4.2.2.
15 See 8.2 above.

Chapter 9

Enforceability in the Internet environment

The questions to be asked of any law or regulation that purports to govern activity on the Internet is not whether it is applicable, but rather whether it is enforceable? Though it may be in vogue to call for regulation, the primary question that should govern whether or how a regulation should be framed is not whether it is applicable – it will almost certainly be so. The question must be whether the regulation is needed, and if so, whether it is enforceable in a coherent and satisfactory manner. If regulations are not needed or do not prove to be enforceable due to the jurisdictional or substantive issues then there is a threat that users of the Internet will hold them in contempt.[1]

This distinction between applicability and enforceability is fundamental to the future development of Internet law. It is a comparatively easy task for a legislator to draft a law which applies to a particular activity undertaken via the Internet, but much more difficult to frame the law so that it is enforceable in practice. Laws which are unenforceable have two major defects; not only do they fail to deal with the mischief which the law seeks to remedy, but the knowledge that they are unenforceable weakens the normative force of other laws.[2]

In discussing the enforceability of law and regulations, it is important to recognise that compliance with law is not solely dependent on that law's enforcement through the courts. In the vast majority of instances, the law is complied with because of its normative force, ie because it *is* the law.[3] Thus most citizens refrain from criminal behaviour because they wish to act lawfully, not because of a fear of prosecution, and similarly in private law matters such as contracts the parties adhere to their bargains because that is what they have agreed. However, the ultimate enforceability of a law is important if it is to have normative force. For this reason, a system of law and regulation which is

---

1   Lars Davies *A Model for Internet Regulation? – Constructing a Framework for Regulating Electronic Commerce* (London: Society for Computers and Law, 1999) p 6 (http://www.scl.org).
2   This chapter assumes that enforceability is a desirable aim, and does not consider the argument occasionally put forward that, for Internet transactions, enforceability is irrelevant. That argument is normally predicated on the assumption that Internet traders who do not respect purchasers' rights will immediately be forced out of business, because the Internet allows customer complaints to be available to all Internet users within minutes or seconds. The author has a number of doubts about the validity of this assumption; but more importantly, we must recognise that the question of enforceability is of real important to national governments, who wish to see their laws obeyed and their citizens' rights protected for political, as well as moral reasons.
3   Kelsen *Pure Theory of the Law* (2nd, University of California Press, 1967) pp 35, 44 ff.

so contradictory that it is, in practical terms, impossible to obey is treated here as unenforceable.[4] Because it is impossible, or excessively burdensome to act in accordance with the law it loses its normative force and ceases to be treated by citizens and businesses as binding on them.

As a final introductory point we must also note that the problems of unenforceability arise largely from the trans-jurisdictional nature of Internet activities. The system of law and regulation which needs to be enforceable is not simply that of a single jurisdiction, but that of all the jurisdictions whose laws are applicable to the activity. Thus although each individual law or regulation may appear to be enforceable, it is the cumulative effect of all the applicable laws which needs to be examined.

This chapter will examine two types of unenforceability:

* laws and regulations which are, in practice unenforceable because the court in question has no effective jurisdiction over the defendant – these will generally be laws creating criminal offences; and
* laws and regulations which are in theory enforceable, but where the cost of enforcement outweighs the benefits of enforcement – these are normally private law matters.

9.1   PUBLIC ORDER RULES

All countries restrict the dissemination of information which is perceived as posing a threat to public order and the general welfare of that country. In the physical world, restrictions of this kind can usually be enforced because the dissemination is undertaken through printed or other physical media. The general distribution of such media has necessarily to be undertaken by persons physically present in the country, thus making enforcement a practicable activity. Admittedly, there may be difficulties in preventing distribution through the mail, particularly via mail sent from outside the jurisdiction, but even in this case foreign mail tends to enter a country through a small number of points and Customs officials may therefore be able to identify unlawful mailings. The same problem arises with information published in journals or magazines which have only a minor circulation in the country, and in practice enforcement against such publications is not undertaken because the small circulation minimises the damage to public order or the general welfare.

Where the Internet is used by a person within the jurisdiction to disseminate unlawful information, enforcement is again not a major problem if the sender can be identified.[5] The position is very different, however, when the information is disseminated from another jurisdiction where it is not unlawful.[6] In such a case the national restrictions on dissemination of that information may be unenforceable because:

* the originator is outside the jurisdiction; and
* there is no identifiable distributor within the jurisdiction against whom action may be taken; or

---

4   'A norm that is not obeyed by anybody anywhere, in other words a norm that is not effective at least to some degree, is not regarded as a valid legal norm.' Kelsen, op cit p 11; see also p 211 ff.
5   Difficulties may arise where anonymising techniques are used by the sender – see Chapter 2.3.3.3.
6   If the information is also unlawful in the other jurisdiction, co-operation between police forces will generally lead to action being taken there.

- there is an identifiable distributor within the jurisdiction, but that person is not liable under the law.

9.1.1   Obscenity

The discussion of obscenity and indecency laws in Chapter 4.2.2 tells us that criminal liability is generally based on (a) possession of unlawful material,[7] or (b) distribution of that material.[8] Because these are criminal offences, a defendant will only be subject to the law if he commits these acts in the jurisdiction unless there are specific provisions relating to distribution from outside the jurisdiction. The problems of enforcing national law can be demonstrated by examining two simple scenarios, relating to the enforcement of UK law – exactly the same problems will arise no matter which country's law is at issue.

The first scenario is where a non-UK individual makes obscene material available via a website. If that website is hosted outside the UK, in a jurisdiction where the material is not unlawful, no possession offence has been committed in the UK by the individual. Has he distributed the material in the UK? The answer will depend on how the UK courts view the Internet technologies, but the following points will be relevant:

- If the website makes the material freely available, without requiring viewers to register and/or pay for access, there is a compelling argument that the distribution takes place where the website is hosted. Viewers request delivery of packets of information by entering the site's URL into their browser software, and that request does not easily identify the jurisdiction from which the request comes.[9] This is most closely analogous to the viewer travelling physically to the hosting jurisdiction and receiving the material there, and thus outside the UK.
- If the website requires registration and/or payment, this may be sufficient information to give the website controller the requisite knowledge that the material will be transmitted to the UK, so that he will have committed the offence of distributing in the UK. However, the 'travelling customer' argument might still be accepted by the courts, enabling them to find that no act of distribution in the UK occurred.[10]

---

7 In the case of child pornography, knowing possession is generally sufficient, whilst for other obscene or indecent material there is normally an additional requirement of intent to distribute – see Chapter 4.2.2.2.

8 The requisite *mens rea* for this offence is normally either knowledge of the material's unlawfulness, or distribution for gain subject to a defence of ignorance and no grounds to suspect unlawfulness – see Chapter 4.2.2.3.

9 The IP address in the viewer's request does not contain direct geographic information, although in theory such information can be obtained by using the nslookup function. However, this only gives the registered address of the viewer's ISP, which may have no connection with the viewer's actual jurisdiction. For example, a request for a page by a UK AOL user would probably give an IP address which appeared to emanate from the US, as AOL's network is US-based. All this assumes that it would be practical to perform geographical investigations into IP addresses – in practice, the web server software has no 'knowledge' about the jurisdiction from which a Web page request originates.

10 This point appears not yet to have come before the courts.

Even supposing a distribution offence to have been committed, there is still the difficulty of bringing effective criminal proceedings against the website controller. His activities are lawful in his home jurisdiction, and so it is unlikely that extradition proceedings would be successful.[11] The UK authorities would therefore need to wait until the controller visited the UK, identify his presence and whereabouts, and then arrest him. The resources required to do this for the numerous websites which infringe the UK's obscenity laws[12] are unlikely to be available. In practical terms, therefore, the website controller runs little or no risk of being convicted of an offence under UK law.

The only real option open to the UK authorities in these circumstances is to take action against the website host, but unless the host is based in the UK such action is unlikely to be successful.[13] Even if the host is UK based, if criminal immunities are introduced along the lines of the civil immunities conferred by the EU Electronic Commerce Directive the host will not be liable unless it has been informed of the unlawful nature of the material (see Chapter 4.3.2.2).

The second, slightly more complex scenario is of a person within the UK who makes obscene material available via a website hosted in a different country where that material is not unlawful. So far as distribution offences are concerned, the analysis above will be identical. However, in those circumstances the UK authorities might wish to proceed on the basis of a possession offence. If the defendant has retained copies of the material on his UK computer and charges for access to the website, the prosecution is likely to succeed, as the existence of the foreign-hosted website demonstrates the necessary intention to distribute for gain under the UK Obscene Publications Act 1964, s 1(2). However, if no copies are retained by the defendant, it will be impossible for the prosecution to prove that he did, at some time, possess copies in the UK. The Internet technologies make it possible to upload material to the website from anywhere in the world, so the mere existence of the website is not sufficient evidence that the defendant ever possessed that material in the UK.

In practice, therefore, the law enforcement bodies of each country will be limited to taking action against websites hosted in the jurisdiction, and website controllers who possess unlawful material in the jurisdiction. Enforcement against those outside the jurisdiction is practically impossible, even though the material in question is just as easily available in the jurisdiction as material hosted or possessed there.

---

11 Extradition normally requires an extradition treaty between the countries concerned, and is only available for crimes listed in the treaty. As a general rule, the list will only cover matters which are offences in both countries. Additionally, information crimes such as the distribution of obscene material may not be seen as sufficiently serious to warrant extradition; the list of extradition crimes under the UK Extradition Acts 1870-1935 does not include non-child-related obscenity offences – *Halsbury's Laws of England* vol 11(1) para 215.

12 On the assumption that images of anal sexual intercourse are obscene under the UK Obscene Publications Act 1959, an AltaVista search was undertaken for Web pages which contained the text 'anal' and 'jpg' or 'jpeg' and were not hosted on .uk domain servers, presuming that these would primarily link to images of that type. The search identified 272,514 pages of which, from an examination of the first 50 page titles, at least 70% were likely to link to such images. This suggests that the number of non-UK website controllers who are, on these assumptions, potentially committing offences under UK law is measured in tens or even hundreds of thousands.

13 See, for example, the largely unsuccessful attempts by Germany to control the availability in Germany of information hosted in the US, discussed in relation to free speech in Chapter 7.3.1.

9.1.2   Advertising controls

Very similar issues arise in relation to those public order rules which control advertising by particular sectors of commercial activity. Rules of this type are often found when the commercial activity itself requires licensing or some other form of approval. Thus advertising restrictions are placed on, inter alia, the regulated professions[14] and the financial services sector.[15]

The existence of these restrictions poses a major problem to any organisation to which they apply and which is considering establishing an Internet presence. Such a presence is very likely to contravene the advertising restrictions of every country other than that in which the organisation is licensed or approved. To achieve global compliance, these organisations have only two options:

- To establish an Internet presence in a way which does not constitute advertising in any jurisdiction that regulates the activity. Such a presence is likely to be so anodyne as not to be worth the effort.
- Alternatively, the organisation could apply to be licensed or authorised in every jurisdiction which regulates its sector of activity. Leaving aside the costs of obtaining global authorisation, this approach is unlikely to be feasible in practice because organisations which require prior authorisation are normally also subject to supervision of their activities. Except where supervision regimes have been harmonised[16] it will always be excessively expensive, and often impossible, to comply with the requirements of all supervisory authorities.

In other words, restrictions of this kind are unenforceable in practice because global compliance is impossible or uneconomic. The effect of this unenforceability is that organisations take the decision to act unlawfully in foreign countries, as can be seen from the numerous websites for lawyers and banks.

The absurdity of the position in which such organisations are placed has been recognised by the authorities who are responsible for enforcing these regulations, some of whom have issued policy statements on their enforcement policy. These seem to demonstrate a trend towards taking enforcement action only against those organisations which seek to do business in the relevant jurisdiction – see further the discussion in Chapter 7.2.1.3. However, a law which requires a formal policy of selective enforcement is by definition a bad law, and will require reform in the near future. In the author's view such reform must, to be effective in the long term, base itself on the twin principles of home (rather than host) country regulation and the convergence of national laws. These concepts have been examined earlier in Chapter 7.2.2, and are also considered in Chapter 10.

9.2   PRIVATE RIGHTS AND CONSUMER PROTECTION

The protection of consumers who purchase goods, services or information products via the Internet has given rise to much discussion. The initial thrust

---

14 Eg in the UK advertising by solicitors is regulated by the Solicitors Practice Rules 1990 and the Solicitors Publicity Code 1990, and advertising using the title of 'architect' is restricted by the Architects (Registration) Act 1931, ss 2–3 and Trade Descriptions Act 1968, s 14(1)(a).
15 See eg UK Financial Services Act 1986, s 57 (investment agreements), s 130 (insurance contracts); UK Banking Act 1987, s 32 (deposit advertisements).
16 As in the EU for the banking sector under the Second Council Directive 89/646/EEC of 15 December 1989 on the coordination of laws, regulations and administrative provisions relating to the taking up and pursuit of the business of credit institutions.

of the debate was towards identifying the additional rights which a consumer would need in these circumstances; but increasingly it is being recognised that the real problem is not the existence of consumer rights but their effective enforcement.

In most jurisdictions, consumers already receive the benefit of a wide range of consumer protection laws. These protect consumers against misleading advertising,[17] control specific types of transaction which are thought to pose special risks to consumers, such as credit transactions,[18] and commonly also impose generic controls on unfair or unconscionable terms in business-to-consumer contracts. A typical example of the latter is the EU Directive on unfair terms in consumer contracts (the Unfair Terms Directive).[19]

The Unfair Terms Directive provides as a general principle that a term in a business-to-consumer contract which is unfair will not be enforceable against the consumer, although the contract will still subsist so far as is possible and its remaining terms will be enforceable.[20] A term is unfair if (a) it has not been individually negotiated, and (b) 'contrary to the requirement of good faith, it causes a significant imbalance in the parties' rights and obligations arising under the contract, to the detriment of the consumer'.[1] The annex to the Directive contains an indicative and non-exhaustive list of terms which 'may be regarded as unfair',[2] several of which may apply to Internet contracts:

(b) inappropriately excluding or limiting the legal rights of the consumer . . . in the event of total or partial non-performance . . .;

(i) irrevocably binding the consumer to terms with which he had no real opportunity of becoming acquainted before the conclusion of the contract;[3]

(q) excluding or hindering the consumer's right to take legal action or exercise any other legal remedy, particularly by . . . unduly restricting the evidence available to him or imposing on him a burden of proof which, according to the applicable law, should lie with another party to the contract.

Additionally, many jurisdictions have enacted consumer protection laws specifically to regulate distance selling, which will thus apply to consumer contracts entered into via the Internet. Typical of these is the EU Directive on the protection of consumers in respect of distance contracts (the Distance Selling Directive).[4] The Directive applies to most[5] 'distance contracts', which

---

17 See eg UK Trade Descriptions Act 1968.
18 See eg UK Consumer Credit Act 1974.
19 Council Directive 93/13/EEC, OJ L 95, April 21 1993.
20 Unfair Terms Directive, art 6(1)
 1 Unfair Terms Directive, art 3(1).
 2 Unfair Terms Directive, art 3(3). Note that the UK Department of Trade and Industry in *Implementation of the EC Directive on Unfair Terms in Consumer Contracts* (London: DTI, October 1993), its consultative document on the implementation of the Directive, takes this wording to mean that the terms in the list may be, but are not necessarily, unfair. Other Member States may take a stronger position on this point, and even under the UK approach including any of the terms in the Annex is likely to give rise to a presumption of unfairness.
 3 See Chapter 6.2.
 4 Directive 97/7/EC on the protection of consumers in respect of distance contracts, OJ L 144, 4 June 1997, p 19.
 5 A list of exemptions is set out in art 3, which includes financial services contracts. These are subject to a separate consumer protection regime under the EU draft directive concerning the distance marketing of consumer financial services and amending Council Directive 90/619/EEC and Directives 97/7/EC and 98/27/EC, OJ C 385, 11 December 1998, p 10, as amended by document 599PC0385, 31.01.2000.

are defined as contracts concerning goods or services which are concluded with a consumer[6] as a consequence of an organised distance sales scheme of the supplier using a means of communicating at a distance.[7]

Where the Directive applies, a number of obligations are placed upon the seller. The most important of these are:

- specified information has to be provided to the consumer prior to the conclusion of the contract,[8] in a clear and comprehensible manner appropriate to the means of communication, and taking into account the principles of good faith in commercial transactions and the rules protecting minors;[9]
- that information must also be provided in writing or in 'another durable medium[10] available and accessible to him' in good time during performance, and at the latest at the time of delivery of goods. Additional information must also be provided, including the supplier's business address for complaints;[11]
- the consumer has an automatic right of withdrawal from the contract for a period of at least seven days from receipt of the required notice, with special rules for services contracts. If no notice is provided, the withdrawal period is three months from making the contract.[12] There is no right of withdrawal for particular contracts listed in art 6(3), among which are included contracts for the supply of audio or video recordings, records or computer software and contracts for the supply of newspapers, periodicals, and magazines. It will be noted that although the supply of information against immediate payment is likely to be one of the most important categories of Internet contract, and that in practice a consumer who exercises his right of withdrawal is likely already to have made use of the information (and probably retained a copy), consumers will still have the right of withdrawal unless that information is packaged in the form of a video recording, computer software, magazine etc;
- performance must be made by the supplier within 30 days unless otherwise agreed;[13]
- where credit card payment is involved, Member States will be required to legislate provisions which allow the consumer to be re-credited on cancellation or in the event of fraudulent use.[14]

Under art 12, these rights may not be waived by the consumer.

6 A natural person not acting in his commercial or professional capacity – Distance Selling Directive, art 2(4).
7 Distance Selling Directive, art 2(1). Such a means is one whereby the supplier and consumer are not physically present at the same place – art 2(4) - and the indicative list of such means in Annex I includes email.
8 Distance Selling Directive, art 4(1). The information to be provided is: the identity of the supplier; the main characteristics of the goods or services; the price including all taxes; delivery costs; payment, delivery and performance arrangements; notification that the consumer has a right of withdrawal under art 6(3); costs of communicating with the supplier 'where it is calculated other than at the basic rate'; period for which offer or price remains valid.
9 Distance Selling Directive, art 4(2).
10 This concept is defined in EU draft directive concerning the distance marketing of consumer financial services and amending Council Directive 90/619/EEC and Directives 97/7/EC and 98/27/EC, OJ C 385, 11 December 1998, p10, art 2(f) as 'any instrument enabling the consumer to store information addressed personally and specifically to him and which is mainly contained on floppy disks, CD-ROMs, and the hard drive of the consumer's computer on which electronic mail is stored'.
11 Distance Selling Directive, art 5(1).
12 Distance Selling Directive, art 6(1).
13 Distance Selling Directive, art 7(1).
14 Distance Selling Directive, art 8.

Furthermore, both Directives recognise that the terms of the contract with the consumer may attempt to make the contract subject to the laws and jurisdiction of the supplier's country, and so provide that such a choice of law is ineffective to remove the consumer's protection.[15]

Although at first sight it appears as if the consumer receives substantial protection from these measures, in fact the protection is only of much value if both consumer and supplier are in the same jurisdiction. This is because where the supplier is in a different jurisdiction and has no assets in the consumer's country against which the judgment can be enforced, the costs of enforcement[16] will normally outweigh the consumer's claim by so substantial a margin that it is not worth bringing a claim.

One possible solution is to allow representative bodies in the supplier's country, such as consumer protection organisations, to bring an action against the supplier on behalf of the consumer.[17] This is the approach adopted in the Distance Selling Directive, art 11 of which provides:

1. Member States shall ensure that adequate and effective means exist to ensure compliance with this Directive in the interests of consumers.
2. The means referred to in paragraph 1 shall include provisions whereby one or more of the following bodies, as determined by national law, may take action under national law before the courts or before the competent administrative bodies to ensure that the national provisions for the implementation of this Directive are applied:
   (a) public bodies or their representatives;
   (b) consumer organizations having a legitimate interest in protecting consumers;
   (c) professional organizations having a legitimate interest in acting.

If this approach proves effective it may make consumer claims in one Member State enforceable against a supplier in another, at least where there are sufficient complainants to justify a class action on their behalf. However, it will be of no assistance where the supplier is outside the EU.

---

15 Article 6 of the Unfair Terms Directive states that its protections apply 'notwithstanding any contract term which applies or purports to apply the law of a non member State, if the contract has a close connection with the territory of the member States' and art 12 of the Distance Selling Directive contains a nearly identical provision. Interestingly, however, the wording of art 6 suggests that a choice of law within the EU is always permissible, though seems probable that any choice of jurisdiction other than the consumer's own is prima facie unfair as in practice it 'excludes or hinders the consumer's right to take legal action or exercise any other legal remedy' and thus falls within Annex item (q) of the Unfair Terms Directive. EU draft directive concerning the distance marketing of consumer financial services and amending Council Directive 90/619/EEC and Directives 97/7/EC and 98/27/EC, OJ C 385, 11 December 1998, p 10, art 11(3) is much clearer; the directive's protections apply 'if the consumer is resident on the territory of a Member State and the contract has a close link with the Community', thus removing the doubt in the other directives whether they apply if the consumer is temporarily in another country when he enters into the transaction.

16 In addition to the costs of bringing a claim before the courts of his own country, once judgment has been given the consumer will need to enforce that judgment in the courts of the supplier's country (assuming both countries are party to a convention which allows such enforcement). In general, the consumer will need to engage the services of a lawyer in that country and pay the costs of the court proceedings which may not be recoverable from the supplier. There are no definitive figures for these costs, but the lowest of the estimates given to the author by practising lawyers for the level of claim at which foreign enforcement would be economic was US $3,000. Most estimates suggested it would not be worth pursuing a claim unless it was for the order of US $15,000–20,000.

17 Or, more likely, a class action on behalf of a group of consumers.

In most cases, therefore, the enforcement of private rights via traditional litigation is unlikely to be effective for Internet transactions. Consumer rights are the most extreme example of this phenomenon, but enforcement is likely to be impracticable for many other kinds of private right where the claim is of low value. For example, many of the misuses of information resources discussed in Chapter 3 are likely to be in practice unenforceable because of the costs of so doing. The question therefore arises whether alternative enforcement methods can be developed to deal with this problem.[18]

9.3   SELF-REGULATION – STICKS AND CARROTS

The most promising candidate as a method of providing some effective enforcement, both in respect of public order regulation and for private rights, is the establishment of self-regulatory schemes. The essence of any such scheme is that:

- membership is voluntary, which increases the normative force of the scheme's rules;
- members agree to abide by the scheme's rules, which are devised so that compliance with the rules also results in a sufficient measure of compliance with the regulations or private rights which the scheme was devised to protect;
- because the rules are devised by members of the industry sector in question, compliance is practicable and compatible with the commercial activities of scheme members; and
- the scheme normally provides a mechanism through which complaints of infringement can be resolved which is cheaper and quicker than court action.

Self-regulatory schemes of this type are already operational in the fields of unlawful information content and privacy protection, and it is likely that new schemes will be devised to cover other areas of Internet activity, most notably to provide consumer protection in electronic commerce transactions.[19]

However, as Sieber demonstrates,[20] a self-regulatory scheme only provides an effective method of enforcement if it is backed up by sanctions for non-compliance with the scheme's rules. If the increase in user confidence and freedom from official enforcement which results from membership of the scheme is the carrot, the sanctions are the corresponding stick with which to beat defaulting members. Sanctions are of two basic types:

- Sanctions imposed by the scheme itself, normally limited to expulsion from the scheme and loss of the privilege to advertise membership. Thus, for example, the Better Business Bureau's BBB*OnLine* privacy seal scheme[1] grants a licence to use the seal on a member's website, but cl 4 of the

---

18 See *Recommendation of the OECD Council concerning Guidelines for Consumer Protection in the Context of Electronic Commerce* (OECD, 1999) guideline VI.

19 See eg the draft Better Business Bureau BBB*OnLine* 'Code of Online Business Practices', http://www.bbbonline.org.

20 Sieber *Legal Regulation, Law Enforcement and Self-Regulation: A new alliance for preventing illegal and harmful contents in the Internet* (Bertelsmann Foundation, 1999) available from http://www.bertelsmann.de – see in particular part 4, p 82 ff.

1 http://www.bbbonline.org

licence permits BBB*OnLine* to suspend membership for non-compliance with the rules and, ultimately, to terminate membership. Suspension or termination requires immediate removal of the seal from that member's website, and may also be publicised by BBB*OnLine*.

• Failure to comply with the scheme may amount to an infringement of national law. This is the case under the Australian Broadcasting Amendment (Online Services) Act 1999, which requires ISPs to follow the rating system for cinematograph films in respect of Internet content. Failure to comply with the rules of an applicable self-regulatory scheme is likely to lead to criminal liability under Sch 5.[2] Similarly, the German Act on the Dissemination of Publications and Media Contents Harmful to Youth[3] establishes a self-regulatory tribunal and makes contravention of its decisions a criminal offence.

9.3.1 Unlawful content

A number of self-regulatory schemes have been introduced by consortia of ISPs to deal with the problem of unlawful content transmitted via the Internet. Although cynics might say that the main aim of the devisers of these schemes was to avoid more stringent regulation of intermediaries,[4] there seems to be a general view amongst law enforcement bodies that these schemes are useful, and may in practice be the only effective way of reducing the volume of unlawful material. Additionally, as the Internet becomes more and more firmly established as a fundamental part of the global communications infrastructure, ISPs need to demonstrate that they are respectable and responsible companies, and membership of self-regulatory content control schemes is one way of doing so.

One of the most effective self-regulatory schemes is the UK's Internet Watch Foundation.[5] It was founded in 1996 through consultation between the UK Government, the police and the main UK ISP organisations, the Internet Service Providers Association and the London Internet Exchange. Its constitution sets out its aims as follows:

> The basic objectives of the Internet Watch Foundation (IWF) are to restrict the availability of criminal content and help consumers prevent access to potentially harmful content on the Internet in the United Kingdom.
>
> The main measures by which these objectives are currently achieved are: operation of a hotline for reporting criminal content; support to international rating and filtering developments and measures to inform and educate Internet users about potential dangers on the Internet and means to avoid them.

Reports of unlawful material are made via the IWF's hotline,[6] the origin of the material is traced, and then it is assessed by IWF for potential illegality. If it is thought to be illegal but emanates from outside the UK, it is reported to the UK police for liaison with the country of origin's authorities. If it is of UK origin, IWF invites the UK host to remove the material in consultation with the

2   See in particular paras 82, 83 and 86.
3   Gesetz über jugendgefährdende Schriften und Medieninhalte, arts 9, 21.
4   If this was the aim, it seems largely to have been successful – see Chapter 4.3 on intermediary immunity.
5   http://www.iwf.org.uk
6   http://www.iwf.org.uk/hotline/hotline.html. At the time of writing, the main focus of action was on child pornography.

originator, and may also report the material to the UK police. There are no direct sanctions for contravention of the scheme. However, because the basis of intermediary criminal liability for the possession of obscene material is generally based on knowledge,[7] an assessment by IWF followed by a report to the ISP in question will give the ISP sufficient knowledge to meet that element of criminal liability.

9.3.2   Privacy

Self-regulatory schemes for privacy form an important part of the EU data protection regime,[8] and receive indirect statutory backing because non-compliance is likely to amount to a breach of the applicable national data protection law. This is particularly so where the code has been approved by the national data protection authority.

However, self-regulatory schemes are of even greater importance in jurisdictions such as the US, which have no comprehensive legislation protecting privacy – see Chapter 7.3.2. One of the most authoritative schemes for protecting online privacy is that devised by the US Better Business Bureau through its BBB*OnLine* Privacy Program.[9] The carrot in this scheme is a licence to use the scheme's Privacy Seal; the stick is removal of that right coupled with publicity.

To join the scheme, potential members must:

- meet the scheme's Eligibility Requirements;[10]
- complete a Compliance Assessment Questionnaire; and
- maintain future compliance with the Eligibility Requirements.

BBB*OnLine* has the right to audit the member for compliance.[11] In addition, members agree to participate in the Program's Dispute Resolution Process Procedures, discussed at 9.3.4 below.

Provided members of such a scheme comply with its rules then, particularly if the scheme incorporates a compulsory dispute resolution mechanism, personal privacy rights are in practice made enforceable. It is noteworthy that the BBB*OnLine* Dispute Resolution Process attempts to go beyond the concept of a simple members/complainants scheme, by accepting complaints against non-members. The main sanction if a complaint is made out against a non-

---

7   See Chapter 4.2.2.
8   Described in Walden, Chapter 11.4.3 and 11.4.4 'Data Protection' in Reed and Angel (eds) *Computer Law* (4th, London: Blackstone Press, 2000).
9   http://www.bbbonline.org/businesses/privacy/
10   http://www.bbbonline.org/businesses/privacy/eligibility.html. In summary, these require the member to:
- engage in lawful activity;
- produce and publicise a privacy policy;
- take appropriate steps to ensure compliance with that policy;
- participate in the Dispute Resolution Program;
- adopt reasonable security measures to ensure privacy;
- not to transfer data to third parties (with certain exceptions);
- allow data subjects to contract out of direct marketing; and
- provide access to the data for the data subject.
11   BBB*OnLine* Privacy Program Participation Agreement, cl 2.

member is reporting the result of the complaint determination to the appropriate government agency and publicising that report.[12]

9.3.3 Consumer protection

Self-regulatory schemes designed to encourage electronic commerce enterprises to comply with consumer protection measures are likely to become increasingly common, both as a mechanism by which the enterprise can instil trust in the consumer, and also as a practical solution to the problems of enforcement.

The UK Which? Webtrader certification scheme[13] is an early example of such a scheme. Under that scheme, traders apply for membership of the scheme and, if accepted, may display the Which? Web Trader logo on their website. To qualify for membership, traders must:

- undergo an audit by Which? of both their website, for compliance with the Webtrader Code of Practice,[14] and their terms and conditions, for compliance with consumer protection law; and
- agree to comply for the future with the Code of Practice.

In addition to the obligations which would be expected in such a Code,[15] the trader also agrees:

- to co-operate with the Which? Legal Service in resolving customer complaints; and
- to invite Which? Online customers to post comments about their experience of dealing with the trader on Which? Online forum discussions.

A further sanction against non-compliant traders is withdrawal of the right to use the Webtrader logo.

There are already signs that, in Europe at least, national laws will soon be modified to permit consumer representative organisations to bring representative actions on behalf of consumers against distance, and particularly

---

12 BBB *OnLine* Privacy Program Dispute Resolution Process, cl 3.6.2. This sanction is also available against a member who refuses to accept the determination, coupled with withdrawal of the Privacy Seal.

13 http://www.which.net/webtrader/index.html

14 http://www.which.net/webtrader/code_of_practice.htm

15 In summary, under the Code suppliers agree to:
- Provide complete and accurate information on pricing and payment, contract terms and conditions, guarantees and contact details.
- Comply with codes for advertising and promotions.
- Meet their obligations under consumer protection law, deliver at the agreed time or offer a refund, and provide the option of a full refund if goods are faulty.
- Provide receipts and correct mistakes promptly.
- Deal with complaints effectively, provide a customer service phone number and details of availability and costs, and provide details about any procedure for solving disputes.
- Provide security for personal information and comply with data protection rules.

on-line, traders.[16] It may soon become the norm, therefore, for operators of self-regulatory schemes to give themselves contractual rights in the scheme rules to take members to court for non-compliance.

9.3.4 Alternative dispute resolution

The cost and effort of resolving a cross-border dispute through the courts[17] means that in practice only the largest claims can be pursued. In effect, small claims are unenforceable. This is a particular problem for electronic commerce because a high proportion of transactions will be cross-border.

Alternative methods of dispute resolution are needed for enforcing the rights of Internet users where these smaller claims are at issue. Possible methods include mediation services, which attempt to broker an agreed resolution of the dispute, or arbitration services which impose a decision on the parties. Whichever type of service is at issue, where there is a cross-border element in an Internet-related dispute then most, perhaps all, elements of the dispute resolution service need to be available on-line.

9.3.4.1   *Mediation*

Examples of on-line mediation already exist. SettleOnline[18] is an interesting mediation service because its primary method of operation is largely automated. In essence, the parties set out the parameters within which they are prepared to reach a settlement in a number of 'demands' or 'offers', and the SettleOnline system then attempts to match these. If a match is found, the parties agree to settle on that basis. SettleOnline is not suitable for very small claims because of its charges, which are US $100 for undertaking the matching process plus an additional US $75–US $200 from each party if a settlement is reached.[19] A similar service of automated offer matching is provided by clickNsettle.com,[1] although its settlement algorithms are different. The other main distinction between clickNsettle and SettleOnline is the former's charging structure, which is based on an initial US $15 registration fee plus a charge to each party for placing an offer on the system. The overall charges for each system are likely to be broadly similar unless a dispute settles straight away.

---

16 Directive 97/7/EC of the European Parliament and of the Council of 20 May 1997 on the Protection of Consumers in respect of Distance Contracts, art 11 (2); see also EU Draft Directive on electronic commerce, Common Position COM(2000) 14263/1/99 REV 1, art 17 for a measure encouraging out-of-court settlement schemes.
17 See note 16 p 259 for estimates.
18 http://www.settleonline.com
19 From the SettleOnline Rules and Procedure document 'Standard Fees':
    '$25 Filing Fee to file a Case, charged to the Filing Party $50 Agreement Fee charged to the Filing Party when the Opposing Party agrees to participate.
    If the Case settles for $10,000 or less during negotiations on SettleOnline, each Party will pay a Settlement Fee of $75. If Case settles for more than $10,000 during negotiations on SettleOnline, each party will pay a Settlement Fee of $200. These fees will automatically be charged to each Party's credit card once a settlement is reached unless a Party has a prearranged credit arrangement.'
 1 http://www.clicknsettle.com

In addition to automated mediation services, on-line mediation moderated by a human specialist is also in operation, such as the work of Professor Ethan Katsh on disputes arising from the eBay auction service.[2]

The problem with on-line mediation, from the point of view of an aggrieved person, is that participation by the defendant is entirely voluntary. Additionally, the requirement that the claimant pay an up-front fee will be a real deterrent for small claims.

9.3.4.2 Arbitration

On-line arbitration is potentially more effective as an enforcement mechanism if the defendant Internet merchant is obliged to submit to the arbitration process. This will be the case where the defendant is a member of a self-regulatory scheme whose rules oblige it to enter into arbitration,[3] or where it is obliged under some other contractual relationship to do so.[4] It seems likely that where the merchant advertises itself as a member of a scheme, a customer who enters into a supply contract with that merchant also forms a collateral contract which obliges the merchant to abide by the scheme rules vis-à-vis the purchaser, at least where the law of a common law jurisdiction applies.[5]

The biggest problem with on-line arbitration is that it is likely to be even more expensive than on-line mediation, as automated determination of complaints is as yet only an aspiration rather than a reality. Arbitration requires the use of a human arbitrator, whose fees must be borne by one or other party.[6] However, where the costs of providing the arbitrator are carried by the self-regulatory scheme, as is the case for the BBB *OnLine* Privacy Program, arbitration may prove suitable for low value complaints. The Privacy Program also aims to reduce the costs of dispute resolution by working primarily on written submissions, and even if a conference is required to enable the parties to make

---

2 http://www.umass.edu/dispute. See also http://www.ResolutionWorks.org for a commercial mediation service.
3 See eg the BBB *OnLine* Privacy Program Participation Agreement, cl 2A.
4 For example, the grant of a domain name will oblige the domain name owner to submit to compulsory dispute resolution – see ICANN Uniform Domain Name Dispute Resolution Policy, cl 4(a) – http://www.icann.org/udrp/udrp-rules-24oct99.htm
5 Under English law it might even be possible for the courts to construct a collateral contract between the complainant and the scheme operator – *Shanklin Pier Ltd v Detel Products Ltd* [1951] 2 KB 854 (manufacturer of paint contractually liable for statements as to the product's suitability, even though purchased from a third party).
6 The ICANN draft Uniform Domain Name Dispute Resolution Policy (http://www.icann.org/udrp/udrp-rules-24oct99.htm) requires arbitration before an approved arbitration Provider, and the parties must bear the Provider's fees – cl 4(a) and (g).
      At the time of writing the fees for participation in an arbitration conducted under the WIPO Expedited Arbitration Rules, which require a hearing, depend on the size of the claim. These fees comprise a Registration Fee of US $1,000 to US $3,000, an Administration Fee of between US $1,000 (for claims up to US $100,000) and US $35,000 (for claims of US $34,800,000 or more), plus the arbitrator's fee.

oral representations, the Program rules provide for this to be achieved through a teleconference or other electronic means.[7]

A further interesting feature of the BBB*OnLine* Privacy Program is that the scheme provides for the review of complaints on a proactive basis, rather than simply mediating or arbitrating the competing claims of the parties.[8] It seems probable that proactive review will be an important element of any successful dispute resolution scheme which deals with consumer complaints.

9.4   THE CHARACTERISTICS OF ENFORCEABILITY

From the discussion above it is possible to deduce three fundamental characteristics of enforceability. These are similar, or at least closely related, to the characteristics of enforceability for laws which apply solely to physical world activities. The fundamental difference is that for Internet activities, these characteristics must be assessed against the complete global pattern of laws or regulations, as Internet activities are visible and potentially have an impact in every jurisdiction.

The first characteristic of enforceability is that compliance with the law or regulation must be feasible, not merely in theoretical but also in practical terms. It is not practically feasible to comply with laws if:

- They impose contradictory obligations on the person subject to that law. Such contradictions are particularly common in public order rules, where different cultural traditions conflict.
- Compliance would remove most or all of the benefits of conducting the activity via the Internet. Financial services regulations which require authorisation and supervision by multiple national authorities will be ignored by many businesses for precisely this reason. Similarly, laws which impose formalities which substantially increase the costs of doing business via the Internet without conferring any real benefit on customers, such as obligations to supply information in non-electronic form, also discourage compliance.

Secondly, the law or regulation must be limited in its application to those over whom the legislator has a legitimate claim. A securities business established in Germany, advertising its services via a German language website and doing business only with German customers, is likely to take the view that the US SEC has no justification for claiming an interest in its activities, and yet (as we have seen in Chapter 7.2.1.3) the German business is almost certainly in breach of US law. Laws and regulations of this type weaken the normative force of all similar laws, and this weakening is not mitigated merely because their lack of legitimate force is recognised through selective prosecution.

---

7   BBB*OnLine* Privacy Program Participation Agreement, cl 3.4.5. However, appeals require a hearing – cls 4.7.1, 4.8 – which will clearly be expensive for a cross-border complaint.
       The ICANN Rules for Uniform Domain Name Dispute Policy are also intended to resolve the dispute on-line, providing in Rule 13 that:
       'There shall be no in-person hearings (including hearings by teleconference, videoconference, and web conference), unless the Panel determines, in its sole discretion and as an exceptional matter, that such a hearing is necessary for deciding the complaint.'
8   BBB*OnLine* Privacy Program Participation Agreement, cl 3.3.

Finally, there must be an effective enforcement mechanism for the law or regulation in question. Without such a mechanism all but the most scrupulous electronic commerce businesses will be tempted to ignore the law, and those which initially comply may be forced by their competitors' non-compliance to cease to do so. An effective enforcement mechanism is particularly difficult to achieve in the field of consumer rights, and it must be recognised that a practically effective but non-binding method, such as self-regulation coupled with alternative dispute resolution, may be more useful in achieving enforcement than a theoretical right which is too difficult and expensive to enforce through the courts.

Chapter 10

Facing the legislative and regulatory challenge

The examination of legal and regulatory issues in the preceding chapters indicates that the challenges posed by the Internet are unlikely to be solved merely by adapting and extending existing legal concepts. The new ways of communicating via the Internet raise legal questions which are fundamentally different for one of two reasons:[1]

- The activity is unknown in the physical world, and is so unlike any current type of activity that no existing legal or regulatory model is appropriate. One of the clearest examples of this is the identity certification infrastructure, examined in detail in Chapter 5.

- Although the problem is present in the physical world and cannot be solved by extending existing concepts, it occurs so infrequently that leaving it unsolved is an acceptable solution. However, the same problem occurs so frequently in the context of Internet activities that it becomes qualitatively different.[2] Examples of this type of challenge to the law include the domain name/trade mark issues examined in Chapter 3 and the application of indirect taxation rules to on-line supplies of information – see Chapter 8.1.1.1.

If we ask ourselves why these activities present fundamentally new challenges to the law, we see that the challenges arise out of two characteristics which are rarely, if ever, exhibited by traditional physical world activities.

The first of these characteristics is the digital nature of all Internet activities, and the consequential ability (and often necessity) for automated decisions to be made in respect of them. Because existing law and regulation has its basis in physical world activities, it assumes the presence of physical world objects and human decision-making. So, for example, the physical world's trade in information products is undertaken by transferring a physical information carrier, such as a book or CD-ROM, from one person to another. This activity can thus be regulated by laws which work on the same basis as those which apply to dealings in other physical goods. These laws also contain an implicit

1   This dichotomy of novelty is explained and illustrated in Kohl 'Legal Reasoning and Legal Change in the Age of the Internet – Why the Ground Rules are still Valid' [1999] 7 International Journal of Law and Information Technology 123, 125 ff.
2   In the same way that torrential rain is qualitatively different from mist, even though the ̱ence is (from one perspective) only that the former consists of more and larger water ̱lets.

assumption that there is necessarily a conscious decision on the part of the human actors to engage in the transfer.

In the Internet world, however, no physical objects are transferred between the parties, and in many cases it is hard to identify a human decision-maker. For example, in the operation of the public key infrastructure used for digital signatures there is only one identifiable piece of human decision-making when the initial identification evidence is taken and an ID Certificate is issued. Thereafter, checking the validity of that certificate and the signature's acceptance or rejection is effected purely through automated means.[3] Similarly, much of the existing law on liability for information content is based on assumptions about conscious dealings with the physical carriers of that information, and the effect of applying those laws to the Internet produces such unexpected consequences that already it has proved necessary to disapply parts of these laws so far as intermediaries are concerned.[4] A further consequence of digitisation and automation is that many Internet activities are widely distributed, both among actors[5] and jurisdictions, thus making it difficult or impossible to apply existing laws to the Internet analogues of physical world activities.[6]

The second characteristic is that the majority of Internet transactions have, in fact or potentially, a cross-border effect. Some, such as posting a Web page, have global reach. Although transactions which have multi-jurisdictional consequences are not uncommon in the physical world, they rarely give rise to the kinds of legal uncertainty found in many Internet transactions. If these physical world dealings are one-to-one transactions, they normally occur between commercial entities who have established their own legal framework for the transaction via a contract. If one-to-many, they tend to be undertaken via already regulated systems such as satellite broadcasting or international voice telephony, where an agreed cross-border regulatory framework already exists.

The cross-border nature of Internet transactions poses two types of challenge to the law:

- national law controls on dealings in information, such as information assets[7] and personal data,[8] become less meaningful and in particular hard (or impossible) to enforce;[9] and
- the multiplicity of overlapping applicable laws and jurisdictions can lead to situations where an activity is subject to multiple and contradictory regulation, or to no regulation at all.[10]

To meet these challenges the global system of laws has to develop new legal concepts and devise techniques for eliminating cross-border conflicts.

3　See Chapters 5 and 6.1.
4　See Chapter 4, especially 4.3.
5　Some of whom undertake roles not previously known in the physical world – see Chapter 2.
6　Some of the consequences of this distribution have been examined in Chapters 6.2 and 8.
7　See Chapters 3 and 4.
8　See Chapter 7.3.
9　See Chapter 9.
10　These issues are examined in depth in Chapters 7 and 8.

10.1   DEVELOPING NEW LEGAL CONCEPTS

One of the most fruitful sources of the new legal concepts which will be necessary to resolve these problems is the activities of private practice lawyers. Electronic commerce activity is growing at a dramatic rate, and on a daily basis specialist commercial lawyers are writing contracts which define the legal relationships between communicating parties. As these contracts are negotiated, the lawyers involved draw on their experience of equivalent terms in other contracts with which they have been involved, and eventually a consensus begins to emerge as to the appropriate relationships and their incidents. From these contracts, the custom and practice of electronic commerce merchants is starting to develop.

The law has always taken account of the custom and practice of merchants – indeed, the commercial laws of most countries are effectively codifications of the commercial practices of the eighteenth and nineteenth centuries. Even at this early stage in the development of electronic commerce we can already detect minor codifications of merchant practice: the UNCITRAL Model Law on Electronic Commerce 1996 is closely based on a number of model Electronic Data Interchange agreements;[11] and the provisions relating to time and place of receipt[12] contained in the US Uniform Electronic Transactions Act 1999 and the Australian Electronic Transactions Act 1999 are based on the most commonly used commercial contract terms.

A second source of new legal concepts is the inventiveness of legislative draftsmen. The first to be faced with a new legal issue has to devise some way to express his solution in legislative terms, and inevitably that becomes a template for later draftsmen. The most striking example of this is the global digital signature legal infrastructure, examined at length in Chapter 5. The shape and much of the detail of the infrastructure was laid down by the drafter of the Utah Digital Signature Act 1996 who worked largely in a legal vacuum, inventing legal relationships which would give effect to the functional description of a working infrastructure set out in the technical document RFC 2527.[13] Thereafter other draftsmen adopted similar solutions, with the result that later, incompatible approaches[14] are unlikely to survive in their incompatible form.[15] The Utah approach was clearly not the only solution, as is demonstrated by the Australian Electronic Transactions Act 1999 which is simpler, less prescriptive and technologically neutral, while at the same time not incompatible with the Utah approach. However, it seems likely that the Australian approach will remain a minority view, simply because Utah was first to invent and thus set the standard.

---

11   See eg the ICC *Uniform Rules of Conduct for Interchange of Trade Data by Teletransmission* (the UNCID Rules); European Commission Recommendation of 19 October 1994 relating to the legal aspects of electronic data interchange (94/820/EC), OJ L338, 1994; American Bar Association *Model Electronic Data Interchange Trading Partner Agreement* (1st edn, 1990).

12   See Chapter 7.1.3.1.

13   Personal communication from Juan Avellan, PhD researcher at Queen Mary and Westfield College, describing his discussions with the draftsman.

14   Such as that taken by the German Digital Signature Act (Signaturgesetz) 1997, which is generally recognised (except perhaps in Germany) to have imposed too prescriptive a technical threshold for signature validity.

15   It is reliably rumoured that the main reason for EU *Directive 1999/93/EC on a Community framework for electronic signatures,* OJ L 13, p 12 was the need to remove the excessive requirements of the German legislation and preempt equally incompatible draft legislation from other EU Member States

10.2   SOLVING PROBLEMS OF GLOBAL REACH – CONVERGENCE OF NATIONAL LAW

The methods of innovation described above cannot, however, solve the legal problems posed by the global reach of Internet activities. Drafters of commercial contracts can negotiate choice of law and forum clauses, but these are unlikely to be enforceable in business-to-consumer transactions and cannot be used to deal with relationships which are not contractual. Legislative drafters can reduce these problems by refraining from drafting in a way which has 'long-arm' effect, but their laws will still apply to activities which take place in those parts of the Internet which are 'inside'[16] their countries.

Most of the problems arising from global reach occur because (a) the applicable national laws differ from each other, and (b) they are often unenforceable in practice. If those laws are substantially identical (in effect if not in wording) the most difficult legal problems under (a) disappear, leaving only the question of which state has jurisdiction in the particular circumstances. In the longer term, the Internet and the commercial and non-commercial activities carried out by means of it will impose substantial pressure on national legislators to eradicate the differences between their own laws and those of other states – a phenomenon described in this chapter by the term 'convergence'.[17] Convergence also reduces the severe difficulties of enforcing laws and regulations against an entity which, whilst very visible in the state in electronic form, has no assets or natural persons there against which enforcement action can be taken,[18] because compliance with its home state laws is likely to mean that it is also compliant abroad. Ultimately, the law will need to recognise as a basic principle that on-line actors can only effectively be regulated in their home countries.[19] Acceptance of this principle in turn demands that the laws converge, for without convergence a legislator will find it politically difficult to remove the (theoretical in most instances) protection that the applicability of host country law gives to its own citizens.

Convergence can happen in one of three ways:

- Through the mechanism of an international convention, implemented into national law by the states who are parties to the convention. So far as the Internet is concerned, this route will only work where there is an existing convention which can be modified in minor respects to deal with Internet-related issues.[20] For completely new problems, the process of negotiating an international convention is so lengthy a task, requiring such a wide range of political compromises, that a brand new convention is likely to require decades rather than years before it is implemented. The Internet evolves rather faster than this, and there is every chance that the convention would

16 Another metaphysical concept, but one which raises serious problems – see eg the discussion of advertising regulation in Chapter 7.2.1.3.
17 'Convergence' is used for two reasons. First, it is a value free term, unlike 'harmonisation' which carries connotations of a supranational legislator. Second, it carries no implications that legislators set out consciously to match their laws with those of another state (usually termed 'approximation'); as explained above in relation to digital signature law, convergence may simply happen, without any overriding plan to produce a uniform, global system of law.
18 Chapter 9 examines the problems of enforcement in depth.
19 See further Chapter 7.2.2.
20 Eg the introduction of a new right of communication to the public in the WIPO Copyright Treaty – see Chapter 4.2.1.3.

be overtaken by new technologies well before its text reached the second or third draft.

- Through harmonisation or approximation of national laws, as the result of a conscious decision of national governments to remove the differences between them. The European Union provides the classic case study for harmonisation, which can be effected with comparative speed because the European Treaty requires Member States to implement harmonising measures which have passed through the legislative process. The degree to which harmonisation within the EU has been successful can be seen in the single passport regime for banking and financial services[1] and the introduction in art 3(2) of the Directive on electronic commerce[2] of the general principle that on-line businesses established in one Member State should not be subject to regulation in another.

  Where powers to enforce the adoption of new laws are lacking, approximation of national laws through bilateral or multilateral agreement is a possible alternative route to home country regulation. This will inevitably be a slower process however, and there are currently few if any concrete examples in the Internet law arena.

- Through what might be described as accidental or fortuitous convergence, as described above for digital signature laws. In fact, such convergence is not really accidental, but is driven by pressure from electronic commerce enterprises and influential policy organisations. Because there is now a growing awareness of the potential for the Internet to impact on almost any area of activity which involves information transfer, governments routinely consult on proposed measures which are likely to raise Internet issues and representative bodies monitor legislative proposals to identify those issues. If the proposal differs too greatly from foreign applicable laws, intense lobbying is likely (from foreign as well as local organisations). It is this process, which is very strong where Internet issues are concerned, that leads to de facto identity of national laws. Exceptions are extremely rare.[3]

10.3   INSOLUBLE PROBLEMS

Will the process of convergence, coupled with home country regulation, lead to solutions for all the new legal problems posed by the Internet, or are there issues to which no solution currently seems possible? The answer is that there

---

1   Discussed in Chapter 7.2.2.

2   EU Directive 2000/31/EC on electronic commerce OJ L 178 p. 1, 17 July 2000. See in particular Recital 22: 'Information Society services should be supervised at the source of the activity, in order to ensure an effective protection of public interest objectives; to that end, it is necessary to ensure that the competent authority provides such protection not only for the citizens of its own country but for all Community citizens; in order to improve mutual trust between Member States, it is essential to state clearly this responsibility on the part of the Member State where the services originate; moreover, in order to effectively guarantee freedom to provide services and legal certainty for suppliers and recipients of services, such Information Society services should in principle be subject to the law of the Member State in which the service provider is established.'

3   One of the most striking exceptions is the Australian legislation imposing broadcasting standards on ISPs – see Chapter 4.2.2. It is reported that many Australian content providers are, as a result, considering moving overseas, thus placing pressure on the Australian government to revise the legislation.

are still insoluble problems, which are caused by the law's inability to reconcile contradictory interests. These fall into three basic categories:

- conflicts between interest groups;
- conflicts between national standards and traditions; and
- conflicts between governmental aspirations and the reality of Internet usage.

One current example of an irreconcilable conflict between interest groups arises in relation to consumer rights. Different countries confer widely differing rights on consumers, some controlling contract terms and some using the criminal law to enforce those rights. Those representing consumers naturally wish to allow consumers to bring actions in their home courts and under their home laws, thus providing them with the level of consumer protection they would otherwise have in physical world dealings. Electronic commerce businesses, faced with the impossible task of complying with nearly 200 different consumer protection regimes, naturally wish to settle on one jurisdiction and comply with its laws alone. If this issue is ever resolved, it is likely to be on a practical rather than a theoretical level, through the self-regulatory and alternative dispute resolution schemes examined in Chapter 9.3. At the theoretical level the consumer's national rights are likely to remain applicable, although unenforceable in practice, at least until self-regulation proves sufficiently effective that consumer representatives are willing to give ground in a compromise on the applicable law.

The clearest example of conflicts between national standards and traditions arises in the field of content liability, particular in relation to obscenity and indecency. As has already been explained in Chapter 4.2.2.1 there is no global consensus on what is and is not unlawful, and no such consensus seems likely to emerge. In part the problem is being resolved for practical purposes by conferring immunities on those most likely to be subjected to criminal liability, the intermediaries who unknowingly carry unlawful information traffic.[4] For the foreseeable future, however, those involved in providing content which is lawful in their home jurisdiction will, in many cases, have no option but to cease operations or to commit criminal offences elsewhere.

The final type of irreconcilable problem is perhaps the most interesting. It arises where the global communications infrastructure provided by the Internet technologies makes it impossible for Governments to achieve their desired policies, although those policies are reasonably practicable in the physical world. Two examples will serve to illustrate this:

- Many, perhaps all, governments wish to retain the ability to monitor communications passing through their countries. The growth in use of electronic communications has, however, led to widespread use of encryption technologies, for purposes of security, confidentiality and identification,[5] and in the arms race between cryptographers and code breakers the current technologies give cryptographers a substantial advantage. Initially governments proposed to deal with this problem by requiring providers of encryption services to escrow encryption keys, so that they would be available to law enforcement and security bodies when

---

4   See Chapter 4.3.
5   Chapter 6.1.2 explains the role of encryption in electronic signatures as an authentication mechanism.

required, but it was soon recognised that the reality of Internet use would make this impracticable.[6] Current efforts to achieve governmental aims in this area have now been reduced to requiring those who possess encryption keys to disclose them on presentation of a properly issued warrant.[7]

- All Governments wish to maintain their tax base, and in recent years there has been a move to increase the revenue from sales or supply taxes and reduce the proportion derived from income and property taxes. However, the reality of electronic commerce via the Internet is that there is no effective way of imposing national sales taxes on information products as they enter the country – indeed, sales to consumers are often, in the current state of the law, legitimately tax-free.[8] No effective solutions have yet been found. The defects in the European Commission's proposal[9] to require non-EU electronic commerce suppliers to register in an EU jurisdiction and collect and account for VAT have already been examined in Chapter 8.1.1.1. Even if businesses were to register voluntarily the proposal would not fully achieve its aim of charging tax in the country of consumption, as the enterprise will be obliged to charge the VAT rate in its country of registration, not that of its customer. Thus most businesses will choose to register in Luxembourg (15% VAT rate) so as, for example, to obtain a 10% price advantage over Danish electronic commerce businesses (currently obliged to charge VAT at 25% to EU consumers). Indeed, a Danish business would be well-advised to conduct its electronic commerce transactions with EU customers via a Luxembourg subsidiary to obtain the benefit of the lower VAT rate. Both will, of course, be undercut by the US business which declines to register, even in Luxembourg, recognising that there are no effective means to enforce its VAT liability against it.

These insoluble problems arise because electronic communications technology facilitates new types of transaction, and new ways of undertaking existing transactions, which transcend the geographical limits of jurisdiction and thus expose conflicts of interest which do not arise in the physical world. Innovation of this type is likely to continue because the pace of development of the Internet technologies shows no sign of slowing down. It is likely that these categories of insoluble problems will be added to in the near future – a desirable result for academic lawyers, if not for legislators.

---

6   See eg the UK DTI document, 'Building Confidence in Electronic Commerce' (URN 99/642, 5 March 1999) http://www.dti.gov.uk/cii/elec/elec_com.html
7   See eg UK Regulation of Investigatory Powers Bill 2000.
8   See Chapter 8.1.1.
9   Proposal for a Council Directive amending Directive 77/388/EEC as regards the value added tax arrangements applicable to certain services supplied by electronic means, COM(2000) 349 final, 7 June 2000.

Index